THE ILLUSTRATED ENCYCLOPEDIA OF CACTI

THE ILLUSTRATED ENCYCLOPEDIA OF CACTI

CLIVE INNES & CHARLES GLASS

A QUANTUM BOOK

Published by Grange Books
An imprint of Grange Books plc
The Grange
Grange Yard
London SE1 3AG

This edition printed 1997

ISBN 1-84013-067-9

This book was produced by
Quantum Books Ltd
6 Blundell Street
London N7 9BH

Senior Editor Kate Kirby
Editor Moyna Kitchen

Designer Carole Perks

Illustrator Anne Savage
Symbols David Kemp

Art Director Moira Clinch
Editorial Director Janet Slingsby

Typeset in Bournemouth by Ampersand Typesetting Ltd
Manufactured in Hong Kong by Regent Publishing Services Ltd
Printed in China by Leefung Asco Printers Ltd

With special thanks to
Philip Gilderdale, Anita Ruddell, Frances Austen

Title page picture: *Rebutia senilis*

CONTENTS

he question most often asked about books on cacti is, 'Where can I find one that is truly informative, with detailed photographs of a wide range of cacti from around the world?' Until now, disappointingly, the answer has been that there isn't one: the aim of this book is to fill that gap.

In producing such a mammoth book, the biggest problem is in organizing the material in a logical and simple way, and the obvious answer is by an alphabetical presentation. As with any branch of the natural sciences, however, the amateur cactus collector soon learns that there is no way of avoiding the botanical or Latin names, and that an understanding of taxonomy, or nomenclature (i.e. the principles of classification of plants etc) will help to make life easier. Only a few cacti have such 'user-friendly' names as 'Bunny Ears', 'Prickly Pear', 'Golden Barrel' or 'Christmas Cactus': for the vast majority one has no alternative but to make one's peace with the Linnaean Binomial System of Nomenclature, foreign as it may sound at first. In this system, the botanical names of plants are in two parts: first the genus, then the species. Plants which closely resemble each other are classified in the same genus. The species name distinguishes different plants belonging to the same genus. In some cases there is a third varietal name, where a plant differs slightly from the species type, but not enough for it to be classed as a separate species.

Related genera are grouped into families, the relationship being based solely on flower structure. Family names end in the suffix *'aceae'*: thus *Cactaceae* is the cactus family. The cactus is a very large family, which including the hybrid genera amounts to over 150 genera and several thousand different species. The more popular the group the greater the proliferation of names and, eventually, the more those names are reshuffled in attempts to make sense of the groups in question. Occasionally, questionable motives have come into play, when a plant has been reclassified merely in order that an individual can have his or her name permanently attached to the plant in question. This has led the science of taxonomy to be unaffectionately referred to as 'the name game'.

In few groups of plants has the 'name game' been so extensively played as in the cactus. Much good work with the classification of cacti has been done by amateurs and, it has to be said, much that is highly questionable to downright outrageous. The result is that some species have been shuffled and reshuffled into so many generic groups that it bewilders both student and botanist as to where, indeed, a particular plant belongs, and a reasonable and consistent classification becomes frustratingly unattainable.

FOREWORD

If we get too caught up in the 'name game', we tend to forget that the plant is more important than what we call it, and that names are meant to be handles for the plants, not the other way round. In our opinion, the best way to put the emphasis back on the plants is through a pictorial compendium such as this one. Of course, those handles are necessary and one is faced with the necessity of espousing some sort of classification. A major classification of the *Cactaceae* was proposed back in the early 1920s by the American botanists, Britton and Rose. This has gained wide acceptance, but of course those species and genera which have been discovered since then are not included in that classification. In the 1960s an amateur German cactus enthusiast, Curt Backeberg, attempted another classification of the cactus family and his mammoth work filled no less than six volumes. His approach was very liberal, resulting in a proliferation of species and mini-genera, and his work did not always conform with proper, accepted procedure, so many of his new genera have to be considered as illegitimate. There have been many other revisions of groups or genera of the *Cactaceae,* but so far no other complete reclassification of the family to the species level.

We have attempted in this book to recognize as far as possible the most popularly accepted and practical classifications, while also recognizing the requirements of those amateur collectors who seek help in identifying their plants, and who may wish to acquire new species and varieties which they have not come across before. The main goal of this book, then, is to represent as many genera, species and varieties of cactus as possible, along with colour photographs, both of habitat and cultivation, and descriptive notes.

CLIVE INNES

CHARLES GLASS

HOW TO LOCATE YOUR PLANT

For those of you who are not familiar with the names of cacti and may have some plants that you would like to try to identify and don't know where to start looking, the guide on this and the following spread may help. It gives a breakdown of the main groups of cactus, according to size and shape, and lists examples of each. Of course some groups have members that may belong in two or more of these categories, so it can be no more than a sometimes fallible guide, but at least it will narrow the field.

Begin by determining which of the basic shape categories your cactus comes under. For example, is it columnar or globular? Once you have established its basic shape, decide to which sub-division the plant belongs. If the plant is globular, does it have very few spines or none at all, or is its dominant characteristic that it has prominent tubercles? (The line illustration above each sub-division will help further with identification.) Once the sub-division has been established look at the globular plants in each of the genera listed, and see if your cactus matches the description or picture. For instance, if you have decided your plant is globular with few spines, look at the globular Astrophytum entries on pages 28–31, does your cactus match picture or text description? If not, look under the globular Aztekium entry on page 32. Work your way through the sub-divisions until you find a match for your plant.

GLOBULAR

Few or no spines

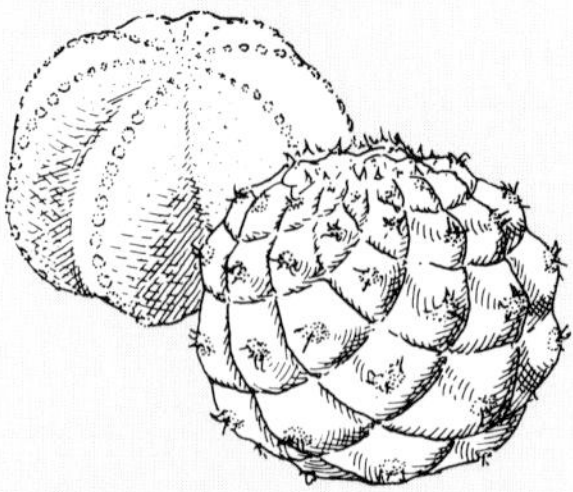

Astrophytum 28-31
Aztekium 32
Blossfeldia 33
Echinocereus 72, 77
Lophophora 150
Turbinicarpus 299-302

With fine spines

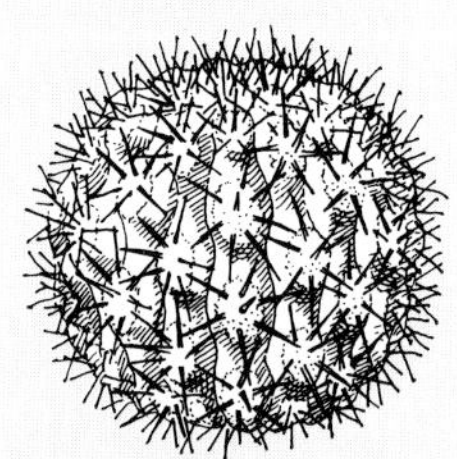

Acanthocalycium 18-19
Echinomastus 82
Epithelantha 103-104
Escobaria 106-107, 109
Frailea 122
Gymnocalycium 126-133
Mammillaria 153-168, 170-185

Spines straight, short

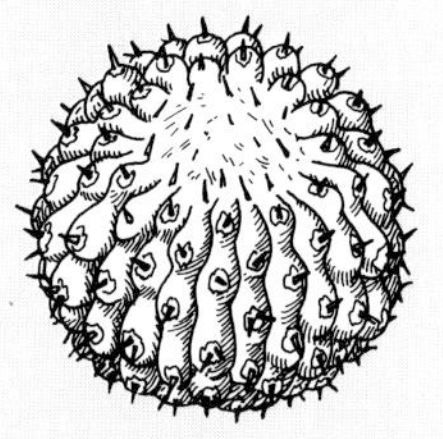

Echinocereus 68, 71, 73
Neolloydia 199
Neoporteria 200-202
Pediocactus 237-239
Pygmaeocereus 252-253
Sclerocactus 270-273
Thelocactus 289-293
Uebelmannia 303-305

Spines in comb-like formation

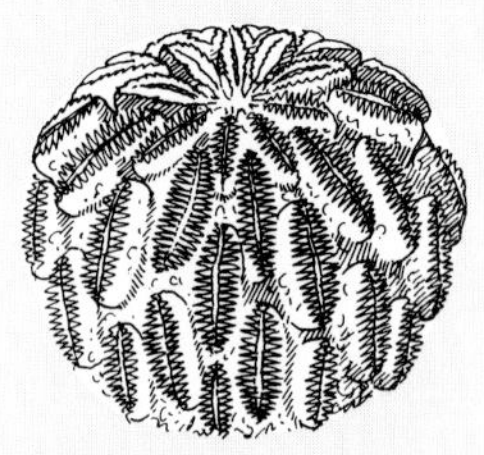

Buiningia 37
Pelecyphora 239

With flat or prominent tubercles (often scale-like)

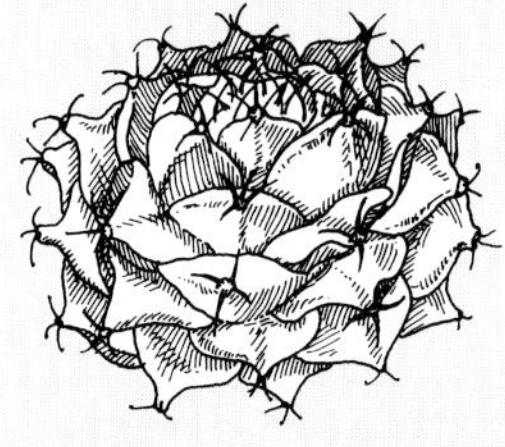

Ariocarpus 23-24
X Ferobergia 113
Leuchtenbergia 144
Neowerdermannia 203
Obregonia 206
Ortegocactus 227
Pelecyphora 239
Strombocactus 281

Woolly or spiny crown

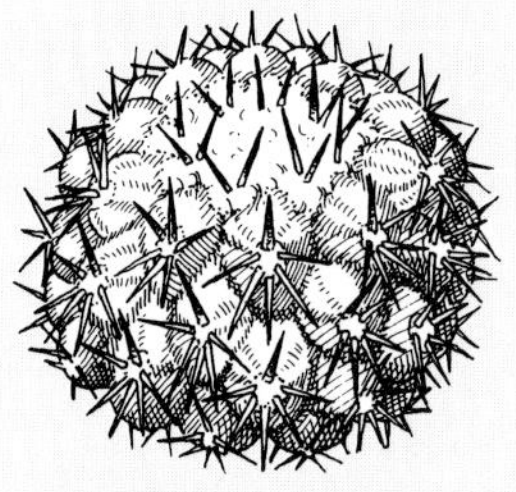

Copiapoa 47-49
Matucana 186-188
Notocactus 204-206
Oroya 226
Parodia 229-237
Weingartia 306-307

Prominent spination

Ancistrocactus 20
Coryphantha 51-58
Denmoza 59
Echinocactus 66-67
Echinocereus 73-76
Echinofossulocactus 80
Echinopsis 84-87
Eriosyce 105
Ferocactus 114-120, 121-122
Gymnocactus 123-125
Homalocephala 139
Lobivia 145-148
X Lobivopsis 148-149
Trichocereus 295

With prominent cephalium

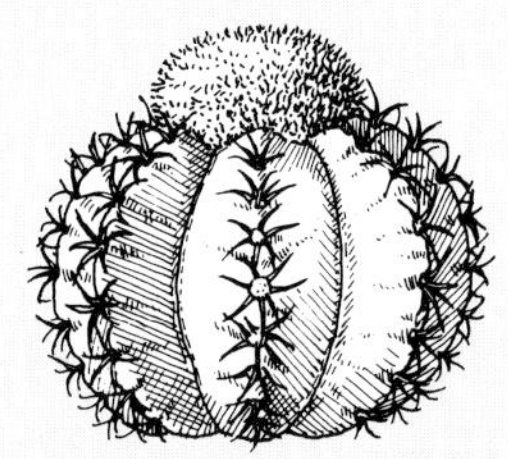

Discocactus 60-63
Melocactus 188-191

HOW TO LOCATE YOUR PLANT

CLIMBING

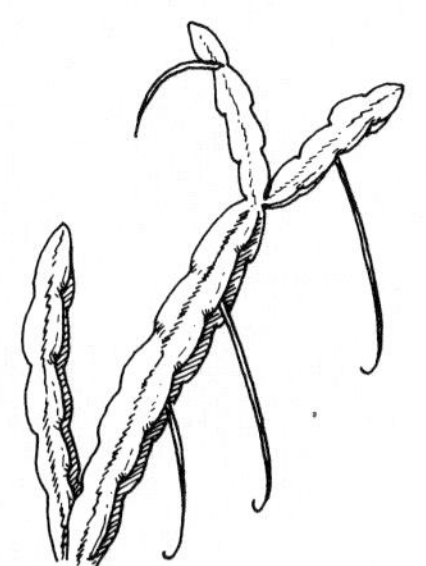

PENDENT

Segmented pendent

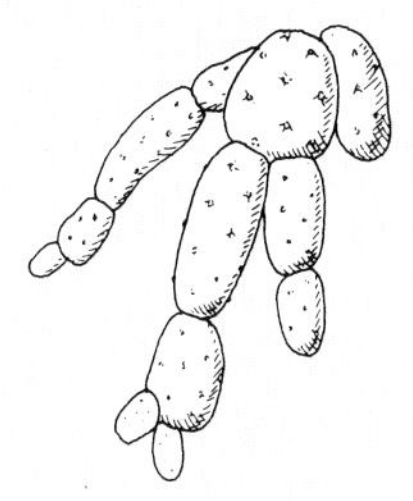

More or less tubular pendent

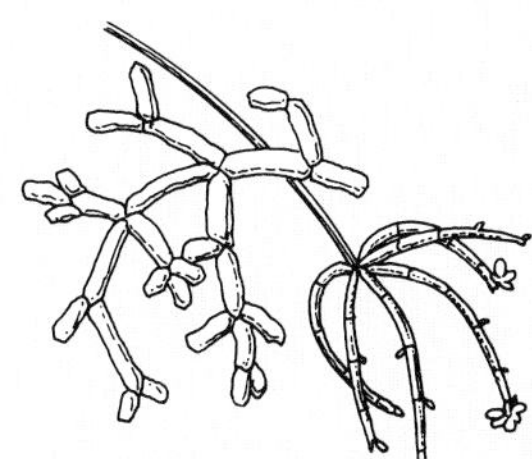

Angular (stems) pendent

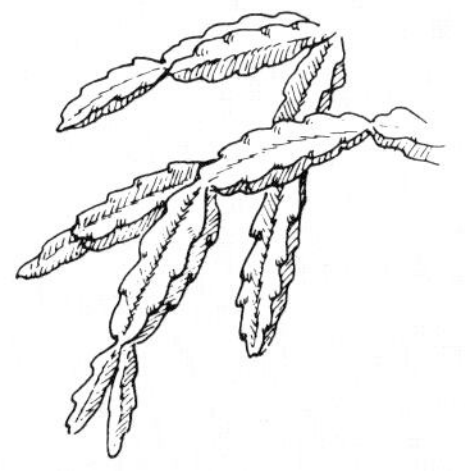

Elongated stems

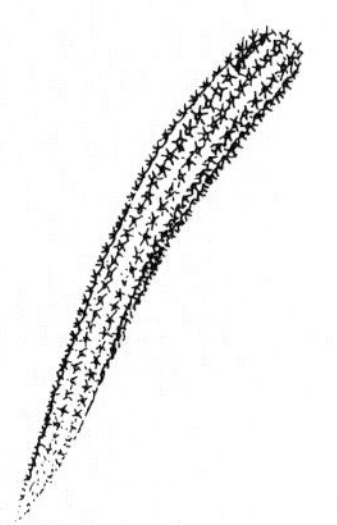

Leaf-like pendent stems

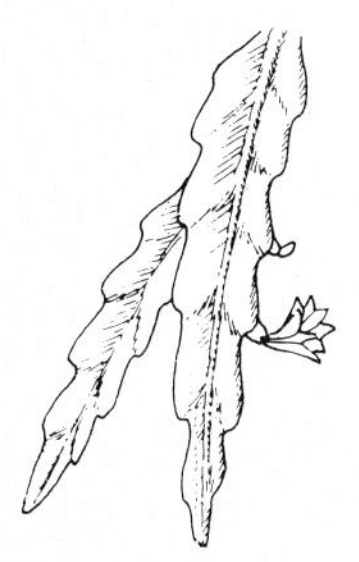

LEAF-LIKE

Broadly leaf-like

Segmented

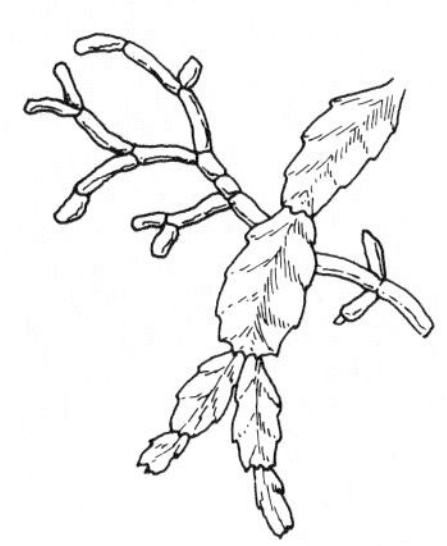

HOW TO LOCATE YOUR PLANT

COLUMNAR

Woolly/hairy

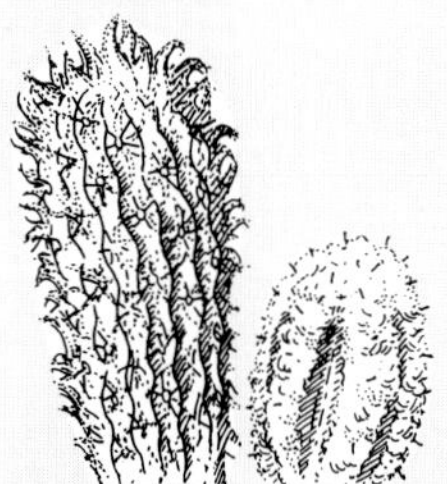

Erect or semi-prostrate

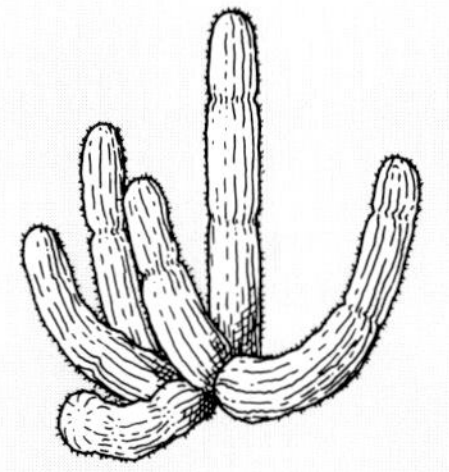

With prominent cephalium

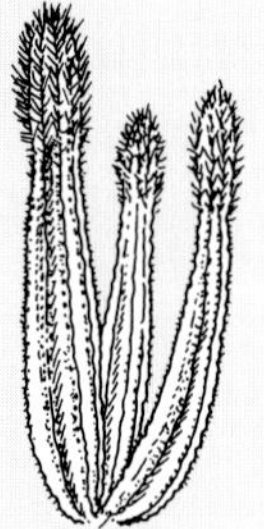

Bushy

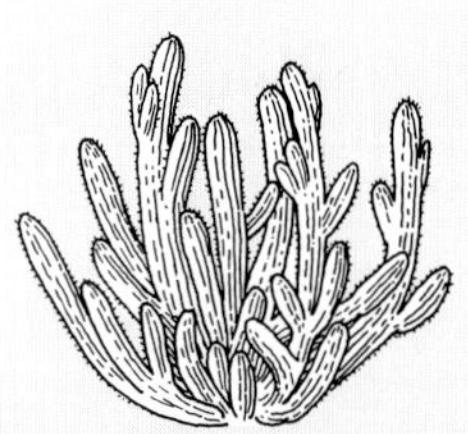

Spiny

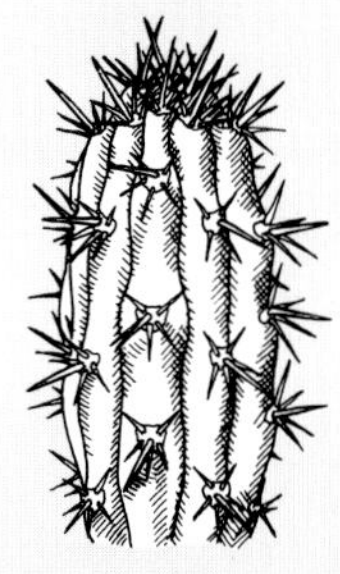

Semi-climbing columnar

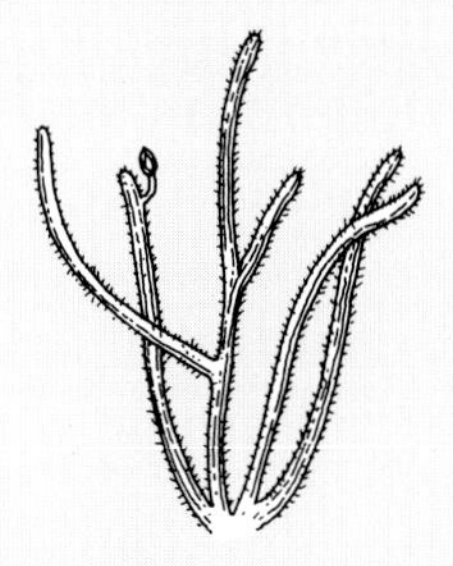

Tree-like, robust

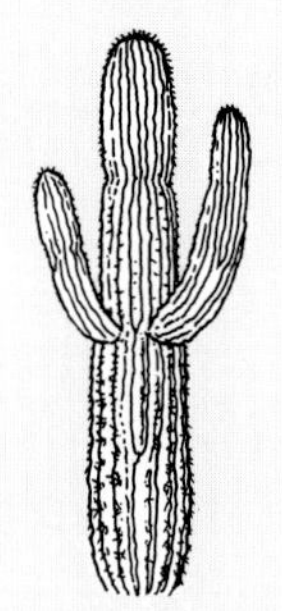

Tree-like, slender

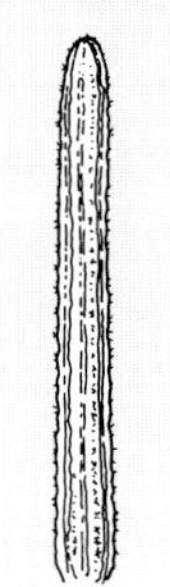

Dense-spiny stems

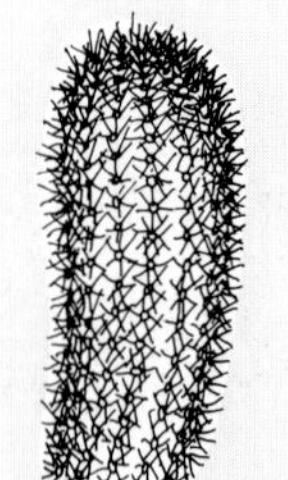

Particularly short columnar

HOW TO LOCATE YOUR PLANT

CLUSTERING

Cushion-like clusters

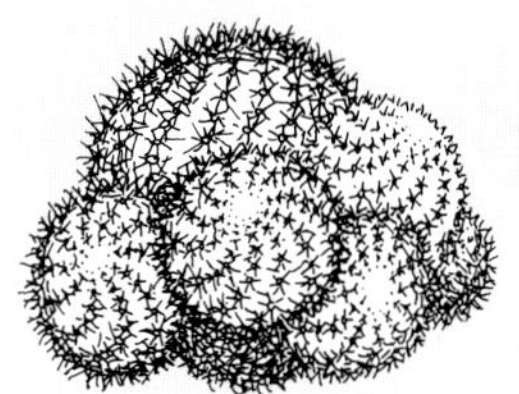

Coryphantha 53-55, 57
Mammillaria..152-155, 157, 159, 162, 164-174, 176-186
Rebutia................254-259
Sulcorebutia 283

Group forming

Echinocereus 68-70, 72-73, 76-77, 78-79
Epithelantha.............. 104
Escobaria 107, 108-109
Ferocactus................. 120
Gymnocalycium ... 126, 130
Pygmaeocereus 253

Sparse clusters

Chamaelobivia 42
Matucana.................. 186
Sulcorebutia 282-284

Sprawling, spreading clusters

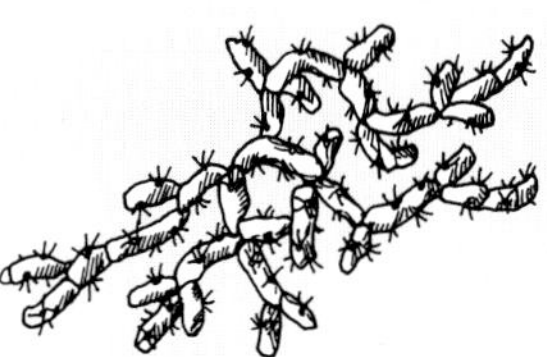

Maihuenia................. 151
Maihueniopsis 152
Mila......................... 193
Tephrocactus........285-288

PADDED/JOINTED

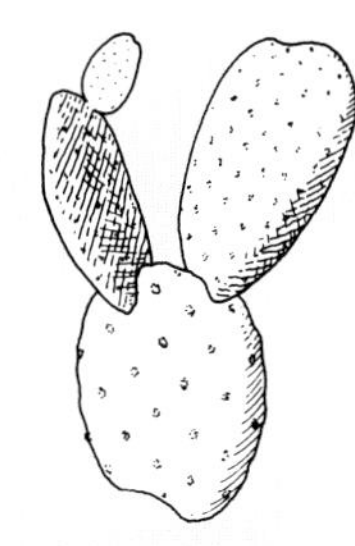

Opuntia...............207-225
Pterocactus................ 251
Tephrocactus............. 287

SPRAWLING/TRAILING

Leafy stems

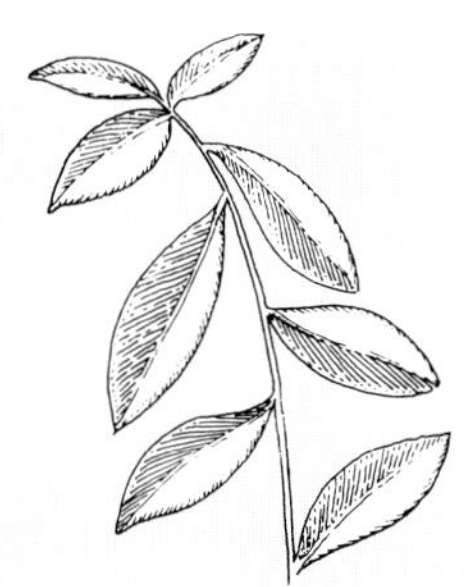

Pereskia.................... 240

Very thin stems

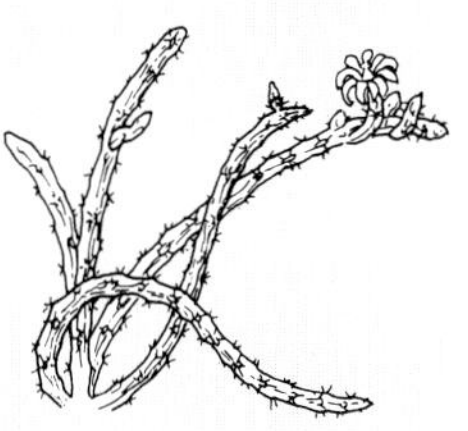

Peniocereus............... 240
Weberocereus 305-306
Wilcoxia 308-309
Wilmattea 309

Firm, sprawling stems

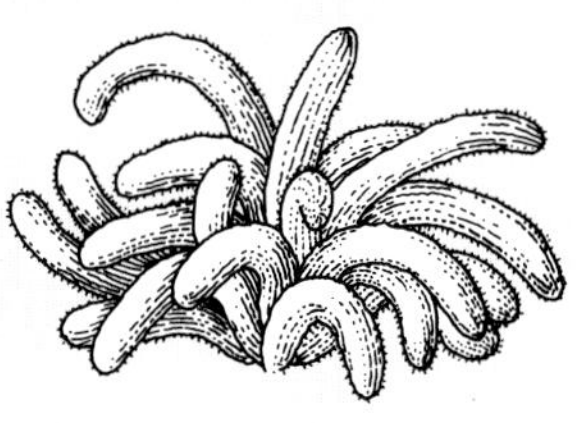

Borzicactus..................34
Echinocereus 70, 74-75
Haageocereus 135
Loxanthocereus.......... 151
Pseudoacanthocereus .. 250
Stenocereus............... 277

Slender, sprawling, strong-spined

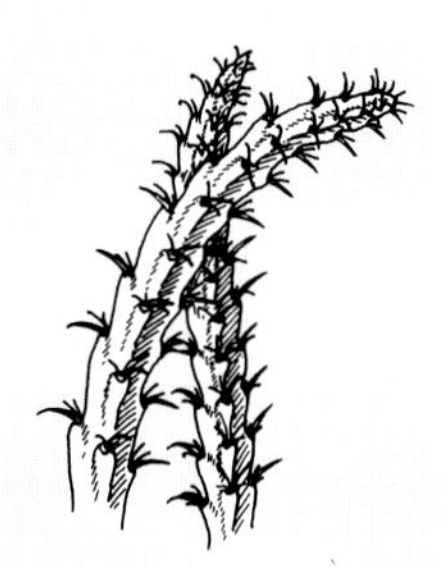

Eriocereus...........104-105
Harrisia 136
Heliocereus 138
Nyctocereus 206
Trichocereus........ 296, 298

HOW TO USE THIS BOOK

The information in the directory section of this book is arranged to supply the reader with as much information as possible about each species. Opposite an explanation is given for the symbols which appear at the base of each plant entry. On this page plant classification is explained.

Understanding nomenclature

The huge diversity of the plant world is such that a system of dividing plants into recognizable groups is necessary in order to make some sense of it. The system of nomenclature and taxonomy is the means by which specialists, collectors and amateurs in different countries can understand each other, the official names and classifications of plants being accepted worldwide.

Plant classification works on the principle of the Russian doll: the broadest classification is the family, which consists of related genera (the relationship being based on flower structure). Family names end in the suffix *'aceae'* – hence cacti belong to the *Cactaceae*. With many plant families, sub-divisions occur, and this certainly applies with the *Cactaceae*, with systematic categories of sub-family, tribe, sub-tribe, and thence to genus, species, sub-species, varieties, cultivars and forms. Where a sub-species occurs, the abbreviation *ssp.* is placed before the sub-species name. Where a variety is distinguished within a species, its name is preceded by the abbreviation *var.* A form is denoted by the abbreviation *fma.* Cultivars are indicated *cv.*; natural hybrids are noted *Hybrid.*

In general, the nomenclature system is fairly straightforward and understandable. In many instances the name given to a plant remains consistent for an indefinite period. However, some species have, through the years, been investigated by various taxonomists and botanists, and this has led far too frequently to plants being reclassified under different genera. All nomenclature bears the name (or the recognized abbreviation of the name) of the author (the person naming the plant). Where a plant has been reclassified by later authors, the name of the original author appears in brackets, followed by the name of the later author or authors. Thus a single species can be known under several names, called synonyms. The example below will help to clarify the system.

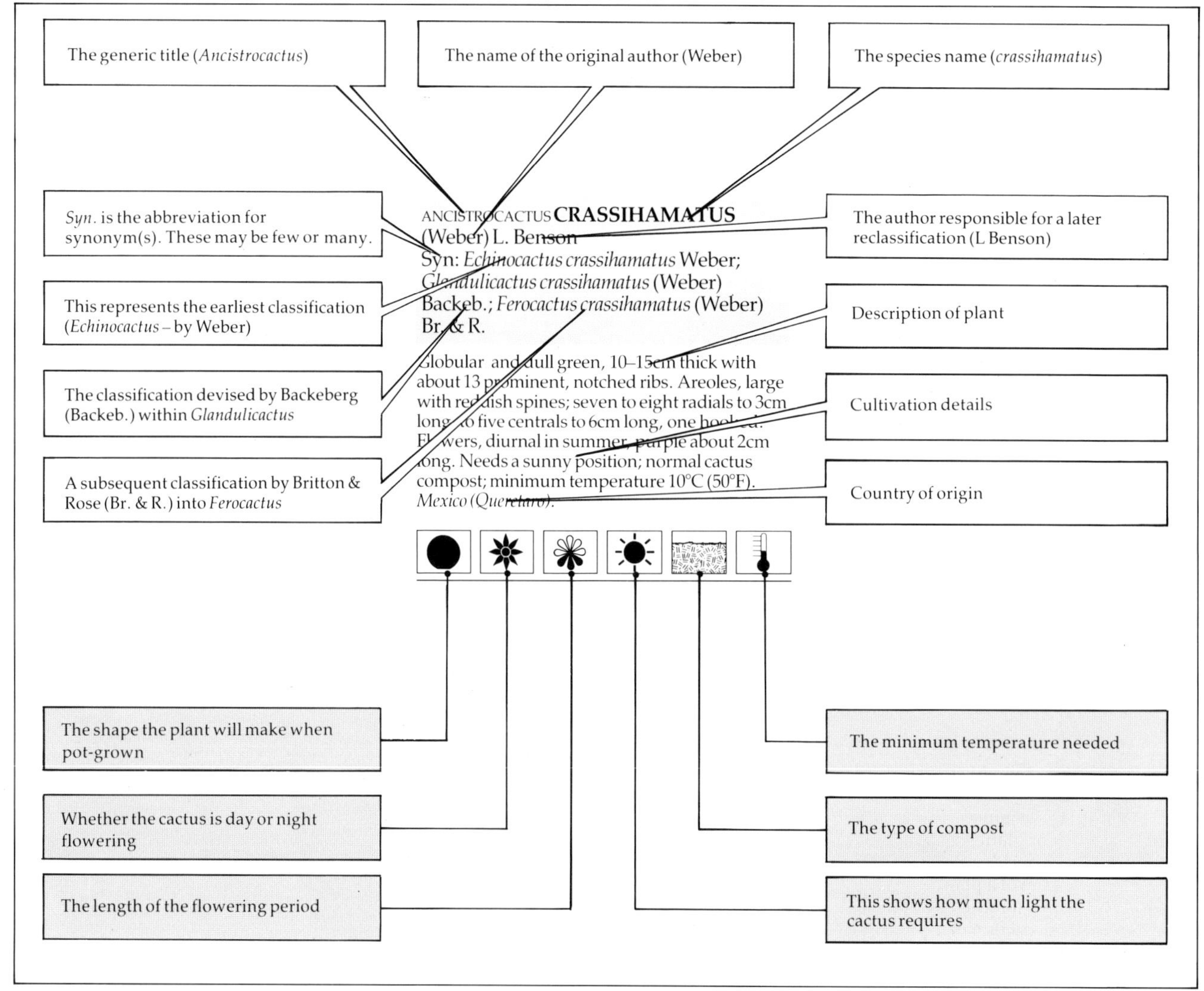

HOW TO USE THIS BOOK

SHAPE

This symbol represents the basic shape the cactus will make when grown in a pot. For the variations within these basic shape categories, see pages 8–11.

 Columnar

 Leaf-like

 Globular

 Pendent

 Padded/jointed

 Sprawling/trailing

 Clustering

 Climbing

FLOWERING TIME

Day flowering
By far the greatest number of cacti are diurnal, or day-flowering. This symbol indicates that the flowers of a particular species are only to be found fully open during daylight hours. Where flowers last for a number of days, they may remain open day and night throughout the period, or close towards evening, then re-open the next morning.

Night flowering
This symbol applies to nocturnal, or night-flowering cacti. These tend to be mainly the columnar plants, particularly those from South American habitats. However, nocturnal flowers also occur on a number of globular plants. The flower buds are tightly closed during the hours of daylight, and commence opening in the late afternoon or early evening, or even during night hours. With the majority of species, the flowers remain open throughout the hours of darkness and begin to close again in early morning. In some cases the blooms last for one night only.

Information unknown
This symbol is used when the information is unknown.

FLOWERING PERIOD

These symbols give a general indication as to when a particular plant should bloom. Sometimes nature decides slightly to vary the flowering season of a plant, but such variation will be minimal. There is also the possibility of a second flowering season occurring later in the same year, but this phenomenon is a more rare event!

 Mid-winter

 Late winter to early spring

 Mid-spring

 Late spring to early summer

 Mid-summer

 Late summer to early autumn

 Mid-autumn

 Late autumn to early winter

LIGHT

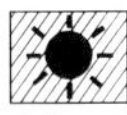

Good but indirect light
A large number of cacti appreciate brief periods of bright sunshine, but not throughout the heat of the day. Place these plants in a position where there is plenty of indirect or filtered light, but not too much shade. In a hot, sunny summer, greenhouse specimens may need protection from scorching. Greenhouse shading can be provided either by using blinds, or by coating the glass with a special substance called 'summer cloud', which provides a thin coating of white that moderates the intensity of the light. On the approach of autumn this should be wiped off.

Partial shade
In the wild, many cacti, especially the smaller species, grow in the protective shade of surrounding desert bushes and scrub. Such plants appreciate semi-shade, even in northern climes, and require protection from the full glare of the midday sun. Indoors, place these plants on a window ledge that does not receive direct sunlight. In the greenhouse, use blinds or other forms of shading to filter out some of the light. Cacti planted in the garden will appreciate the shade provided by overhanging tree branches or a nearby wall.

Full shade
Rainforest and jungle cacti can be grown in shade. This does not mean the total exclusion of light, but these species do best in a position where the light is finely shaded at all times. Many such plants are grown 'under the bench' in greenhouses; in the home, they can be stood in windows which do not get too much sunlight, or brought away from the window altogether.

Direct sunlight
Some cactus species can withstand extended periods of full sun without coming to any harm. Plants grown indoors should be placed on a bright, sunny window ledge; in a greenhouse, place them as near to the glass as possible; in the garden, choose a sheltered, sunny aspect.

COMPOST

Slightly acid compost
The basic mixture consists of equal parts sterilized loam, shredded peat and coarse washed sand, or sand and perlite. To achieve the required acidity, mix a small quantity of thoroughly decomposed leafmould or cow manure in granulated form with the peat: about one quarter in bulk of the peat content is sufficient. Suitable for forest cacti such as *Disocactus, Epiphyllums, Rhipsalis, Schlumbergera etc.*.

Proprietary cactus compost
This is the type of compost invariably offered commercially for cactus and succulent plant culture. Normally composed of equal parts sterilized loam, shredded sphagnum peat and sharp gritty sand, to which is added a slow-release base fertilizer. If a soil-less compost is considered, add one part coarse washed sand to three parts compost to increase porosity and aid drainage.

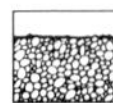

Enriched mineral compost
This consists of normal cactus compost with an extra sand or grit content. The suggested formula is one part sterilized loam, one part shredded peat, and two parts sharp gritty sand or fine gravel, enriched with thoroughly decomposed leafmould in granulated form at the rate of three parts prepared compost to one part leafmould. Suitable for cacti from rocky, sloping habitats, where decomposed leaves from the surrounding scrub and low trees, plus minerals washed from the rocks, provide the necessary nutrients.

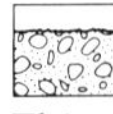

Calcareous compost
This consists of normal cactus compost with the addition of limestone gravel or chippings (never powdered lime or chalk). The quantity of limestone added depends on the species concerned, but in general one part limestone gravel to six parts compost is sufficient. Suitable for the spiny or woolly type of desert cacti. The addition of limestone assists in strong spine formation.

TEMPERATURE

The temperatures stated pertain to night-time conditions, and are recommended as a *minimum* for the well-being of the plant.

 7°C

 15–16°C

 10°C

 18°C

 13°C

19°C and over

Some superb examples of cacti growing behind glass.

This book is carefully planned to provide ease of use, even by a complete cactus novice. The core of the work is the illustrated reference directory of this exotic family, the *Cactaceae*. Here you will find over 1,200 examples of individual cactus species, suitably arranged in the standard generic groupings, and these species, together with any varieties which occur, can be identified alphabetically according to their botanical nomenclature. This means that, even if you know nothing about a particular plant other than its name, you will be able to locate it easily and quickly.

Each entry is illustrated with a colour photograph of the plant, sometimes depicted in the wild or, more frequently, in domestic conditions, and invariably showing the flower as well as the plant form. Each entry is accompanied by a visual ready-reference chart, in which specially devised symbols act as an instant and useful checklist. These symbols indicate the preferred type of soil, the degree of sun or shade the plant requires, the optimum temperatures for successful domestic cultivation, whether the plant is day or night flowering, the season of the year when flowering takes place, and, finally, the shape the plant will develop when grown in cultivation, this frequently differing from its shape in the wild.

The text which accompanies each entry in the directory section gives cultivation advice specific to the plant featured. However, there are a number of general guidelines to cultivation that will assist you along the way, and ensure success when raising and caring for individual species and varieties, as well as mixed plantings. What follows applies to all cacti which are being grown as typical houseplants – that is, in normal domestic conditions rather than in specialist greenhouses or conservatories.

Planting in containers

Clay and plastic containers are equally suitable for cacti, although clay pots dry out more quickly. The most important thing is that the pot should be large enough comfortably to accommodate the plant or plants, and deep enough to allow for drainage and for the roots to spread naturally. If the container is too small, root growth is restricted, resulting in weak growth and possibly the eventual loss of the plant. If the container is too large, there is a danger of either under-watering or over-watering, with adverse effects on the plant. Also, because the roots of the plant do not fill the pot, the unused soil may become sour. Lastly, a small cactus in an over-large container does not look aesthetically pleasing!

The best time to plant or re-pot is in spring, during the early part of the growing season, before any buds have developed. Good drainage is of paramount importance, so start by placing a layer of broken crocks in the base of the container to a depth of 1–2cm (½–¾in) or more, depending on the size of the container. This prevents the drainage holes from becoming blocked with compost. A few pieces of charcoal can be mixed with the crocks to keep the compost sweet.

Place a thin covering of compost over the crocks, then hold the plant in position with the roots hanging just above the compost. Protect hands from very prickly specimens by holding the plant wrapped in newspaper. Fill in around the plant with slightly moist compost, repeatedly tapping the container to encourage the compost to settle around the roots without any air pockets. Finally firm the surface with thumb and fingers. The soil should not reach higher than a centimetre or so below the rim of the pot, to allow for watering. After planting, no water should be given at all for several days, so that any broken roots can heal over, preventing the risk of root rot. Leave the plant in a bright, airy position, but not in direct sunlight.

Mixed planting

If mixed plantings of cacti are desired, be careful to select species which have similar requirements in terms of soil type, temperature, light and general cultivation. This is particularly important when planting bowl gardens, where plants are closely confined.

Never plant any species of cactus in a bottle garden. It may seem an attractive idea initially, but cacti simply would not survive, as the micro-climate in a bottle garden is far too extreme.

Compost

As the directory section of this book indicates, different species of cactus prefer different types of soil, but one essential requirement common to all is that the soil must be of an open texture to permit free drainage and circulation of air; a waterlogged soil is certain to spell disaster. If a soil-less compost is used, it is a good idea to mix in a quantity of washed, gritty sand, to the ratio of one part sand to two parts compost.

Plants from certain habitats may have additional soil requirements. Some desert species, such as *Mammillaria plumosa*, will benefit from the addition of limestone chippings to the planting mixture since, in nature, many such plants flourish on calcareous rocky slopes.

Forest cacti, such as *Epiphyllums*, require a richer, more acid soil.

Watering and feeding

When plants are well established and are firmly set in the compost, watering can commence, but with extreme care. Success in growing cacti is dependent upon correct watering more than any other factor. Overwatering can lead to black rot and should be avoided at all costs. If in doubt – don't water! Having said that, and while acknowledging that cacti are naturally constructed to withstand periods of drought in the wild, most cacti grown in cultivation will benefit from regular watering during the growing period. Lack of water at this time may result in the rootstock becoming dehydrated, hampering development of the plants. During the dormant period, however, water should be withheld – either partially or totally, depending on the species – and the plant should be kept cool.

In the wild, cacti are subject to seasonal rainstorms, followed by periods of drought. When watering, it makes sense to follow this natural pattern. Soak the compost well, then wait until it has dried out before watering again. The best time to water is in the early morning, or late evening – never in the heat of the day, as this can cause scorching. In hot, dry weather, cacti will benefit from a gentle spraying with water in the evening, which simulates the dew to which they are accustomed in their natural habitat.

Follow this routine throughout the growing season, until mid- to late autumn, then gradually reduce the amount and frequency of watering as winter approaches. The majority of desert species can survive without water during the dormant period (although plants kept in a warm, centrally heated room should be watered occasionally, just sufficient to moisten the soil). Jungle and rainforest plants should be kept slightly moist, so that the rootstock does not become dehydrated.

In early spring watering can be resumed. Start with only a small amount, as the plants are incapable of absorbing much water at this stage. Gradually increase the amount and frequency of watering as summer approaches.

Proper feeding is also important. Without it growth will become retarded and, if the flowers develop at all, they will be of poor quality. Feeding is best combined with watering, the fertilizer being applied in diluted form every three to five weeks during the growing season. Choose what is termed a comprehensive fertilizer – that is, one containing the essential trace elements of iron, magnesium, boron, copper, cobalt, manganese and molybdenum, together with the standard nitrogen, potassium and potash. Fertilizers specially prepared for cactus growing are available from garden centres and specialist nurseries.

ABOVE The Huntington Botanic Garden in California.

LEFT Part of the collection assembled by the co-author at his Sussex home.

Light

Different species of cacti require different amounts of light, depending on their original habitat. Desert species require the brightest and sunniest positions possible, otherwise they become etiolated and misshapen, the spines become weak, and they are unlikely to flower successfully. Jungle and rainforest cacti, on the other hand, dislike direct sunlight. Regardless of their individual requirements, however, all cacti need a reasonable amount of light, which is essential for photosynthesis to take place. For further information on the light requirements of different species, see page 13.

Temperature

One of the all-important factors in the cultivation of cacti is temperature, and it is well to remember that there may be widely variable demands, depending on the season and on the origins of the individual plants in your collection. During the summer months, normal room temperature is usually adequate for plants used for home decor. For plants kept in a greenhouse, good ventilation is essential: a close, damp atmosphere encourages the growth of harmful fungi. With certain species, some form of greenhouse shading will be necessary.

Any major problems are likely to develop during the winter months. When discussing temperatures, we are referring to measurements taken in the shade: only in this way can the minimum required temperature be ensured.

With the majority of desert cacti a minimum temperature of 8–10°C (46–50°F) throughout the dormant period of winter will suffice. Plants which originate from extremely hot climates, such as many of the *Melocactus* and *Discocactus*, require a minimum temperature of around 15°C (59°F). Other types of cacti are normally happy so long as the winter temperature does not fall below about 5°C (40°F).

With desert plants in general, a day-time maximum temperature in springtime of 22°C–27°C (70°–80°F) will help to promote growth and flowering.

A different approach is required when it comes to jungle or rainforest cacti. During the time when bud formation is in progress, and when flowering commences, temperatures must never be allowed to fall below 10°C (50°F): ideally, they should be a few degrees higher.

Since rainforest and jungle plants are accustomed to humid conditions in their natural habitats, it will prove most beneficial if something similar can be arranged in cultivation. This can be provided by fairly regular overhead misting of the plants, using tepid, preferably rain water: this will help to emulate natural conditions by increasing the humidity in the air.

Once flowering is over – usually by late spring – rainforest species will happily accept much the same temperature range as their desert counterparts, with but slight variation in watering procedures.

Pests and diseases

All plants are vulnerable to attack by insect pests, and cacti are no exception. The most common pests associated with cacti are mealy bugs, root mealy bugs, red spider mites, scale insects, sciarid flies and their larvae, aphids. Infestation can be prevented by providing good growing conditions: for example, red spider mites may attack if the atmosphere is excessively dry and hot, and regular spraying with water is recommended as a deterrent. Another preventative measure is to water in to the soil some diluted systemic insecticide, following the manufacturer's instructions, about three or four times during the growing season (though never do this when the rootstock is dry). If the pests are already established, spray the actual plant as well.

Over-watering and insufficient drainage can lead to a bacterial infection known as black rot, in which the base of the plant literally blackens. Such a condition must be treated promptly or it will prove fatal. Cut away the infected area with a very sharp knife and treat the wound with sulphur powder. Be thorough, otherwise the trouble may re-occur.

Reddish spots on your plants are not a sign of disease, but are the result of overhead watering in the full heat of the day, which causes scorching.

ACANTHOCALYCIUM **AURANTIACUM** Rausch

A globular species to about 5cm high, 9cm in diameter, dark greyish-green in colour with 10–16 ribs. Spines are dark, almost blackish-brown, with five to seven radials to 4cm long, rarely one central slightly longer, but more often absent. Flowers are borne on lateral areoles, to about 5cm long and across, diurnal, in summer. The inner petals are yellowish orange in the lower part, reddish towards the top; outer petals are usually totally red. A bright airy position is essential; normal cactus compost and winter temperature 7°C (45°F). *Argentina (Catamarca).*

▲

ACANTHOCALYCIUM **GLAUCUM** Ritter

Globular bluish-green plants about 15cm high, 7cm in diameter with eight to fourteen ribs over 1cm high. Spines are more or less erect; usually there are five to ten radials, rarely one to two centrals. Flowers are golden yellow, with reddish-tipped petals about 6cm long and across. Day flowering in mid-summer, they need a bright location and normal cactus compost; minimum temperature 10°C (50°F). *Argentina (Catamarca).*

ACANTHOCALYCIUM **PEITSCHERIANUM** Backeb.

A greyish-green, globular plant to about 8cm high, 10cm wide, having about 17 prominent ribs. Spines varying from pale to dark-brown, with seven to nine radials and usually one central, all to 2cm in length. Flowers are diurnal, whitish or pale pinkish-white, 6cm long, appearing in late summer. Needs bright light; normal cactus compost; minimum temperature 10°C (50°F). *Argentina (Cordoba).*

     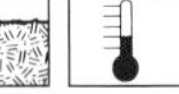

ACANTHOCALYCIUM

ACANTHOCALYCIUM **THIONANTHUM** (Speg.) Backeb.

A short cylindrical, dark-green species 12cm or more high, 6–10cm thick with about 14 ribs. The pale brownish spines are curved upwards, about 1.5cm long; about 10 radials, one to four centrals. Day flowering in mid-summer, the flowers are citron yellow, 4.5cm long. Requires a bright, airy position; normal cactus compost; minimum temperature 10°C (50°F). *Argentina (Salta).*

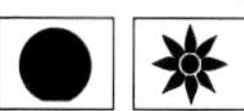    

ACANTHOCALYCIUM **VIOLACEUM** (Werd.) Backeb.
Syn: *Echinopsis violacea* Werd.

The plants are solitary, more or less globular to 20cm high, 13cm diameter, and dull green, having about 15 ribs with areoles bearing 12 or more slender yellowish-brown radial spines and three to four slightly longer centrals. Flowering in summer, from near or at the crown of the plant, the blooms are diurnal, pale violet to 7.5cm long, 6cm across. A bright airy position is required, with normal cactus compost and minimum winter temperature 7°C (45°F). *Argentina (Cordoba).*

   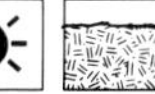 

ACANTHOCEREUS

ACANTHOCEREUS **HORRIDUS** Br. & R.
Syn: *Acanthocereus horribilis* Berger

A semi-erect, many-branched species. The dark green stems which are about 10cm thick have three broad wing-like ribs with crenate margins. Areoles, set 3–6cm apart and bearing up to six radial spines to 1cm long and one to two thick centrals about 5cm in length, are brownish, becoming grey. Night flowering in summer, the flowers are white with greenish-brown outer segments, about 20cm long. Requires a bright position; normal cactus compost; minimum temperature 13°C (55°F). *Guatemala.*

  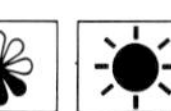 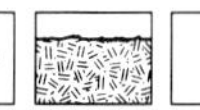 

ACANTHOCEREUS **sp. nova.** (aff. *A. colombianus)*

This would appear to resemble *A. colombianus* Br. & R., which is the only other recorded species known from that country. It was discovered by Professor W. Rauh in Magdalena which is in the north of the country. The erect plant has three-angled stems, about 9cm thick, with greyish or brownish spines of unequal length. Flowers are unknown. A very bright position is necessary, with normal cactus soil; minimum temperature 13°C (55°F). *Colombia.*

    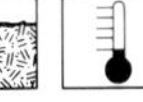

ACANTHORHIPSALIS

ACANTHOCEREUS **PENTAGONUS** (L.) Br. & R.
Syn: *Acanthocereus tetragonus* (L.) Humlk.

A tall columnar species around 5m high. The branches are dark green, 6–7cm in diameter with three to five angular ribs, deeply crenate. Areoles are greyish, 2–3cm apart, bearing brownish spines, six to eight radials 1–2.5cm long, one or more centrals about 4cm long. Flowers, white with greenish outer segments, about 20cm long, are nocturnal in late summer. Requires bright light; normal cactus compost; minimum temperature 13°C (55°F). *USA (Florida), Mexico, Central and South America, West Indies.*

 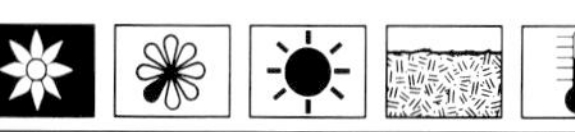

ACANTHORHIPSALIS **MONOCANTHA** (Griseb.) Br. & R.
Syn: *Rhipsalis monocantha* Griseb.; *Lepismium monocanthum* (Griseb.) Barthlott

A branching epiphyte with spiny three-angled or flat and leaf-like stems up to 45cm long, having crenate margins and yellowish-woolly areoles. It differs from species of *Rhipsalis* in having one, rarely two, 1cm long yellowish spines to each areole, persisting. Orange flowers appear in spring and summer. These are diurnal, about 1.5cm long and 1.3cm across. Filtered light preferable; normal cactus compost; minimum temperature 13°C (55°F). *N. Argentina.*

   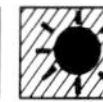 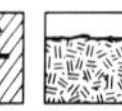  

ANCISTROCACTUS

ANCISTROCACTUS **CRASSIHAMATUS** (Weber) L. Benson
Syn: *Echinocactus crassihamatus* Weber; *Glandulicactus crassihamatus* (Weber) Backeb.; *Ferocactus crassihamatus* (Weber) Br. & R.

Globular and dull green, 10–15cm thick with about 13 prominent, notched ribs. Areoles, large with reddish spines; seven to eight radials to 3cm long, to five centrals to 6cm long, one hooked. Flowers, diurnal in summer, purple about 2cm long. Needs a sunny position; normal cactus compost; minimum temperature 10°C (50°F). *Mexico (Queretaro).*

ANCISTROCACTUS **SCHEERII** (Salm-Dyck) Br. & R.
Syn: *Echinocactus scheeri* Salm-Dyck

Bright-green stems are more or less globular, generally solitary, up to about 12cm tall, 7–8cm across. Ribs number about 13; these are divided into conical tubercles set with areoles at the tips. Radial spines are whitish or straw-coloured, 15–18 to 1cm long; three to four centrals 2-5cm long are yellow with a brownish base, the lowest hooked. Flowers are diurnal, greenish yellow, to 3cm long in summer. Requires bright light; normal cactus compost; minimum temperature 10°C (50°F). *Mexico (Chihuahua), USA (S. Texas).*

   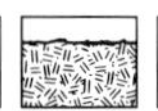 

ANCISTROCACTUS **TOBUSCHII** Marsh

Stems are globular, about 7cm long and in diameter, dark glossy green, solitary and divided into a series of spirally arranged prominent tubercles, each tipped with a conspicuous areole. There are about seven greyish-white radial spines 1–1.5cm long, spreading, and three centrals to 3cm in length. Flowers are greenish yellow to 4cm long in summer, diurnal. A comparatively uncommon species, it requires slight shade; normal cactus compost; minimum temperature 10°C (50°F). *USA (Texas).*

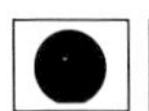     

ANCISTROCACTUS **UNCINATUS** (Gal.) L. Benson
Syn: *Echinocactus uncinatus* Gal.; *Hamatocactus uncinatus* (Gal.) Buxb.; *Glandulicactus uncinatus* (Gal.) Backeb.

Short columnar, bluish-green, 20cm high, 7cm thick, 13 straight ribs. Areoles surrounded by yellowish hairs; spines are reddish. The brownish flowers are diurnal appearing in mid-summer, to 2.5cm long. Needs bright light; normal cactus compost with added grit; minimum temperature 10°C (50°F). *USA (Texas), Mexico (Northern to Central).*

 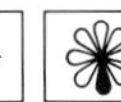  

APOROCACTUS

APOROCACTUS **CONZATTII** (Berger) Br. & R.
Syn: *Cereus conzattii* Berger

Creeping or pendant plants, with stems to 1m long, 1–2.5cm thick with eight to ten low tuberculate ribs and fairly close-set areoles with many pale-brown spines. Flowers diurnal, appearing in summer, are bright red, 8–9cm long. The petals are in two series, the inner slightly incurving, the outer rather reflexed; the style and stamens are white. Suitable for hanging baskets. Requires partial shade; normal cactus compost; minimum temperature 13°C (55°F). *Mexico (Oaxaca).*

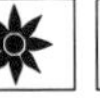  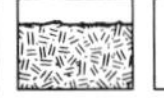 

APOROCACTUS **FLAGELLIFORMIS** (L.) Lemaire
Syn: *Cactus flagelliformis* L. (1753)

Greyish-green stems are creeping or pendant up to 2m in length, 1–2cm thick, with 10–14 low-set ribs and close-set areoles each with 15 or more yellow spines. Day flowering, in early summer, the red blooms are zygomorphic, 7–8cm long, and last for several days. Outer petals are narrow, reflexed; inner petals are wider and partially spreading. Ideal for hanging baskets. Needs a sunny position; rich acid compost; minimum temperature 10°C (50°F). *Mexico, Central America.*

    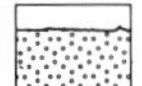 

APOROCACTUS **FLAGELLIFORMIS** (Mill.) Lem. **'Cristata'**

On rare occasions, a monstrose growth develops to form an unusual hand-shaped crest from which normal growth is very likely to appear. To maintain the cristated form it is best to graft on to robust stock. *Mexico.*

APOROCACTUS **MARTIANUS** (Zucc.) Br. & R.
Syn: *Cereus martianus* Zucc.; *Eriocereus martianus* Ricco.

A creeping, pendant plant with stems over 1m long, to 2cm in diameter. There are eight low ribs with six to eight radials and two or more yellowish, rather bristle-like central spines. Flowers are red, diurnal, appearing in early summer, about 10cm long, 6cm across, and are somewhat funnel-shaped. A bright location is important; requires normal cactus compost; minimum temperature 13°C (55°F). *Mexico (Oaxaca).*

APOROCACTUS × **WILLIAMSONII** Knebel

One of the earliest recorded hybrids within the genus, the parentage is believed to be *Aporocactus flagriformis* × *Aporocactus martianus.* It flowers in spring; the petals are suffused violet-pink. Suitable for hanging baskets. Requires slight shade; normal cactus compost; minimum temperature 13°C (55°F).

     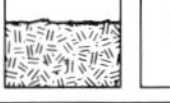 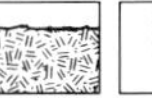 

APOROCACTUS **FLAGRIFORMIS** (Zucc.) Lem.

The greyish-green stems are about 1.5cm thick, to 75cm or more long and of pendant habit. Ribs, seven to ten with areoles set 1–1.5cm apart, are yellowish. Spines consist of six to eight weak radials and four to five centrals up to 1cm long. Day flowering in late spring, the flowers are slightly irregular, crimson with pinkish-edged inner petals, 7.5cm broad, 10cm long. An epiphyte, it is suitable for hanging baskets. Requires slight shade; normal cactus compost; minimum temperature 13°C (55°F). *Mexico.*

    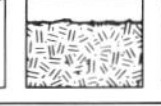 

APOROCACTUS **MOENNINGHOFFII** Fischer

Reputedly a hybrid between *Aporocactus flagelliformis* and *Aporocactus martianus.* The stems and flowers are more similar to the latter species, but the coloration of flowers can be most variable. It is day flowering, in early spring. Needs slight shade; normal cactus compost; minimum temperature 10°C (50°F).

   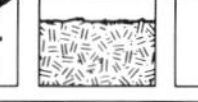 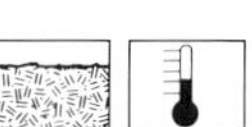

× APOROHELIOCEREUS **SMITHII** (Pfeiff.) Rowley
Syn: *Aporocactus mallisonii* hort.; *Cereus mallisonii* Pfeiff.; *Cereus smithii* Pfeiff.

An inter-generic hybrid of *Aporocactus flagelliformis* and *Heliocereus speciosa.* The stem is dark green, pendant, with six to eight ribs and dark-brown areoles with many radiating dark spines. Flowers are diurnal, in summer, to 7cm long, 4–6cm across, with reddish pink petals in three series. It is suitable for hanging baskets. A bright position is essential. Requires normal cactus compost; minimum temperature 10°C (50°F).

    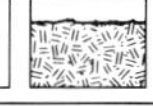 

APOROPHYLLUM × **CASCADE** Barber

An inter-generic hybrid reputed to be between *Aporocactus martianus* and *Nopalxochia phyllanthoides*. The pale-green, three-to-five-angled stems very much resemble those of the former species, the main stems reaching 30–40cm in length. The diurnal flowers appear in late spring and early summer, and are about 4cm long and in diameter. The paler inner petals and the richer deep rose outer segments are representative of both parents. Requires a bright position; normal cactus compost; minimum temperature 13°C (55°F).

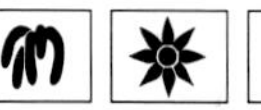    

APOROPHYLLUM × **HELENA** Innes

An inter-generic hybrid of *Aporocactus martianus* and *Epicactus* × *Scheherazade*, one of the more remarkable results of cross-pollinating. Stems are bright green, four to five angled, with prominent tubercles tipped with woolly areoles. The spines, fine and bristly, soon fall. Flowers occur in late spring and early summer, up to 10cm diameter when fully open. The deep magenta colouring of both parents is very apparent but the petal structure is unique. Requires bright light; normal cactus compost; minimum temperature 13°C (55°F).

APOROPHYLLUM × **RETTIGII** (?) Knebel

Parentage is uncertain. The stems are trailing or pendant, to about 60cm long and 2cm thick, and four to five angled with prominent tubercles tipped with minutely woolly areoles and a few grey bristly spines. Flowering by day in late spring and early summer, the blooms are about 6cm long, 6–8cm across when fully expanded, and somewhat funnel-shaped. Petals are lilac pink, rarely a deeper shade, and last for several days. Requires a bright position; normal cactus compost; minimum temperature 13°C (55°F).

     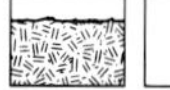  

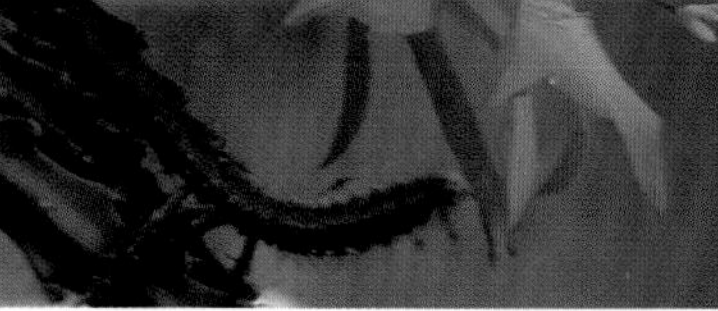

APOROPHYLLUM × **SABRA** Innes

An inter-generic hybrid of *Aporocactus martianus* and *Epicactus 'Dreamland'* which depicts the flower shape of the former and the colouring of the latter. Stems are dark green, four to five angled with wart-like prominences and the areoles bear a few yellowish-grey spines. Flowering in late spring, it is diurnal. Flowers are 5–6cm in diameter with a well-exserted style of deep magenta. Needs a bright position but out of direct sun; normal cactus compost; minimum temperature 13°C (55°F).

 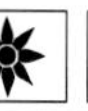  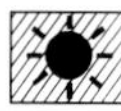 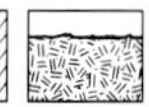 

ARIOCARPUS **AGAVOIDES** (Castañ.) And.
Syn: *Neogomesia agavoides* Castañ.

Plants are 4–8cm in diameter with only few tubercles to 4 cm long, about 6mm wide, resembling the leaves of the *Agave*. Tubercles have a flat upper surface and are rounded below with pointed tips. Tips of tubercles bear areoles from about 1cm, rarely with one to three very short spines. Occurring in mid-summer, the flowers are diurnal, deep pink and 2.5–4cm across. Water in moderation in summer from below, keep dry in winter. Requires full sun; a rich open mineral compost; minimum temperature 13°C (55°F). *Mexico (Tamaulipas).*

ARIOCARPUS **FISSURATUS** (Engelm.) K. Sch.
Syn: *Roseocactus fissuratus* (Engelm.) Berger

Somewhat flat and globular in shape to about 15cm in diameter. The whole surface is covered with three-edged greyish-green tubercles to 2.5cm thick at the base, narrowing to a blunted tip, and deeply wrinkled on the uppermost surface. Day flowering in mid-summer; the flowers are pink, about 4cm in diameter. Requires full sun; an enriched mineral compost; minimum temperature 10°C (50°F). *Mexico (Coahuila), USA (Texas).*

ARIOCARPUS **KOTSCHOUBEYANUS** (Lem.) K. Sch.
Syn: *Roseocactus kotschoubeyanus* (Lem.) Berger; *Anhalonium kotschoubeyanus* Lem.

Plants are up to about 7cm in diameter with close-set, three-angled tubercles to about 1.3cm long, 7–8mm broad, flat on the upper surface and dark green, with a woolly furrow. Flowers are diurnal, growing from the centre of the plant, to 3.5cm long and 5cm across, purplish or pink in colour, appearing in early summer. Water in moderation late spring and summer; keep dry in winter. Requires very bright light; an enriched porous mineral compost; minimum temperature 10°C (50°F). *Mexico (Coahuila).*

    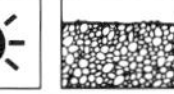

ARIOCARPUS **KOTSCHOUBEYANUS var. ALBIFLORUS** Backeb.

Differs only in respect of the flower colour, which is white. *Mexico (Nuevo Leon).*

    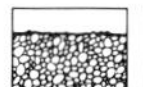 

ARIOCARPUS **KOTSCHOUBEYANUS**
'Cristate form'

An unusual fasciated form with magenta flowers set well apart.

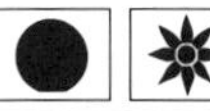 

ARIOCARPUS **TRIGONUS** (Weber) K. Sch.
Syn: *Anhalonium trigonum* Weber

The plants vary in size from 10–15cm in diameter with many semi-erect, greyish-green tubercles to 5cm long, 2.5cm broad at the base. They are acutely triangular with a flat, unfurrowed upper surface and acute tips. Areoles are spineless. The flowers arise from the axils of the tubercles and are yellowish, about 5cm across, diurnal, and appearing in mid-summer. Needs a bright, sunny location; a gritty, but enriched compost; no water in winter; minimum temperature 13°C (55°F). *Mexico (Nuevo Leon, Tamaulipas).*

    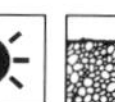 

ARIOCARPUS **RETUSUS** Scheidw.
Syn: *Anhalonium retusum* Salm-Dyck; *Ariocarpus furfuraceus* Thomson

Plants are up to 25cm in diameter and are covered with spreading bluish-green tubercles with horny tips. Each tubercle is about 2cm long, flat on the upper surface. Flowers are diurnal in summer, 4–5cm in diameter, varying in colour from white to pale pink. As with all *Ariocarpus*, plants arise from a thickish tap root, so require careful watering in summer. Keep completely dry in winter. Requires sun; porous rich soil; minimum temperature 10°C (50°F). *Mexico (San Luis Potosi, Nuevo Leon).*

    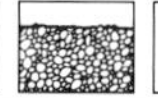 

ARIOCARPUS **SCAPHAROSTRUS** Böed.

A miniature species to about 9cm in diameter with thick, dull greyish-green tubercles to 5cm in length, flat on the upper surface with blunted tip, and no furrow. Plants seemingly are without areoles and definitely spineless, but are lined with thick greyish-white wool between the tubercles. Flowers appear from the centre of the plant in summer and are diurnal, bright rose purple and 3–4cm across, with a creamy-white style and golden-yellow stamens. Keep dry in winter. Flourishes in bright sun; needs a coarse, porous compost; minimum temperature 13°C (55°F). *Mexico (Nuevo Leon).*

ARMATOCEREUS **CARTWRIGHTIANUS** (Br. & R.) Backeb.
Syn: *Lemaireocereus cartwrightianus* Br. & R.

Columnar plants 3–5m high, branching freely. The branches consist of dull green joints 15–60cm in length, 8–15cm thick, with seven to eight prominent ribs. Large brown areoles bear about 20 whitish or dark brownish spines 1–2cm long – on fully mature growth these are often up to 12cm in length. Flowers, appearing in summer, are nocturnal; the inner petals are white, outer petals reddish, and they are 7–8cm long. Requires slight shade; normal cactus compost; minimum temperature 13°C (55°F). *Ecuador, Northern Peru.*

    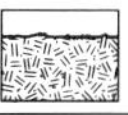 

ARMATOCEREUS **LAETUS** (HBK.) Backeb.
Syn: *Lemaireocereus laetus* (HBK.) Br. & R.

Greyish-green columnar plants 4–6m high, branching freely from the base, with four to eight ribs. The branches are formed of joints which indicate the growth of successive years. Areoles, 2–3cm apart, bear up to 12 brownish-grey spines, 1–2cm long, sometimes much longer. Flowering is in summer, and nocturnal; the flowers are white, 6.5cm long, 5cm across. Requires good light; normal cactus compost; minimum temperature 13°C (55°F). *Northern Peru.*

   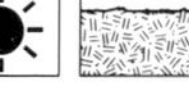 

ARMATOCEREUS **OLIGOGONUS** Rauh & Backeb.

Closely allied to *A. ghiesbreghtii* and *A. laetus*. A tree-like columnar plant about 3m tall; the stems have four to five prominently angled ribs, dull greenish in colour. Areoles bear grey spines, eight to twelve radials up to 1.5cm long and one to two centrals, usually considerably longer. Nocturnal flowering in summer; the flowers are white, about 6cm long, 4–5.5cm in diameter. Needs sun; normal cactus compost; minimum temperature 13°C (55°F). *Peru (Huancabamba).*

ARMATOCEREUS **PROCERUS** Rauh & Backeb.

Columnar plants to 7m high, dark green or grey-green, with eight to ten ribs and large areoles bearing many whitish or brownish spines of varying lengths: 15–20 radials up to 2cm long and four centrals to 12cm in length. Flowering is in summer, and nocturnal. The flowers are white, 10cm long, 5cm across, from the tips of the stems. Bright light is essential; normal cactus compost; minimum temperature 13°C (55°F). *Southern Peru (Nazca).*

ARMATOCEREUS

ARMATOCEREUS **RAUHII** Backeb.

Columnar tree-like plants 4–6m high. The branches are bluish grey-green with prominent joint-like constrictions. There are 10–13 ribs with small whitish areoles bearing six to ten radial spines 1–2mm long and sometimes a few centrals varying from 6mm to 3cm in length. Flowering in mid-summer, the flowers are carmine red. Requires a bright position; normal cactus compost; minimum temperature 13°C (55°F). *Northern Peru.*

    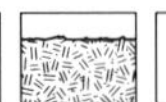 

ARMATOCEREUS **RIOMAJENSIS** Rauh & Backeb.

Columnar plants up to about 2m high, they are dark greyish green with seven to nine narrow ribs about 2cm high. The areoles are round and brownish, bearing 10–15 greyish radial spines to 1cm long and usually one to four centrals which are longer. The plant is night flowering, in summer; flowers are white, 8–10cm long. Bright light is needed; normal cactus compost; minimum temperature 13°C (55°F). *Southern Peru (Rio Majes-Tal).*

ARROJADOA

ARROJADOA **AUREISPINA var. ANGUINEA** Braun & Esteves

A thin-stemmed, often creeping plant to about 1m long, 1.5–3cm thick with 13–15 ribs bearing more or less flexible yellowish or brownish spines consisting of 10-15 radials 1–5mm long and four centrals 3–7mm in length. Flowers are semi-nocturnal in summer, rose to pink, up to 4.2cm long. Requires bright light; normal cactus compost; minimum temperature 10°C (50°F). *Brazil (Bahia).*

    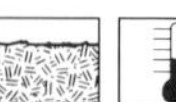  

ARROJADOA **AUREISPINA var. AUREISPINA** Buin. & Bred.

An erect plant to about 1m tall, with 5–5.5cm diameter stems. Spines are golden yellow, with many radials and about nine centrals up to 1.4cm long. Flowers are rose pink, somewhat tubular in shape, 2.8–3.1cm long, appearing by day in summer. Needs bright light but not direct sun; normal cactus compost; minimum temperature 10°C (50°F). *Brazil (Bahia).*

ARROJADOA **AUREISPINA var. GUANAMBENSIS** Braun & Heimen

An erect to creeping species with stems to about 30cm long and 3.5cm thick with 10–11 ribs bearing many brownish spines to 1.5cm in length, including five to seven centrals. Flowers are diurnal in summer, deep rose pink and 3.5cm long. Requires filtered light; normal cactus compost; minimum temperature 10°C (50°F). *Brazil (Bahia).*

ARROJADOA **BEATEAE** Braun & Esteves

An unusual species only discovered in 1987. It has more or less erect stems with about 10 ribs, many yellowish-brown spines and bicoloured flowers of rose pink and yellowish white arising from the terminal dark-brown spiny cephalium. Needs slight shade; normal cactus compost; minimum temperature 10°C (50°F). *Brazil (Minas Gerais).*

ARROJADOA **HORSTIANA** Braun & Heimen

One of the more remarkable species of the genus and a native of high mountainous regions. Stems are almost globular between the cephalia and carry only very short spines. Flowers are small, almost tubular in shape, purplish red, and day flowering in summer. Needs bright light; normal cactus compost; minimum temperature 10°C (50°F). Very careful watering is essential. *Brazil (Minas Gerais).*

ARROJADOA **PENICILLATA** (Gürke) Br. & R.

A bushy, clustering species with semi-erect or prostrate stems up to 2m in length, about 1.5cm in diameter, with 10–12 shallow ribs. Spines are yellowish, eventually grey, consisting of eight to twelve radials and one or two centrals from 1–3cm long. Flowers appear in clusters from a reddish-brown, bristly cephalium in summer, and are diurnal, bright deep pink, 2cm long and across. Needs good light; normal cactus compost; minimum temperature 10°C (50°F). *Brazil (Bahia).*

ARROJADOA **RHODANTHA** (Gürke) Br. & R.

An erect, often climbing plant to about 2m tall. The stems are more or less cylindrical, dark green and 2–4cm thick. There are 10–14 low-set ribs with areoles arranged about 1cm apart. Spines are at first yellowish, then become brown, of which about 20 are radials and five to six centrals, all very similar at 1–3cm long. Flowers arise in early summer from a brown woolly, reddish-brown bristly cephalium. The blooms are tubular, 3–3.5cm long and 1–1.2cm wide, purplish pink and are diurnal. Stems then continue to grow through the cephalium to form another flowering apex the following year. Very occasionally an unusual form occurs when the cephalium becomes cristated with bristles and wool running laterally on the stem. Requires full sun; normal cactus compost; minimum temperature 13°C (55°F). *Brazil (Bahia, Minas Gerais).*

    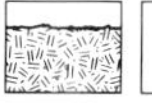 

ARTHROCEREUS Sp. nova

A small genus of Brazilian columnar plants, some decumbent, others more or less erect in habit. The one featured appears to be a new discovery and closely related to *A. rondonianus* which has bright green stems 20–50cm tall and up to 4cm thick with about 13 ribs and many fine yellowish radial spines about 2–5mm long, with one or two centrals usually much longer. Flowers, which are nocturnal and appear in mid-summer, are lilac pink, about 10cm long. Requires bright light; normal cactus compost; minimum temperature 13°C (55°F). *Brazil (Minas Gerais).*

ARTHROCEREUS **MELANURUS var. ESTEVESII** Diers & Braun

The species was earlier included in *Cereus* and *Leocereus*. Stems are cylindrical to 50cm long, 3cm or more thick, branching from the base. Ribs number about 15, the areoles bearing golden-yellow spines varying from 2mm to 5cm in length. Flowers are funnel-shaped, yellowish, and about 6cm long. The plant is night flowering, in summer. Bright light is essential; normal cactus compost; minimum temperature 13°C (55°F). *Brazil (Minas Gerais).*

ARTHROCEREUS **SPINOSISSIMUS** (Buin. & Bred.) Ritter.
Syn: *Eriocereus spinosissimus* Buin. & Bred.

A rare and unusual species which frequents an area thousands of kilometres away from the generally accepted habitat of the genus. The erect green plants, branching from the base with 16 or more ribs, close-set areoles and numerous spines, are night flowering in mid-summer. The flowers are pale pink(?) but has not yet flowered in cultivation. Needs good light; slightly calcareous cactus compost; minimum temperature 13°C (55°F). *Brazil (Mato Grosso).*

      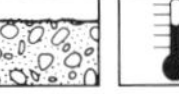 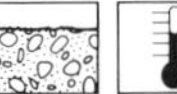

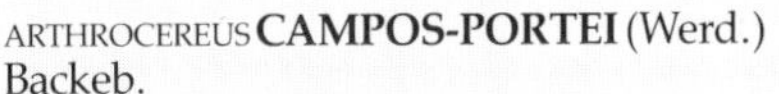

ARTHROCEREUS **CAMPOS-PORTEI** (Werd.) Backeb.

A semi-decumbent, clustering species with stems to 15cm long, 3cm thick and about 12 ribs. Spines are brownish becoming white, consisting of 25–35 radials 7mm long and one or two centrals to 4cm in length. Night flowering in summer, the flowers are white, about 8cm long. Needs fairly bright light; normal cactus compost; minimum temperature 13°C (55°F). *Brazil (Minas Gerais).*

  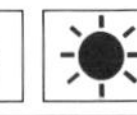 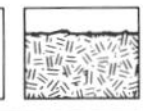 

ASTROPHYTUM **ASTERIAS** (Zucc.) Lem.
Syn: *Echinocereus asterias* Zucc.

A globular, solitary species, slightly flat on the top, about 10cm in diameter with six to eight or more totally flat ribs with straight grooves between and white, conspicuous spineless areoles set lengthwise on the ribs. Stems are purplish brown and the flowers are diurnal in early summer, about 3cm long and 4cm across, yellow, slightly reddish in the throat, but pollen tends to disguise this coloration. Requires a sunny position; normal cactus compost; minimum temperature 7°C (45°F). *Mexico (Tamaulipas).*

ASTROPHYTUM **ASTERIAS fma 'Mirakuru Kabuto'**

An extraordinary variant known from just one individual field-collected plant and sold at a high price in Japan. Propagations have been made possible by cross-pollinating with the typical form or by grafting. The title is Japanese for 'miracle plant'.

ASTROPHYTUM **CAPRICORNE var. CRASSISPINUM** (Möll.) Ok.

A rare variety mainly found in Coahuila which has particularly thick spines. Day flowering in summer, the flowers are long, red and yellow. *Northern Mexico.*

ASTROPHYTUM **MYRIOSTIGMA** (Salm-Dyck) Lem.
Syn: *Echinocactus myriostigma* Salm-Dyck

A high-altitude species found at over 2000m (6563ft), the plant is more or less rounded and 10–20cm in diameter, basically green but totally covered with minute whitish scales which obliterate the green. It has four to eight ribs with brownish, woolly areoles, but no spines. Flowers appear in summer, and are diurnal, 4–6cm long and across, yellow, sometimes with a red centre. Requires a bright location; normal cactus compost; minimum temperature 10°C (50°F). *Northern and Central Mexico.*

      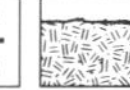  

ASTROPHYTUM **CAPRICORNE** (Dietr.) Br. & R.
Syn: *Echinocactus capricornis* Dietr.; *Maierocactus capricornis* Rost.

Plants are globular, becoming oval to about 20cm high, 10cm broad with about eight to nine acute ribs, deeply grooved between with brownish areoles and dotted with many whitish scales. There are many long and twisted spines, 3–10cm long, yellowish to brownish-black. Flowers, yellow with a reddish centre, are diurnal, in early summer, growing from areoles near to the top, and are 6–7cm long. Requires full sun; normal cactus compost; minimum temperature 10°C (50°F). *Northern Mexico.*

    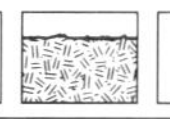 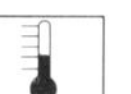

ASTROPHYTUM **MYRIOSTIGMA var. COAHUILENSIS** Möll
Syn: *Astrophytum coahuilense* (Möll.) Kayser

A somewhat conical species with five straight, broad ribs densely covered with whitish scale-like dots. The areoles are spineless. Flowers are produced from near the crown of the plant, and are diurnal in mid-summer. The blooms are bright sulphur-yellow with a minute reddish blotch in the throat. A sun-loving plant; requires normal cactus compost; minimum temperature 7°C (45°F). *Mexico (Coahuila).*

ASTROPHYTUM **MYRIOSTIGMA fma 'LOTUSLAND'**

A peculiar monstrose form which was developed in cultivation in the Botanic Garden, Lotusland, at Santa Barbara, California. It flowers infrequently; the flowers are yellow.

ASTROPHYTUM **MYRIOSTIGMA var. POTOSINUM** (Möll.) Krzgr.

A variant of the species, similar in shape but with far fewer whitish scales, giving the body a dark greyish-green colour. It has five to seven straight, acute or rounded ribs; the areoles are spineless. Flowers are diurnal, in summer; they are a bright, clear golden yellow with no red blotch in the centre, 3–5cm across when fully open. Requirements are the same as for the species. *Mexico (San Luis Potosi).*

ASTROPHYTUM **MYRIOSTIGMA var. COLUMNARE** (K. Sch.) Tsuda
Syn: *Astrophytum columnare* (K. Sch.) Sadovsky & Schütz

An unusual, rather columnar plant. The stem is elongated to about 25cm high, about 8cm in diameter with seven to eight prominent ribs with furrows between and the whole body is covered with fine, whitish scales. Areoles are spineless. Flowers are about 6cm long and across when fully open, yellow with a red blotch in the throat, and appear by day in summer. Needs a bright position; normal cactus compost; minimum temperature 10°C (50°F). *Mexico.*

ASTROPHYTUM **MYRIOSTIGMA var. QUADRICOSTATUM** (Möll.) Baum.

An interesting variety in respect to the rib formation. The greyish-green body is divided into four almost even, broad ribs with a distinct furrow between. The flowers and requirements are the same as for the species. *Mexico (Central areas).*

ASTROPHYTUM **MYRIOSTIGMA var. POTOSINUM** Backeb.

This variety is similar to the species in shape and other characteristics except that the body of the plant has few or no whitish scales or wool, remaining completely green, and is possibly synonymous with the variety *nudum* (R. Mey.) Backeb. Flowers and requirements are the same as for the species. *Mexico (Central areas).*

    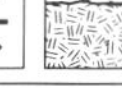  

ASTROPHYTUM **MYRIOSTIGMA × ASTERIAS**

Several interesting and unusual hybrids have been developed by cross-pollination of these two fascinating species, many being the work of Gil Tegelberg of the USA. Cultivation requirements are as for the species.

     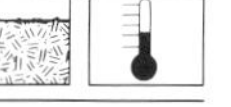

ASTROPHYTUM **ORNATUM** (DC.) Weber
Syn: *Echinocactus ornatus* DC.

An attractive species with a more cylindrical stem reaching 30–35cm high, to 15cm in diameter. The whole body is dotted with silvery scales arranged in bands. There are eight ribs, straight or slightly spiralled; the close-set areoles bear five to eleven straight yellowish-brown spines to 4cm long. Flowers are diurnal, pale yellow, 7–9cm long and broad, and appear in early summer. Requires a truly bright position; normal cactus compost; minimum temperature 10°C (50°F). *Mexico (Hidalgo, Queretaro).*

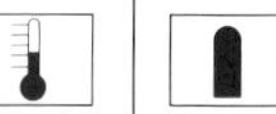   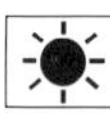 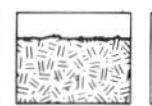 

AUSTROCACTUS **HIBERNUS** Ritter

A short, erect, greenish plant to 10cm long, 3cm in diameter, with seven to eight distinct ribs to 6mm high. Areoles are pale yellow, bearing five to eight whitish radial spines 3–10cm long, the upper one about 2cm and yellowish brown; one to four central spines 1–3cm long. The diurnal flowers are borne on the tips of the stems in summer; they are yellowish brown, about 5cm long. The plant needs careful cultivation: good light; normal cactus compost; minimum temperature best at 10°C (50°F). *Chile.*

  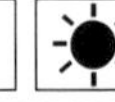  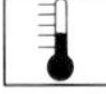

AUSTROCEPHALOCEREUS **DYBOWSKII** (Goss.) Backeb.
Syn: *Cephalocereus dybowskii* (Goss.) Br. & R.; *Cereus dybowskii* Goss.

An erect columnar plant 2–4m high, 8–10cm thick. There are 20–28 low ribs densely covered with fine spines and matted yellowish wool; many fine radial spines and two to three yellowish centrals, 2–3cm long. The cephalium is of white wool, 20–60cm long, from which protrude whitish bell-shaped flowers 4–6cm long. These are nocturnal, in summer. Needs sun; normal cactus compost; minimum temperature 15°C (59°F). *Brazil (Bahia).*

    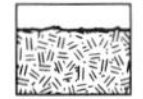 

AUSTROCEPHALOCEREUS **LEHMANNIANUS** (Werd.) Backeb.

Columnar plants up to about 2m tall with branches around 8cm thick. They are bluish green, with about 20 ribs 5–8mm high, the thick areoles bearing about 40 whitish spines to 2cm in length. The dense woolly, bristly cephalium is about 50cm long; flowers are nocturnal in summer, and are about 3.5cm long, with white inner petals, externally reddish pink and scaly. Needs a bright sunny position; normal cactus compost; minimum temperature 15°C (59°F). *Brazil (Bahia).*

AZTEKIUM **RITTERI** Böed.
Syn: *Echinocactus ritteri* Böed.

A unique species of a flattened, globular shape to about 5cm thick, often sprouting from the base to form compact groups. The nine to eleven ribs, about 1cm high, 8mm broad, are olive green. Areoles are minute and closely set with one to four flat, papery, twisting spines to 4mm long which soon fall. Flowers arise from new areoles in the centre and are white or pink, 1cm long, 8mm wide. Requires full sun; a porous mineral-based soil; minimum temperature 10°C (50°F). *Mexico (Nuevo Leon on stony, slate slopes).*

    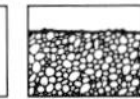 

BACKEBERGIA

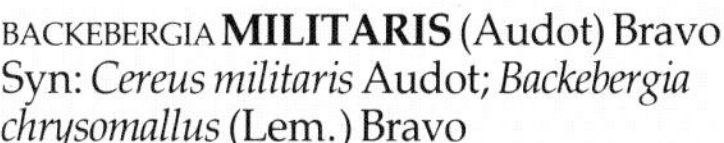

BACKEBERGIA **MILITARIS** (Audot) Bravo
Syn: *Cereus militaris* Audot; *Backebergia chrysomallus* (Lem.) Bravo

A tree-like columnar plant to 6m tall, with stems up to 12cm thick and five to eleven ribs. Areoles have greyish spines, seven to thirteen radials and one to four centrals, 1cm long. There is a terminal, dome-like cephalium of orange-brown bristles. Flowers are nocturnal, in summer, and are orange red opening to creamy whites, up to 7cm long, 4cm wide. Requires full sun; normal cactus compost; minimum temperature 13°C (55°F). *Mexico (Guerrero, Michoacan).*

   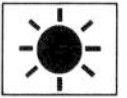 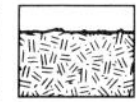 

BERGEROCACTUS

BERGEROCACTUS **EMORYI** (Engelm.) Br. & R.
Syn: *Cereus emoryi* Engelm.; *Echinocereus emoryi* Rümpl.

A pale green bushy, columnar plant with stems 20–60cm long, 3–6cm thick, offsetting from the base, with 14–20 or more low ribs. The areoles are fairly closely set, each with 10–30 golden-yellow spines including one to four centrals. Flowers are diurnal, in summer, growing from the tips of the stems, 2–4cm long and across and are bright yellow. A sunny position is essential; needs normal cactus compost; minimum temperature 10°C (50°F). *USA (California), Mexico.*

    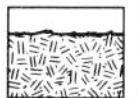 

BLOSSFELDIA

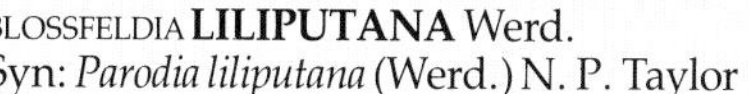

BLOSSFELDIA **LILIPUTANA** Werd.
Syn: *Parodia liliputana* (Werd.) N. P. Taylor

A very small, greyish-green globular plant about 1cm in diameter. There are no ribs and no spines. Flowers are diurnal in mid-summer, whitish yellow, and up to 1cm wide when fully open. Best grafted on to robust stock. Requires very bright light; normal cactus compost; minimum temperature 13°C (55°F). *Argentina, Bolivia.*

   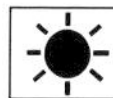 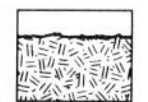 

BORZICACTUS **FIELDIANUS** Br. & R.
Syn: *Clistanthocereus fieldianus* (Br. & R.) Backeb.

Erect or semi-prostrate plants with stems 3–6m in length, branching from the base, and six to seven ribs with large areoles notched between. Spines are white, six to ten in number, varying in size to about 4cm long. Day flowering in summer; the flowers are red, 6–7cm long. Needs slight shade; normal cactus compost; minimum temperature 10°C (50°F). *Peru (Huaraz).*

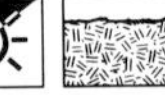
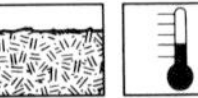

BORZICACTUS **ROEZLII** Backeb.
Syn: *Seticereus roezlii* (Haage Jr.) Backeb.

Columnar, greyish green and 1–2m high, about 7cm thick. Seven to fourteen ribs, notched above each areole. Areoles are yellowish with nine to fourteen brownish radial spines to 1cm long and one greyish central 1–4cm in length. The tips of the stems are covered with tufts of bristles through which flowers appear in summer. These are diurnal, tubular, red, 6–7cm long. Bright light essential; normal cactus compost; minimum temperature 13°C (55°F). *Northern Peru.*

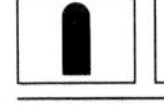

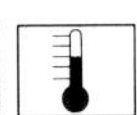

BORZICACTUS **LEUCOTRICHUS** (Phil.) Kimnach.
Syn: *Arequipa leucotricha* (Phil.) Br. & R.

A short columnar species to about 60cm high. The stem is about 10cm thick, greyish green, with yellowish wool at the tips and about 20 prominent, bumpy ribs. The white areoles have eight to twelve yellow radial spines up to 3cm long and three to four reddish-brown centrals to 4.5cm in length. It is summer flowering and diurnal; the flowers are bright scarlet, up to 7.5cm long, 3.5cm across. Needs sun; normal cactus compost with added grit; minimum temperature 10°C (50°F). *Chile (Tarapaca).*

BORZICACTUS **NANUS** (Akers)
Syn: *Loxanthocereus nanus* (Akers) Backeb.; *Maritimocereus nana* Akers

A species which apparently belongs to this genus, but is not yet reclassified. It is low growing with a short stem of about 10cm, and 12–14 ribs. The whitish areoles bear about eight pale brownish radial spines to 1cm long and one to three centrals of similar length. Flowers are zygomorphic, deep scarlet-orange and are diurnal, in summer. Requires sun; normal cactus compost; minimum temperature 13°C (55°F). *Southern Peru.*

BORZICACTUS **ROSEIFLORUS** (Buin.) Kimnach
Syn: *Akersia roseiflora* Buin.

A low, spreading plant with rather trailing, 4–5cm thick pale green stems to 1m long and 16–17 low ribs. Spines are yellowish, 30–40 in number, about 1cm long, but longer in the flowering area. Day flowering in summer; the flowers are lilac pink, about 5cm long, 3cm across. Needs full sun; normal cactus compost; minimum temperature 10°C (50°F). *Northern Peru.*

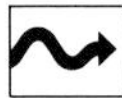

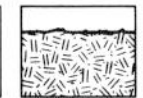

BORZICACTUS **SAMAIPATANUS** Card.
Syn: *Bolivicereus samaipatanus* Card.; *Cleistocactus samaipatanus* (Card.) D. R. Hunt

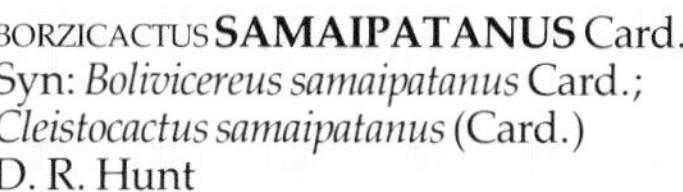

An erect, later pendant plant with bright green stems to 1.5m long, 3–5cm thick, and 14–16 ribs. The areoles are brownish, set 3–4mm apart and bearing 13–22 slender yellowish-brown spines from 4mm to about 3cm in length. Day flowering in summer, the flowers are tubular, curved, and 4–6cm long; deep red with paler edges. Requires sun; normal cactus compost; minimum temperature 10°C (50°F). *Bolivia (Santa Cruz).*

   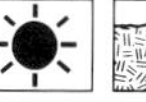 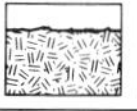 

BRACHYCEREUS **NESIOTICUS** (K. Sch.) Backeb.

Rather short columnar, clustering plants. The stems are 30-60cm in length, greenish, with dense spines which are initially yellowish brown, becoming grey. There are 13–16 ribs with pale brownish areoles 2.5mm wide, each bearing around 40 or more spines up to 3cm long. It is nocturnal flowering in summer. The flowers are borne from the sides of the stems and are 4–6.5cm long, 2.5–3cm in diameter with narrow, white petals. Needs full sun; slightly calcareous compost; minimum temperature 15°C (59°F). *Galapagos Islands.*

   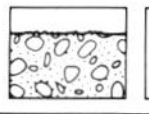 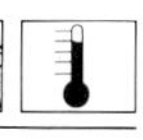

BROWNINGIA **CANDELARIS** (Meyen) Br. & R.

A tree-like columnar species to 5m high with a base of about 50cm in diameter, branching from above. Mature branches develop about 50 ribs. Areoles are closely set, bearing 20 or more yellowish-brown spines up to 1cm long. The main trunk produces spines 10–15cm in length. Flowers are nocturnal in summer, tubular and 8–12cm in length. The inner petals are whitish, the outer segments darkish pink. The oval fruits are about 7cm long. Requires bright light; normal cactus compost; minimum temperature 13°C (55°F). *Southern Peru, Northern Chile.*

    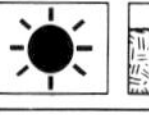 

BROWNINGIA **HERTLINGIANA** (Backeb.) Buxb.
Syn: *Azureocereus hertlingianus* (Backeb.) Backeb.; *Azureocereus nobilis* Akers

Columnar, bluish green, to 8m tall, 30cm wide. The 18 or more ribs have prominent areoles, grey-felted, with four to seven radial spines and up to three centrals about 8cm long. As plants mature, more spines develop; yellowish grey with brown tips. Flowers in summer, nocturnal; inner petals white, purplish externally, about 5cm wide. Needs a bright position; normal cactus compost with a little lime; minimum temperature 13°C (55°F). *Peru (Mantaro Valley).*

   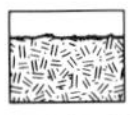 

BROWNINGIA **HERTLINGIANA** (Backeb.) Buxb. fma. *'monstrosus'*

An interesting malformed feature occurs on many cacti, and invariably this is most spectacular, especially when it is seen in the wild.

BROWNINGIA **MICROSPERMA** (Werd. & Backeb.) Borg
Syn: *Gymnocereus microspermus* (Werd. & Backeb.) Backeb.

A tree-like columnar plant to about 6m high and about 30cm in diameter. The branches have 12–20 rounded ribs, about 5mm high. Areoles are about 5mm apart, yellowish, bearing numerous yellowish-brown or reddish-brown spines from 5mm to 2.5cm in length. Flowers are 3–4cm long and across, white with brownish-red sepals. Flowers in summer, nocturnal. Needs sun; normal cactus compost; minimum temperature 13°C (55°F). *Northern Peru.*

BUININGIA **AUREA** (Ritter) Buxb.
Syn: *Coleocephalocereus aureus* Ritter

A short, columnar plant to about 60cm tall in the wild, branching freely from the base to form clumps. Individual stems are 7–10cm thick, dull green, with 10–16 ribs and golden-yellow spines consisting of 10–15 radials 1–2cm long, and one to four centrals 5–7cm in length. A pseudocephalium develops laterally which is composed of white wool and yellow bristles from which flowers appear. These are nocturnal, occurring in summer, pale yellowish-green in colour and very small. Requires full sun; normal cactus compost; minimum temperature 13°C (55°F). *Brazil (Minas Gerais).*

BUININGIA **BREVICYLINDRICA** Buin.
Syn: *Coleocephalocereus brevicylindricus* (Buin.) Ritter

Globular at first, the plant later becomes short and cylindrical, often clustering around the base. Stems are deep green, about 17cm in diameter, eventually up to 30cm tall, and have 12–18 ribs. Areoles are whitish, bearing about seven yellowish-grey radial spines 1–3cm long, and usually four straight or slightly curved yellowish centrals, the lower ones up to 6cm in length, the others 2.5–3cm long. The semi-terminal cephalium of white wool and yellowish bristly spines is about 8cm in diameter with creamy-yellow tubular flowers about 3cm long, 1.5cm wide, protruding in summer; these are nocturnal. Needs sun; an enriched mineral compost; minimum temperature 15°C (59°F). *Brazil (Minas Gerais).*

    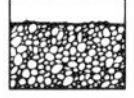

CALYMMANTHIUM **SUBSTERILE** Ritter

A tree-like, bushy columnar plant to about 8m tall in the wild. The stems are pale green, 4–8cm thick and have three to four ribs. Areoles are whitish, bearing three to eight radial spines to 1cm in length, and one to six centrals, 1.5cm long, all white. Flowers are nocturnal, occurring in summer. The buds initially appear as small shoots, then open to a white flower 9.5–11cm long and 3–5cm across, with reddish-brown outer petals. Requires bright light; normal cactus compost; minimum temperature 13°C (55°F). *Peru (Jaen).*

CARNEGIEA **GIGANTEA** (Engelm.) Br. & R.

The celebrated 'Saguaro' of the Arizona desert. An erect, dark-green tree-like giant, to about 14m tall, 65cm thick. There are 12–24 ribs with areoles about 2cm apart bearing 12 or more brownish-grey radial spines 1–2cm in length, and three to six thicker brownish centrals 7–8cm long. Flowers are nocturnal, appearing in early summer from the end of the branches; the inner petals are white, greenish externally, about 12cm long and across. The plant is slow growing. Requires full sun; normal cactus compost; minimum temperature 10°C (50°F). *USA (Arizona, California), Mexico (Sonora).*

CEPHALOCEREUS **HOPPENSTEDTII** (Weber) K. Sch.
Syn: *Haseltonia columna-trajani* (Karw.) Backeb.

Columnar, unbranched, 6–10m high to 30cm thick in middle, greyish green. About 16 ribs bear areoles 5mm apart, with 14–18 whitish radial spines to 1cm long and five to eight centrals to 8cm. Flowers appear in summer from near top of stems, through the whitish wool and yellowish spines of the pseudocephalium. They are nocturnal, white or pale yellow. Needs full sun; calcareous cactus compost; minimum temperature 13°C (55°F). *Mexico (Oaxaca).*

   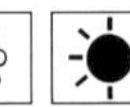 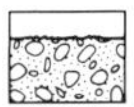 

CEPHALOCEREUS **SENILIS** (Haw.) Pfeiff.
Syn: *Cereus senilis* DC.

Known as the 'Old Man Cactus'. A columnar plant frequently branching from the base, it reaches to 15m tall and 40cm thick. 12-30 ribs are low and rounded, with close-set areoles bearing 20–30 hair-like white radial spines 6–12cm long, and one to five central spines 1.2–5cm in length. A cephalium forms in maturity, which produces whitish-yellow flowers about 8.5cm long, 7cm across. These are nocturnal, in summer. Requires full sun; normal cactus compost with a little lime; minimum temperature 13°C (55°F). *Mexico (Hidalgo, Guanajuato).*

CEREUS **AETHIOPS** Haw.
Syn: *Cereus coerulescens* Salm-Dyck

An erect, rarely branching columnar plant to 2m tall, 3–4cm in diameter, dark bluish later becoming dark green, with eight ribs bearing small warts. Areoles are about 1.5cm apart and are almost black, with nine to twelve usually black radial spines to 1.2cm long and two to four black centrals up to 2cm in length. The flowers, up to 20cm long, with white or pale pink inner petals and greenish-brown outer petals, are nocturnal, appearing in summer. Requires normal cactus compost; bright light; minimum temperature 10°C (50°F). *Argentina (Mendoza).*

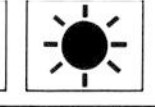
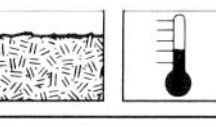

CEREUS **ARGENTINENSIS** Br. & R.

A much-branching columnar plant to 12m high. The branches are 10–15cm thick and a pale bluish green. There are four to five ribs to 5cm high which are broadly furrowed and five to eight brownish radial spines up to 5cm in length, with one or two centrals to 10cm long. The funnel-shaped flowers are about 22cm long, with white inner petals and green outer petals tinged red. These are nocturnal appearing in summer. Needs a sunny position; normal cactus compost; minimum temperature 10°C (50°F). *Argentina (Chaco).*

    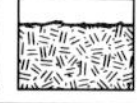  

CEREUS **CHALYBAEUS** Otto

A tall columnar plant to 3m high with few branches 5–10cm thick, bluish to dark green in colour. There are five to six ribs with areoles set about 2cm apart bearing seven to nine blackish radial spines to 1.4cm long and three to four similarly coloured centrals slightly longer. Flowering in summer, the flowers are white, reddish externally, to 20cm long, and are nocturnal. Requires full sun; normal cactus compost; minimum temperature 10°C (50°F). *Brazil, Argentina.*

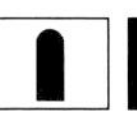    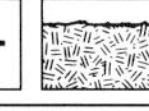 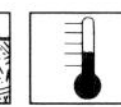

CEREUS **FORBESII** Otto

A columnar species, frequently branching with erect branches, reaching up to 4m high in its habitat; the dull bluish-green branches are 7–12cm thick. Ribs usually number six and are often notched with large areoles set about 3cm apart, bearing five to seven radial spines 1–2cm long, and one or two centrals up to 5cm in length. These are all yellowish brown, awl-shaped, with blackish bases. Nocturnal flowering in summer, the flowers are about 6cm long, trumpet-shaped and white. Requires bright light; normal cactus compost; minimum temperature 13°C (55°F). *Argentina* .

CEREUS **INSULARIS** Hemsl.
Syn: *Monvillea insularis* (Hemsl.) Br. & R.

A much-branching, usually trailing plant, the stems are about 3cm thick, deep green. Ribs are straight, six to eight in number with fairly close-set grey areoles bearing 12–15 slender, brownish-yellow to greyish-brown spines to 1cm in length. Flowers are yellow, about 12–15cm long, and are nocturnal, appearing in summer. Needs slight shade; normal cactus compost, kept slightly moist throughout the year; minimum temperature 15°C (59°F). *Northern Brazil (St. Michael's Island).*

    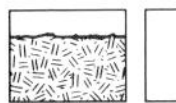 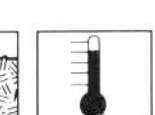

CEREUS **PERUVIANUS** (L.) Mill.

A tall columnar, branching species, 3–5m tall, 10–25cm thick, bluish to dull green. It has five to eight ribs, acutely furrowed, and the areoles are brown, about 2cm apart, bearing four to seven brown radial spines 1cm long with one reddish-brown central 2cm long. Nocturnal flowers appear in summer; these are white with greenish-brown outer petals, about 16cm long. Requires bright light; normal cactus compost; minimum temperature 10°C (50°F). *Argentina, Brazil (very uncertain).*

    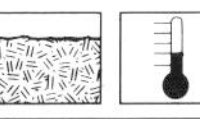

CHAMAELOBIVIA **'Calvini'**

A cultivar of *Chamaecereus (Lobivia) silvestrii* and a colour form of *L. jajoiana* reputed to have been developed in Holland. Flowering early to midsummer, it is diurnal. Needs good light; normal cactus compost; minimum temperature 10°C (50°F).

    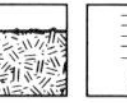

CHAMAELOBIVIA **'Joanne'**

A brilliantly coloured cultivar of *Lobivia (Chamaecereus) silvestrii* and *Lobivia jajoiana*. The 'peanut'-like stems of the first parent are more stunted, but the vivid flower clearly depicts the other parent, *L. jajoiana*. Flowering in midsummer, it is diurnal. Needs good light; normal cactus compost; minimum temperature 10°C (50°F).

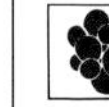 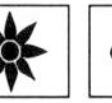 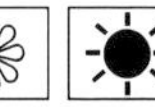 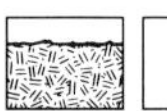

CHAMAELOBIVIA **'Fire Chief'**

A colourful hybrid of *Lobivia* × *Echinopsis* × *Chamaecereus (Lobivia) silvestrii* developed by Harry Johnson of the USA. One of the most startling cultivars yet produced.

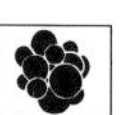    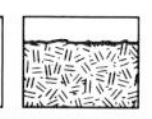 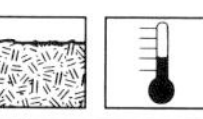

CHAMAELOBIVIA **'Yellow Flame'**

A hybrid between *Chamaecereus (Lobivia) silvestrii* and *Lobivia famatimensis* which was developed about 1945. The stems are similar to those of a typical 'peanut cactus', the flowers reminiscent of the *L. famatimensis*. They appear by day, in summer. Requires bright light; normal cactus compost; minimum temperature 7°C (45°F).

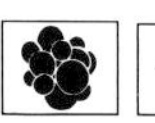    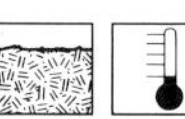

CIPOCEREUS **AURISETUS** (Werd.)

A short, bluish-green columnar plant to about 1m tall, the stems about 6cm in diameter. This is a freely branching species having about 15 ribs with greyish-white areoles bearing numerous fine spines up to 2.5cm long. Flowers are borne laterally from often elongated pseudocephaliums comprised of whitish wool and bristly yellow spines up to 5cm in length. The flowers are whitish, about 5cm long, nocturnal, and appear in summer. Requires sun; normal cactus compost; minimum temperature 13°C (55°F). *Brazil (Serra do Cipo).*

CIPOCEREUS **MENIENSIS** (Werd.) Ritter

Also spelt *'minensis'*. Green columnar plants 1m or more high, 5cm in diameter with 12 or more ribs. The areoles are round and white felted with greyish-white or yellowish spines, about 20 in all to 2cm long, one often longer to 3cm. Flowers are produced laterally; greenish white in colour and about 5cm long, 3cm across, they appear in mid-summer and are nocturnal. Carries blue fruit. Requires bright light; normal cactus compost; minimum temperature 13°C (55°F). *Brazil (Minas Gerais).*

   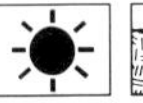 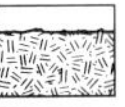 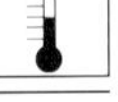

CIPOCEREUS **PLEUROCARPUS** Ritter

A fairly short columnar plant about 3cm in diameter, dull greenish, with 10–16 ribs 3–5mm high. Areoles are brownish white bearing eight to eleven brown radial spines up to 1cm in length, and four or more prominent centrals up to 2.5cm long. Night flowering in mid-summer, the creamy white flowers are produced laterally, about 5cm long, and are slightly scented. Needs good light; normal cactus compost; minimum temperature 13°C (55°F). *Brazil (Serra do Cipo, Minas Gerais).*

    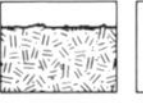 

CLEISTOCACTUS **AZERENSIS** Card.

A slender columnar plant branching from the base. The stems are greyish green, about 4cm thick with about 23 straight ribs. Areoles are brownish with 16–24 whitish or pale yellowish spines about 5mm in length. The flowers, diurnal in mid- to late summer, are violet red, somewhat tubular in shape, and are about 5cm long to 7mm in diameter. Needs good light; normal cactus compost; minimum temperature 10°C (50°F). *Bolivia (Chuquisaca).*

   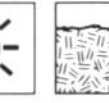  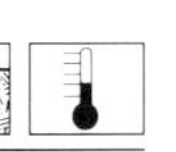

CLEISTOCACTUS **BAUMANNII** (Lem.) Lem.
Syn: *Cereus baumannii* Lem.

An erect columnar plant with stiff stems to 1m high, 3–4cm thick. About 14 ribs have regularly placed areoles each with 15–20 yellowish-brown radial spines to 1.5cm long and one longer central to 2.5cm, yellowish or dark brown. A day-flowering species in summer, the flowers are brilliant red or orange-red, 6–7cm long, curved, with reddish stamens just protruding. Requires sunshine; normal cactus compost; minimum temperature 10°C (50°F). *Argentina, Uruguay, Paraguay.*

CLEISTOCACTUS **HORSTII** P. J. Braub

A rare, recently introduced columnar plant often found near swampy territory. Stems are slender, 1m or more in length, dark green with about 10–11 ribs and regularly arranged brown areoles with greyish spines. Flowers are bright red, about 6cm long. The plant is day flowering, in summer. Water freely in summer, keep barely moist in winter. Needs normal cactus compost; a fairly sunny position; minimum temperature 15°C (59°F). *Brazil (Matto Grosso do Sul).*

CLEISTOCACTUS **RITTERI** Backeb.
Syn: *Cephalocleistocactus ritteri* (Backeb.) Backeb.

A more or less erect columnar plant to about 1m tall. The stems are 3cm in diameter and bright green, with 12–14 or more ribs. Areoles are dull brown, bearing about 30 fine whitish radial spines and about five longer centrals. Mature plants have a more densely whitish-spined flowering zone. The flowers are greenish yellow, about 4cm long and slightly downward pointing, and are diurnal, in summer. Requires good light; normal cactus compost; minimum temperature 13°C (55°F). *Bolivia (Yungas).*

CLEISTOCACTUS **BROOKEI** Card.
Syn: *Cleistocactus wendlandiorum* Backeb.

A semi-erect or somewhat sprawling columnar plant with greenish stems to about 50cm long, 4–5cm thick, with about 25 ribs. Areoles are greyish brown bearing 30–40 greyish-white or slightly yellowish spines 4–9mm in length. Day flowering in late summer, the flowers are about 5cm long and mostly carmine red. Needs good light; normal cactus compost; minimum temperature 13°C (55°F). *Bolivia (Santa Cruz).*

CLEISTOCACTUS **JUJUYENSIS** (Backeb.) Backeb.
Syn: *Cleistocactus strausii* var. *jujuyensis* Fric

A greyish-green columnar plant, freely branching from the base, with 15–25 ribs. The stems reach 1m or more in length. The areoles, fairly closely set, bear many hair-like radial spines, almost bristly, up to 1.5cm long, and four yellowish-brown central spines. Flowers are pale red and straight, to 4cm long, and are diurnal, appearing in summer. Requires full sun; normal cactus compost; minimum temperature 10°C (50°F). *Argentina, Bolivia.*

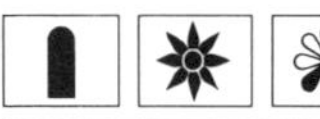

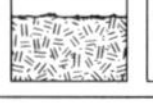

CLEISTOCACTUS **SMARAGDIFLORUS** (Weber) Speg.

An erect, stiff columnar species to about 2m tall, later becoming rather decumbent. The stems are 4–6cm thick with closely arranged yellowish-brown areoles set along 12-16 ribs. There are numerous pale to dark-brown spines, the upper ones to 3cm in length. Flowers are tubular, red with green tips, up to 5cm long. The plant is diurnal flowering in summer and should be kept moist when in bloom. Requires full sun; normal cactus compost; minimum temperature 13°C (55°F). *Argentina, Uruguay, Paraguay.*

    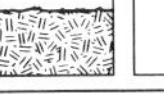 

CLEISTOCACTUS **STRAUSII** (Heese) Backeb.
Syn: *Pilocereus strausii* Heese

A branching, columnar plant with stems 1m or more high, 4–8cm thick, totally covered with silvery white spines. The light green stems have about 25 ribs; the areoles, set about 5mm apart, have 30 or more snow-white bristly spines to 1.5cm long and four longer pale yellowish spines to 4cm in length. Flowers are carmine red, straight, and 8–9cm long; these are diurnal, appearing in summer. Requires full sun; normal cactus compost; minimum temperature 10°C (50°F). *Bolivia.*

   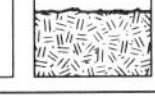 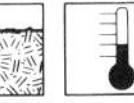 

▲

▲

COLEOCEPHALOCEREUS **BRAUNII** Diers & Esteves

A recent discovery by L. Horst, Esteves Pereira and Pierre Braun (pictured). Up to about 1m tall. The stems have 12 or more notched ribs and the areoles are pale brownish with yellowish spination. The cephalium, apparent when plants reach about 15cm tall, consists of yellowish spines and wool. Night flowering in summer, the greenish white flowers are followed by purple fruits. Needs sun and warmth; normal cactus compost; minimum temperature 13°C (55°F). *Brazil (Espirito Santo).*

    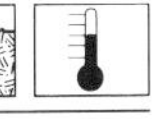

COLEOCEPHALOCEREUS **DIERSIANUS** Braun & Esteves

Discovered in 1983 growing on high granite mountain slopes. A fairly erect deep-green plant with about 15 straight ribs. The areoles are closely set, with brownish-yellow spines becoming greyish; the cephalium is somewhat blackish. Night flowering in summer, the flowers are creamy white to greenish white. Needs very careful watering at all times; a sunny and airy position; normal cactus compost; minimum temperature 13°C (55°F). *Brazil (Minas Gerais).*

COLEOCEPHALOCEREUS **ELONGATUS** (Buin.) Braun
Syn: *Buiningia elongata* Buin.

A tall columnar species with stems to about 1m high with 15–20 straight ribs, deeply furrowed between, having whitish woolly areoles bearing prominent yellowish-brown spines. The flowers are green, borne in a white woolly and yellowish bristly cephalium, and appear at night in summer. Needs bright light which is essential; normal cactus compost; minimum temperature 13°C (55°F). *Brazil (Minas Gerais).*

  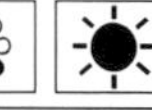 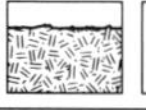 

COLEOCEPHALOCEREUS **ESTEVESII** Diers

An erect columnar plant of bright green dominated by a mass of yellowish, widely spreading spines. The 18–20 ribs have fairly close-set areoles. The whitish flowers, borne in a lateral cephalium, are long and tubular in shape and are nocturnal, appearing in summer. This is one of a number of fascinating species discovered by E. Esteves Pereira for whom it is named. Requires full sun; mineral-based cactus compost; minimum temperature 13°C (55°F). *Brazil (Goiania).*

    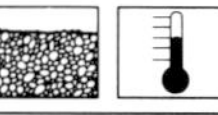 

COLEOCEPHALOCEREUS **FLUMINENSIS var. BRAAMHAARII** Braun

The type species, *Coleocephalocereus fluminensis* (Miquel) Backeb., was one of the earliest introductions of cacti from Brazil. This is a columnar plant to about 1m tall, 10cm thick, with about 15 ribs. Areoles bear orange-brown spines, both radial and central, up to 3cm in length. Flowers are whitish with pinkish outer petals, appearing from a whitish woolly cephalium. They are nocturnal, flowering in summer. Needs full sun; slightly calcareous cactus compost; minimum temperature 13°C (55°F). *Brazil (Espirito Santo).*

  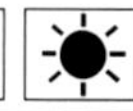 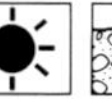 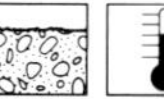

COLEOCEPHALOCEREUS **GOEBELIANUS** (Vaup.) Ritter

Tall columnar plants to about 2m high, 6cm in diameter with 10–20 ribs and close-set areoles bearing 10–12 brown, needle-like spines to 1cm long. The lateral cephalium is about 20cm wide, densely woolly, dark and bristly. Flowers are bell-shaped, about 5cm long, with very pale pinkish-white short petals, widely spreading and nocturnal flowering in summer. Requires sun and warmth; normal cactus compost; minimum temperature 15°C (59°F). *Brazil.*

COLEOCEPHALOCEREUS **PURPUREUS** (Buin. & Bred.) Ritter
Syn: *Buiningia purpurea* Buin. & Bred.

A short or long columnar plant to about 90cm tall, 10cm thick. The deep green stems have 13 ribs with about 12 radial spines up to 2.5cm long and about four centrals to 7cm. Spines are brownish, later greyish. The woolly cephalium is greyish with yellow or reddish-grey bristles. Flowers are purplish red, 3cm long, appearing at night in summer. Requires slightly calcareous cactus compost; bright sunshine; minimum temperature 13°C (55°F). Also featured is the tall *Brasilicereus phaeacanthus* var. *breviflorus*. *Brazil.*

   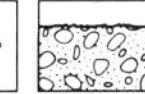 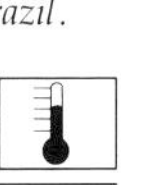

COPIAPOA **BARQUITENSIS** Ritter

Closely allied to and possibly synonymous with *C. hypogaea*. It has a rather flattened, rounded stem which offsets from the base and is dark brownish green, 6–7cm wide. The ribs are divided into tubercles spirally arranged. Areoles are clothed in white wool and bear a few very short spines. Flowers are borne in the densely woolly crown and are yellow, about 2cm long; these are diurnal, appearing in summer. Bright sun is advisable; normal cactus compost; minimum temperature 10°C (50°F). *Chile.*

COPIAPOA **BRUNNESCENS** Backeb.

An illegitimate specific title – the plant has certain features peculiar to itself, but might better be classified as *Copiapoa krainziana* var. *brunnescens*. The globular greyish-green stem is 8–12cm wide, offsetting from the base to form large clumps. About 14 ribs have prominent greyish-white areoles bearing many greyish-white, spreading radial spines and a few centrals 1–2cm in length. The flowers are yellow, diurnal, appearing in summer and are up to about 3cm long. Requires sun; an open, slightly calcareous compost; minimum temperature 10°C (50°F). *Chile.*

    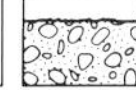 

COPIAPOA **CINEREA (Phil.)** Br. & R.

The plants are globular when young, later cylindrical, to 10cm in diameter, eventually reaching over 1m tall, and are whitish grey. There are 14–30 ribs with one or two black spines to 2cm or more in length. Flowers are bright yellow, diurnal in late summer, and about 3.5cm long and wide. Needs bright light, which is essential; calcareous cactus compost; minimum temperature 10°C (50°F). *Chile (Taltal).*

COPIAPOA **HASELTONIANA** Backeb.

An almost cylindrical plant to about 20cm in diameter and 30cm high; possibly a natural hybrid of *C. cinerea*. It is totally greyish in colour with 20 or more pronounced ribs, and areoles set well apart with few spreading radial spines, rarely one central, which are dark brown. The crown of the plant is covered with creamy yellow wool and fine hairs. Flowers are golden yellow, diurnal in summer, 3–3.5cm long. Requires a slightly shaded position; normal cactus compost; minimum temperature 10°C (50°F). *Chile (Taltal).*

    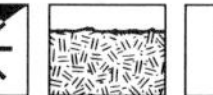

COPIAPOA **HYPOGAEA** Ritter

A globular species 4–6.5cm in diameter with a fairly rough, dull brownish-green skin, and 10–14 slightly spiralled ribs regularly divided into tubercles. The crown of the plant is set with white wool. Areoles at the tips of tubercles bear one to six brownish spines 2–4mm long, which soon fall. Flowering in late summer, the flowers arise from the crown. They are diurnal, golden yellow in colour and about 2cm long, 4cm across. Very careful watering is demanded. Requires filtered light; normal cactus compost; minimum temperature 10°C (50°F). *Chile (Antofagasta).*

COPIAPOA **KRAINZIANA** Ritter

A greyish-green globular plant to about 12cm in diameter, forming clusters to 1m or more across. The crown is grey and woolly, and there are 13–24 ribs with greyish areoles bearing 10–12 white to greyish radial spines, 1–2cm in length, and 14–20 centrals 2–3cm long. Day flowering in summer, the flowers are yellow, about 3.5cm long. Requires bright light; normal cactus compost; minimum temperature 10°C (50°F). *Chile (Taltal).*

    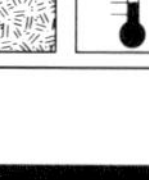

COPIAPOA **MOLLICULA** Ritter

A grey-green globular plant about 7cm in diameter having 10–14 somewhat blunt ribs set with white woolly areoles. These have five to nine greyish-brown radial spines 5mm to 1.5cm long, and one to three blackish-brown centrals, 1–3cm in length. Summer flowering, the flowers are diurnal and rich yellow, about 3cm long. Needs good light; normal cactus compost; minimum temperature 10°C (50°F). *Northern Chile.*

COPIAPOA **LAUI** Diers

A true miniature species only 1–3cm in diameter. It is somewhat similar to species of *Blossfeldia* or *Frailea*. The round stem is brownish in colour with about 20 or more well-defined ribs somewhat spirally arranged and tuberculate. The areoles have white wool and fine hairs and bear a few insignificant spines. Flowers appear diurnally in mid-summer, and are rich glossy yellow to 3cm across. Probably best grafted on *Cereus* stock. Requires partial shade; normal cactus compost; minimum temperature 10°C (50°F). *Chile (Esmeralda).*

     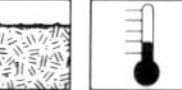

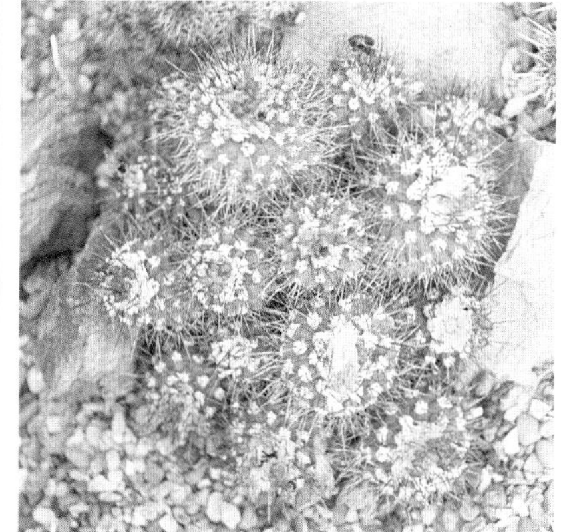

COPIAPOA **SERPENTISULCATA** Ritter

A clustering, clumping species with greyish-green individual stems up to 15cm in diameter and yellowish-brown crowns. Ribs vary from about 20 to often over 30 in the wild. The areoles are brown (white in cultivation) with yellowish-brown or greyish spines 2–3cm in length consisting of six to ten radials, one to four centrals. Flowers are pale yellow, to 3cm long, and are diurnal, appearing in late summer. Requires good light; normal cactus compost; minimum temperature 10°C (50°F). *Chile (Chanaral).*

CORRYOCACTUS **AUREUS** (Meyen) P. C. Hutch
Syn: *Erdisia meyenii* Br. & R.

More or less cylindrical plants with stems 50cm or more tall. These are pale brownish green, 3–5cm thick with five to eight ribs; the areoles are set fairly close together. The spines are brownish, consisting of nine to eleven radials to about 2cm long, often with one, rarely two, longer centrals to 6cm. A day-flowering plant, in summer, the flowers are yellow to orange, about 4cm long. Requires bright light; normal cactus compost; minimum temperature 13°C (55°F). *Peru (Arequipa).*

CORRYOCACTUS **BRACHYPETALUS** (Vaup.) Br. & R.

Columnar, dull green plants to about 4m high, usually branching from the base. The ribs are fairly prominent, generally seven to eight in number with areoles to 1cm wide, set at intervals of approximately 2cm. The spines are brownish black, about 20 to each areole, and from about 7mm to 10cm or more long. Flowers appear in early summer; these are diurnal and broadly funnel-shaped, 4–6cm across, and deep orange. In the foothills of southern Peru at altitudes of around 600m, clumps of these long, slender stems provide an imposing sight, growing as they do almost in isolation. Needs sun; an enriched mineral compost; minimum temperature 13°C (55°F). *Southern Peru.*

    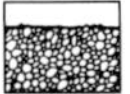

CORRYOCACTUS **BREVISTYLUS** (K. Sch.) Br. & R.

A dark-green columnar species, branching freely from the base. Individual stems are from 3–4m high in its habitat, to 15cm thick, and it has six to seven ribs with densely woolly areoles set about 3cm apart. Their spines are dark brown, about 15 in number, varying from 1–3cm long; others are very much longer. Day flowering in summer, the flowers are golden yellow, up to 10cm broad, and fragrant. Needs full sun; normal cactus compost; minimum temperature 13°C (55°F). *Peru (at 2000m).*

CORRYOCACTUS **SQUARROSUS** (Vaup.) P. C. Hutch.
Syn: *Erdisia squarrosa* (Vaup.) Br. & R.

Plants with long, branching deep-green stems 1–2m in length and 1–3cm thick, with five to eight ribs and brownish areoles. The spines are yellowish, consisting of nine to thirteen radials about 1.2cm long and often one central to 3cm in length. Summer flowering and diurnal, the flowers are bright red, about 4cm long and across, and appear from the tips of the branches. Requires a sunny position; normal cactus compost; minimum temperature 13°C (55°F). *Peru (Tarma).*

    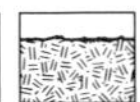 

CORYPHANTHA **ANDREAE** (Purp. & Böed.) Böed.
Syn: *Mammillaria andreae* Böed.

A more or less globular plant to 9cm in diameter, it is a dark, glossy green with wool in the crown and axils. Tubercles are 2cm high, 2.5cm thick. The radial spines are yellowish grey, about 10 in number, to 1.2cm long; there are five to seven curved centrals up to 2.5cm long. Flowers are diurnal in summer and are bright yellow, opening 5–6cm wide. Requires sun; normal cactus compost; minimum temperature 10°C (50°F). *Mexico (Veracruz).*

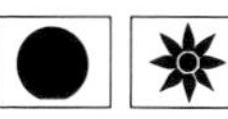    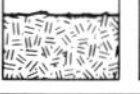 

▲

CORYPHANTHA **CALIPENSIS** Bravo

An almost globular plant, but slightly elongated, up to 9cm high, 5–8cm wide. It is greyish-green with prominent tubercles 3cm long and wide. The spines are brownish, becoming grey, and consist of 10–16 radials 1–1.5cm long and one central, slightly curved and 1.5cm in length. Summer flowering, the flowers are diurnal, 5–6cm across and creamy with deep red filaments. Requires sun; normal cactus compost with a few lime chippings added; minimum temperature 13°C (55°F). *Mexico (Puebla).*

   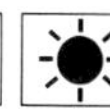 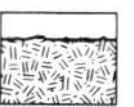 

CORYPHANTHA **BORWIGII** Purp.
Syn: *Coryphantha difficilis* (Quehl) Berger

Bluish-green, globular, with four-angled, conical tubercles. The stems are 6–10cm high, 5–7cm thick with tubercles to 1.5cm high. The axils are initially woolly, later bare. There are nine to ten radial spines and one to three centrals, all brownish and to 2cm long. Day flowering in summer, the flowers are about 6cm long, with petals in three rows, the inner yellow with a dark median line, the middle yellow with frilled tips and the outer pale reddish purple. Requires bright light; normal cactus compost; minimum temperature 10°C (50°F). *Mexico (Coahuila).*

      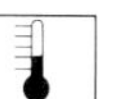

CORYPHANTHA **CALOCHLORA** Böed.

A somewhat oval-shaped plant of dark, almost blackish green, 9–10cm high and about 8cm wide with almost rounded tubercles and bare axils. The areoles are initially woolly, later bare, with 12–15 thin whitish radial spines to 1.5cm long and three to five longer greyish centrals. Day flowering in summer, the flowers are yellow, with outer segments brownish purple, and 3–4cm wide when fully open. Requires full sun; normal cactus compost; minimum temperature 10°C (50°F). *Mexico.*

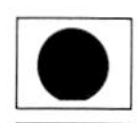     

CORYPHANTHA **CHLORANTHA** (Engelm.) Br. & R.

A globular to cylindrical-shaped, dark-green plant, about 20cm high, 8cm in diameter. The tubercles are closely set and covered with densely matted spines; the axils are bare. There are 20 or more radial spines, whitish with pale brown tips 1–2cm long, and three to five centrals of similar colour, to 2.5cm in length. Flowering in summer and diurnal, the narrow yellow petals have a greenish mid-rib, and are 3cm long, 4cm across. Requires sun; normal cactus compost; minimum temperature 10°C (50°F). *USA (Utah, Nevada, Arizona).*

CORYPHANTHA **CLAVATA** (Scheidw.) Backeb.
Syn: *Coryphantha raphidacantha* (Lem.) Berger; *Mammillaria clavata* Scheidw.

A conical, bluish-green plant 15–30cm high and 4–7cm thick with tubercles up to 2cm long and white woolly axils. The six to nine radial spines are whitish, tipped brown, 8–15mm long and one yellowish-brown, slightly hooked central to 2cm long. Day flowering in summer, the flowers are glossy yellow with brownish outer segments, 2–3cm long. Requires very slight shade; normal cactus compost; minimum temperature 10°C (50°F). *Mexico (Hidalgo, Queretaro).*

    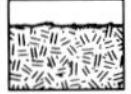 

▲

CORYPHANTHA **CLAVATA var. RADICANTISSIMA** (Quehl.) Heinr.
Syn: *Mammillaria radicantissima* Quehl.

The stems are more or less globular covered with tubercles about 1cm long, and white woolly axils. Areoles carry about nine to eleven radial spines, more or less greyish in colour, to 1cm long, with usually one central of similar length and colour, tipped blackish. The plant flowers diurnally in summer; the flowers are yellow, 2–2.5cm long, 1.8–2.5cm across. Cultivation is the same as for the species. *Mexico (San Luis Potosi).*

CORYPHANTHA **COMPACTA** (Engelm.) Br. & R.

A dark-green globular plant 3–6cm high and 5–8cm thick. The tubercles and areoles are close-set together, each tubercle about 8mm long. Areoles bear 14–16 spreading whitish radial spines 1–2cm long, generally without centrals. Summer flowering, the flowers are diurnal, and about 2cm long and wide; the inner petals are yellow, outer ones reddish externally. Requires full sun; normal cactus compost; minimum temperature 10°C (50°F). *Mexico (Chihuahua).*

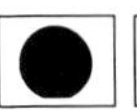    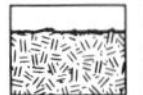 

CORYPHANTHA **DURANGENSIS** (Rge.) Br. & R.

The plant is cylindrical, greyish green and 10–15cm high, 4–6cm thick, freely clustering. Tubercles are four-angled at the base, almost pointed at the tips, with white woolly axils. The radial spines are whitish grey to 1cm long, and there is one slender, black central spine slightly longer. Day flowering in summer, the flowers are creamy white to pale yellow, up to 2cm long, with reddish-brown outer segments. Needs careful watering and good light; normal cactus compost with lime chippings; minimum temperature 10°C (50°F). *Mexico (Durango).*

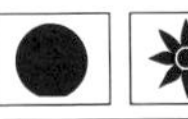    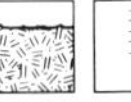

CORYPHANTHA **ELEPHANTIDENS** (Lem.) Lem.
Syn: *Mammillaria elephantidens* Lem.

A globular, dark glossy-green plant, solitary or offsetting. Stems reach up to 14cm high, 20cm in diameter, and the large rounded tubercles are up to 4cm long, 6cm wide at the base with white woolly axils. Areoles bear six to eight curved, brownish radial spines to 2cm in length, no centrals. Pink to carmine flowers appear in summer, and are diurnal, 8–10cm across. Needs full sun; normal cactus compost; minimum temperature 13°C (55°F). *Mexico (Michoacan).*

     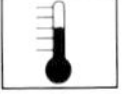

CORYPHANTHA **ERECTA** (Lem.) Lem.

The stems are cylindrical, clustering from the base, each reaching up to 30cm high, 6–8cm in diameter. These are yellowish green with conical tubercles 7–8mm long, 1.5cm wide at the base, and the axils and crown of the stems are woolly. The spines are yellowish brown and consist of eight to fourteen radials about 1cm long and two to four centrals, up to 2cm in length. Flowering in summer, the flowers are diurnal, pale yellow and up to 6cm long and wide. Requires sun; normal cactus compost; minimum temperature 10°C (50°F). *Mexico (Hidalgo).*

CORYPHANTHA **GLADIISPINA** (Böed.) Berger

Plants are solitary, oval in shape and a dark greyish green, 10cm high and 6cm thick, with a very spiny crown. They have fairly prominent tubercles and areoles bearing 17–20 black-tipped greyish radial spines, the upper ones clustering and brush-like, the lower ones shorter and spreading, to 2cm long. There are four central spines similarly coloured and up to 2.5cm in length. Day flowering, in summer, the flowers are chrome yellow, 4–4.5cm in diameter. Needs bright light; normal cactus compost; minimum temperature 10°C (50°F). *Mexico (Coahuila).*

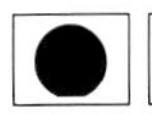   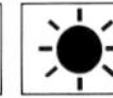 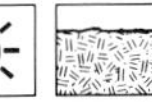 

CORYPHANTHA **MACROMERIS var. RUNYONII** (Br. & R.) L. Benson
Syn: *Lepidocoryphantha runyonii* (Br. & R.) Backeb.

The greyish-green stems are small and cylindrical, in dense clumps to about 50cm wide. They have rounded tubercles 1–2cm long. Radial spines are yellowish to reddish orange; there are six to seven up to 3cm long and one to three central spines the same colour and size. Flowers appear in mid-summer, are diurnal, pinkish purple and up to 5cm wide. Requires full sun; slightly calcareous cactus compost; minimum temperature 10°C (50°F). *USA (Eastern Texas).*

  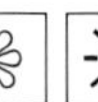   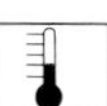

▲

CORYPHANTHA **LONGICORNIS** Böed.

More or less globular in shape and up to 20cm long, 10cm in diameter, this plant is greyish green with cone-shaped tubercles 1.5–2cm long and bare axils. Areoles carry about 12 dull whitish radial spines to 1cm long and three centrals, which are brown, from 1–2.5cm in length. Flowering in summer, the diurnal flowers are pale to deep yellow, about 3.5cm across. Requires good light; normal cactus compost with a few lime chippings added; minimum temperature 10°C (50°F). *Mexico (Durango).*

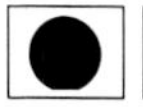   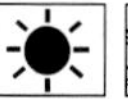  

CORYPHANTHA **MACROMERIS** (Engelm.) Lem.

A clustering globular species. Each stem is up to 20cm tall, 7–8cm thick, and is greyish green, with cylindrical tubercles up to 3cm long. Areoles bear 10–17 reddish radial spines which become white, tipped brown, and are 1–4cm long; there are one to four blackish-brown centrals 2–5cm in length. Flowering in summer, the flowers are diurnal, and about 8cm across, with toothed, deep pink petals. Needs good light; normal cactus compost; minimum temperature 10°C (50°F). *USA (Texas, New Mexico), Mexico.*

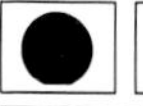      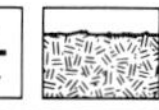 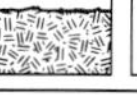

CORYPHANTHA **MAIZ-TABLASENSIS** Backeb.

A globular species which clusters freely. Each bluish-green stem is up to 5.5cm wide with tubercles about 1cm long. The six to seven greyish-white spines are all radials, about 1.2cm long. The plant flowers in summer, and is diurnal; the flowers are pale yellow. Requires bright light; normal cactus compost; minimum temperature 10°C (50°F). *Mexico (San Luis Potosi).*

 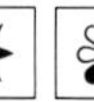  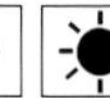 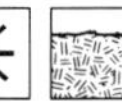 

CORYPHANTHA **ODORATA** Böed.
Syn: *Neolloydia odorata* Backeb.; *Neobesseya odorata* Böed.

A clustering species; the stems are dark green, about 3cm in diameter, tipped with dark spines. The tubercles are cylindrical, about 1cm long, the axils are slightly hairy. Areoles bear seven to nine brown-tipped, white radial spines to 1cm long and three to four brownish-yellow centrals, hooked, up to 2.5cm in length. Day flowering in summer; the flowers are pale yellowish pink, 1.5cm long, 1cm across. Needs sun; normal cactus compost; minimum temperature 10°C (50°F). *Mexico (Tamaulipas, San Luis Potosi).*

CORYPHANTHA **OTTONIS** (Pfeiff.) Lem.
Syn: *Mammillaria golziana* Haage

A short cylindrical plant to 12cm high and about 8cm thick, it is dark greyish green, with very thick grooved tubercles and woolly axils. Spines are yellowish; there are eight or more radials to 1cm long, and one or more centrals, usually longer. Flowers are white or pale yellowish, about 5cm across, and appear by day, in summer. Needs good light; normal cactus compost; minimum temperature 10°C (50°F). *Mexico (Hidalgo).*

  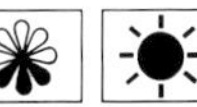 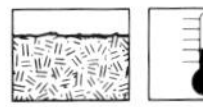 

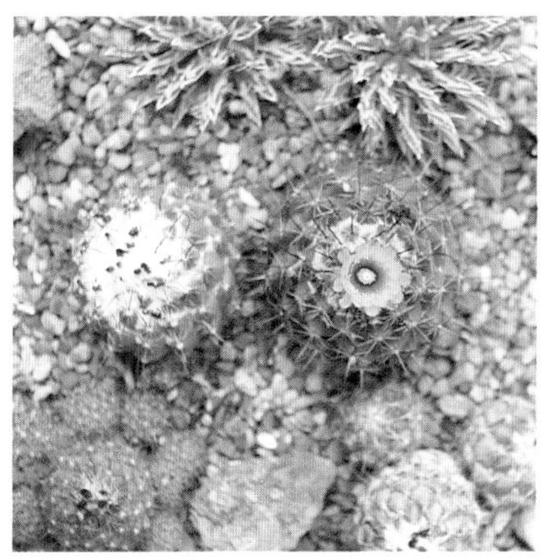

CORYPHANTHA **PALLIDA** Br. & R.

A globular, bluish-green plant to about 12cm thick, enclosed with closely set tubercles. There are about 20 whitish radial spines and one to three centrals, the lowest one tipped reddish-brown and downward pointing. Day flowering in summer, the flowers are 5–7cm across and are bright yellow, with reddish stamens and yellow style and stigma lobes. Requires bright light; normal cactus compost; minimum temperature 10°C (50°F). *Mexico (Tehuacan).*

         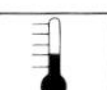 

CORYPHANTHA **PALMERI** Br. & R.

The plants are solitary or offsetting, with pale-green, globular-elongated stems 8–10cm thick. Tubercles are spirally arranged, and the areoles, which are white and woolly when young, carry 11–14 black-tipped yellowish radial spines and one hooked, downward-pointing, brownish central 1–2cm long. The plant is summer flowering and diurnal, with yellow flowers 3–4cm long. Requires bright light; normal cactus compost; minimum temperature 10°C (50°F). *Mexico (Durango).*

   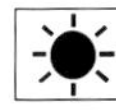 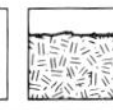 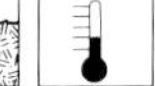

CORYPHANTHA **PULLEINEANA** (Backeb.) Glass
Syn: *Neolloydia pulleineana* Backeb.

A somewhat cylindrical, dull green plant to 20cm long, 1.5cm thick, with roundish-conical tubercles. Spines are brownish to black; there are about 18 radials to 1.2cm long and three to four centrals to 2cm long. It is diurnal, flowering in summer, with bright yellow to orangish flowers. Requires sun; normal cactus compost with few lime chippings added; minimum temperature 13°C (55°F). *Mexico (San Luis Potosi).*

CORYPHANTHA **POSELGERIANA** (Dietr.) Br. & R.
Syn: *Echinocactus poselgeriana* Dietr.

Globular plants of bluish greyish green to 20cm high with angular tubercles to 2cm long and bare axils. The radial spines are reddish brown, five to seven in number and 2–5cm long. There is one similarly coloured central but it has a white tip, to 5cm long. Summer flowering, and diurnal, the flowers are 4–6cm long and deep pink, rarely yellow. Requires sun; normal cactus compost; minimum temperature 10°C (50°F). *Mexico (Coahuila).*

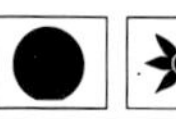     

CORYPHANTHA **POTOSIANA** (Jacobi) Glass & Foster
Syn: *Mammillaria potosiana* Jacobi

More or less globular, greyish-green plants to 8cm in diameter. The tubercles are conical, 8mm long, 7mm wide at the base, and the grooves at the base of the tubercles bear two to three pale orange glands; the axils are woolly. There are 12–18 radial spines which are whitish, tipped brown and rarely a central spine; all are 1.5–2.3cm long. Flowering in summer, the flowers are diurnal and about 2cm long and wide. The inner petals are pale tan to cream, and the outer segments purplish red with cream margins. Requires full sun; normal cactus compost; minimum temperature 13°C (55°F). *Mexico (San Luis Potosi).*

    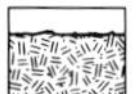

CORYPHANTHA **RADIANS** (DC.) Br. & R.
Syn: *Mammillaria radians* DC.

Dull green, globular or oval-shaped plants, 5–7cm in diameter, offsetting in maturity. The tubercles are cone-shaped, and the axils woolly but becoming bare. Spines are yellowish white tipped brown, consisting of 12–20 fine radials to 1.2cm long but no centrals. Appearing in mid-summer, the flowers are diurnal, 6–7cm broad, and citron yellow in colour, the outer segments tipped reddish with a greenish median line. Requires full sun; normal cactus compost; minimum temperature 10°C (50°F). *Mexico (Hidalgo).*

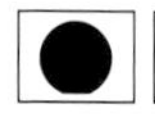     

CORYPHANTHA **RECURVATA** (Engelm.) Br. & R.
Syn: *Mammillaria recurvata* Engelm.

A densely clustering species; each globular stem is 10–20cm thick, and bluish green. The tubercles are conical, about 1cm long, with bare axils. There are 20–25 yellowish-grey radial spines, arranged comb-like, up to 1.2cm long, and one to two similarly coloured central spines, to 2cm in length. Flowers appear in summer, and are diurnal, yellow in colour, funnel-shaped and 3.5cm long. Requires full sun; slightly calcareous cactus compost; minimum temperature 10°C (50°F). *USA (Arizona), Mexico (Nogales).*

   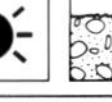 

CORYPHANTHA **SALM-DYCKIANA** (Scheer) Br. & R.

A globular plant 10–15cm broad, often offsetting from the base. The tubercles are four-edged, about 1cm long, pale to greyish green, and the axils are woolly. There are seven to fifteen greyish-white radial spines 1–1.5cm long and one to four almost black centrals, 2–2.5cm in length. Flowering in summer, diurnal; flowers are about 4cm long, funnel-shaped, with yellow inner petals and outer segments yellowish green edged reddish. Needs bright light; slightly calcareous cactus compost; minimum temperature 10°C (50°F). *Mexico (Chihuahua).*

    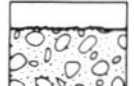  

▲

CORYPHANTHA **SCOLYMOIDES** (Scheidw.) Berger
Syn: *Coryphantha cornifera* (DC.) Lem. var. *scolymoides* (Scheidw.) Borg

A rather bluish-green globular species, the stems set very closely together, tending to be upward pointing. Areoles are woolly with 12–20 yellowish radial spines to 2cm long and one to four darker coloured centrals about 3.5cm in length. It is day flowering in summer; the blooms are yellow, about 5cm in diameter. Needs sun; normal cactus compost; minimum temperature 10°C (50°F). *Northern Mexico.*

CORYPHANTHA **VILLARENSIS** Backeb.

A dark greyish-green solitary, globular species up to about 15cm high, 13cm in diameter. The tubercles, about 3cm long, are cone-shaped, and the axils initially woolly, later bare. The yellowish-grey radial spines number nine to eleven and are 5mm–1.5cm long; there is one similarly coloured central to 3cm in length. It is a summer-flowering plant, and diurnal; the flowers are bright yellow, 4cm long, 5cm in diameter. Requires sun; normal cactus compost; minimum temperature 13°C (55°F). *Mexico (San Luis Potosi).*

CORYPHANTHA **VIVIPARA** (Nutt.) Engelm
Syn: *Escobaria vivipara* (Nutt.) Buxb.

The plants are globular to short cylindrical and are about 13cm high, 5cm in diameter, greyish with tubercles somewhat cylindrical in shape, and white woolly axils. The radial spines are white, about 16 in number, with one to six brownish centrals, all to about 2cm long. Summer flowering and diurnal, the flowers are a pale reddish purple, about 3.5cm long and 4–5cm broad. Must be kept dry in winter. Requires bright light; normal cactus compost; minimum temperature 7°C (45°F). *Canada (Manitoba, Alberta), USA (Kansas to Northern Texas).*

 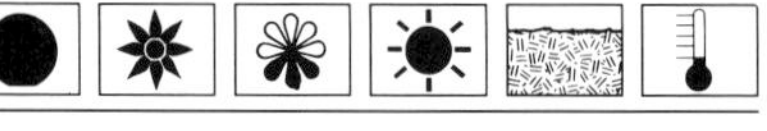 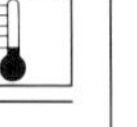

CORYPHANTHA **VIVIPARA var. ROSEA** (Clokey) L. Benson
Syn: *Coryphantha rosea* Clokey

A solitary, rarely branching plant, 8–13cm long, 8–10cm in diameter. It is dark green and densely covered with white spines consisting of 12–18 radials to 2cm long and 10–12 centrals, usually tipped red, to 2.5cm in length. The flowers, about 5cm in diameter, are magenta to purplish; they appear in summer, and are diurnal. Requirements are similar to those for the species, but compost should have lime added. *USA (California, Nevada etc).*

      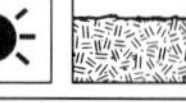  

CORYPHANTHA **WERDERMANNII** Böed.

Stems are almost oval in shape to about 6cm in diameter, greyish green and rarely offsetting. The tubercles are pyramid-shaped, 5mm long, and the axils bare. There are 15–20 or more whitish radial spines to 6mm long and one to four brownish-grey centrals, 2cm or more long. Appearing in summer, the funnel-shaped flowers are diurnal and a pale golden yellow up to 6cm long. Requires full sun; normal cactus compost with a little lime added; minimum temperature 10°C (50°F). *Mexico (Coahuila).*

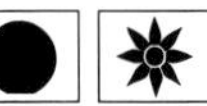  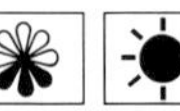  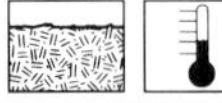 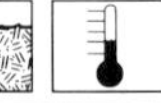

CORYPHANTHA **VIVIPARA var. DESERTII** (Engelm.) W. T. Marsh.
Syn: *Coryphantha desertii* Br. & R.

A globular, elongating plant 10–14cm high, 6–8cm wide. Glaucous green and usually solitary, it is densely covered with numerous spines, 12–20 white radials 1cm or more long and four to six white, red-tipped centrals, to 2cm in length. The flowers, yellowish green and about 2.5cm in diameter, are diurnal, appearing in summer. Requirements are the same as for the species. *USA (Arizona, South-eastern California).*

CRYPTOCEREUS

CRYPTOCEREUS **ANTHONYANUS** Alex.

An epiphytic species with bright green leaf-like, flat stems 30–45cm or more long, 7–15cm wide. The stem margins have indentations 3.5–4.5cm deep, forming lobes. Areoles bear minute spines, which are often absent. Flowers are nocturnal in summer, about 12cm long, with yellowish or creamy white inner petals, maroon-red outer petals. Requires partial shade; a fairly acid, orchid-like, compost; minimum temperature 15°C (59°F). *Mexico (Chiapas).*

   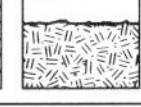 

CRYPTOCEREUS **IMITANS** (Kimnach & P. C. Hutch.) Backeb.
Syn: *Werckleocereus imitans* Kimnach & P.C. Hutch.; *Weberocereus imitans* (Kimn. & P.C. Hutch.) D. R. Hunt

Thick, leaf-like stems to 90cm long, 10-15cm wide, often serrated, forming lobes. Areoles of white wool, rarely bearing one to three spines 2–4mm long. The flowers are creamy, up to 7cm long, the inner petals form a trumpet shape, the maroon outer segments recurved. An epiphyte, night flowering in spring, it needs partial shade; normal cactus compost plus leafmould; minimum temperature 15°C (59°F). *Costa Rica.*

DENDROCEREUS

DENDROCEREUS **NUDIFLORUS** (Engelm.) Br. & R.

Likely to be reclassified within *Acanthocereus.* A night-flowering columnar plant to about 10m high, almost tree-like with branches developing from the top. The trunk is about 1m long, 60cm thick with three to five dull-green ribbed branches about 12cm thick. Areoles are white felted bearing two to fifteen spines up to 4cm in length. The flowers, appearing in summer, are 10–12cm long, with white, widely spreading petals and a ring of numerous stamens. Requires full sun; normal cactus compost; minimum temperature 18°C (64°F). *Cuba.*

    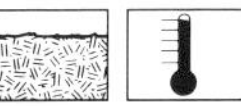

DENMOZA

DENMOZA **ERYTHROCEPHALA** (K. Sch.) Berger

A greyish-green globular to elongated species, up to 1.5m high in the wild, 15–30cm in diameter. Always solitary, with 20–30 low, rounded ribs, deeply furrowed. There are 30 or more reddish-brown spines, up to 6cm long; the younger brown areoles have flexible, hair-like bristles and whitish wool. Day flowering in summer. Flowers are tubular to 7.5cm long; the petals, 1cm long, are closed together with style, stamens and stigma lobes exserted. All are red. Needs sun; normal cactus compost; minimum temperature 10°C (50°F). *Argentina (Mendoza).*

DENMOZA **RHODANTHA** (Salm-Dyck) Br. & R.

Considered by certain taxonomists as being synonymous with *D. erythrocephala.* Generally a smaller plant up to 16cm wide and tall, having about 15 deeply furrowed ribs. Areoles bear brownish-red, later greyish, spines, eight to ten radials and often one central, all to about 3cm long. The flowers are red, 7cm long, and more or less tubular in shape, with protruding style, stamens and stigma lobes. They appear by day in summer. Requires a sunny and airy position; normal cactus compost; minimum temperature 10°C (50°F). *Argentina (Mendoza).*

    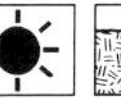 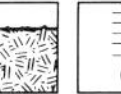 

DISCOCACTUS **BAHIENSIS** Br. & R.

Globular plants about 8cm in diameter with up to 10 ribs. The areoles bear seven to nine spreading spines 1–3cm in length, and the cephalium is composed of short bristles. Night flowering in summer, the flowers are yellowish white and 4–5cm long. Careful watering is essential at all times. Requires bright light; normal cactus compost; minimum temperature 16°C (61°F). *Brazil (Bahia).*

DISCOCACTUS **CANGAENSIS** Diers & Esteves

Named from the iron oxide outcrop formation called 'Canga'. Rather flat to 14cm in diameter, greyish green, with 10–14 ribs divided into rounded tubercles. Areoles bear greyish, brownish or reddish spines, five to nine radials up to 5cm long, and rarely one thick central 2.5cm in length. The cephalium is whitish to yellowish with yellowish or brownish bristles. The flowers, funnel-shaped to 7.5cm long, are white and nocturnal in summer. Needs careful watering; an enriched gritty compost; full sun; minimum temperature 16°C (61°F). *Brazil (Goias).*

  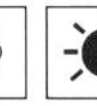  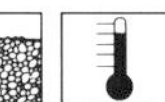

DISCOCACTUS **CEPHALIACICULOSUS** Buin. & Bred.

A somewhat flattened globular plant 13cm high, 20–26cm in diameter with 13–18 prominent tuberculate ribs. The spines are horn-coloured becoming dark grey, consisting of up to six radials 3.7cm long, and rarely one central to 2.5cm, and the cephalium is covered in white wool with protruding reddish spines. Night flowering in summer, the flowers are white, to 4cm long, about 3cm across. Requires normal cactus compost; a bright location; minimum temperature 16°C (61°F). *Brazil (Goias).*

    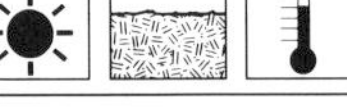

DISCOCACTUS **BOLIVIENSIS** Backeb. Buin. & Bred.

A dark-green, compressed globular species 25–29cm in diameter, to 15cm high. It has 12–13 ribs with four to five areoles along each rib bearing five white or yellow, later grey, spines to 3cm long. The cephalium, up to 7cm high, is white and hairy but has no bristles. The flowers are 5cm long, white with pale pink outer petals, and appear at night in summer. Needs very careful watering; a fairly sunny position; normal cactus compost; minimum temperature 16°C (61°F). *Border area of Brazil and Bolivia.*

    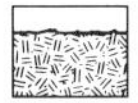 

DISCOCACTUS **CRASSISPINUS** Braun & Esteves

A dull-green plant from mountainous areas, it is a flattened globular shape and about 15cm in diameter, with about 15 bumpy ribs and prominent and rounded tubercles. Spines are brownish with transverse lines, four to six in number and widely spreading. The cephalium is of white wool with slightly protruding reddish-brown bristles. Night flowering in summer, the flowers are white. Needs a bright sunny position; normal cactus compost; minimum temperature 16°C (61°F). *Brazil (Goias).*

  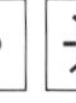  

DISCOCACTUS **CRYSTALLOPHILUS** Diers & Esteves

A dark-green globular species about 9cm in diameter with 10–12 ribs, slightly tubercled. The areoles bear about four blackish-grey spines and the cephalium is covered in dense white wool. Flowers, nocturnal in summer, are white with widely spreading segments. The plant is so named on account of its habitat of pure quartz crystals. Requires full sun; slightly calcareous cactus compost; minimum temperature 16°C (61°F). *Brazil (Minas Gerais).*

DISCOCACTUS **DIERSIANUS** Esteves

A flattened globose plant of olive to dark green, up to 25cm wide, 10cm high with 14–18 rounded, tuberculate ribs each bearing four to six areoles. Spines are greyish to blackish, and consist of four to ten radials up to 8cm long, with occasionally one central to 4cm in length. The cephalium, up to 10cm high, 9cm wide, consists of greyish yellowish-white wool and reddish-brown to black bristles. Flowers are nocturnal in summer; they are 6cm long, white, and have 55 or more flower segments. Needs full sun; an enriched mineral compost; minimum temperature 16°C (61°F). *Brazil (Goias).*

DISCOCACTUS **HARTMANNII** (K. Sch.) Br. & R. **var. GIGANTEUS** Braun

(Featured on the left.) More or less globular plants to 25cm wide, 9cm high or more, with 18 or more ribs. Flowers are nocturnal, occurring in summer. Description is limited as the plant depicted was discovered in a fire-damaged area. Requires full sun; an enriched mineral compost; minimum temperature 16°C (61°F). The smaller plant portrayed is an undescribed species from Northern Mato Grosso. *Paraguay/Brazil.*

    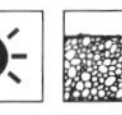 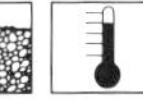

DISCOCACTUS **HEPTACANTHUS** (Rodr.) Br. & R.

A dull-green, somewhat rounded stem to 6cm high, 16cm in diameter, the whole stem divided into a series of prominent warts. The five to eleven spines, all radials, are greyish white and about 1–1.5cm or more long. Flowers are nocturnal, appearing in summer from a cephalium about 5cm wide, 3.5cm high consisting of wool and brownish bristles. The blooms are white, 6.5cm long, 5cm across. Requires bright light; normal cactus compost; minimum temperature 16°C (61°F). *Brazil (Matto Grosso).*

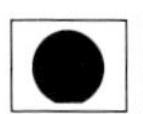   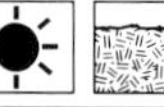  

DISCOCACTUS **HORSTII fma CRISTATA** hort.

On rare occasions a cristated form develops which is best maintained by grafting it on to *Trichocereus* stock. This procedure invariably results in several flowers appearing at one time. Requirements are the same as for the species.

DISCOCACTUS **HORSTII** Buin. & Bred.

Flattened globular plants up to 6cm in diameter, 2cm high, they are brownish green with up to 20 prominent ribs. Areoles are fairly close-set having about eight to ten greyish-white or brownish spines to 3.5mm long, arranged like a comb. The cephalium is of white wool and bristly, about 2cm wide, 1.5cm high. The nocturnal flowers are white, to 7.5cm long, 6cm across, occurring in summer. Requires full sun; an enriched mineral compost; minimum temperature 16°C (61°F). *Brazil (Minas Gerais).*

    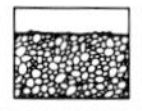 

DISCOCACTUS **MULTICOLORISPINUS** Braun & Bred.

A novel species with a globular stem of dull green with 16 or more ribs and strong, multicoloured spination, the spines mostly incurving. The cephalium is of white wool with few protruding reddish-brown spines. Night flowering in summer, the flowers are pale yellowish. Needs full sun; an enriched mineral compost; minimum temperature 16°C (61°F). *Brazil (Minas Gerais).*

DISCOCACTUS **PSEUDOLATISPINUS** Diers & Esteves

A dark-green, flattened globose species, reportedly nearing extinction. Up to 20cm in diameter with about 20 ribs, the spines are yellowish grey or brownish yellow. The nocturnal flowers are white arising in summer from a somewhat flattened cephalium. The picture of its habitat shows the plant hidden by leaves in an area endangered by development. Requires a fairly sunny position; normal cactus compost; minimum temperature 16°C (61°F). *Brazil.*

    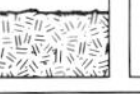 

▲

DISCOCACTUS **TRICORNIS** Monv.

The deep green stem is globular, depressed, and up to 7cm high, 10cm in diameter. There are 10–12 or more ribs with areoles bearing five to seven brownish-white spines, one being a very short central, the others curved to 2cm in length. The white, woolly cephalium is 3–4cm wide, about 1cm high, and bears white flowers, 7–8cm long. These are nocturnal, appearing in summer. Requires sun; normal cactus compost; minimum temperature 16°C (61°F). *Brazil (Minas Gerais).*

DISCOCACTUS **SUBTERRANEO-PROLIFERANS** Diers & Esteves

Now considered totally extinct in its native habitat, the area having been turned into pasture, this species is only rarely encountered in cultivation. It is a slightly flattened globular plant of greyish green covered completely with prominent rounded tubercles. There are five to seven pale brownish-white spines of varying size and there are spines protruding from the white woolly cephalium. Flowers are white, night flowering in summer. Requires full sun; normal cactus compost; minimum temperature 16°C (61°F). *Brazil (Rio Araguaia).*

    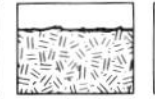 

DISCOCACTUS **ZEHNTNERI var. BOOMIANUS** (Buin. & Bred.) Braun
Syn: *Discocactus boomianus* Buin. & Bred.

A dull green, more or less globular plant to 6cm high, 10cm in diameter. The 16-20 ribs are densely covered with yellow to pale-brownish spines, 10 radial spines 3cm in length, arranged like a comb, and usually no centrals, only rarely one about 3.5cm long. Flowers are nocturnal arising from a terminal cephalium in summer. They are white, trumpet-shaped, and up to 9cm across when fully open. Requires very bright light; an enriched mineral compost; minimum temperature 16°C (61°F). *Brazil (Bahia).*

    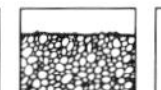 

DISOCACTUS **ALATUS** (K. Sch.) Kimnach

Syn: *Pseudorhipsalis alata* (K. Sch.) Br. & R.
Rhipsalis coriacea Polak

A branching epiphytic shrub with cylindrical stems and flat, lanceolate branches 15–25cm long and about 2cm wide. The marginal, grey woolly areoles are without spines or bristles. Flowering diurnally in late spring, the flowers are greenish white to yellowish white, and about 1.5cm long. Requires slight shade; normal cactus compost; minimum temperature 15°C (59°F). *Jamaica.*

DISOCACTUS **BIFORMIS** Lindley

Syn: *Phyllocactus biformis* Lab.

An epiphytic species with long, flat, leaf-like branches to 20cm long issuing from a fairly long cylindrical stem. The branches have regular, serrate margins where very small areoles are situated; these are spineless. Daytime flowers which are pale red and 5–6cm long appear in early spring from the side areoles. Requires a position in filtered light; an acid, free-draining compost; minimum temperature 15°C (59°F). *Honduras, Guatemala.*

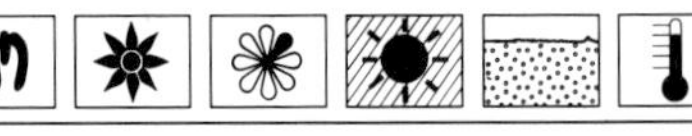

DISOCACTUS **EICHLAMII** (Weingt.) Br. & R.

Syn: *Phyllocactus eichlamii* Weingt.

Plants with a cylindrical, slender stem with many flattened branches about 30cm long, 5cm wide. They are slightly fleshy, with crenate margins, along which small areoles occur which are spineless. This is an epiphyte with carmine-red flowers opening in succession in late winter and early spring in daytime, each about 6cm long with a slender, trumpet-like tube. Needs partial shade; porous acid compost; minimum temperature 15°C (59°F). *Guatemala.*

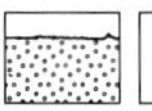

DISOCACTUS **MACRANTHA** (Alex.) Kimnach & P. C. Hutch.
Syn: *Pseudorhipsalis macrantha* Alex.

An epiphyte with pendant, flat, leaf-like stems to about 90cm long, 4.5cm wide with notched margins which carry minute, spineless areoles. Flowers appear in early summer from the side areoles. They are diurnal, and pale lemon yellow, about 5cm long, 3cm across when expanded. Requires partial shade; a porous acid compost and minimum temperature 15°C (59°F). *Mexico (Oaxaca).*

DISOCACTUS **NELSONII** (Br. & R.) Lindinger
Syn: *Chiapasia nelsonii* Br. & R.

A high-altitude epiphytic species with many dark-green flattened branches 60cm or more long. These are somewhat terete at the base, but becoming 3–4cm wide above; the margins are obtusely crenate. Flowers are diurnal, occurring in early summer and borne on a long tube 2–3cm long; they are trumpet-shaped with purplish-pink petals about 6cm long. Requires semi-shade; a porous acid compost; minimum temperature 15°C (59°F). *Mexico (Chiapas), Guatemala.*

DISOCACTUS **NELSONII var. HONDURENSIS** (Kimnach) Kimnach
Syn: *Chiapasia nelsonii* var. *hondurensis* (Kimnach) Backeb.

An epiphyte with elongated, flat, leaf-like stems to 50cm long, 5–6cm broad. Flowers are similarly coloured to those of the species, but with wider petals which tend to recurve. Requirements are as for the species. *Honduras.*

DISOCACTUS **QUEZALTECUS** (Standley & Steyermark) Kimnach
Syn: *Bonifazia quezalteca* Standley & Steyermark

An epiphytic with stems up to 35cm long, terete, with three rows of areoles bearing up to 15 white bristles to 1.5cm long, then becoming flat and leaf-like for 10–45cm. Lance-shaped stems initially reddish, becoming green, with serrate margins and areoles bearing one to three bristles. Flowers are tubular, to 9cm long, pale purplish, and day flowering in early summer. Requires normal cactus compost; partial shade; minimum temperature 16°C (61°F). *Guatemala.*

    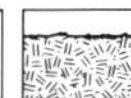 

ECHINOCACTUS **GRUSONII var. INERMIS** hort.
Syn: *Echinocactus grusonii subinermis* hort.; *Echinocactus grusonii* × *'L. J. van Veen'* Janse

A curiosity plant more or less identical to the species but totally without the golden-yellow spines.

   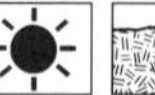

ECHINOCACTUS **GRUSONII** Hildm.

The 'Golden Barrel' or 'Mother-in-law's Cushion'. A large globose plant to over 1m high, 40–80cm thick, and pale green in colour. It has 20–35 or more sharply defined ribs with comparatively small, felted areoles carrying golden-yellow spines consisting of eight to ten radials and three to five centrals 3–5cm long. Flowers occur by day in summer only on mature plants from the crown of the plant; these are bright yellow, 4–6cm long. Requires bright sun; normal cactus compost; minimum temperature 10°C (50°F). *Mexico (San Luis Potosi to Hidalgo).*

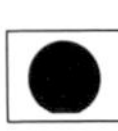    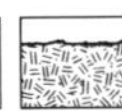 

ECHINOCACTUS **HORIZONTHALONIUS** Lem.

A glaucous-green globular plant to 25cm high, 40cm in diameter, with seven to thirteen ribs often spirally arranged. Areoles bear six to nine brownish radial spines and one central, 2–4cm long; the radials are sometimes curved. Summer flowering, the rose or pink flowers are 5–7cm long, and diurnal. Requires full sun; slightly calcareous cactus compost; minimum temperature 15°C (59°F). *USA (Texas, New Mexico), Northern Mexico.*

     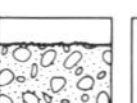 

ECHINOCACTUS **INGENS** Zucc.
Syn: *Echinocactus platyacanthus* Link & Otto

A thick, semi-globular plant to 1.5m tall, 1.25m in diameter, purplish grey in colour, with grey wool on top. About 50 ribs have yellowish-woolly areoles bearing eight straight brown radial spines about 2cm long, and one central slightly longer. Flowers are yellow, diurnal in summer, about 2cm long, 3cm across when expanded. Full sun is essential; needs slightly calcareous porous, enriched soil; minimum temperature 15°C (59°F). *Mexico (Hidalgo).*

ECHINOCACTUS **PLATYACANTHUS** Link & Otto

A large, fresh green, broadly globular plant to about 50cm in diameter with 21–24 very pronounced ribs. The greyish areoles bear greyish-brown spines, about four radials and three to four longer centrals. Flowers are diurnal in summer. Golden yellow and about 4cm long, they are centred in the woolly crown. Needs a bright position; normal cactus compost with lime added; minimum temperature 15°C (59°F). *Mexico (Central areas).*

ECHINOCACTUS **POLYCEPHALUS** Engelm. & Bigelow

Globular, sometimes elongating plants 40–70cm high, 18–25cm thick, starting solitary but later forming large clumps. There are 13–21 ribs with whitish-grey areoles set at intervals of about 3cm. Spines are reddish brown consisting of four to eight somewhat flat, spreading radials to 5cm long, and four centrals 4–9cm in length. Day flowering in summer, flowers are yellow, 5–6cm long. Needs full sun, which is essential; normal cactus compost; minimum temperature 10°C (50°F). *USA (California, Nevada), Mexico (Sonora).*

ECHINOCACTUS **PALMERI** Rose
Syn: *Echinocactus platyacanthus* Link & Otto

The plants are globular and elongated to 2m high, 50cm in diameter with 12–26 or more slightly notched, broad ribs. The areoles are brownish, bearing yellowish-brown spines; four to six radials 2–3cm long, and four centrals 6–8cm long. Flowers are diurnal in summer; they are yellow, 2.5–4cm long, and the petals have 'laced' edges. Requires full sun; normal cactus compost; minimum temperature 13°C (55°F). *Mexico (Zacatecas).*

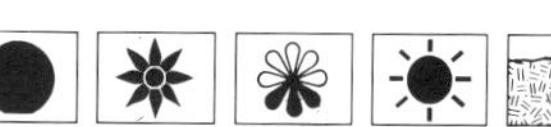

ECHINOCEREUS **ADUSTUS** Engelm.
Syn: *Echinocereus caespitosus* var. *adustus* Engelm.

A short cylindrical, rarely caespitose species, 4–6cm high, and dark green. It has 13–15 ribs, and closely set areoles with dark brownish-red spines which are yellowish near the base, consisting of 16–20 widely spreading radials and one central about 1.5cm long. Flowers are diurnal appearing in early summer; they are 3–4cm long, and are pinkish purple often with a slightly paler edge to the inner petals. Requires bright light; normal cactus compost; minimum temperature 7°C (45°F). *Northern Mexico.*

ECHINOCEREUS **ADUSTUS var. SCHWARZII** (Lau) N. P. Taylor
Syn: *Echinocereus schwarzii* Lau

Similar in most respects to the species, the dark-green stems are up to 8cm high, and 12cm in diameter, with 11–14 ribs. The spines are yellowish with reddish tips; there are 26–31 radials to 1.5cm long and one to two centrals, the upper one 5mm, the lower 2cm in length. A summer, day-flowering plant, the flowers are 5–6cm long, 5cm across, pale purple sometimes with a darker centre area. Requires sun; normal cactus compost; minimum temperature 10°C (50°F). *Mexico (Durango).*

    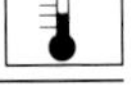

ECHINOCEREUS **BARTHELOWIANUS** Br. & R.

A clustering species, the cylindrical stems are up to 20cm long, 4–5cm wide with about 10 ribs, slightly tuberculate towards the base. Areoles are fairly close-set and bear numerous white or pinkish-white spines, later turning grey, with brownish-black tips, consisting of both radials and centrals, often to 7cm long. Summer flowering, and diurnal, the flowers are purple, up to 1.3cm long, the petals only 3–4mm long. Needs full sun; normal cactus compost; minimum temperature 13°C (55°F). *Mexico (Baja).*

    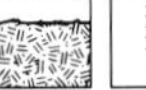 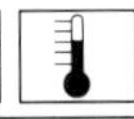

ECHINOCEREUS **BRANDEGEEI** (Coult.) K. Sch.
Syn: *Cereus brandegeei* Coult.

A dull-green, more or less erect, stiff plant to 35cm tall, 4–5cm thick, becoming cylindrical in shape and forming clumps. There are about six ribs with prominent tubercles bearing circular areoles with about 12 radial spines and four thicker centrals which are yellowish red and are frequently 8cm in length. The flowers are purplish pink with a reddish throat, and about 5cm long; they appear by day in summer. Needs bright light; normal cactus compost; minimum temperature 10°C (50°F). *Mexico (Baja).*

    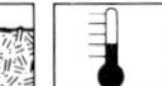

ECHINOCEREUS **CONGLOMERATUS** Först.

A group-forming species: the dark-green individual stems are 10–20cm long each with 11–13 ribs. The areoles are about 1cm apart, bearing pale brownish-white spines which almost cover the plant. These consist of nine to ten radials 1.5–2.5cm long and several flexible centrals, to 7cm in length. Flowering by day in mid-summer, the flowers are purple, 6–7cm long and wide, the tube and ovary with dense long spines. Needs full sun; slightly calcareous compost; minimum temperature 10°C (50°F). *Mexico (Coahuila).*

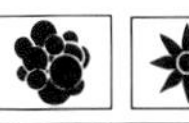    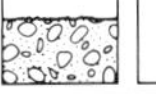 

▲

ECHINOCEREUS **ENGELMANNII** (Parry) Rümpl.
Syn: *Cereus engelmannii* Parry

A clump-forming plant to about 25cm high; individual stems are 5–7cm thick with 10–14 ribs. Large round areoles are set about 1cm apart with variously coloured spines: 10–12 radial spines about 1cm in length, and two to six centrals to 7cm long. The typical colouring is white. Flowers are 5–8cm long and over 7cm across, and are pinkish red, occurring by day in summer. Requires a sunny position; normal cactus compost; minimum temperature 10°C (50°F). *USA (South-western States), Mexico (Northern).*

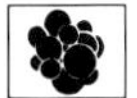    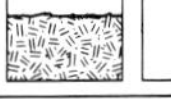

ECHINOCEREUS **DELAETII** Gürke

A clustering species with stems 10–25cm high, 5–7cm thick, pale green and entirely covered with long white hairs. There are 18–24 ribs with areoles bearing 18–36 pale yellowish radial spines to 1cm long, and four to five red-tipped centrals to 3cm in length, plus numerous hairs which almost obscure the stems. Flowers are diurnal in early summer; they are pale purplish pink, 7cm long, 6cm or more across, with the green stigma very much in evidence. Requires a sunny position; normal cactus compost with a little lime added; minimum temperature 10°C (50°F). *Mexico (Coahuila).*

  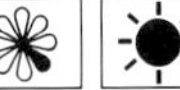   

ECHINOCEREUS **ENGELMANNII var. ACICULARIS** L. Benson

A spine-colour variety found on rocky hillsides at up to 1000m elevation. Stems can reach up to 60cm long, 5cm in diameter, forming clusters. The pinkish or yellowish spines vary in length up to 4cm. Day flowering in summer, the flowers are purple or magenta, and are about 6cm across. Requirements are the same as for the type species. *USA (Arizona).*

   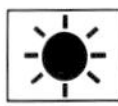 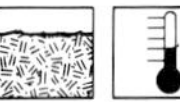 

ECHINOCEREUS **ENGELMANNII var. CHRYSOCENTRUS** (Engelm.) Engelm. ex Rümpl.

A long-spined variety from low to high elevations in desert regions. Stems are usually up to 20cm high, about 6cm thick and forming groups of three to ten. The spines are various shades of reddish or yellowish colouring, the lower central being white, all straight or twisted, to about 5cm long. Flowers are purplish to magenta, to 8cm in diameter, and occur by day in summer. Requirements as for the species. *USA (Arizona, California).*

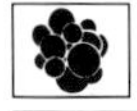    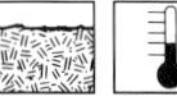 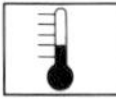

ECHINOCEREUS **ENGELMANNII var. VARIEGATUS** (Engelm.) Engelm. ex Rümpl.

Habitats vary from grassy, gravelly hillsides to high-altitude deserts. These are clustering plants with stems 8–15cm long, to 5cm thick. Spines are reddish black, the radials sometimes almost white, as is the lower central; all are about 4cm in length. Diurnal, in summer, flowers are purplish to magenta, about 5cm diameter. Requirements as for the species. *USA (Arizona).*

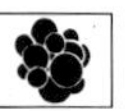    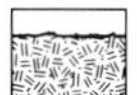 

▲

ECHINOCEREUS **ENNEACANTHUS** Engelm.

A clustering, somewhat prostrate species with stems to 20cm long, 3–7cm thick with eight to ten prominent blunt ribs. The whitish round areoles are set about 1cm apart. Radial spines are white, numbering seven to ten or more, up to 1.5cm long, and spreading; there are one to three yellowish-brown centrals 4–6.5cm in length. The pale purplish-red flowers, 5–6cm long, about 7cm across, appear by day in mid-summer. Requires a bright sunny position; normal cactus compost; minimum temperature 10°C (50°F). *Mexico (Chihuahua, Coahuila).*

ECHINOCEREUS **FENDLERI** (Engelm.) Rümpl.
Syn: *Cereus fendleri* Engelm.

Stems are 10–15cm long, 5–6cm thick, dull or brownish green with nine to twelve ribs. Areoles are about 1–1.5cm apart bearing about eight brownish radial spines 1–2cm long and a single, much longer central. The purplish-violet flowers are about 8cm long, with petals 'toothed' at the edges. They are diurnal, appearing in summer. Requires full sun; normal cactus compost with a little lime added; minimum temperature 10°C (50°F). *USA (Arizona, New Mexico), Mexico (Sonora and Chihuahua).*

    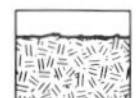 

ECHINOCEREUS **FENDLERI var. KUENZLERI** (Castetter *et al*) L. Benson
Syn: *Echinocereus kuenzleri*, Castetter, Pierce & Schwerin

Solitary or branching, dark green to reddish brown, conical, to 15cm long and up to 10cm in diameter. They have about 10 prominent ribs and conspicuous tubercles. Areoles bear four to six whitish radial spines about 6–9mm long, and occasionally one longer blackish central. Flowers are diurnal, in summer; purplish pink to violet, 5.7–10cm long and across. Requires good light; normal cactus compost; minimum temperature 10°C (50°F). *USA (New Mexico).*

 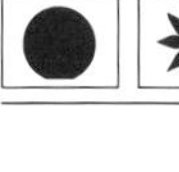      

ECHINOCEREUS **FERREIRIANUS** Gat.

An erect, somewhat globular plant often up to 30cm high in its habitat and 8cm thick. Dull grey-green in colour it has nine to thirteen ribs. The areoles bear nine to thirteen greyish-brown radial spines up to 2cm long, and the long centrals, first brown but becoming grey, are very prominent, about 5cm long. Flowering in summer by day, the blooms are a deep rose pink about 4cm across, 6cm long. Requires a bright sunny position; normal cactus compost; minimum temperature 10°C (50°F). *Mexico (Baja).*

   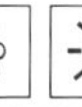  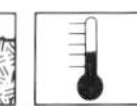

ECHINOCEREUS **FLORESII** Backeb.

A cylindrical-stemmed species to about 10cm high, 3cm in diameter, deep green in colour with about 14 ribs. The areoles bear many whitish or brownish radial spines about 1.5cm long, and more rarely one to two longer centrals. Flowers are bright red, 4.5cm long, 7cm across, appearing by day in mid-summer. Requires careful watering at all times; a fairly sunny position; an enriched mineral compost; minimum temperature 10°C (50°F). *Mexico (Sinaloa).*

ECHINOCEREUS **FENDLERI var. NOVA**

A most colourful variant discovered in the Clark Mountains. It has been recently considered a form of var. *rectispinus*, but the flower colouring fails to meet the necessary description. The flowers, 5cm long, are funnel-shaped with pale pink petals shading down to a rich deep reddish-purple throat, and appear by day in summer. Requires full sun; normal cactus compost; minimum temperature 10°C (50°F). *USA (California, Nevada).*

     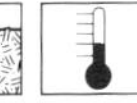 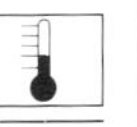

ECHINOCEREUS **KNIPPELIANUS var. REYESII** Lau

Very similar in most respects to var. *kruegeri* the four spines are whitish to pale yellow, the upper three tipped brown, to 8mm long, the lowest spines to 2.5cm. Flowers are purple, 5–6.5cm wide when fully open. Day flowering in the summer. Requires full sun; normal cactus compost; minimum temperature 10°C (50°F). *Mexico (Nuevo Leon).*

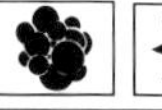    

▲

ECHINOCEREUS **KNIPPELIANUS** Liebn.

A very dark green globular, almost oval plant about 5cm in diameter, with five to six rounded ribs divided by broad furrows. The areoles are very small with one to three yellowish, bristly spines to 1.5cm long, these quickly falling. Flowering diurnally in spring and early summer, the flowers are pink, about 4cm long. Requires sun; normal cactus compost; minimum temperature 10°C (50°F). *Mexico (Coahuila).*

    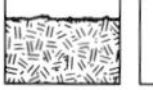 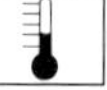

ECHINOCEREUS **KNIPPELIANUS var. KRUEGERI** Glass & Foster

Similar in most respects to the species, but more readily forming clusters. The stems, 5cm or more thick, have more ribs, and the areoles bear three to four spines to 1cm long. Flowers are whitish, the outer segments tinged tan to pale purple. Requires bright light; normal cactus compost; minimum temperature 13°C (55°F). *Mexico (Nuevo Leon).*

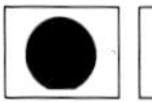      

ECHINOCEREUS **LEONENSIS** Mathsson
Syn: *Echinocereus pentalophus* var. *leonensis* (Mathsson) N. P. Taylor

A stiff, erect grey-green species with stems to 25cm long, 4–5cm thick. There are six to seven ribs with whitish areoles set with white spines, eight radials to 1.5cm long and one central 2.5–3cm in length. Day flowering in summer, the flowers are 8cm long, purplish red with a centre line a deeper shade. Requires bright light; normal cactus compost; minimum temperature 10°C (50°F). *Mexico (Nuevo Leon).*

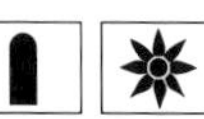   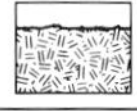 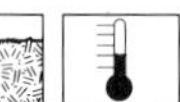

ECHINOCEREUS **LINDSAYI** Meyran
Syn: *Echinocereus ferreirianus* var. *lindsayi* (Meyran) N. P. Taylor

A dull-green almost globose plant, 20cm or more tall and about 8cm thick. It has eight to thirteen ribs and areoles bearing long, white tortuous spines tipped black; the radials are about 2cm long, the centrals 4–5cm. Flowering in summer, the plant is diurnal and the flowers are about 5cm long, rose pink with an orange-red throat. Requires full sun; normal cactus compost; minimum temperature 13°C (55°F). *Mexico (Baja).*

ECHINOCEREUS **MERKERI** Hildm.

An erect or semi-prostrate species with stems of greyish green 12–15cm thick, up to 30cm or more high and with eight to nine rounded ribs with prominent tubercles. The areoles are greyish white set about 2cm apart with six to nine white radial spines and one to two centrals up to 5cm long. Flowers are purplish red, about 6cm long, and are diurnal, in summer. Needs good light; normal cactus compost; minimum temperature 10°C (50°F). *Northern Mexico.*

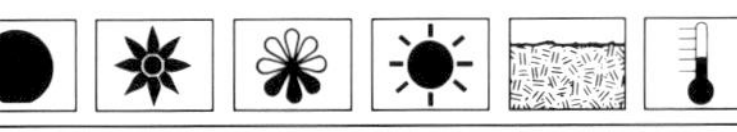

ECHINOCEREUS **NIVOSUS** Glass & Foster
Syn: *Echinocereus albatus* Backeb. (?)

A clump-forming species, the individual stems are pale green and up to 4cm in diameter, with about 12 low ribs. Areoles are on slight prominences set 7mm apart. The spines are white or greyish, tipped black, of which there are about 30 radials, 4–9mm long and 11–12 centrals, 9–12mm, rarely one longer to 2cm. Flowers are diurnal, in summer, magenta in colour and 3–3.5cm across. Requires full sun; slightly calcareous cactus compost; minimum temperature 10°C (50°F). *Mexico (Coahuila).*

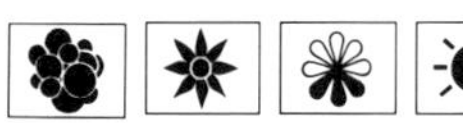  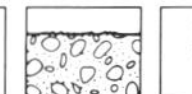 

ECHINOCEREUS **MARITIMUS** (Jones) K. Sch.

A rather variable species with roundish or somewhat cylindrical stems 5–15cm long, 2–2.5cm thick and clustering freely. Coloured bright green passing to grey, there are eight to ten ribs with areoles set about 2cm apart bearing greyish-white spines, nine to ten radials to 2.5cm long, and one to four centrals to 3.5cm. The flowers are yellow, about 4cm long, and bloom by day, in summer. Requires full sun; normal cactus compost with lime added; minimum temperature 13°C (55°F). *Mexico (Baja).*

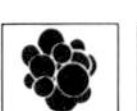     

ECHINOCEREUS **PAPILLOSUS** A. Linke
Syn: *Echinocereus blanckii* var. *angusticeps* (Clov.) L. Benson

The earlier title still persists regardless of the reclassification. A sprawling, branching pale green plant with stems up to 24cm long, 2.5cm thick and seven to nine ribs. Areoles are yellowish with about seven brownish-white radial spines to 1cm long and one yellow central to 2cm. Flowering diurnally in summer, the blooms are yellow, to 10cm in diameter. Requires a sunny position; normal cactus compost; minimum temperature 10°C (50°F). *USA (Texas).*

ECHINOCEREUS **PECTINATUS** (Scheidw.) Engelm

The 'type' of a most variable species. Globose or short cylindrical plants to 15cm high, 6–8cm thick with about 20 ribs. The 22–30 radial spines are whitish or pinkish, to 9mm long, arranged like a comb, and there are about three very short centrals to 3mm long. Flowers are diurnal, appearing in summer; 6–8cm across, they are pale pinkish lavender with a white throat. Requires sun; normal cactus compost; minimum temperature 10°C (50°F). *USA (Texas), Mexico (Northern States).*

     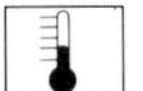

ECHINOCEREUS **PECTINATUS var. CTENOIDES** (Engelm.) Weniger
Syn: *Echinocereus ctenoides* Engelm.

A dark-green, cylindrical-shaped plant to 30–35cm high, with 20 or more ribs. The areoles are close-set bearing 12–25 greyish or brownish radial spines more or less adpressed, with two to five or more brownish centrals about 2cm long. Flowers appear in summer, and are diurnal. Up to 10cm diameter, they are generally yellow, rarely pink or purplish. Requires sun; normal cactus compost; minimum temperature 10°C (50°F). *Mexico (Sonora), USA (Texas).*

        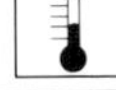

ECHINOCEREUS **PECTINATUS var. DASYACANTHUS** (Engelm.) N. P. Taylor
Syn: *Echinocereus dasyacanthus* Engelm.
Echinocereus pectinatus var. *neomexicanus* L. Benson

Cylindrical, to 20cm high and 7–8cm thick, with 18–20 ribs. Brownish areoles bear 18–22 brown or pink radial spines to 1.2cm long and three to eight centrals to 8mm. Flowers are yellow, to 10cm long, 12cm in diameter, diurnal, in summer. Needs sun; normal cactus compost with a little lime; minimum temperature 10°C (50°F). *USA (Arizona, New Mexico), Mexico.*

ECHINOCEREUS **PECTINATUS var. MINOR** (Engelm.) L. Benson
Syn: *Echinocereus dasyacanthus* var. *minor* Engelm.; *Echinocereus scopulorum* Br. & R.

Stems are usually solitary, 10–30cm or more tall and about 7cm thick with 14–16 straight ribs. The closely set areoles carry up to 15 pink or greyish radial spines 4.5–15mm long and two or more centrals 5mm or a little more in length. Flowering in early summer, the plant is diurnal, with magenta flowers 5.2–7.5cm in diameter. Requires bright sun; normal cactus compost with a little lime added; minimum temperature 10°C (50°F). *USA (Southern States), Mexico (Northern States).*

    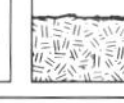 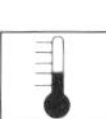

ECHINOCEREUS **PENTALOPHUS** (DC.) Rümpl.

A somewhat sprawling, pale to dark-green plant with stems 12–14cm long, about 2cm thick, and four to five ribs set with whitish areoles. The yellowish or whitish spines are all radials, to 2cm in length. Flowering early to mid-summer, the flowers are diurnal, lilac to carmine, and up to 10cm long and across. Requires bright light; normal cactus compost; minimum temperature 10°C (50°F). *USA (Texas), Mexico (Northern States).*

ECHINOCEREUS **PECTINATUS var. WENIGERI** L. Benson

More or less cylindrical plants, 7–10cm long, 5cm thick, with up to 14 straight ribs. The areoles bear 14–16 ashy-white radial spines 6mm long and one to three similarly coloured centrals in a vertical series, 2–3mm in length. Day flowering in mid-summer, the flowers are magenta with a yellowish throat, 5–7.5cm in diameter. Needs a bright sunny position; normal cactus compost with a little lime added; minimum temperature 10°C (50°F). *USA (Texas), Mexico (Coahuila).*

    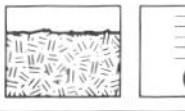

ECHINOCEREUS **PULCHELLUS** (Mart.) K. Sch.

More or less globular plants, branching from the base. The individual stems are 4–5cm thick, bluish green, with 11–13 low ribs notched into small prominences bearing whitish areoles. There are three to four yellowish to greyish spines, all radials, to 1cm long. Flowers are a bright rose pink with white-edged petals, about 4cm long, and are diurnal in summer. Requires bright light; normal cactus compost; minimum temperature 10°C (50°F). *Mexico (Hidalgo).*

    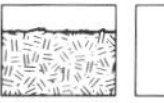 

ECHINOCEREUS **PULCHELLUS var. WEINBERGII** (Weingt.) N. P. Taylor
Syn: *Echinocereus weinbergii* Weingt.

The greyish-green stems are globular becoming slightly elongated, about 12cm in diameter, with about 15 ribs. Areoles, about 8mm apart, bear about 10 short, thick white radial spines with brownish tips to 1cm long; there are no centrals. Flowering diurnally in summer, the flowers are bright pink, about 5cm long. Requires bright light; normal cactus compost; minimum temperature 10°C (50°F). *Mexico (Zacatecas).*

    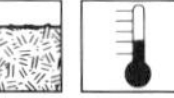

ECHINOCEREUS **SPINIGEMMATUS** Lau

A clustering species, offsetting from the base. The stems are dark green, 3–5cm thick with 10–12 slightly bumpy ribs. Areoles are brownish bearing yellowish-brown spines, six to eight radials 5–8mm long and one to three longer centrals. Flowering by day in summer, the blooms are about 5cm across, and deep pink. Requires bright light; normal cactus compost; minimum temperature 10°C (50°F). *Mexico.*

ECHINOCEREUS **RIGIDISSIMUS** (Engelm.) Rose
Syn: *Echinocereus pectinatus* (Engelm.) var. *rigidissimus* Engelm.

A globular to cylindrical plant to 30cm high, 4–9cm thick, rarely offsetting, with 16–23 straight ribs bearing elongated areoles. The spines are whitish or in shades of red or brown made up of 15–23 radials, 6–10mm long and spreading like a comb; no centrals. Flowering early summer, bright pink to magenta, 6–7cm long, diurnal. Requires bright light; normal cactus compost; minimum temperature 10°C (50°F). *USA (Arizona, New Mexico), Mexico (Sonora).*

    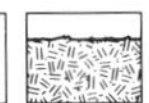 

ECHINOCEREUS **SCHEERI** (Salm-Dyck) **var. GENTRYI** (Clov.) N. P. Taylor
Syn: *Echinocereus gentryi* Clov.; *Echinocereus nocturniflorus* Hort.

A slender cylindrical plant with creeping or erect stems to 15cm or more long, 1.5–4cm thick. Dull green, it has four to five ribs, scarcely tuberculate, with areoles bearing eight to twelve radial spines hardly 1mm long and rarely one central. Summer flowering, the flowers are diurnal, bright pink and about 8cm long. Requires bright light; normal cactus compost; minimum temperature 10°C (50°F). *Mexico (Sonora, Chihuahua).*

ECHINOCEREUS **STOLONIFERUS** W. T. Marsh

A greyish-green, stoloniferous plant with cylindrical stems to 30cm high, 5cm in diameter, and 12–16 finely tuberculate ribs. Areoles 4–5mm apart bear 10–12 whitish radial spines to 6mm long; there are three to four brownish centrals 1–2.5cm in length. Flowers are borne laterally; they are bright yellow and funnel-shaped, up to 7.5cm long, 8–9cm across when fully open. They appear by day in summer. Requires sun; normal cactus compost; minimum temperature 10°C (50°F). *Mexico (Sonora).*

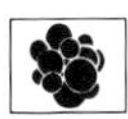     

ECHINOCEREUS **STRAMINEUS** (Engelm.) Rümpl.

A clump-forming species, each pale-green stem is up to 25cm long, 8cm wide at the base, with 10–13 rather tuberculate, deeply furrowed ribs. The areoles are round, small and white, about 1.5cm apart, bearing seven to fourteen whitish radial spines to 3cm long and one to four centrals 4–8.5cm long. The purple-pink flowers are funnel-shaped, 6–12cm long and wide, appearing by day in mid-summer. Requires good light; slightly calcareous cactus compost; minimum temperature 10°C (50°F). *USA (New Mexico, Texas), Mexico.*

   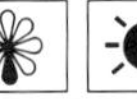 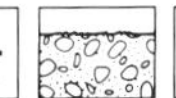

ECHINOCEREUS **SUBINERMIS** Salm-Dyck

The stems are globular becoming elongated and clustering occasionally. Dull green, they are about 15cm long, 7–9cm thick, with five to nine prominent ribs with narrow furrows between. Small woolly areoles bear three to eight radial spines and one central to 5mm long, later becoming almost spineless. Day flowering in summer, the flowers are yellow, about 8cm long and wide. Requires sun; normal cactus compost; minimum temperature 10°C (50°F). *Mexico (Central and Northern States).*

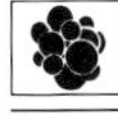   

ECHINOCEREUS **STOLONIFERUS var. TAYOPENSIS** (W. T. Marsh) N. P. Taylor
Syn: *Echinocereus tayopensis* W. T. Marsh

The greyish-green stems are cylindrical and up to 15cm high, 6–8cm thick, occasionally offsetting, with 11–13 ribs bearing areoles set 5–9mm apart. Spines are greyish: there are numerous radial spines, one to 1.5cm long, and one to three centrals to 2.5cm in length. Flowering by day in summer, the blooms are bright yellow, 7cm long, 6cm across. Requires bright light; normal cactus compost; minimum temperature 10°C (50°F). *Mexico (Sonora, Chihuahua).*

    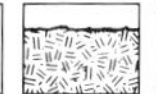 

ECHINOCEREUS **TRIGLOCHIDIATUS** Engelm. **var. GONACANTHUS** Boiss.
Syn: *Echinocereus gonacanthus* (Engelm. & Bigelow) Lem.

Stems are cylindrical and up to about 6cm thick, dull greenish with seven to nine more or less acute ribs. Areoles bear eight thick, greyish yellow radial spines 1.5–2cm long and one yellowish, black-tipped central about 6cm in length. Day flowering in summer, the 4–5cm long flowers are a vivid yellowish orange. Requires sun; normal cactus compost; minimum temperature 10°C (50°F). *USA (Southern States).*

    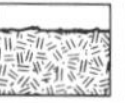 

ECHINOCEREUS **TRIGLOCHIDIATUS var. MELANACANTHUS** (Engelm.) L. Benson
Syn: *Echinocereus melanacanthus* Engelm. ex W. H. Earle

A freely clumping plant with many stems 7–15cm long, 2.5–5cm thick, and nine to ten tuberculate ribs. Spines mostly greyish, 2–6cm in length, of which there are five to eleven radials and one to three centrals. Flowers are bright red, 2.2–6cm long, 2.5–4cm across, and are day flowering in mid-summer. Needs sun; normal cactus compost; minimum temperature 7°C (45°F). *USA (California).*

   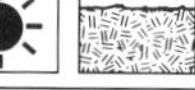 

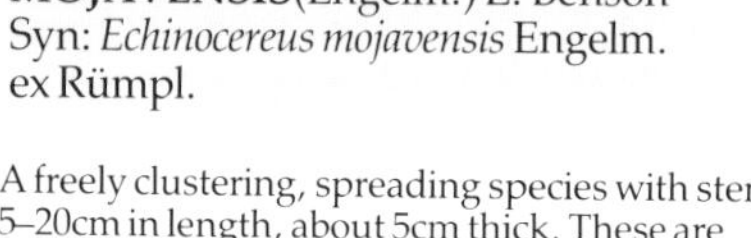

ECHINOCEREUS **TRIGLOCHIDIATUS var. MOJAVENSIS**(Engelm.) L. Benson
Syn: *Echinocereus mojavensis* Engelm. ex Rümpl.

A freely clustering, spreading species with stems 5–20cm in length, about 5cm thick. These are pale to greyish green, with whitish areoles set about 1cm apart. The spines, initially reddish but soon turning grey, include about ten radials to 2.5cm long and one central to 5cm. Flowers are carmine red, 4–5cm long and across; they are diurnal, flowering in mid-summer. Requires sun; normal cactus compost; minimum temperature 10°C (50°F). *USA.*

ECHINOCEREUS **TULENSIS** Bravo

A species which it seems should be rightfully placed, possibly with *E. enneacanthus*. Stems, to about 5cm in diameter, are dull green with five to six bumpy ribs. Spines are greyish or brownish; there are about five to six radials and one to three centrals to 1.5–2cm long. Flowering in summer, and diurnal, the flowers are 5–6cm long, purplish-pink. Requires sun; normal cactus compost; minimum temperature 10°C (50°F). *Mexico (Northern States).*

    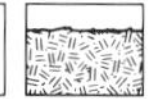 

ECHINOCEREUS **VIERECKII** Werd.

A semi-prostrate species with long, pale green stems to about 20cm, 3–4.5cm thick, with seven to nine tuberculate ribs. Areoles are 5–8mm apart bearing whitish or yellowish spines: seven to eleven radials up to about 1cm long and three to five centrals to 2cm or more long. Summer flowering, the diurnal flowers are about 7–11cm in diameter, deep pink or magenta. Requires bright light; normal cactus compost; minimum temperature 10°C (50°F). *Mexico (Tamaulipas).*

ECHINOCEREUS **VIRIDIFLORUS** Engelm.

A dull to fresh green plant with somewhat globular stems to 7.5cm long, 2–5cm thick, and 13–15 ribs. The spines are white or brownish arising from elongated areoles. There are 13–15 radials about 5mm long, and nought to three central spines, up to 2.5cm in length when present. Flowering by day in summer, the flowers are up to 3cm long and across and greenish-yellow with a darker midstripe. Requires bright sun; normal cactus compost; minimum temperature 10°C (50°F). *USA (Southern States).*

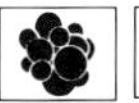       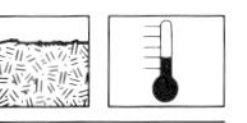 

ECHINOCEREUS **VIRIDIFLORUS var. DAVISII** (Houghton) Marsh.

Very short, dull-green stems of a depressed globular shape. There are six to seven ribs with areoles bearing nine to twelve radial spines, rarely one central; these are reddish or greyish and up to 1.7cm long. The flowers are greenish yellow, 2.5cm long, 2cm across, and appear diurnally, in summer. Requirements as for the species. *USA (Texas).*

  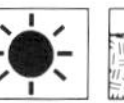 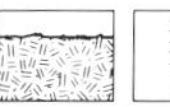 

▲

ECHINOFOSSULOCACTUS **COPTONOGONUS** (Lem.) Lawr.
Syn: *Stenocactus coptonogonus* (Lem.) Berger

A globular, greyish-green plant with 10–15 straight, notched ribs, 5–10cm high, to 11cm in diameter. The areoles are set 2–3cm apart in the notches. Spines are reddish, becoming yellowish, about 3cm long and always curved upwards; there are three to five in number. Spring flowering, and diurnal, the flowers are a whitish purple with a prominent pinkish-brown median line to the petals. Requires full sunlight; normal cactus compost; minimum temperature 10°C (50°F). *Mexico (Hidalgo etc.)*

   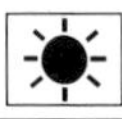 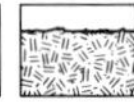 

ECHINOFOSSULOCACTUS **COPTONOGONUS fma CRISTATE FORM**

Only on rare occasions is a crested form of this species discovered, and frequently only the spination reveals its specific status.

ECHINOFOSSULOCACTUS
DICHROACANTHUS (Mart.) Br. & R.
Syn: *Stenocactus dichroacanthus* (Mart.) Berger

A somewhat oval-shaped, pale green plant to 15cm high, 10cm wide with about 32 acute, wavy ribs. The roundish areoles are set at intervals of 2–4cm, and bear four to six reddish or greyish spines, some to 2cm in length. Late spring flowering, and diurnal, the flowers are pinkish violet. Needs a sunny position; normal cactus compost; minimum temperature 10°C (50°F). *Mexico (Hidalgo).*

ECHINOFOSSULOCACTUS **ERECTOCENTRUS** Backeb.

A more or less globular plant to about 5cm high, 8cm in diameter, dark greyish green in colour with about 50 or more ribs. The areoles are about 2cm apart, bearing five to six or more pale, yellowish-brown radial spines about 1cm long, but one of these up to about 5cm in length. There are two yellowish central spines, about 2cm long. Flowers are whitish, around 2cm long, and diurnal in summer. Needs good light; normal cactus compost; minimum temperature 10°C (50°F). *Mexico.*

    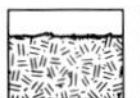 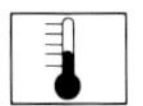

ECHINOFOSSULOCACTUS **MULTICOSTATUS** (Hildm.) Br. & R.
Syn: *Stenocactus multicostatus* (Hildm.) Berger

Dark green globular species about 10cm wide, flattened on top, with up to 100 ribs, each with about two white woolly areoles. Six to nine spines, up to 4cm in length and yellowish or greyish. Day flowering in late spring, the flowers are 2.5cm long, whitish with a purplish-violet median line. Requires a bright, sunny position; normal cactus compost; minimum temperature 7°C (45°F). *Mexico (Durango, Coahuila).*

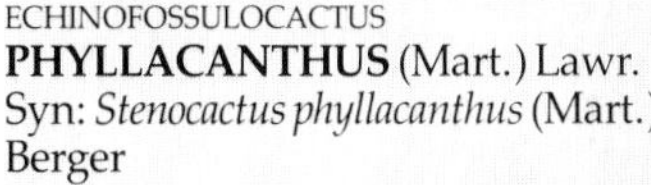

ECHINOFOSSULOCACTUS **PHYLLACANTHUS** (Mart.) Lawr.
Syn: *Stenocactus phyllacanthus* (Mart.) Berger

A dark bluish-green globular plant about 8cm in diameter with 30–35 thin, wavy-edged ribs bearing areoles set about 2.5cm apart. The spines are red, passing to brown. There are two to seven in all, the upper three, 4–8cm long, are flat, the others slender and spreading. Day flowering in late spring, the blooms are up to 2cm long and yellowish white with a brownish-red throat. Requires sun; normal cactus compost; minimum temperature 10°C (50°F). *Mexico (Hidalgo).*

    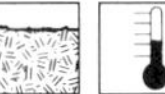

ECHINOFOSSULOCACTUS **OCHOTERENAUS** Tiegel.

A bluish-green globular plant 7cm high, 10cm in diameter, with about 30 wavy-edged ribs. The yellowish areoles bear many glassy-white radial spines 1.2cm long and four brownish-yellow centrals, the uppermost often to 6cm in length. Spring flowering, and diurnal, the flowers are pale pink or whitish with a purplish median line and throat. Requires full sun; normal cactus compost; minimum temperature 13°C (55°F). *Mexico (Guanajuato).*

ECHINOFOSSULOCACTUS **PENTACANTHUS** (Lem.) Br. & R.
Syn: *Stenocactus pentacanthus* (Lem.) Berger

Greyish-green globular plants 7–8cm in diameter with 30–40 wavy-edged ribs bearing very few greyish areoles. These have five greyish-brown spines, the upper ones to 5cm long, the lower to 1cm. Flowering diurnally in spring, the flowers are 2cm long, whitish with a pale purple midstripe. Requires full sun; normal cactus compost; minimum temperature 10°C (50°F). *Central Mexico.*

    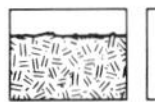 

ECHINOMASTUS **ACUNENSIS** Marsh.

A short cylindrical plant about 17cm high, 10cm in diameter with a spindle-shaped rootstock. There are 18 low-set ribs with white woolly areoles, 12 whitish spreading radial spines and three to four reddish-tipped centrals about 2.5cm long. Flowers are diurnal in summer, with pale pink inner petals shaded deeper in the throat, reddish-pink externally on the outer ones, about 2.5cm long and across. Requires bright sun; enriched porous compost plus a little lime and humus; minimum temperature 10°C (50°F). *USA (Arizona).*

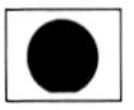    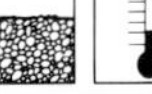 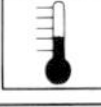

ECHINOMASTUS **DURANGENSIS** (Runge) Br. & R.
Syn: *Neolloydia durangensis* (Runge) L. Benson

Plants are solitary 7.5–10cm high, 5–7.5cm broad, dark green, with 18 ribs divided into warts up to 8mm high. The areoles bear about 30 greyish-black radial spines, 1.5–3cm long, and four upward-pointing centrals of similar length and colour. Flowering diurnally in summer, the flowers are 2–2.5cm with reddish purple petals edged with pink. Requires full sun; normal cactus compost; minimum temperature 10°C (50°F). *Mexico (Durango).*

    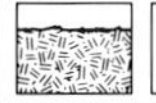 

ECHINOMASTUS **ERECTOCANTRUS** (Coult.) Br. & R.
Syn: *Sclerocactus erectocentrus* (Coult.) N. P. Taylor; *Echinocactus erectocentrus* Coult.

Globular, bluish-green to 20cm tall, 10cm in diameter, covered in whitish spines. 14–21 notched ribs carry elongated areoles with 14–21 radial spines, 1.25cm long, and one longer central. Flowering in summer, diurnal, flowers are 3–5cm long, 2cm across, pink with a dark throat. Needs full sun; normal cactus compost with a little lime; minimum temperature 10°C (50°F). *USA (Arizona).*

ECHINOMASTUS **INTERTEXTUS** (Engelm.) Br. & R.
Syn: *Echinocactus intertextus* Engelm.; *Neolloydia intertexta* (Engelm.) L. Benson

A green globular plant about 9cm high, 7cm in diameter, with 13 tuberculate ribs and numerous spines covering the body of the plant. The spines are whitish red consisting of 16–25 radials 1–1.5cm long, and four centrals 2cm in length. Flowers are diurnal in summer, 2cm long and across. Requires full sun; slightly calcareous cactus compost; minimum temperature 10°C (50°F). *USA (Southern States).*

    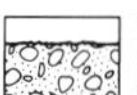

ECHINOMASTUS **MARIPOSENSIS** Hester
Syn: *Neolloydia mariposensis* (Hester) L. Benson; *Sclerocactus mariposensis* (Hester) N. P. Taylor

A short cylindrical plant to 9cm high, 6cm wide, covered with spines. It has 21 ribs with areoles bearing 25–35 whitish radial spines 4–6mm long and four to six brownish tipped centrals to 1.5cm long. Flowers which are diurnal and summer flowering, are rose pink, pale pink or pinkish white, 2.5cm long and 2–3cm across. Needs a sunny position; a slightly calcareous cactus compost; minimum temperature 10°C (50°F). *USA (Texas).*

ECHINOMASTUS **UNGUISPINUS** (Engelm.) Br. & R.
Syn: *Neolloydia unguispina* (Engelm.) L. Benson

Bluish-green plants globular, to 12cm high and about 10cm wide. They have large woolly areoles bearing about 25 whitish radial spines to 2cm long, and four to eight thicker brownish centrals. Flowers are a deep reddish brown, about 2.5cm long, 2cm across, and are day flowering in summer. Requires bright light; a permeable, slightly calcareous but enriched compost; minimum temperature 10°C (50°F). *Mexico (Chihuahua, Zacatecas).*

    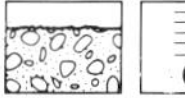 

ECHINOMASTUS **UNGUISPINUS var. LAUI** (Frank & Zecher) Glass & Foster
Syn: *Echinomastus laui* Frank & Zecher

This has a more flattened stem than the species, but is generally globular to about 10cm in diameter. It has about 20 tubercled ribs with whitish areoles having around 20 radial spines 2cm long and four to six centrals to 3cm; these are reddish brown. Flowers are pale yellowish green with a violet-brownish median stripe to the petals, appearing by day in summer. Requires a sunny position; normal cactus compost; minimum temperature 13°C (55°F). *Mexico (San Luis Potosi).*

    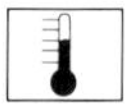

ECHINOMASTUS **WARNOCKII** (L. Benson) Glass & Foster
Syn: *Neolloydia warnockii* L. Benson; *Sclerocactus warnockii* (L. Benson) N. P. Taylor

Stems are solitary, globose or ovoid, and spiny. Up to 11cm long, 7.5cm wide. Ribs divided into tubercles with areoles bearing 12–14 radial and two or more central spines, whitish with brownish tips, 1.2–2.5cm long. Flowering by day in mid-summer, yellowish white, 2.5cm across. Requires bright light; slightly calcareous compost; minimum temperature 10°C (50°F). *USA (Texas), Mexico (Chihuahua).*

    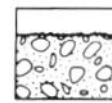 

ECHINOPSIS **ARACHNACANTHA** (Buin. & Ritter) Friedr.
Syn: *Lobivia arachnacantha* Buin. & Ritter

A roundish plant about 2cm high, 4cm thick, dark green in colour with 14 ribs. The areoles bear about 15 dark-brownish radial spines which later turn whitish, and one dark central spine, all about 5mm long. Flowers are yellow to orange, 3–4cm across, appearing by day in summer. Requires bright light which is essential; normal cactus compost; minimum temperature 10°C (50°F). *Bolivia (Samaipata).*

ECHINOPSIS **AUREA var. ALBIFLORA** Rausch
Syn: *Lobivia aurea* var. *albiflora* Rausch

Very similar to the type species, this globular dark green plant 6–7cm or more in diameter has six to eight or more pale brown radial spines and one to three longer centrals which are initially dark reddish brown, but later similar to radials. Flowers are white, with the petals slightly tinged pinkish at the tips. They are diurnal, flowering in summer. Requires normal cactus compost; bright light; minimum temperature 10°C (50°F). *Argentina (Cordoba).*

ECHINOPSIS **AUREA** Br. & R. **var. AURANTIACA** (Backeb.) Rausch
Syn: *Lobivia famatimensis* var. *aurantiaca* (Backeb.) Backeb.

Dark green, more or less globular plants 7–8cm in diameter, with about 16 ribs. The areoles are large, bearing six to eight or more pale brown radial spines and one to three or four dark brown centrals. Flowers, which are diurnal, appearing in summer, are 5–6cm long and a deep orange-yellow or pale reddish orange. Requires bright light; normal cactus compost; minimum temperature 10°C (50°F). *Argentina.*

▲

ECHINOPSIS **AUREA** Br. & R.
Syn: *Lobivia aurea* (Br. & R.) Backeb.

A more or less globular plant to 10cm high, 6–7cm thick, offsetting from the base. The stems are dark green with 14–15 ribs; areoles, set about 1cm apart, bear eight to ten pale brown radial spines and about four blackish-brown centrals to 3cm long. Flowering in summer, and diurnal, the flowers are bright yellow, about 9cm long, 8cm across. Needs sun; normal cactus compost; minimum temperature 10°C (50°F). *Argentina (Cordoba).*

ECHINOPSIS **AUREA** Br. & R. **var. LEUCOMALLA** (Wessn.) Rausch
Syn: *Lobivia famatimensis* var. *leucomalla* (Wessn.) Backeb.

A dark green globular species 5–6cm in diameter, with about 20 ribs. The areoles bear numerous whitish-grey spines which densely cover the whole body of the plant. Flowers are bright yellow, 6cm or more long and across: they are summer flowering, and diurnal. Requires slight shade; normal cactus compost; minimum temperature 10°C (50°F). *Argentina.*

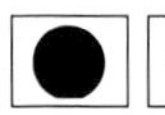

ECHINOPSIS **CANDICANS** (Gillies ex Salm-Dyck) F. A. C. Weber ex D. R. Hunt
Syn: *Trichocereus candicans* (Gillies) Br. & R.

Erect or semi-prostrate bright-green plants to about 75cm high, 16cm thick, with nine to eleven prominent ribs. Areoles are large and whitish, bearing 10–14 yellowish-brown radial spines up to 4cm long and one or more longer centrals to 10cm in length. Nocturnal flowering in summer, the flowers are white, 18–25cm long. Requires a bright position; normal cactus compost; minimum temperature 10°C (50°F). *Argentina.*

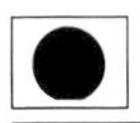     

ECHINOPSIS **EYRIESII** Zucc.

A popular dark green globular species, later elongating to become somewhat cylindrical and ultimately 12–15cm thick, offsetting freely. It has 11–18 deeply furrowed ribs. Areoles are about 3cm apart, greyish, and bearing up to 10 radial and four to eight brown central spines, up to 5mm in length. Flowers are nocturnal, opening late afternoon in summer; they are white, and 17–25cm long, 10–12cm across. Requires bright light; normal cactus compost; minimum temperature 10°C (50°F). *Argentina, Uruguay, Southern Brazil.*

    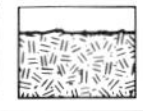 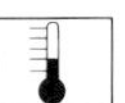

ECHINOPSIS **'Haku-jo'**

This plant is an oddity originating from Japan, but how the bizarre and abnormal growth was developed has still to be revealed. Obviously related to *E. multiplex* and *E. tubiflora,* it might just prove to be a mutation. Flowers are creamy white, about 10cm long and about 7cm diameter, and bloom by day in summer. Requires slight shade; normal cactus compost; minimum temperature 13°C (55°F).

    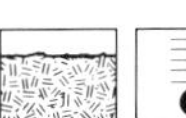

ECHINOPSIS **'Haku-jo cristata'**

Another oddity depicting the additional abnormal growth termed 'monstrose' or 'cristate'. Flowers and requirements are the same as for E. 'Haku-jo'.

    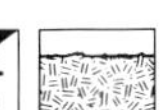 

ECHINOPSIS **LEUCANTHA fma CRISTATA**

An unusual monstrose form discovered at Maradona, San Juan, Argentina. Spine and flower colour are similar to type. Cultural requirements are as for the species.

ECHINOPSIS **KERMESINA** Krainz

Currently considered a variety of *E. mammillosa* Gürke. The plants are globular, up to 15cm in diameter and a rich green, having 15–23 ribs with areoles bearing 11–16 reddish-yellow radial spines about 1.2cm long and four to six darker centrals to 2.5cm. Day flowering in mid-summer, the flowers are carmine red, up to 18cm long, 9cm across. Needs bright light which is essential; normal cactus compost; minimum temperature 13°C (55°F). *Argentina.*

  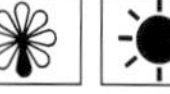   

ECHINOPSIS **LEUCANTHA** Walp.
Syn: *Echinopsis salpingophora* Lem.

Globular to elongating greyish-green plants about 12cm in diameter. There are about 14 ribs, slightly notched with areoles 1–1.5cm apart bearing about 10 radial spines to 2.5cm long, and one thick central, curved upwards to 10cm in length. Flowers are white with orange tips, the outer segments brownish green. Night flowering in summer, it requires filtered light; normal cactus compost; minimum temperature 10°C (50°F). *Western Argentina (Catamarca).*

ECHINOPSIS **MULTIPLEX** (Pfeiff.) Zucc.

A pale green or yellowish-green globular plant up to 15cm or more tall, freely offsetting from the base and sides. It has 12–15 deeply furrowed ribs with white woolly areoles set about 2cm apart. Spines are yellowish brown tipped darker, made up of five to fifteen (usually 10) radial spines to 2cm long and two to five centrals up to 4cm. Free flowering and diurnal in summer, the flowers are white to pink, fragrant, and 15–20cm long, 12–15cm across. Requires good light; normal cactus compost; minimum temperature 10°C (50°F). *Southern Brazil.*

   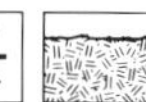 

ECHINOPSIS **OBREPANDA** Salm-Dyck **var. FIEBRIGII** (Gürke) Friedr.
Syn: *Echinopsis fiebrigii* Gürke

Greyish-green plants with globular stems 15–18cm in diameter, with 18–24 irregular ribs. The areoles are yellowish grey, about 3cm apart, bearing eight to ten pale yellow, becoming greyish radial spines to 2.5cm long, and one curved central to 3.5cm. Day flowering in summer, the blooms are 17–19cm long and pure white, with a slender green scaly and white hairy tube. Needs bright light; normal cactus compost; minimum temperature 10°C (50°F). *Bolivia.*

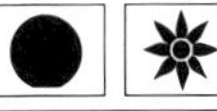    

ECHINOPSIS **OXYGONA** (Link) Zucc.

Globular stems becoming cylindrical to 25cm or more high, 20cm wide, and offsetting from around the sides. There are 13–15 ribs with large, short woolly areoles set 2cm or more apart. The pale-brownish spines consist of 13–15 radials to 1.5cm long and two to seven centrals 2–4cm in length. Diurnal, and summer flowering, the blooms are about 25cm long, to 12cm across, pale pink internally and reddish externally. Needs full sun; normal cactus compost; minimum temperature 10°C (50°F). *Southern Brazil, Argentina, Uruguay.*

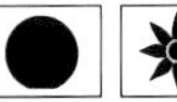   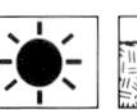  

ECHINOPSIS **SILVESTRII** Speg.

A greyish-green globular plant to about 15cm diameter with a depressed crown. It has 20 or more ribs with areoles bearing five to nine radial spines, and one central, initially yellow becoming grey and up to 1cm long. The flowers are white, about 20cm long to 15cm across and are day flowering in summer. Needs bright light; normal cactus compost; minimum temperature 10°C (50°F). *Argentina (Salta).*

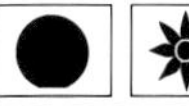      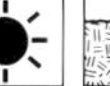  

× EPICACTUS **'Absintha'** Passmore

An attractive cultivar produced about 1946 in the UK, the parents being 'Marseillaise' crossed with 'Augusta von Szombathy', two of the few hybrids available at that time. The stem growth is similar to the majority of epicacti, being elongated and leaf-like. Flowering in spring, it is diurnal. Needs filtered light; normal cactus compost; minimum temperature 10°C (50°F).

   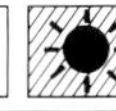 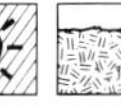 

x EPICACTUS **'Achievement'** Innes

One of the earliest yellow-flowering cultivars to be developed in the UK, the product of *Echinopsis aurea* and *Epiphyllum crenatum*. Flowers are about 14cm in diameter with slightly frilled petals, and appear by day in late spring. Requires filtered light; an acid, porous compost; minimum temperature 10°C (50°F).

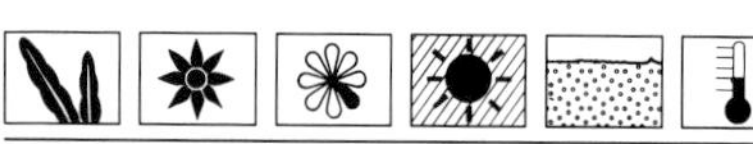

x EPICACTUS **'Alba Superbus'** Beahm

A large-flowering white cultivar developed in the USA by Sherman Beahm. The large bloom, 10–12cm in diameter, is pure white, the outer segments pinkish white, and it lasts for three to four days, appearing by day in late spring and early summer. Requires semi-shade with brief periods of brighter light; a permeable acid compost; minimum temperature 10°C (50°F).

x EPICACTUS **'Ackermannii'** Haworth (?)

The early-day hybrid well known for very many years as a popular houseplant. Its origin remains uncertain but it is seemingly a hybrid of an *Epiphyllum* and *Heliocereus*. A medium- to large-sized flower of dazzling red, about 8cm long, it remains open for several days. The flowers, borne on either flat or three-angled stems, appear in late spring. Needs slight shade; normal cactus compost; minimum temperature 10°C (50°F).

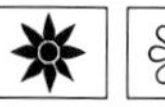

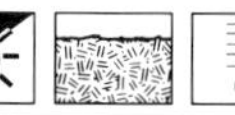

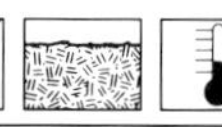

x EPICACTUS **'Ashlea'** Barber

The product of the late J. T. Barber, a British nurseryman specializing in epiphytic cacti. The rich, deep-orange colouring is derived from one of the parents, the cultivar 'Amber Queen'. Flowering in early summer, the flowers, which are diurnal, are 12–14cm across, the petals always tending to recurve at the edges. Requires indirect light; normal cactus compost; minimum temperature 10°C (50°F).

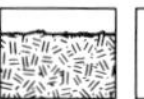

x EPICACTUS **'Astronaut'** Cactus Pete

A product of the eminent rare plant nursery in the USA, a result which was achieved in 1960. The large, bell-shaped flower is rich orange throughout, 12–15cm in diameter, and lasts for three to four days. It is day flowering in late spring. Needs indirect light but not too shaded; normal cactus compost; minimum temperature 10°C (50°F).

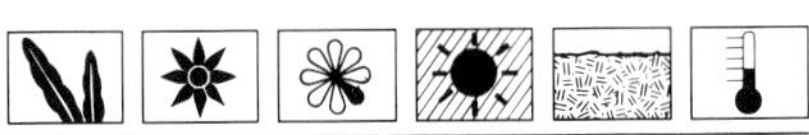

x EPICACTUS **'Augusta von Szombathy'** Knebel

One of the outstanding hybridizers of all time, Curt Knebel of Germany developed this outstanding plant in about 1935. The varying shades of colour in this funnel-shaped bloom are very much in evidence. A medium-sized flower, 10–11cm long, 9–11cm across at the tips, it lasts for four or five days, flowering late in spring in the day time. Needs protection from full sun; normal cactus compost; minimum temperature 10°C (50°F).

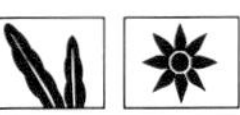    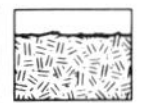 

x EPICACTUS **'Ballyshavel'**

This very colourful cultivar originated from the USA, possibly produced by Hummel, but this remains uncertain. A richly coloured flower, it appears in late spring, the blend of deep lilac and purple giving a startling effect. The flowers are 10–12cm in diameter and last up to three days, opening in mid-morning, and partially closing near dusk. Needs a slightly shaded position; normal cactus compost; minimum temperature 10°C (50°F).

    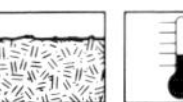

x EPICACTUS **'Bambi'** Monmonier

A product of Ventura Gardens, USA. The trumpet-shaped flowers vary from quite small to medium sized and are up to 12cm long. Colouring is in shades of fuchsia and carmine, and it is very free flowering in late spring. Requires indirect light; normal cactus compost; minimum temperature 10°C (50°F).

   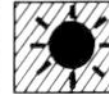  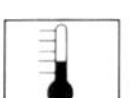

x EPICACTUS **'Calypso'** Innes

A low-growing plant with large lilac-pinkish flowers about 12cm across. This was developed in the UK at the Holly Gate Nurseries in 1965 and was the result of crossing the cultivars 'Padre' and 'Flirtation', the latter being the 'mother' plant. It is day flowering in late spring, the flowers lasting for three to four days. Requires a slightly shaded position; normal cactus compost; minimum temperature 10°C (50°F).

   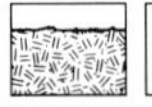 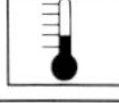

▲

x EPICACTUS **'Carolyn Haupt'** Daly

A choice variety with cherry-red flowers developed by Leo M. Daly of the USA. The more or less ruffled structure of the flower is particularly significant, coupled with its very large size. Flowering from mid-spring to early summer, it is diurnal. Requires indirect light: with shade too dense it loses its colouring; normal cactus compost; minimum temperature 10°C (50°F).

   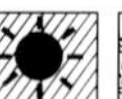 

x EPICACTUS **'Carnation'** C. Steele

A most intriguing cultivar from the USA. The broad, overlapping pinkish petals are enhanced by the rich rose throat. The flower, 12–14cm across, opens early in the day during late spring and is long-lasting. Requires filtered light; normal cactus compost; minimum temperature 10°C (50°F).

x EPICACTUS **'Celeste'** Coolidge

An excellent cultivar produced in 1950. The outstanding feature is the cup and saucer-shaped flower with the distinctive three to four rows of lilac-pink petals. The flowers, about 14cm in diameter, appear during late spring and remain open for three or four days or more. Requires a bright position out of direct sun; normal cactus compost; minimum temperature 10°C (50°F).

   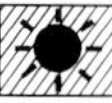 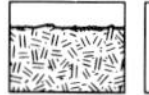 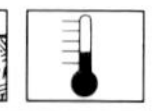

× EPICACTUS **'Celestine'** C. Steele

A cultivar which appeared in 1939 and has maintained its popularity ever since, both in the USA where it was produced and equally so in Europe. The almost 'ruffled', funnel-shaped flower of pale purplish pink is about 12cm across and is diurnal, at its best in late spring. Needs protection from full sun; normal cactus compost; minimum temperature 10°C (50°F)

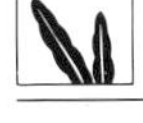   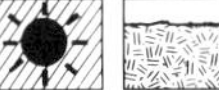 

× EPICACTUS **'Cleona'** Beahm

A striking cultivar developed in 1945 and offered by the Beahm Gardens, it is a hybrid of the cultivars 'Montezuma' and 'Sun Goddess'. The large, dark orange-red petals are widely spreading and enhanced by the violet throat. It flowers by day in early summer. Requires only slight shade; normal cactus compost; minimum temperature 10°C (50°F).

 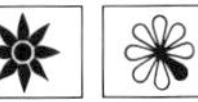  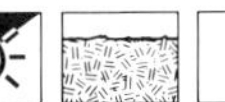

× EPICACTUS **'Crinoline Lady'** Innes

An erect cultivar produced about 1958 in the UK. The stems are either flat or three-angled and the flowers are produced in spring; their somewhat ruffled petals are pale orange-pink throughout and last up to five days. Requires filtered light; normal cactus compost; minimum temperature 10°C (50°F).

 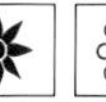 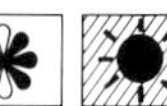 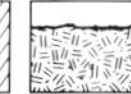 

× EPICACTUS **'Chauncey'** Stoddard

A most impressive cultivar developed in the USA in 1940. It is a tall plant with stems to over 60cm long with large flowers about 15cm across. The broad inner petals are purple with a reddish median line and suffused with white along the margins; the outer segments are dark reddish. The plant is day flowering in late spring. Requires slight shade; normal cactus compost; minimum temperature 10°C (50°F).

    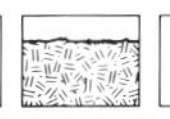 

× EPICACTUS **'Communion'** Fort & O'Barr

An outstanding and impressive cultivar from the USA produced by Country Garden Nursery in 1950, the result of cross-pollinating the epicacti 'Harmony' and 'Garden'. The flowers are 9–10cm across, with white inner petals suffused with pale pink and lilac-pink outer ones. It is day flowering in early to mid-spring. Requires filtered light; normal cactus compost; minimum temperature 10°C (50°F).

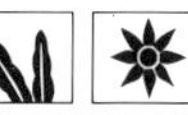 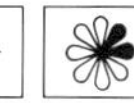  

× EPICACTUS **'Deutsche Kaiserin'**

This popular cultivar appears to be an improved form of *Nopalxochia phyllanthoides* and would seem to be of German origin. The bright pink flowers are larger than those of the species and are produced in greater abundance during late spring until mid-summer; they are diurnal. An ideal plant for hanging baskets. Requires protection from direct sun; normal cactus compost; minimum temperature 13°C (55°F).

    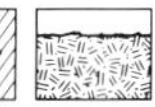 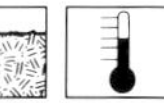

x EPICACTUS **'Dobson's Yellow'** Dobson

An early-day yellowish hybrid developed by the late Mr Dobson of Scarborough, UK. A very free-flowering plant from early to late spring, the rich creamy-yellow flowers are highly scented, and about 16cm in diameter when fully open. Needs partial shade, which is essential; normal cactus compost; minimum temperature best at 13°C (55°F).

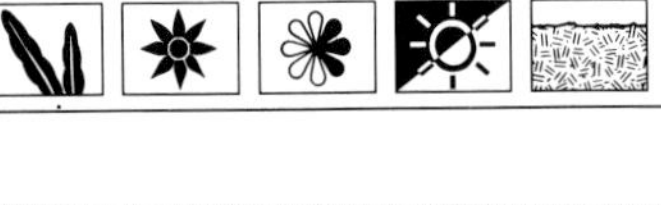

x EPICACTUS **'Dreamland'** Beahm

An outstanding cultivar produced in 1953, the parents being the epicacti 'Sherman E. Beahm' and 'Pride of Bell'. The spring flowers, which last for three or four days, are about 12cm across with pinkish-orange petals and a deeper, almost reddish median line and a rose-red 'eye'. Needs filtered light; normal cactus compost; minimum temperature 10°C (50°F).

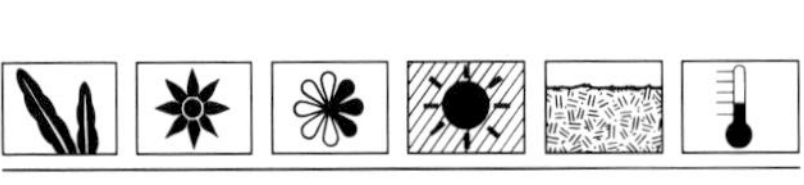

x EPICACTUS **'Don Juan'** Cactus Pete

A cultivar introduced in 1946 having been developed in the USA. Flowers are 10–12cm across, with evenly coloured burnt-orange petals with a slightly shaded reddish-pink throat. They are diurnal, appearing in late spring. Needs slight shade; normal cactus compost; minimum temperature 10°C (50°F).

x EPICACTUS **'Dr Werdemann'** Knebel

One of several hybrids produced by Curt Knebel of Germany, which has maintained its popularity since the early 1930s. The carmine-pink petals have a paler edge and very pale orange veining. The flowers, which appear by day in spring, are 16–20cm across. Requires slight shade; normal cactus compost; minimum temperature 10°C (50°F).

x EPICACTUS **'Giant Empress'**

Another improved form of *Nopalxochia phyllanthoides* reputed to have been developed by Curt Knebel, the German authority. Very similar to 'Deutsche Kaiserin' but with flowers half as big again and a slightly deeper colour; the individual flowers are often 8–10cm long. They are day flowering, in spring. Requires slight shade; normal cactus compost; minimum temperature 13°C (55°F).

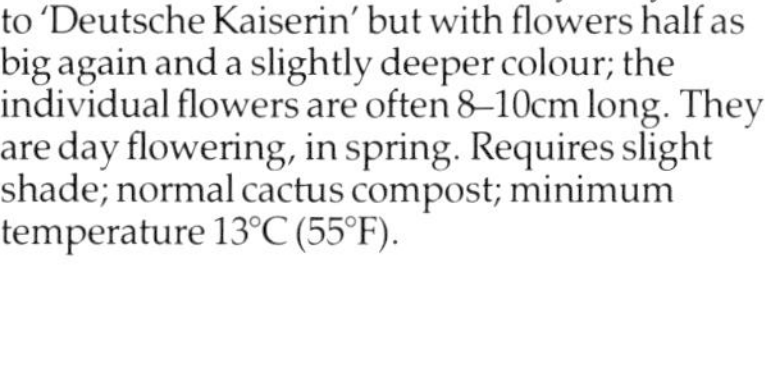

x EPICACTUS **'Helena'** Innes

A sturdy, erect plant with three-angled stems to 45cm high; the flowers appear by day in late spring. Blooms are reddish to violet and about 12cm wide, and the somewhat frilled petals are a special feature. Needs fairly bright light; normal cactus compost; minimum temperature 13°C (55°F).

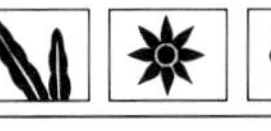

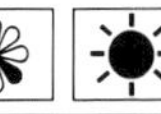
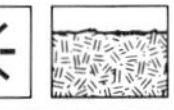
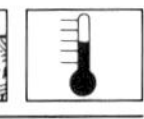

x EPICACTUS **'Holly Gate'** Innes

A cultivar produced in the UK in 1969 and perhaps better named x *Heliochia*, an intergeneric title proposed by Rowley. The parents are *Epicactus (Heliochia) ackermannii* and *Heliocereus speciosus* var. *serratus*. Day flowering in late spring, the blooms are 16–18cm across with bright purple inner petals with a reddish median line, purple and red outer petals, and reddish-orange, outspread sepals. Needs only partial shade; normal cactus compost; minimum temperature 13°C (55°F).

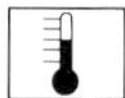
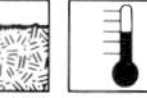

x EPICACTUS **'Hecla'** Passmore

One of the earlier cultivars produced by an English enthusiast. The day-flowering plant is tall, growing to nearly 75cm high, producing the brownish-red flowers in late spring; each bloom is about 14cm across. Needs fairly good light, but not full sun; normal cactus compost; minimum temperature 7°C (45°F).

x EPICACTUS **'Helianthus'** C. Steele

An excellent cultivar introduced in 1951 by a US nurseryman at a period when efforts were being made in America and Europe to produce a really good yellow variety. The cup-shaped flower is predominantly yellow with a whitish throat, the petals being somewhat feathery. Flowers are 9–11cm in diameter, appearing by day in spring. Requires very bright light, but not direct sun; normal cactus compost; minimum temperature 13°C (55°F).

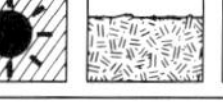

x EPICACTUS **'Impello'** Innes

A delicately shaded cultivar produced in 1964 in the UK. Fairly low growing, the stems are about 40cm long with early spring, day flowering blooms of varying shades of pale lilac to mauve and rose red. The flowers are about 14cm across. Requires filtered light; normal cactus compost; minimum temperature 10°C (50°F).

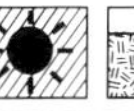
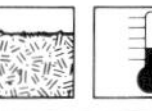

x EPICACTUS **'Jenkinsonii'** Walton

One of the earliest cultivars on record, developed by F. A. Walton in 1845 in Britain. The actual origin is uncertain, but it is believed to be with *Heliocereus* parentage cross-pollinated with the hybrid *Epiphyllum ackermannii*, this being apparent in the angled, spiny stems. Flowers appear by day in spring and early summer, and are up to 15cm in diameter, of a brilliant dark orange or purplish red with deeper shading in the throat. Requires bright light but not full sun; normal cactus compost; minimum temperature 10°C (50°F).

   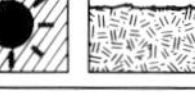 

x EPICACTUS **'King Midas'** Cactus Pete

One of the most sensational cultivars made available in 1939, and considered one of the finest yellow-flowering epicacti produced to date. Plants are tall, the angled or flattened stems up to 1m or more long with the very large terminal flower 16–20cm across when fully open. The bright yellow petals have a deep golden-yellow midstripe; the sepals are yellowish orange. The flowers are diurnal, in spring. Only slight shade is required; normal cactus compost; minimum temperature 13°C (55°F).

x EPICACTUS **'Little Sister'** Fort & O'Barr

Produced in the USA in 1950, this colourful cup-and-saucer flower is about 15cm in diameter when fully open. The 'cup' is light violet with darker veining and sepals of a slightly deeper purple. Flowering in early spring in partial shade, it is diurnal. Requires a rich cactus compost; minimum temperature 10°C (50°F).

      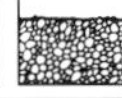   

x EPICACTUS **'Jersey Beauty'** Fort & O'Barr

A one-toned bright, glistening orange cultivar introduced in the USA in 1950, resulting from a cross-pollinating of the two cultivars 'Dr. A. D. Houghton' and 'Garden'. Flowers, 14cm or more across, appear in spring and last for three to four days. Requires filtered light; normal cactus compost; minimum temperature 13°C (55°F).

   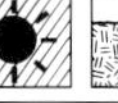 

x EPICACTUS **'Kismet'** Innes

One of the early Innes hybrids of about 1947. The flower is widely cup-shaped, about 16cm in diameter, in shades of palest purple in the throat and deepening to deeper red outer segments. It is diurnal, spring and early summer flowering. Requires slight shade; normal cactus compost; minimum temperature 10°C (50°F).

x EPICACTUS **'Marseillaise'** Knebel & C. Steele

An extraordinary richly coloured cultivar introduced in 1938 of German/American origin. The flowers appear in late spring and are diurnal, 15cm or more in diameter. The deep reddish-purple inner petals have paler, sometimes almost whitish, edges and a darker reddish centre stripe; outer petals are bright red. Requires a semi-shaded position; normal cactus compost; minimum temperature 10°C (50°F).

x EPICACTUS **'Mdme. G. M. Peach'** Barber

This is recorded as having been produced in about 1957 by the British nurseryman, the late J. T. Barber. The large lilac-pink flower measures almost 30cm in diameter, and blooms freely during the weeks of early spring to early summer. Requires a slightly shaded position; normal cactus compost; minimum temperature 10°C (50°F).

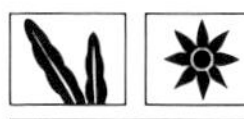 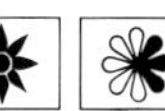   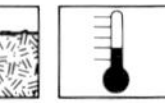 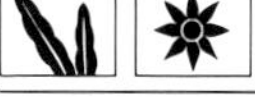  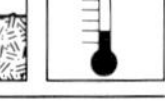

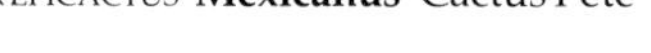

x EPICACTUS **'Mexicanus'** Cactus Pete

A very showy cultivar from the USA. The large flower, 15–17cm in diameter when fully open, blooms during spring and individual flowers last for several days. Shades of pink and rose are very evident. Requires a bright position away from direct sun; normal cactus compost; minimum temperature 10°C (50°F).

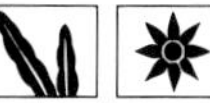  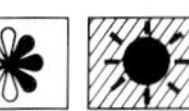 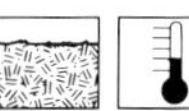       

x EPICACTUS **'Moonlight Sonata'** Fort & O'Barr

A rather choice cultivar introduced from the USA in 1950, the product of crossing the cultivars 'Eleonora Prochaska' and 'Garden'. The flowers, described as beautiful, lacquered blooms in a base of white, shading to orchid petals and dark violet sepals, appear in early to mid-spring, and are diurnal. Requires filtered light; normal cactus compost; minimum temperature 10°C (50°F).

   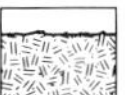    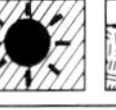 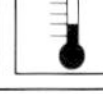

x EPICACTUS **'Oriole'**

A large-flowered cultivar of unknown origin, but probably developed by European hybridizers in about 1950. The whitish-cream inner petals and the creamy-yellow outer segments form a cup-and-saucer-shaped flower about 14cm in diameter. A day flowering plant, it is usually at its best in late spring. Requires semi-shade; normal cactus compost; minimum temperature 10°C (50°F).

    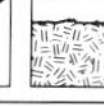 

x EPICACTUS **'Pegasus'** Coolidge

An attractive cultivar from the USA, a product of the Coolidge Rare Plant Nursery. The reddish-orange petals and sepals have brownish-violet edges, and when fully open the bloom is about 20cm across. Late spring flowering, it is diurnal. Requires only slight shade; normal cactus compost; minimum temperature 10°C (50°F).

x EPICACTUS **'Phosper'** C. Steele

A lovely, open white-flowering plant developed in the USA in 1939. The broad, pure-white inner petals surrounded by the golden-yellow sepals make a splendid daytime flower for late spring display: each bloom is at least 15cm in diameter. Needs a bright position away from full sun; normal cactus compost; minimum temperature 13°C (55°F).

x EPICACTUS **'Polar Bear'** Steele

An American hybrid from Clarion Steele. It produces a large, almost star-like flower of pure white with a pale greenish 'eye' and yellowish sepals. Flowering by day in late spring, the blooms are up to about 20cm wide and are slightly scented. Needs filtered light; normal cactus compost; minimum temperature 10°C (50°F).

x EPICACTUS **'Prince Charming'** Monmonier

A richly coloured bloom of deep blood red with bright-purple suffusions, about 20cm in diameter. Produced in the USA in 1943, its popularity still persists. Appearing by day, mid-spring to early summer is the flowering period. Requires partial shade; normal cactus compost; minimum temperature 13°C (55°F).

x EPICACTUS **'Prince Regent'** Innes

A cultivar raised in 1950 between the epicacti 'Deutsche Kaiserin' and 'Amber Queen'. It is a day flowering plant well suited for hanging baskets which blooms in profusion from mid-spring to the early days of summer. Requires bright light, but not full sun; normal cactus compost; minimum temperature 10°C (50°F).

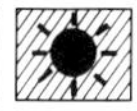
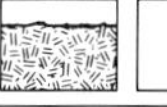

x EPICACTUS **'Purple Dwarf'** Innes

A fairly dwarf cultivar which rarely exceeds 30cm tall but produces flowers about 10cm across. It was derived from a hybrid of *Discocactus nelsonii* cross-pollinated with *Heliocereus schrankii*. Suitable for hanging baskets, the flowers continue in succession over a period of several weeks in spring. Requires humidity, especially in early spring; filtered light; normal cactus compost; minimum temperature 13°C (55°F).

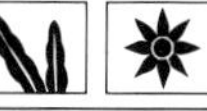

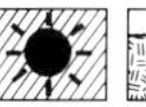

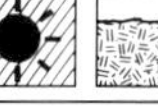
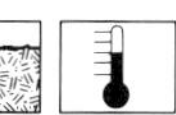
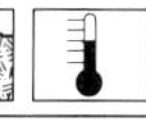
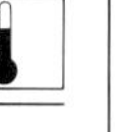

x EPICACTUS **'Regency'** Innes

A large-flowered cultivar produced in the UK in 1949 which owes its origin to crossing *Epiphyllum crenatum* and *Hylocereus undatus*. The creamy-white blooms are diurnal and last two to three days in late spring; each bloom is 14–16cm in diameter. Requires bright light but not full sun; normal cactus compost; minimum temperature 13°C (55°F).

x EPICACTUS **'Princess Grace'** Innes

Introduced in 1956 commemorating the marriage of Princess Grace in the April of that year and exhibited at the Chelsea Flower Show in May. Delicate, pale pink petals form an attractive flower about 12cm across; often a slight tinge of orange can be observed on the sepals which are pale purplish externally. Day flowering in spring, it needs partial shade; normal cactus compost; minimum temperature 10°C (50°F).

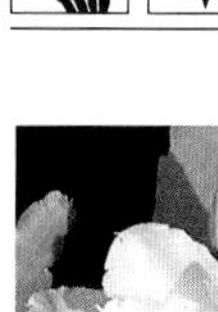

x EPICACTUS **'Queen Anne'** Ed. Stephans

Several efforts were made both in the USA and the UK between 1950–1952 to produce a fine yellow-flowering epicactus and by coincidence hybridizers from both countries decided on the same title for their result. Flowering by day in spring, this is an ideal plant for hanging-basket culture, requiring filtered light; normal cactus compost; minimum temperature 13°C (55°F).

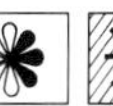
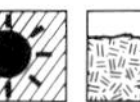
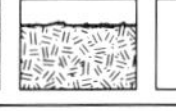
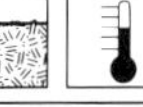

x EPICACTUS **'Reward'** Fort & O'Barr

Recorded as a cross between epicacti 'Thorinne' and 'Madonna', this is a splendid yellow-flowering cultivar acclaimed 'the best' when distributed in 1952. These two American enthusiasts provided many beautiful cultivars, and this is certainly outstanding. Flowering by day in spring, the blooms are a soft yellow with widely opening petals, each with a deeper yellow centre line, and 15–18cm overall in diameter. Requires bright filtered light; normal cactus compost; minimum temperature 13°C (55°F).

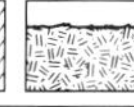

x EPICACTUS **'Scarlet Emblem'** Innes

A miniature plant developed in the UK about 1950, it remains up to 45cm tall with flat or three-angled stems. The flowers are rich scarlet with three to four rows of petals and are about 8cm in diameter when fully open. Flowering in early summer, they are diurnal. Requires only partial shade; normal cactus compost; minimum temperature 10°C (50°F).

x EPICACTUS **'Sky Rocket'** Steele

A cultivar created in the USA in 1937. The large, pinkish-orange flowers are over 15cm across when fully expanded, a striking feature being the prominent dark-red style. The flowers are diurnal, in spring. Needs protection from full sun; normal cactus compost; minimum temperature 10°C (50°F).

 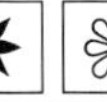 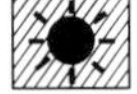 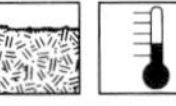

x EPICACTUS **'Soft Lights'** Wressey Cocke

Produced in the USA in 1977 and developed in conjunction with Hawke Nursery, this is a fine yellow hybrid with pale inner petals and deeper yellow outer segments. The flowers are funnel-shaped up to 20–23cm in diameter when fully expanded; day flowering, they appear in late spring to early summer. Needs filtered light; normal cactus compost; minimum temperature 10°C (50°F).

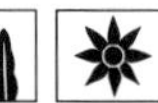  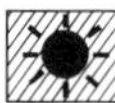 

x EPICACTUS **'Shasta'** Steele

An American cultivar of consequence, the parentage being epicacti 'Peacockii' and 'Garden'. The unusual narrow and slightly twisted arrangement of the white petals produces a unique flower of up to about 15cm across when fully open, flowering by day in mid- to late spring. Needs good light, but not full sun; normal cactus compost; minimum temperature 10°C (50°F).

   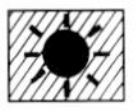 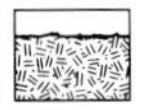 

x EPICACTUS **'Soraya'** Innes

Developed in the UK in 1965 this is a somewhat dwarf spring-flowering plant with brilliant deep-scarlet, cup-shaped blooms. The broad, almost oval-shaped petals are similar throughout, creating a flower about 11cm across when expanded, which last three to four days. Requires slight shade; normal cactus compost; minimum temperature 13°C (55°F).

x EPICACTUS **'Space Rocket'** Monmonier

Produced by the Ventura Epiphyllum Gardens in the USA, this has proved one of the most exciting cultivars yet developed. It flowers by day in spring, producing a large, open blossom of pinkish red, with overlapping petals frilled and shading to a paler pink. Flowers are up to 18cm in diameter. Requires slight shade; normal cactus compost; minimum temperature 13°C (55°F).

x EPICACTUS **'Sweet Alibi'** Monmonier

A beautiful, somewhat funnel-shaped bloom, 13–15cm in diameter at the perimeter. It is a product of Theresa M. Monmonier of Ventura Gardens, USA, and is an extremely fascinating cultivar, day flowering in spring, with slender rose-cerise petals shading to a deeper colour on the outer edges. Requires indirect light; normal cactus compost; minimum temperature 10°C (50°F).

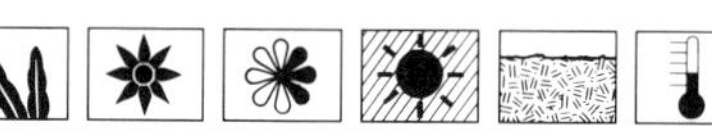

x EPICACTUS **'Tyke'** Passmore

Developed in the UK about 1935 and subsequently propagated for distribution by Holly Gate Nurseries. An extraordinarily 'untidy' flower, about 12cm in diameter, the reddish or orange-red petals are widely spreading in a twisting fashion. The flowers, which appear in spring, last for nearly one week. Needs slight shade; normal cactus compost; minimum temperature 13°C (55°F).

x EPICACTUS **'Ventura Jubilee'** Monmonier

This lovely intense rhodamine-purple flower opens almost flat, the sepals being of an even more intense cardinal red, and are 18cm or even more in diameter. Produced in the USA, it continues to be a popular favourite. It is diurnal, and requires slight shade and certainly protection from full sun during the spring flowering season; normal cactus compost; minimum temperature 13°C (55°F).

×EPICACTUS **'Wrayii'** Walton

An early-day cultivar produced in 1845 by the botanist F. A. Walton and given a latinized title. The flowers are very large, often up to 20cm in diameter, and highly scented, the whitish-yellow petals contrasting with the brown and yellow of the sepals. It is day flowering from early spring to early summer. Requires partial shade; normal cactus compost; minimum temperature 13°C (55°F).

×EPICACTUS **'Zoe'** Innes

A low-growing, semi-prostrate cultivar produced in 1958. It flowers over a period of several weeks from very early spring to early summer, each bloom lasting for three or four days. The peach-orange cup-and-saucer flower is set in three rows of petals, and when fully expanded is about 12cm across. Requires good light, but not full sun; normal cactus compost; minimum temperature 13°C (55°F).

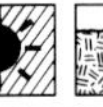

EPIPHYLLUM **ANGULIGER** (Lem.) G. Don
Syn: *Phyllocactus anguliger* Lem.

A bushy, much-branched epiphyte with flat, deeply notched, green and fleshy stems to about 60cm long, 6cm in diameter. The spineless areoles are set between and at the base of the tooth-like notches. Flowers are diurnal in late spring and early summer, fragrant, and about 15cm long on a slender tube. The inner segments are white or yellowish, the outer segments narrow and yellowish. Requires semi-shade; enriched open compost; minimum temperature 13°C (55°F). *Southern Mexico.*

EPIPHYLLUM **CARTAGENSE** (Weber) Br. & R.
Syn: *Phyllocactus cartagensis* Weber

A tall-growing, much-branched epiphyte. The stems, more or less flat, are up to and over 2m high, the branches also becoming elongated, 4–6cm broad with serrated margins. The areoles are spineless. Appearing in late spring, the nocturnal flowers, about 20cm long on a slender tube, have white inner segments and yellowish outer segments. The style and stamens are white, with pale yellow stigma lobes. Requires semi-shade; normal cactus compost; minimum temperature 15°C (59°F). *Costa Rica (Cartago).*

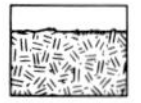
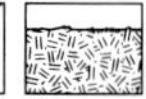

EPIPHYLLUM **CHRYSOCARDIUM** Alex.
Syn: *Marniera chrysocardium* (Alex.) Backeb.

A spectacular epiphyte with broad, flat, serrated stems and branches to about 30cm broad. The serrations form deep-set lobes, 3–4cm wide, indented to the midrib. The areoles are either spineless or have two to three bristles. Flowers are 32cm long with wide-spreading petals, the inner petals pure white, the outer ones pinkish externally; the style is white, and there are golden-yellow stamens. They are nocturnal, in spring to early summer. Requires semi-shade; enriched open compost; minimum temperature 15°C (59°F). *Mexico (Chiapas).*

EPIPHYLLUM **CRENATUM** (Lem.) Br. & R.
Syn: *Phyllocactus crenatus* Lem.

An erect, semi-epiphytic species to about 1m tall. It has a cylindrical main stem and thick, leaf-like branches of greyish green up to 60cm long, 6–8cm broad, the margins undulating and notched and spineless. The flowers are diurnal in summer, about 20cm long and across when fully open. The inner petals are creamy white, the outer segments greenish or pinkish yellow. Requires only slight shade; normal cactus compost; minimum temperature 13°C (55°F). *Guatemala, Honduras.*

EPIPHYLLUM **CRENATUM var. KIMNACHII** Bravo
Syn: *Phyllocactus cooperi* Regel; × *Seleniphyllum cooperi*

For years this was presumed to be a hybrid of *Epiphyllum* × *Selenicereus*, a fact which remains undecided. The stems are leaf-like, 4–6cm wide, with crenate edges and semi-circular lobes. The flowers bear a remarkable resemblance to both *Selenicereus grandiflorus* and *E. crenatum*. Requirements are the same as for the species. *Southern Mexico?*

    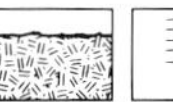

EPIPHYLLUM **CRENATUM var. KINCHINJUNGA** Backeb.

An unusual variety of *E. crenatum*, recorded as being native to mountainous forest areas supposedly named Kinchinjunga. The stem and branch formation is very similar to the species, generally greenish grey in colour with pronounced crenate margins, and the small, whitish woolly areoles are spineless. The pale, creamy-yellow flowers are diurnal in early summer, and about 12cm long, 8cm across when fully open. Requires only slight shade; normal cactus compost; minimum temperature 13°C (55°F). *Guatemala.*

EPIPHYLLUM **CRENATUM var. CHICHICASTENANGO** Backeb.

A variety with stems and branches to about 60cm long with a prominent midrib and large, rounded, lobe-like crenations. The small areoles are spineless. Flowers are diurnal, appearing in early summer, and are about 10cm long borne on a long green tube. The creamy-white petals are slightly incurving, and the outer petals are golden yellow and spreading. Requires partial shade; normal cactus compost; minimum temperature 13°C (55°F). *Guatemala.*

    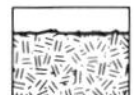 

EPIPHYLLUM **DARRAHII** (K. Sch.) Br. & R.
Syn: *Phyllocactus darrahii* K. Sch.

A bushy, branching epiphyte. The fresh green branches are 20–40cm long, 3–5cm broad, and quite fleshy, the margins deeply toothed with rounded notches forming lobes. Flowers are diurnal in early summer. Pure white with yellowish outer petals and 6–7cm across, they are fragrant and borne on a greenish-pink tube about 11cm in length. Requires semi-shade; a porous, fairly acid compost; minimum temperature 13°C (55°F). *Mexico (Chiapas).*

EPIPHYLLUM **PHYLLANTHUS** (L.) Haw.
Syn: *Cactus phyllanthus* L.; *Phyllocactus phyllanthus* Link

Cylindrical main stems and flat, thin, leaf-like green branches with purple-shaded margins. These are up to 7cm broad and are broadly serrated. Flowers, nocturnal in mid-summer, are 25–30cm long with a slender, long, greenish-pink tube. The glistening white petals are all narrow, 2–2.5cm wide, and the style varies in colour, being red, orange, pink, or rarely white. Needs shade, which is essential; an acid compost; minimum temperature 15°C (59°F). *Panama to Peru, Brazil.*

    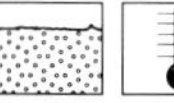 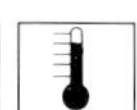

EPIPHYLLUM **RUESTII** Weingt.
Syn: *Phyllocactus ruestii* Weingt.

A semi-epiphytic species to 1m tall. The stems are often three-angled, the branches flat and up to 50cm long, 10cm broad, lance-shaped and with slightly notched margins. The areoles are very small and generally spineless. Flowers, nocturnal in early summer, are 26–30cm long, greenish or pinkish white. Inner segments are about 1.5cm wide, outer segments narrower and partially spreading. Requires filtered light; normal cactus compost; minimum temperature 15°C (59°F). *Honduras.*

   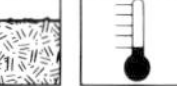

EPIPHYLLUM **OXYPETALUM** (DC.) Haw
Syn: *Cereus oxypetalus* DC.; *Phyllocactus latifrons* Link; *Epiphyllum latifrons* (Link) Zucc.

A much-branching epiphyte up to 3m long. The stems are cylindrical, the branches, 10–12cm broad, are flat and leaf-like. The flowers are nocturnal, appearing in mid-summer, and are 25–30cm long and 12cm across with a long curved, arching tube. The petals are white. Requires a humid, shaded position; enriched porous compost; minimum temperature 13°C (55°F). *Mexico, Guatemala, Venezuela, Brazil.*

  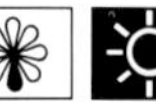 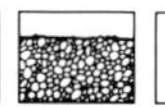 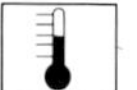

EPIPHYLLUM **PUMILUM** (Vaup.) Br. & R.
Syn: *Phyllocactus pumilus* Vaup.

A semi-erect or pendant epiphyte with long, flat, leaf-like stems and branches. The main stem is usually terete at the base, otherwise this and the branches are 3–8cm broad, often tapering to an almost pointed tip, and the margins have shallow crenations. Flowers are small and fragrant, creamy white, and borne on a greenish tube 6cm long. They are nocturnal, appearing in mid-summer. Filtered light is essential; a porous acid compost; minimum temperature 18°C (64°F). *Guatemala.*

EPIPHYLLUM **STENOPETALUM** (Förster) Br. & R.
Syn: *Phyllocactus stenopetalus* Förster

A forest epiphyte up to 2m high. It has terete stems and flat, dark green branches, shallowly notched along the margins, 6–8cm broad and spineless. The flowers are nocturnal in summer; they are 25–28cm long on a long, red-scaled tube. Petals are narrow and spreading, the inner ones white and the outer ones greenish white and only 4mm broad. There is a prominent red style with deep yellow stigma lobes. Semi-shade is essential, and a porous acid compost; minimum temperature 15°C (59°F). *Mexico (Oaxaca).*

EPIPHYLLUM **STRICTUM** (Lem.) Br. & R.
Syn: *Phyllocactus strictus* Lem.

Some authorities place this as a variety of *E. phyllanthus*. It is a forest epiphyte to 2m high with a cylindrical main stem and narrow, flat, bluish-green branches up to 8cm broad. These are spineless and the margins are coarsely serrated. The flowers, nocturnal in mid-summer, are up to 25cm long and borne on a slender green tube 15cm long. Of the very narrow petals, the inner ones are white, the outer pale greenish externally, and there is a pinkish style. Requires semi-shade; normal cactus compost; minimum temperature 15°C (59°F). *Honduras, Guatemala.*

    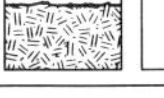 

EPITHELANTHA **MICROMERIS var. BOKEI** (L. Benson) Glass & Foster

Originally described as a distinct species. The plants are 2.5–5cm thick and covered with minute tubercles. The areoles bear numerous densely set spines which obscure the stem. Flowers are very pale pink and about 1cm across. Requirements are the same as for the species. *Mexico (Chihuahua), USA (Texas).*

    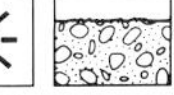 

EPITHELANTHA **MICROMERIS var. GREGGII** (Engelm.) Borg

Previously considered a species in its own right, this is a larger-growing variety up to about 8cm high, frequently offsetting. The tubercles are longer, the radial spines are up to 7mm long and there are frequently one or more longer centrals. The flowers, too, are a deeper pink. Requirements are the same as for the species. *Mexico (Coahuila).*

 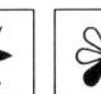  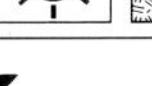 

EPITHELANTHA **MICROMERIS** (Engelm.) Weber
Syn: *Mammillaria micromeris* Engelm.

Unusual globular plants, solitary or grouped, up to about 6cm. They are thick set with spiralling rows of small tubercles set close together. Small areoles bear tufts of about 20 white spreading spines up to 2mm long. Flowers appear in summer; these are diurnal, arising from the centre of the white woolly crown, and are about 1cm across, white or pale pink. Requires sun and warmth; a calcareous compost; minimum temperature 10°C (50°F). *Mexico (Coahuila, Nuevo Leon), USA (Texas).*

   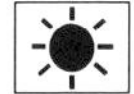 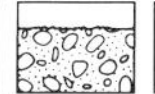 

EPITHELANTHA **MICROMERIS var. PACHYRHIZA** (Backeb.) Bravo
Syn: *Epithelantha pachyrhiza* (Marsh.) Backeb.

The stems are somewhat cylindrical, up to about 4cm thick, and usually clustering. They are covered with minute tubercles from which arise numerous minute white spines. Flowers are whitish pink. Requirements are the same as for the species. *Mexico (Coahuila).*

    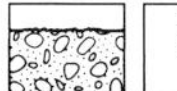 

EPITHELANTHA **MICROMERIS var. UNGUISPINA** (Böed.) Backeb.

Very similar in size to the species, but the green body is more exposed. The white hairy areoles bear numerous white radial spines, the lower ones considerably longer than those of the species, up to 1cm in length. The rose to pale pink flowers spring from the tubercles in the crown of the plant, not from the areoles. Requirements are similar to those for the species. *Mexico (Nuevo Leon).*

   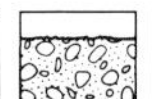 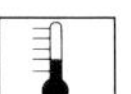

ERIOCEREUS **BONPLANDII** (Parment.) Ricco.
Syn: *Harrisia bonplandii* (Parment.) Br. & R.

A climbing species with stems 2–3m in length, 3–8cm thick. The colour is bluish-green. There are four to six ribs with broad furrows between and the areoles are greyish arranged 1.5–3cm apart with three to eight greyish-white spines. Flowering at night in summer, the flowers are about 25cm long, with white inner petals. Requires good light but not necessarily full sun; normal cactus compost; minimum temperature 13°C (55°F). *Brazil, Argentina, Paraguay.*

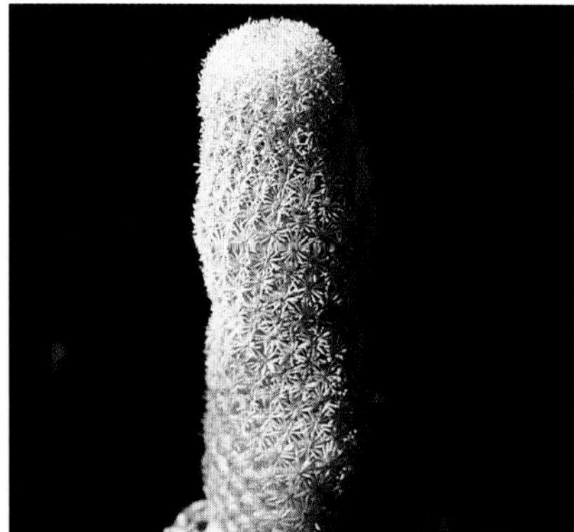

EPITHELANTHA **MICROMERIS var. POLYCEPHALA** (Backeb.) Glass & Foster
Syn: *Epithelantha polycephala* Backeb.

A small clustering plant with stems 7cm or more long, to 2cm thick, covered with minute green tubercles, spirally arranged. Areoles with very short white hairs and numerous whitish spines. Day flowering in summer, flowers are pinkish, about 1cm long, 5mm wide, and funnel-shaped. Needs full sun; enriched mineral compost; minimum temperature 10°C (50°F). *Mexico (Coahuila).*

   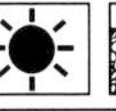 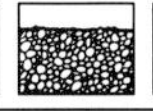 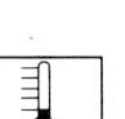

ERIOCEREUS **JUSBERTII** (Rebut) Ricco.
Syn: *Harrisia jusbertii* (Rebut) Br. & R.

Plants are usually solitary. The dark green stems are 4–6cm thick with five to six broad ribs along which yellowish-grey areoles are set at 2cm intervals. Spines are brownish to black, consisting of about seven radials 5mm long and one to four slightly longer centrals. The flowers are nocturnal, appearing in mid-summer. They are up to about 15cm long, and 18–20cm in diameter, with pure white inner petals and brownish-green outer segments. Requires filtered light; normal cactus compost; minimum temperature 10°C (50°F). *Argentina or Paraguay.*

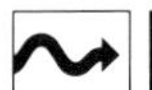   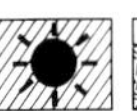  

ERIOCEREUS **POMANENSIS** (Weber) Berger
Syn: *Harrisia pomanensis* (Weber) Br. & R.

The greyish-green stems are more or less erect, with three to six rather angled ribs. Areoles are brown, and about 2cm apart with greyish-white, black-tipped spines, of which up to seven are radials about 1cm in length and one or two are centrals to 2cm long. The plant is nocturnal flowering in early summer; flowers are white and about 16cm long and across, with pinkish-green outer segments. Needs partial shade; normal cactus compost; minimum temperature 13°C (55°F). *Argentina.*

   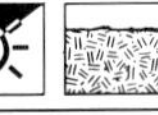 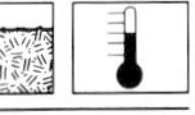

ERIOSYCE **AUSSELIANA** Ritter

A grey-green, more or less globular plant up to 40cm in diameter. It has about 37 ribs, divided into prominent tubercles. The areoles bear 12–14 radial spines about 2cm long and there are six to twelve centrals, slightly longer. All are greyish brown, and the newer spines brownish yellow. Flowers are unknown; possibly they are pinkish purple, about 3cm long, diurnal and blooming in summer. Needs bright light; normal cactus compost; minimum temperature 10°C (50°F). *Chile (La Serena).*

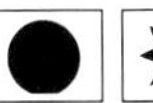     

ERIOSYCE **IHOTZKYANA** Ritter

A globular plant which in its habitat can reach 40cm in diameter, but is considerably smaller in cultivation. It has up to 37 ribs with areoles bearing thick, sturdy dark-greyish to yellowish spines, of which eight to twelve are radials 2–4cm long, and generally two to three centrals. It is day flowering in summer. The flowers are purple with pale yellow or whitish margins, 3–4cm long, and are borne only on mature plants. Needs sun; normal cactus compost; minimum temperature 10°C (50°F). *Chile (Coquimbo).*

    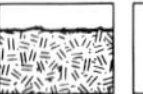 

ERYTHRORHIPSALIS **PILOCARPA** (Loefgr.) Berger

An epiphyte with long, greyish-green, cylindrical stems, branching in whorls and becoming pendant. The branchlets are 3–12cm long, 3–6mm thick, with eight to ten indistinct ribs. The white, woolly areoles bear three to ten minute bristly spines. Flowers are fragrant and diurnal, coming out in winter or early spring. They are yellowish white and about 2.5cm wide. The plant is an ideal choice for hanging baskets. Needs partial shade; normal cactus compost; minimum temperature 10°C (50°F). *Brazil (Rio de Janeiro, Sao Paulo).*

   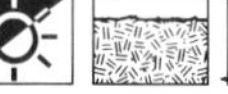

ESCOBARIA **AGUIRREANA** (Glass & Foster) N. P. Taylor
Syn: *Gymnocactus aguirreanus* Glass & Foster; *Thelocactus aguirreanus* (Glass & Foster) Bravo

This medium-green species is globular to 5cm high, 7cm in diameter. The tubercles are 1cm long, 1.5cm wide, and the spines, greyish pink with dark tips, are composed of 13–16 radials. Summer flowering and diurnal, the flowers are yellow with a cerise midstripe, and the outer segments have a broad reddish-purple centre line. Requires sun; normal cactus compost; minimum temperature 10°C (50°F). *Mexico.*

   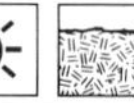 

ESCOBARIA **ASPERISPINA** (Böed.) D. R. Hunt
Syn: *Coryphantha asperispina* Böed.; *Neobesseya asperispina* Böed.

The stems are a dull bluish green and are globular, about 6cm thick. There are conical tubercles about 1.8cm long, and bare axils. The areoles bear nine to ten stiff radial spines to 1cm long. Flowering in summer, and diurnal, the flowers are whitish yellow with a pale brownish or olive-green centre stripe to the petals, which are 3cm long, 2.5cm across. Requires bright light; normal cactus compost; minimum temperature 10°C (50°F). *Mexico (Coahuila).*

    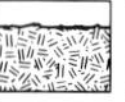 

ESCOBARIA **CHAFFEYI** Br. & R.
Syn: *Escobaria dasyacantha* var. *chaffeyi* (Br. & R.) N. P. Taylor

An oval-shaped plant, solitary or clustering, the dark green stems are up to 12cm high, 5–6cm wide. Tubercles bear 18 or more white bristle-like radial spines, and one or more shorter white, brown-tipped centrals. It flowers in summer, and is diurnal. The blooms are yellowish white with a broad reddish-brown centre area to the petals, which are about 1.5cm long, 1cm wide. Requires full sun; normal cactus compost; minimum temperature 10°C (50°F). *Mexico (Zacatecas, Cedros).*

   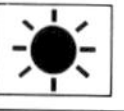 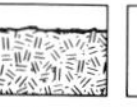 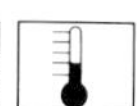

ESCOBARIA **CUBENSIS** (Br. & R.) D. R. Hunt
Syn: *Neolloydia cubensis* (Br. & R.) Backeb.; *Coryphantha cubensis* Br. & R.

The plants are globose, 2–3cm in diameter and pale green in colour, offsetting to form small clumps. The conical tubercles are 6–7mm long, 4–5mm wide at the base, and grooved on the upper side. White areoles bear about 10 whitish radial spines 3–4mm long. Flowering during summer, and diurnal, the flowers are pale yellowish green, about 1.6cm long. Requires sun; normal cactus compost; minimum temperature 13°C (55°F). *Cuba.*

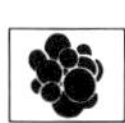     

ESCOBARIA **HENRICKSONII** Glass & Foster
Syn: *Coryphantha henricksonii* (Glass & Foster) Glass & Foster

A pale green, tuberous-rooted plant with a few cylindrical stems up to 8cm high, 3cm in diameter. The tubercles are about 6mm long, 5mm wide, and the axils are bare. There are about 32 whitish radial spines, 4–5mm long, and ten centrals, 3–4mm long, with one only 1.5mm. Flowers are diurnal, appearing in summer; they are cerise, and about 2.5cm in diameter. Requires sun; normal cactus compost; minimum temperature 10°C (50°F). *Mexico (Chihuahua).*

    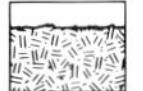 

▲

ESCOBARIA **HESTERI** (Y. Wright) Buxb.
Syn: *Coryphantha hesteri* Y. Wright

A small, globular, clustering species, it often forms clumps up to 30cm in diameter in the wild. The stems, 2.5–4cm high, are dull green, with conical tubercles to 1.2cm long. There are 14–16 pale brownish-yellow radial spines about 1.5cm long, but with no centrals. Flowering in summer, it is diurnal. The flowers are bright purple, about 2.5cm long and in diameter. Requires bright light; normal cactus compost; minimum temperature 10°C (50°F). *USA (Texas).*

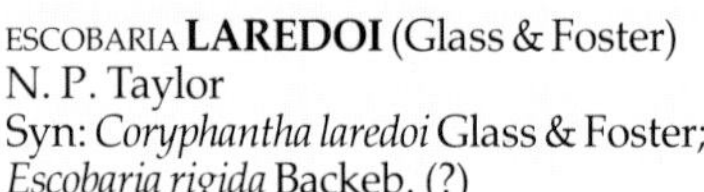

ESCOBARIA **LAREDOI** (Glass & Foster) N. P. Taylor
Syn: *Coryphantha laredoi* Glass & Foster; *Escobaria rigida* Backeb. (?)

The stems are globose, forming clusters, and pale green in colour. Individual stems are 4–4.5cm thick. The tubercles are 1–1.2cm long and 4mm thick with a woolly groove at the base. There are about 33 white, stiff, radial spines 5–12mm long and four to five central spines 1.1–1.4cm in length, similarly coloured but with a yellowish base. Flowering by day in summer, the blooms are 1.5–1.7cm long, to 1cm wide, with pinkish-tan outer segments and magenta inner petals. Requires sun; a calcareous cactus compost; minimum temperature 10°C (50°F). *Mexico (Coahuila).*

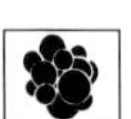 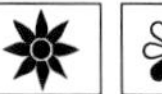  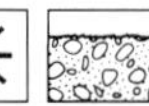 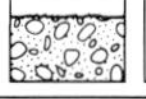 

ESCOBARIA **MINIMA** (Baird) D. R. Hunt
Syn: *Coryphantha minima* Baird; *Coryphantha nellieae* Croiz.

The dark-green stems are more or less oval, about 2.5cm tall, 2cm wide, solitary or clustering. The tubercles are conical, 2mm long, and the grooves bare. There are 13–15 radial spines about 3mm long and three centrals about 6mm in length: these spines are pinkish, becoming grey. The plant is diurnal, flowering in summer, with blooms about 2cm long, to 1cm in diameter, and rose pink in colour. Requires slight shade; normal cactus compost; minimum temperature 10°C (50°F). *USA (Texas).*

     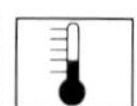

ESCOBARIA **ROBBINSORUM** (W. M. Earle) D. R. Hunt
Syn: *Coryphantha robbinsorum* (W. M. Earle) Zimm.; *Cochiseia robbinsorum* W. M. Earle

A dark-green cylindrical-shaped plant 2–6cm long, with tubercles 5–8mm long, and 4–6mm wide. Spines are white; 11–17 of these are radials, up to 1.8cm long, with rarely one central up to 1.4cm. The flowers, yellowish green with a brown centre stripe, are around 2cm long, 1.5cm wide, and are day flowering in the late spring and early summer. Careful watering is essential. Requires sun; normal cactus compost; minimum temperature 10°C (50°F). *USA (Arizona).*

    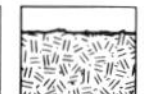 

ESCOBARIA **ROSEANA** (Böed) Backeb.

An oval-shaped plant of bright green and up to 4cm high, 3cm wide, with tubercles 8mm long and broad. The areoles are yellow, bearing 15 pale yellow radial spines to 1.5cm long, and four to six centrals, similarly coloured. Flowering is in early summer, and is diurnal. The flowers are small; the inner petals are yellowish with a reddish midstripe, the outer segments are more reddish. Requires sun; normal cactus compost; minimum temperature 10°C (50°F). *Mexico (Coahuila).*

ESCOBARIA **RUNYONII** Br. & R.
Syn: *Coryphantha robertii* Berger

A free-clustering species comprising many greyish-green, more or less globose stems 3–5cm long, with terete tubercles 5mm in length and slightly grooved above. Radial spines are numerous and 4–5mm long, and there are five to seven dark brownish-tipped centrals 6–8mm in length. Day flowering in mid-summer, the blooms are very pale purple with a darker midstripe on all the petals. Requires bright light; normal cactus compost; minimum temperature 10°C (50°F). *USA (New Mexico, Texas).*

     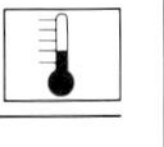

ESCOBARIA **SNEEDII var. SNEEDII** Br. & R.
Syn: *Coryphantha sneedii* Berger

A clustering species with small, rather cylindrical stems 6cm high, 1–2cm thick. These are covered with numerous white spines about 6mm long which are at first reddish, then change colour. Day flowering, in summer, the flowers are small, and pale pinkish. Needs good light; normal cactus compost; minimum temperature 10°C (50°F). *USA (Texas).*

   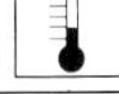

ESCOBARIA **ROSEANA var. NOVA**

This is a grouping plant, collected by A. Lau near Saltillo in Coahuila, Mexico. It is a densely clustering variety with offsets arising from around the base, and has about 12 tubercled ribs, spirally arranged and bearing many yellowish-brown spines. The flowers are unknown. Requirements are the same as for the species. *Mexico (Coahuila).*

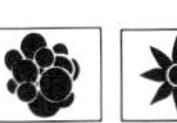   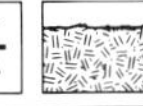 

ESCOBARIA **SNEEDII** Br. & R. **var. LEEI** (Rose ex Böed.) D. R. Hunt
Syn: *Escobaria leei* Rose ex Böed.; *Coryphantha sneedii* var. *leei* (Rose) L. Benson

Miniature to medium-sized plants, which cluster freely, with closely set tubercles. Areoles bear many greyish-white 2–3mm long spines. The flowers are a dull brownish pink with a deeper pinkish median line to the petals. Flowering in early summer, they are diurnal. Requires sun; normal cactus compost with limestone chippings added; minimum temperature 10°C (50°F). *USA (New Mexico).*

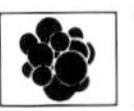  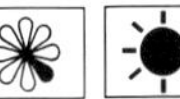 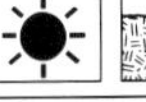 

ESCONTRIA **CHIOTILLA** (Weber) Br. & R.

A tree-like columnar species reaching 6–7m high in its habitat, with the trunk often up to 40cm in diameter. The branches are dark green with seven to eight prominently crenate ribs and greyish woolly areoles about 1cm long. Spines are yellowish brown, consisting of 10–15 radials to 1cm long and one, rarely more, central spine 5–7cm in length. It is day flowering, in mid-summer; the flowers are yellow, with brownish outer segments, 3–4cm long, and funnel-shaped. Requires sun; normal cactus compost; minimum temperature 13°C (55°F). *Guatemala, Mexico (Puebla).*

   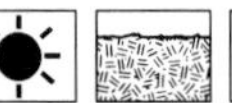 

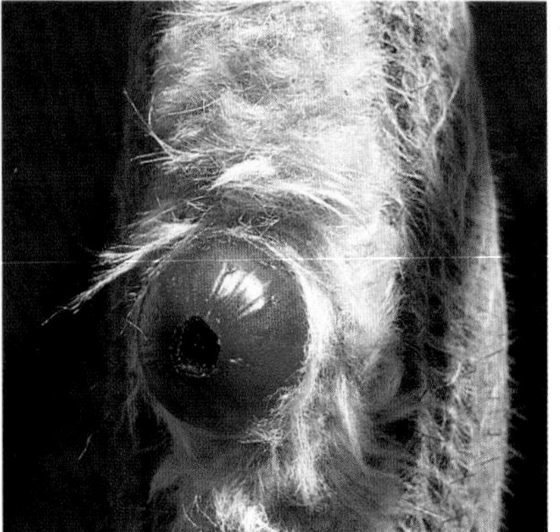

ESPOSTOA **LANATA** (HBK.) Br. & R.

A tree-like columnar plant to about 4m high and 15cm thick in its own habitat, in cultivation 1–1.5m tall, 6–7cm thick. It has 20–30 ribs with white areoles set about 5mm apart. The spines are white or pale yellowish, often red and very short. The central spines are up to 8cm long, and an abundance of long, whitish hairs entirely cover the green stem. Flowers are nocturnal, produced in summer from a lateral cephalium; they are white, 5–6cm long. The large, red, berry-like fruits are 4–6cm in diameter. Needs full sun; normal cactus compost; minimum temperature 10°C (50°F). *Northern Peru.*

    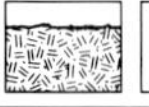

ESPOSTOA **MELANOSTELE** Vaup.

A tall, greyish-green columnar plant to about 2m high, 10cm in diameter. It has about 25 ribs with fairly close-set areoles, bearing numerous golden-yellow spines about 5mm long. Flowers appear through the pseudocephalium which is very woolly and has longer yellow spines to 4cm in length. The blooms, which are nocturnal, occurring in summer, are white, 5.4cm long. Requires bright light; slightly calcareous cactus compost; minimum temperature 10°C (50°F). *Peru (Chosica).*

    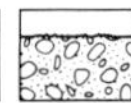 

ESPOSTOA **NANA** Ritter

Probably a variety of *E. melanostele*. This is a short columnar species to 1.5m high, with 8–9cm thick stems, branching from the base. With many closely set ribs, the whitish areoles have about 30 very pale yellowish radial spines about 7mm long and one slightly longer central and the whole plant is densely coated with white woolly hairs, especially at the tips of the stems. The flowers are nocturnal, appearing in summer from a whitish cephalium; they are whitish, about 4–5cm long. Needs careful watering at all times; bright light; calcareous cactus compost; minimum temperature 13°C (55°F). *Peru (Ancash).*

   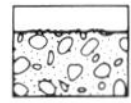 

ESPOSTOA **RITTERI** Buin.

Dark-green columnar plants attaining 2–4m high and 6–7cm thick, having 18–24 ribs and white roundish areoles. The spines are about 25 in number, very fine, reddish brown or yellowish white and from 8mm to 2cm in length. Nocturnal flowers appear in summer from a whitish-yellow cephalium. These are 6–8cm long, 6cm wide. Requires sunlight; normal cactus compost; minimum temperature 13°C (55°F). *Peru (Amazonas).*

EULYCHNIA **IQUIQUENSIS** (K. Sch.) Br. & R.

A tall columnar, almost tree-like plant up to 7m high in its habitat, the stem up to 25cm in diameter. Grey-green in colour, it has 12–15 rounded, warty ribs, narrowly furrowed between. The white woolly areoles are closely set, bearing 12–15 greyish spines about 1cm long, and one or two to 12cm in length. Flowers are white, 6–7cm long, arising from the top of the stem in summer, and are diurnal. Needs sun; normal cactus compost; minimum temperature 10°C (50°F). *Chile (Atacama).*

    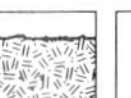 

EULYCHNIA **SAINT-PIEANA** Ritter

A columnar, tree-like plant 2–4m high in its habitat. The stems are 7–10cm thick, dark green, with 10–15 ribs. Areoles are very obvious with greyish felt and long white woolly hairs. There are eight to twelve radial spines and one central. These are dark brown, becoming grey, and varying in length from 2.5 to 10cm. Day flowering in mid-summer, the flowers are 6–7.5cm long, white sometimes with a pinkish midstripe to the petals, and opening to about 6cm in diameter. Needs sun; normal cactus compost; minimum temperature 10°C (50°F). *Chile (Atacama).*

  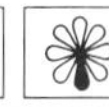   

FACHEIROA Br. & R. Sp. nova

A further introduction of Dr Werner Rauh's. A much-branching, columnar plant with about 15 ribs. The areoles bear many yellowish-brown spines, both radials and centrals. The cephalium consists of much white wool which forms laterally from near the top of the stems. Flowers are not known. *Brazil.*

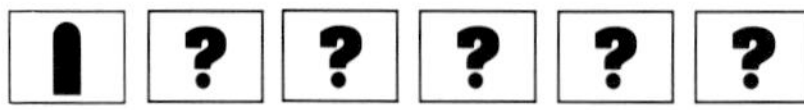

FACHEIROA Br. & R. Sp. nova

A tall-growing, columnar plant discovered by Dr Werner Rauh. It produces few branches, which are about 7cm in diameter. The ribs number about 18 and the areoles are set well apart, with particularly attractive brown spination. The brownish-white cephalium composed of wool and bristles extends downwards from the top with small pinkish-white flowers protruding from red-scaled tubes. Temperatures are best maintained at a minimum 15°C (59°F). *Brazil (Bahia).*

FACHEIROA **DEINACANTHUS** Rauh

A comparatively recent discovery, the tree-like growth very much resembling another species, *F. ulei* (Gürke) Werd. There are about 15 greyish-green ribs with yellowish-brown spines and almost tubular flowers with short inner perianth segments. As yet, the plant is not known in cultivation. *Brazil.*

FACHEIROA **ESTEVESII** Braun

A discovery of E. Esteves Pereira (pictured) for whom it was named. A much-branching plant to 2m or more in height with 20 or more ribs and golden-yellow spines which later become greyish yellow, and a long lateral cephalium. The flowers are pinkish, often appearing from the stems with or without a cephalium. Not yet known in cultivation. *Brazil (Bahia).*

FACHEIROA **TENEBROSA** Braun & Esteves

Erect columnar plants with many branches, sometimes up to 200 on one plant! There are up to 20 or more ribs and both radial and central spines, which are brownish black. Flowers are borne on the cephalium, the red tube more or less naked; flower colour is unknown, but is probably white. A rare species, not as yet known in cultivation. *Brazil (South-western Bahia).*

× FEROBERGIA **'Gil Tegelberg'** Glass

A rather fascinating hybrid between a species of *Ferocactus* and *Leuchtenbergia principis* produced by Gil Tegelberg, a prominent and well-known American cactus authority, and subsequently named for him. The plants are about 12cm in diameter, the stem bearing elongated tubercles, with long, spreading spines and terminal silky yellow flowers which are diurnal, appearing in summer. Flourishes in sunny locations; normal cactus compost; minimum temperature 10°C (50°F).

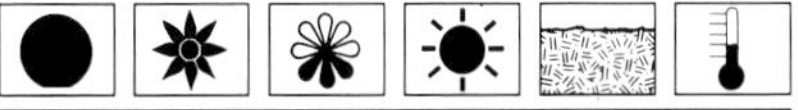

× FEROBERGIA **'Gil Tegelberg'** Glass

Another product of the same two genera: in the former illustration the *Ferocactus* parentage is dominant. With this unflowered plant, that of *Leuchtenbergia* is obvious.

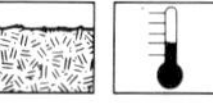

FEROCACTUS **ACANTHODES** (Lem.) Br. & R.
Syn: *Echinocactus acanthodes* Lem.

Plants are solitary, rarely offsetting. The oval stem becomes columnar and up to 3m tall, 80cm in diameter, and there are 13–27 glaucous-green ribs. Areoles, set about 2cm apart, are up to 1cm long and bear nine to thirteen reddish radial spines 4cm long, and one to four flat centrals to 12cm in length. Flowers are diurnal in summer, yellow or orange, about 5cm long. Needs a bright sunny location; a porous enriched compost; minimum temperature 10°C (50°F). *Mexico (Baja California).*

FEROCACTUS **CHRYSACANTHUS** (Orc.) Br. & R.
Syn: *Echinocactus chrysanthus* Orc.

A globose to cylindrical plant up to about 1m high, 30–40cm in diameter, and dark green in colour. There are 13–22 tubercled ribs and the areoles carry four to six slender white radial spines and four to ten curved yellow or red centrals 5–7cm long. Flowers are diurnal, in summer, up to 3cm long and to 5cm across, the inner petals yellow with jagged edges, and outer petals pale brownish pink. Requires full sun; normal cactus compost; minimum temperature 10°C (50°F). *Mexico (Baja California).*

FEROCACTUS **DIGUETII** (Weber) Br. & R.
Syn: *Echinocactus diguetii* Weber

A large species eventually reaching to 4m tall, 80 cm in diameter and more or less globular as a young plant. The stems are dark green with about 34 ribs when fully grown, the areoles bearing six to seven reddish-yellow radial spines and one central, slightly curved, to 7cm long. Flowers, diurnal in summer, are funnel-shaped, to 7cm long, with yellow inner petals and reddish-brown outer ones. Requires a sunny position; normal cactus compost; minimum temperature 10°C (50°F). *Mexico (Santa Catalina Island).*

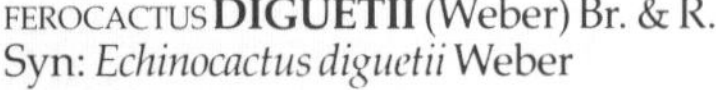

FEROCACTUS **ACANTHODES var. LECONTEI** (Engelm.) Lindsay

A globular plant, later becoming cylindrical, up to 2m or more high with 20–30 undulating ribs, dark to greyish green. The large areoles, set 2–3cm apart, have short yellowish-brown wool. The whitish to reddish spines, up to 6cm long, are most variable: some of the radials are thread-like and bristly, while others, are flexible, partially flattened, and curved but not hooked. Day flowering, and diurnal, the flowers are yellow, about 4cm long. Cultivation requirements are the same as for the species. *USA (California, Nevada, Arizona).*

FEROCACTUS **ECHIDNE** (DC.) Br. & R.
Syn: *Echinocactus echidne* DC.

A greyish-green, solitary, rarely grouping species. The globular stem is up to 20cm in diameter, and there are 14–16 acute-edged ribs, often wavy, with areoles set 2–3cm apart. The five to seven radial spines are yellow, becoming greyish, and there is one longer recurved central. Flowers are diurnal in mid-summer, about 3cm long and slightly more across, with many glossy yellow-toothed petals. Needs full sun; normal cactus compost; minimum temperature 10°C (50°F). *Mexico (Hidalgo).*

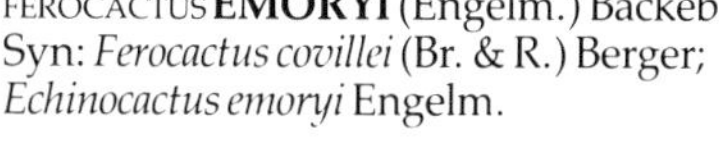
FEROCACTUS **EMORYI** (Engelm.) Backeb.
Syn: *Ferocactus covillei* (Br. & R.) Berger;
Echinocactus emoryi Engelm.

A large globular, later cylindrical, plant up to 1.5m tall and 60cm thick. It has 30–32 ribs with large oval brown woolly areoles, set 2–3cm apart and bearing five to eight white or reddish radial spines up to 6cm long, and one flat, hooked central to 8cm in length. Day flowering in summer, the flowers are centred towards the crown of the plant; these are red with yellow-tipped petals, or entirely yellow, 6–7cm long. Requires a fully sunny position; slightly calcareous porous cactus compost; minimum temperature 10°C (50°F). *Mexico (Sonora), USA (Arizona).*

     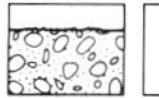

FEROCACTUS **FLAVOVIRENS** (Scheidw.) Br. & R.
Syn: *Echinocactus flavovirens* Scheidw.

Dull-green globular, short-columnar plants up to 40cm high, starting as solitary but later offsetting to form groups. The greyish areoles are set about 2cm apart with about 14 grey, spreading radial spines up to 2cm long and four centrals, the lowest of which is up to 8cm in length. Flowers are diurnal, in summer, produced at the top of the plant, and are about 3cm long, funnel-shaped and yellowish red. Requires full sun; normal cactus compost; minimum temperature 10°C (50°F). *Mexico (Puebla, Tehuacan)*

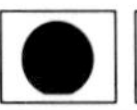    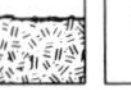 

FEROCACTUS **FORDII** (Orc.) Br. & R.
Syn: *Echinocactus fordii* Orc.

Large globular plants of greyish green, up to 40cm high, and slightly depressed in the centre. About 21 ribs have grey woolly areoles set at 2cm intervals bearing about 15 white, spreading radial spines and four centrals, one hooked, to 4cm long. The flowers are diurnal, in summer, and are pink, up to 4cm long. Needs really good light; normal cactus compost; minimum temperature 13°C (55°F). *Mexico (Baja).*

    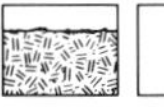 

▲

FEROCACTUS **GLAUCESCENS** (DC.) Br. & R.
Syn: *Echinocactus glaucescens* DC.

A solitary, globular plant with an attractive bluish-green body which becomes slightly elongated to about 40cm high, 30–50cm in diameter. There are 11–15 ribs, straight but deeply grooved between, and the closely set white woolly areoles bear six to seven yellow radial spines, 3–4cm long, and one central which is often absent. Flowers are glossy yellow, 3–3.5cm long, and appear by day in summer. Requires bright sunlight; normal cactus compost; minimum temperature 10°C (50°F). *Mexico (Central and Eastern).*

    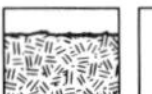

FEROCACTUS **GRACILIS** Gat.

A globular to cylindrical plant, reaching to 1.5m high in its habitat, 30cm in diameter, but usually globular in cultivation. There are 24 ribs and the elliptical-shaped areoles bear five to six reddish-brown radial spines, 2.5–4cm long, and seven to thirteen centrals, mostly longer. Summer flowering, the plant is diurnal, with golden-yellow flowers, the petals usually with a reddish mid-stripe. Needs bright light, which is essential; normal cactus compost; minimum temperature 10°C (50°F).

    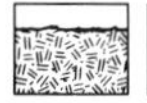 

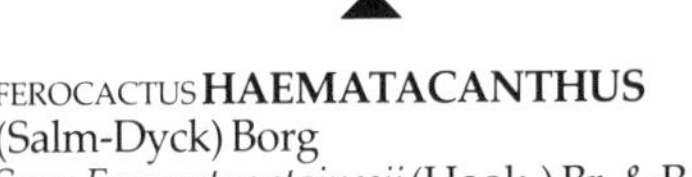

FEROCACTUS **HAEMATACANTHUS**
(Salm-Dyck) Borg
Syn: *Ferocactus stainesii* (Hook.) Br. & R.
var. *haematacanthus* (Salm-Dyck) Backeb.

The plants are globose to cylindrical, up to 1m or more tall in the wild and 35cm or more thick. They are deep green with 13–27 prominent ribs and the areoles are about 4cm apart. These bear spines in two series, the six reddish radials with whitish tips (the two laterals white only), and 2–3.5cm long. Day flowering in summer, the flowers are funnel-shaped, about 7cm long and wide and rose purple in colour. Requires full sun; slightly calcareous cactus compost; minimum temperature 10°C (50°F). *Mexico (Vera Cruz).*

    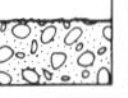 

FEROCACTUS **HAMATACANTHUS**
(Mühlpf.) Br. & R.
Syn: *Hamatocactus hamatacanthus* (Mühlpf.) Br. & R.

A globular species becoming elongated, up to 60cm tall and 30cm in diameter with 13-18 broad ribs. The areoles bear six to twelve brownish-red radial spines and four centrals, the lowest hooked and up to 12cm long. Flowers are diurnal, appearing in summer; they are pale yellow, often with a reddish throat, to 7cm long. Requires bright light; normal cactus compost; minimum temperature 7°C (45°F). *Mexico (Northern), USA (Texas).*

    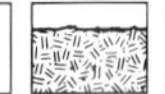 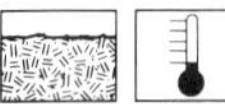

FEROCACTUS **HERRERAE** G. Ort.

A globular plant, becoming cylindrical to about 2m high, and a greyish dull green. It has 13–14 slightly wavy ribs with long white areoles bearing eight to ten whitish radial spines and one hooked central, 2–3cm long. The flowers, diurnal and appearing in summer, are funnel-shaped, 7cm long and 7cm across, reddish with yellowish edges. Requires a sunny position; normal cactus compost; minimum temperature 10°C (50°F). *Mexico (Sonora and Sinaloa).*

   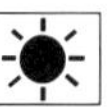  

FEROCACTUS **HISTRIX** (DC.) Linds.
Syn: *Echinocactus histrix* DC.

Globular plants, often elongating to about 70cm tall, they are dull green in colour. Ribs number about 24 with areoles carrying seven to twelve thin, brownish radials, more or less spreading, and three to four centrals to 6cm in length. Flowers are diurnal, in mid-summer, and are bright yellow, and up to 3.5cm long. Requires very bright light; slightly calcareous compost; minimum temperature 13°C (55°F). *Mexico (Central and Eastern).*

    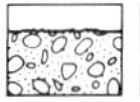 

FEROCACTUS **LATISPINUS** (Haw.) Br. & R.
Syn: *Cactus latispinus* Haw.

A broadly globular species of greyish green, 25–40cm in diameter with a slightly flattened top. The 15–23 ribs are rather notched with large grey areoles carrying six to twelve pale radial spines, and four reddish centrals up to 3.5cm long, the lower one hooked with a flattened surface and 7mm wide. Flowers are diurnal, appearing in summer, and are whitish, reddish or purplish, and 3.5cm long. This is a popular, easily grown plant which requires a sunny position; normal cactus compost; minimum temperature 10°C (50°F). *Mexico (Central areas).*

  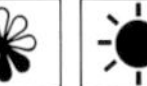  

FEROCACTUS **MACRODISCUS** (Mart.) Br. & R.
Syn: *Echinocactus macrodiscus* Mart.

Stem globular but flattened at the top, and up to about 30cm diameter; it is a pale, dull green. There are 16–21 ribs with deep grooves between them. The areoles bear six to eight yellow or red radial spines up to 2cm long and four curved centrals to 3.5cm in length. Flowers are reddish-purple with a deeper median stripe along the petals; they are diurnal, blooming in late summer. Requires a sunny position; normal cactus compost; minimum temperature 10°C (50°F). *Mexico (San Luis Potosi to Oaxaca).*

   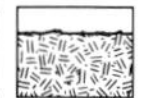

FEROCACTUS **MACRODISCUS var. SEPTENTRIONALIS** Meyran

Very similar to the species but a deeper green in colour. The areoles are rather smaller than those of the species and have much paler spines. The flowers are more pinkish purple, and about 5cm long; they are diurnal, and summer flowering. Requirements are similar to those for the species. *Mexico (Guanajuato).*

     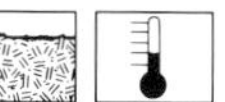

FEROCACTUS **POTTSII** (Salm-Dyck) Backeb.
Syn: *Thelocactus pottsii* Salm-Dyck.

A globular, solitary plant up to about 30cm in diameter, and a dull glaucous green. It has nine to sixteen ribs with long, white-felted areoles bearing seven to ten straight radial spines 1–2cm long and one to four centrals 3–4cm in length. These are reddish or greyish red, often banded in a deeper red. Flowers are diurnal, appearing in mid-summer; cup-shaped, they are yellow and 4–6cm long. Requires a sunny location; normal cactus compost; minimum temperature 7°C (45°F). *Mexico (Chihuahua).*

FEROCACTUS **POTTSII var. ALAMOSANUS** (Br. & R.) Unger
Syn: *Echinocactus alamosanus* Br. & R.; *Ferocactus alamosanus* Br. & R.

These plants are solitary, rarely forming groups. Green in colour, they reach 30cm or more in diameter. The ribs are narrow, about 20 in number with dull yellowish spines consisting of about eight radials 3–4cm long and one more or less erect central to 6cm in length. Flowers are a rich yellow, about 5cm long and across; flowering in summer, they are diurnal. Requirements are the same as for the species. *Mexico (Alamos Mountains, Sonora).*

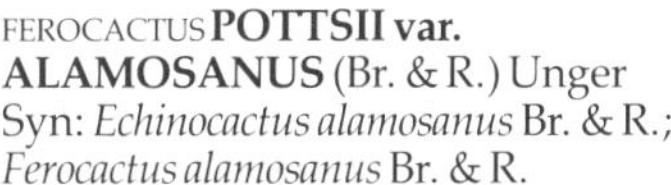

FEROCACTUS **RECTISPINUS** Br. & R.
Syn: *Ferocactus emoryii* var. *rectispinus* N. P. Taylor

A deep-green species more than 2m tall and 60cm in diameter. Ribs are straight, tuberculate, and up to 24 or more. Areoles are round and woolly with white bristles and seven to nine reddish radial spines, 3–6cm long, and one straight or curved reddish-brown central spine, longer than the radials. Flowers, which appear in summer, are diurnal; 6–7cm long, they are yellow, enhanced by the vivid purplish stigma-lobes. Requires full sun; normal cactus compost; minimum temperature 10°C (50°F). *Mexico (Baja).*

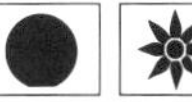

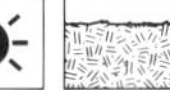

FEROCACTUS **RECURVUS** (Mill.) Berger
Syn: *Ferocactus nobilis* (L.) Br. & R.

Globular or slightly cylindrical, solitary plants to 25cm high, 20cm wide, they are greyish green with 10–15 prominent ribs up to 3cm high. The round, greyish areoles have eight stiff reddish-grey radial spines to 2.5cm long, and one strongly hooked central, flat on its upper surface, to about 5cm in length. The diurnal flowers, appearing in mid-summer, are pink with a deeper shade median line and throat; they are bell-shaped and 5cm long. Needs a bright position; normal cactus compost; minimum temperature 13°C (55°F). *Mexico (Puebla, Oaxaca).*

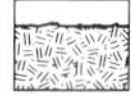

FEROCACTUS **RECURVUS var. GREENWOODII** C. Glass
Syn: *Ferocactus latispinus* var. *greenwoodii* N. P. Taylor

Dark green in colour, rarely exceeding 15cm in diameter. Ribs, of which there are 13, tuberculate with long areoles 2cm in length bearing greyish-red spines. These are both radial and central, 1.5–2.5cm long, with the single central up to 4cm long. The flowers are straw-yellow and bell-shaped, 6cm long, 3cm across, and are diurnal in late summer. Requires slight shade; slightly calcareous compost; minimum temperature 13°C (55°F). *Mexico (Oaxaca).*

    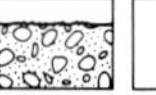 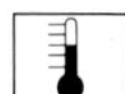

FEROCACTUS **RECURVUS var. SPIRALIS** (Karw.) K. Sch.
Syn: *Echinocactus spiralis* Karw.; *Ferocactus latispinus* var. *spiralis* (Karw.) N. P. Taylor

A globular, often cylindrical greyish-green plant, larger than the species, with about 15 somewhat spiralled ribs with brownish-red spines which are more vivid at the upper part of the stem. In general, the flowers and cultivation requirements are the same as for the species. *Mexico (Oaxaca).*

FEROCACTUS **ROBUSTUS** (Link & Otto) Br. & R.
Syn: *Echinocactus robustus* Link & Otto

A prolific, group-forming species with stems offsetting from the base. Each stem is 10–20cm in diameter, dull green and somewhat oval in shape. There are eight ribs and areoles set about 2–3cm apart, with 10–14 bristly yellowish radial spines about 2.5–3cm long and four to six straight, slightly flat centrals up to 6cm long. The diurnal flowers are yellow or orange-yellow, about 4cm long, and bloom in summer. Requires a sunny position; normal cactus compost; minimum temperature 10°C (50°F). *Mexico.*

     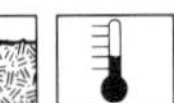

FEROCACTUS **SCHWARZII** Linds.

Tall, solitary plants to about 80cm high, 50cm in diameter, and apple green in colour. With 13–19 ribs about 5cm high, the long brownish-grey areoles bear three to five radial spines and one to three centrals, all yellowish brown and varying from 1.5 to 5cm long. The golden-yellow flowers are diurnal, appearing in summer, and are about 5cm long, 4cm across, with many petals. Needs full sun; normal cactus compost; minimum temperature 13°C (55°F). *Mexico (Sinaloa).*

FEROCACTUS **SETISPINUS** (Engelm.) L. Benson
Syn: *Hamatocactus setispinus* (Engelm.) Br. & R.

A globular, later elongating, species to 15cm high and 10cm across. Dark green, it offsets when old. There are 13 ribs, notched and often wavy, with areoles set about 1cm apart. The spines are white or brown, consisting of six to fifteen radial spines and one to three centrals, hooked. Day flowering in summer; flowers are yellow with a red centre. Needs full sun; normal cactus compost; minimum temperature 10°C (50°F). *USA (Texas), Northern Mexico.*

    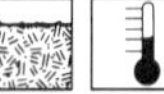 

FEROCACTUS **STAINESII** (Hook.) Br. & R.
Syn: *Echinocactus stainesii* Hook.

A globular species, becoming cylindrical and clustering, in maturity up to 3m tall, 60cm in diameter. The 15–20 ribs, up to 4cm high, have areoles set 3–4cm apart. Spines are reddish; there are six to eight radials to 2cm long, and four curved centrals to 4cm in length. The flowers, which are diurnal, bell-shaped, orange-red and 4cm long, are produced in mid-summer. Requires really bright sunshine; normal cactus compost; minimum temperature 10°C (50°F). *Mexico (San Luis Potosi).*

FEROCACTUS **STAINESII var. PILOSUS** (Gal.) Backeb.
Syn: *Echinocactus pilosus* Gal.

In general, this is very similar to the species in size, rib formation and spination. It is peculiar insofar as the body of the plant is densely covered with fine whitish hairs from the areoles. The flowers and the requirements are the same as for the species. *Mexico (San Luis Potosi).*

FEROCACTUS **ECHIDNE var. VICTORIENSIS** (Rose) Linds. Backeb.
Syn: *Ferocactus victoriensis* Rose

Probably better described as a variety of *F. echidne*. These are globular plants to about 18cm in diameter, bluish green, with 20 or more ribs. The areoles bear five to seven stiff yellowish radial spines up to about 2cm long, and one central 3–5cm in length. The golden-yellow flowers appear in summer; they are day flowering, and are 3–4cm long. Requires good light at all times; normal cactus compost; minimum temperature 10°C (50°F). *Mexico (Ciudad, Tamaulipas, Victoria).*

FEROCACTUS **VIRIDESCENS** (Torrey & A. Gray) Br. & R.
Syn: *Echinocactus viridescens* Torrey & A. Gray

A globular species, often offsetting from the base, reaching to about 45cm high, 35cm in diameter, and a glossy deep green. It has 13–21 ribs with short, whitish woolly areoles carrying nine to twenty greenish-red radial spines 2cm long, some curved, and four similarly coloured centrals up to 4cm long. Flowers are diurnal, in summer, yellowish green and 3–4cm long. Requires full sun; normal cactus compost; minimum temperature 10°C (50°F). *Mexico (Baja).*

   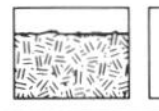 

FEROCACTUS **WISLIZENII var. TIBURONENSIS** Linds.
Syn: *Ferocactus tiburonensis* (Linds.) Backeb.

The dark-green stems are more or less cylindrical, up to 1m tall and 35cm in diameter. There are about 21 ribs, rather notched and with areoles bearing about 20 bristly greyish radial spines and one or more reddish hooked centrals, 7–9cm long. The flowers, diurnal, in summer, are golden yellow deepening to orange and about 6cm long, 5cm across. Requires bright light, which is essential; normal cactus compost; minimum temperature 7°C (45°F). *Mexico (Baja).*

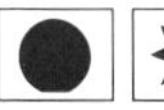    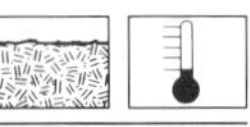

FRAILEA **ASTEROIDES** Werd.
Syn: *Frailea castanea* Backeb.

A rather dwarf, dark reddish-brown species to about 3cm in diameter. It has 10–15 ribs with diminutive areoles bearing about eight minute brownish spines which are hardly visible. The flowers are pale yellow and 4cm across. They bloom by day, in summer, several appearing together. Requires full sun at flowering time; slightly acid, porous compost; minimum temperature 13°C (55°F). *Uruguay, Brazil.*

FRAILEA **CURVISPINA** Buin. & Bred.

A comparatively new discovery. The plants are up to 5cm high and about 3cm in diameter, and are a deep grey-green. There are about 32 more or less straight and warty ribs and small, yellowish-brown areoles which bear about 14 dense, curved yellow or white radial spines to about 6mm long with one central spine. Flowers, about 3cm across, are clear yellow, and diurnal in summer. Needs sun and warmth, which are very necessary; slightly acid, porous compost; minimum temperature 13°C (55°F). *Brazil (Rio Grande do Sul).*

   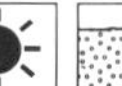 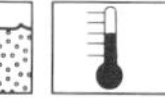

FRAILEA **PYGMAEA var. PHAEODISCA** (Speg.) Y. Ito
Syn: *Frailea phaeodisca* Speg.

A small species with a very dark greyish-green stem 3–4cm in diameter. About 30 ribs have brownish-black minutely tufted areoles bearing a few, scarcely discernible spines. Flowers appear in summer from near the crown of the plant; these are yellow, about 3cm across, and can pollinate without opening! Requires full sun at flowering time; a normal, but slightly acid cactus compost; minimum temperature 13°C (55°F). *Uruguay.*

    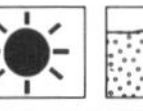 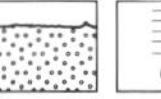

GYMNOCACTUS **BEGUINII var. nova**

A more recent introduction, currently unnamed, which bears many features common to the species, the principal difference being the colourful flowers of pale yellow with the reddish midstripe. It was discovered during the expeditions of Charles Glass and Robert Foster.

GYMNOCACTUS **GIELSDORFIANUS** (Werd.) Backeb.
Syn: *Neolloydia gielsdorfianus* (Werd.) F. Knuth; *Thelocactus gielsdorfiana* (Werd.) Bravo

A globular plant to 7.5cm high, 5cm wide, and bluish grey. The areoles are pyramid-shaped and spirally arranged, and the axils bare. Spines are brown or black: there are six to eight radials to 2cm long but no centrals. Day flowering in summer, flowers are creamy white to about 2.5cm long. Requires sun; a permeable, enriched mineral compost; minimum temperature 10°C (50°F). *Mexico (Tamaulipas).*

   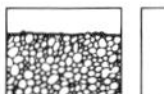 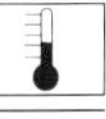

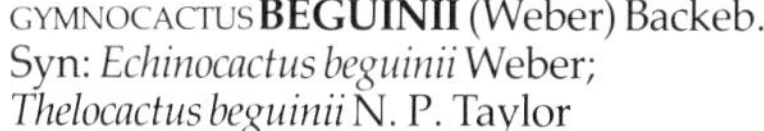

GYMNOCACTUS **BEGUINII** (Weber) Backeb.
Syn: *Echinocactus beguinii* Weber; *Thelocactus beguinii* N. P. Taylor

The bluish-green stem is usually solitary, globular in shape and up to 15cm tall, 8cm in diameter with 13–21 tubercled ribs. The tubercles are somewhat conical and close-set, and there are 12–20 greyish, black-tipped radial spines 1.5cm long, and one or two centrals to 3cm. Flowering in summer, the blooms are diurnal, pinkish purple in colour and 3–4cm long. Requires sun; normal cactus compost; minimum temperature 10°C (50°F). *Mexico (Coahuila).*

    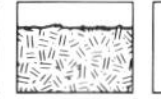 

GYMNOCACTUS **BEGUINII var. SENILIS** Hort.

A very pleasing attractive form, of uncertain origin. In most respects it is similar to the species but is more densely spined, and the spines are brownish and longer. Flowers are the same as those of the type. Requirements are the same as for the species.

   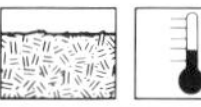

GYMNOCACTUS **HORRIPILUS** (Lem.) Backeb.
Syn: *Thelocactus horripilus* (Lem.) Kladiwa & Fittkau; *Neolloydia horripila* Br. & R.

A globular, bluish-green plant about 9cm high and thick with 15–18 ribs divided into close-set tubercles about 1cm high. The spines are whitish, sometimes with brownish tips: there are nine to fifteen radials up to 1.5cm long and one longer central. Day flowering in summer, the flowers are a deep purple-red, about 3cm long. Requires sun; a slightly calcareous cactus compost; minimum temperature 10°C (50°F). *Mexico (Hidalgo).*

   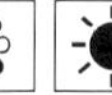  

GYMNOCACTUS **hybrid** Glass

An inter-generic hybrid of *Gymnocactus viereckii* and *Turbinicarpus schmiedickeanus*. It is a charming globular plant of dwarf dimensions with a white woolly crown and attractive spination. Flowers are pale pink with a deeper midstripe to the petals and appear by day in summer. Needs a sunny position; normal cactus compost; minimum temperature 10°C (50°F).

GYMNOCACTUS **KNUTHIANUS** (Böed.) Backeb.
Syn: *Thelocactus knuthianus* (Bravo)Backeb.

A bright-green, solitary or group-forming plant with globular stems about 9cm high and in diameter. It has 13 ribs divided into slender tubercles and white woolly areoles bearing nine to twenty whitish radial spines up to 1.5cm long, and one slightly longer central. Summer flowering, and diurnal, the flowers are in shades of pink, 2.5–3.5cm long. Requires full sun; normal cactus compost; minimum temperature 10°C (50°F). *Mexico (San Luis Potosi).*

     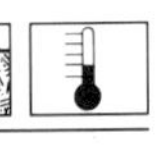

GYMNOCACTUS **MANDRAGORA** (Frič ex Berger) Backeb.
Syn: *Neolloydia mandragora* (Frič) E. F. Anderson

Grey-green, globular plants 4–6cm wide, with four-angled, close-set tubercles. Woolly areoles carry 12 radial spines 6–8mm long, and there are two thicker, brown-tipped white centrals. Day flowering in summer, flowers to 2cm long, 2.5cm across, white with reddish or greenish outer segments. Requires sun; normal cactus compost; minimum temperature 10°C (50°F). *Mexico.*

GYMNOCACTUS **SAUERI** (Böed.) Backeb.
Syn: *Thelocactus saueri* (Böed.) Berger

Small grey-green plants which are more or less globular, solitary, and about 3cm high, 5.5cm in diameter. There are 13 ribs divided into short six-sided tubercles and 14–18 white, brown-tipped radial spines 1.5cm long with one or two brown centrals 2cm in length. Flowers are white, 2.5cm long, and appear by day, in early summer. Requires sun; normal cactus compost; minimum temperature 10°C (50°F). *Mexico (Tamaulipas).*

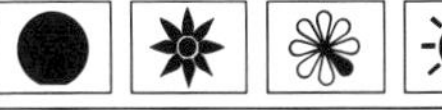

GYMNOCACTUS **SUBTERRANEUS** (Backeb.)
Syn: *Neolloydia subterranea* Backeb

Arising from a tuberous rootstock, the bright-green stems are up to about 5cm long, 3cm in diameter. The white woolly areoles carry about 16 white radial spines 6mm in length, and two dark-greyish centrals about 2cm long and whitish bristles 3cm in length. Flowers are pinkish violet, 3cm across; these occur in summer, and are diurnal. Requires full sun; slightly calcareous, enriched and porous compost; minimum temperature 10°C (50°F). *Mexico (Tamaulipas).*

▲

▲

GYMNOCACTUS **SUBTERRANEUS var. ZARAGOSAE** Glass & Foster
Syn: *Neolloydia subterranea;* var. *zaragosae* (Glass & Foster) E.F. Anderson

The long stems, tapering towards the base, are about 3–4cm thick with a long tuberous rootstock. Areoles are very woolly at flowering time; they bear 21–25 brown-tipped white radial spines 3–6mm long and two to three sub-centrals up to 2cm in length. There are two brownish-black centrals, the upper longer than the lower, and up to 1.7cm long. Day flowering in summer, the flowers are up to 2cm long, 1.5cm across, and are yellowish with a greenish-violet or pink midstripe. The peculiarly long tap roots afford anchorage to almost perpendicular gypsum cliffs near to Zaragosa. Requires sun; a slightly calcareous, enriched compost; minimum temperature 10°C (50°F). *Mexico (Nuevo Leon).*

GYMNOCACTUS **VIERECKII** (Werd.) Backeb.
Syn: *Neolloydia viereckii* (Werd.) F. Knuth

Stems are globose, 3cm high, 4.5cm thick, and freely offsetting. Dull bluish green in colour, they are divided into about 15–18 tuberculate ribs. The white woolly areoles carry up to 20 white radial spines up to 1cm long and there are four to five black-tipped centrals to 2cm in length. Flowers are magenta, 2cm long and wide, occurring diurnally, in summer. Requires bright light; enriched calcareous mineral compost; minimum temperature 10°C (50°F). *Mexico (Tamaulipas).*

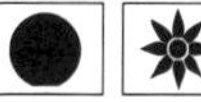    

GYMNOCACTUS **VIERECKII var. MAJOR** Glass & Foster
Syn: *Neolloydia viereckii* var. *major* (Glass & Foster) E. F. Anderson

A greenish, globose plant to 7cm high, 4–6.5cm wide. Tubercles are pyramidal in shape, to 7mm high, with bare axils. Spines are grey to brown, 13–16 radials 6–12mm long, two to four sub-centrals 5–8mm in length, and four centrals to 2.2cm long. Flowers are white, 3cm long, 3.5cm across, diurnal, in summer. Needs sun; normal cactus compost with lime added; minimum temperature 10°C (50°F). *Mexico (San Luis Potosi).*

    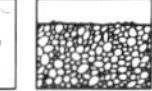 

GYMNOCALYCIUM **BRUCHII** (Speg.) Hoss.
Syn: *Gymnocalycium lafaldense* Vaup.

A dark-green clustering plant with globular stems 2.5–6cm thick with about 12 ribs divided into roundish tubercles. The elongated white areoles have 10–15 white radial spines 5mm long and one brownish and longer central spine, which is often absent. Flowering by day in summer, the flowers are pale pink, about 3cm long. Requires slight shade; normal cactus compost; minimum temperature 10°C (50°F). *Argentina (Cordoba).*

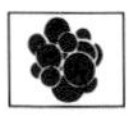   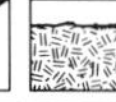 

GYMNOCALYCIUM **CASTELLANOSII** Backeb.

A solitary, globular species, velvety bluish green in colour and up to 15cm tall, 10cm in diameter with 10–12 broad ribs. The white woolly areoles are set about 2cm apart, and bear five to seven dark-tipped whitish radial spines to 2.5cm long, with sometimes one central. Flowers are white flushed pink, about 4.5cm across. Day flowering in summer, it requires normal cactus compost; slight shade; minimum temperature 10°C (50°F). *Northern Argentina.*

GYMNOCALYCIUM **BRUCHII** ***albispinum*** hort.

This appears to have come from the same locality as the species. The areoles are brownish with prominent white spines, both radials and centrals. Flowers are white, the outer petals slightly suffused purple pink. Requirements are the same as for the species.

GYMNOCALYCIUM **CARDENASIANUM** Ritter

Greyish-green, large globular plants 12–24cm in diameter with about eight to ten ribs. Areoles are whitish with two to six whitish or pale-brownish radial spines up to 6cm long and one or two centrals to 8cm. The flowers vary from pink to white, and are about 5cm long, 8–9cm across; they appear in early summer, and are diurnal. Needs slight shade; normal cactus compost; minimum temperature 10°C (50°F). *Bolivia (Tarija).*

GYMNOCALYCIUM **DENUDATUM** (Link & Otto) Pfeiff.

Dark, almost greyish-green globular plants 8–15cm in diameter with five to eight prominent ribs set with only a few areoles. The spines are whitish or greyish, five to eight in number and up to 1.5cm long. Day flowering in mid-summer, the blooms are pure white, 5cm long and 7cm in diameter. Requires slight shade, normal cactus compost; minimum temperature 10°C (50°F). *Argentina, Uruguay, Brazil.*

GYMNOCALYCIUM **HORRIDISPINUM** Frank

Dark greyish-green globular plants to 8cm wide, sometimes becoming slightly elongated. There are 10–13 ribs bearing brownish areoles with 10–12 creamy-brown radial spines and four rigid centrals, 3–4cm in length. Summer flowering, it is diurnal; the flowers are pale purplish pink or white with pinkish edges, 6cm long and across. Requires slight shade; normal cactus compost; minimum temperature 10°C (50°F). *Argentina (Cordoba).*

GYMNOCALYCIUM **HYBOPLEURUM** (K. Sch.) Backeb.

The spines are very variable in this species. Globular in shape, the plants are greyish green, with usually 13 ribs and brownish areoles bearing incurved greyish-white or pale brownish spines, usually nine radials but no centrals. Flowers are white to greenish white with a slightly pinkish throat, and about 4cm long. Summer flowering, it is diurnal, and requires normal cactus compost; slight shade; minimum temperature 10°C (50°F). *Argentina (Cordoba).*

GYMNOCALYCIUM **GIBBOSUM** (Haw.) Pfeiff.

A dark bluish-green, globular plant generally up to 30cm high, 10–15cm wide. It has 12–19 notched, rounded ribs. The areoles, up to 2cm apart, bear seven to ten pale brown radial spines to 3.5cm long and one to three centrals, which are often absent. Flowers are whitish or reddish, and up to 6.5cm long. Day flowering in summer, it requires indirect light; normal cactus compost; minimum temperature 10°C (50°F). *Argentina (La Plata, Mendoza, San Luis).*

GYMNOCALYCIUM **HORSTII** Buin.

Bright green globular plants up to about 11cm in diameter with five to six wide ribs, often bumpy. The areoles are whitish with about five yellowish-white radial spines to 3cm long, and occasionally one or two brown centrals of unequal length. Day flowering in early summer, the flowers are creamy white or pale purplish pink to 11cm long and across. Requires a position in filtered light; normal cactus compost; minimum temperature 13°C (55°F). *Brazil (Rio Grande do Sul).*

GYMNOCALYCIUM **HYBOPLEURUM var. FEROCIOR** Backeb.

This very long-spined plant appears to be that described by Backeberg as a new variety. The long, twisted, pale brownish spines are particularly significant, these being both radials and centrals. Flowers and requirements are the same as those for the species. *Argentina (Catamarca).*

    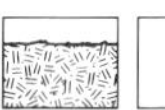 

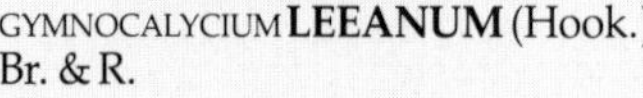

GYMNOCALYCIUM **LEEANUM** (Hook.) Br. & R.

A bluish-green, rather flattened globular plant to 7.5cm wide with up to 15 ribs divided into more or less six-sided tubercles. There are up to about 11 radial spines, 1.2cm long, and occasionally one central. Flowers are yellowish-white, 5–6cm long and wide, blooming in early summer, and are diurnal. Requires slight shade; normal cactus compost; minimum temperature 10°C (50°F). *Argentina, Uruguay.*

    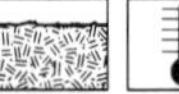 

GYMNOCALYCIUM **LEEANUM var. NETRELIANUM** (Monv.) Backeb.

Slightly more globular in shape than the species with fewer and shorter spines, amounting to about five to seven radials 8–9mm long, but usually no centrals. The flowers are citron yellow, 4–4.5cm long and across. Requirements are the same as for the species. *Uruguay.*

    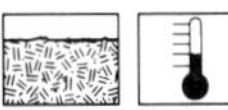

GYMNOCALYCIUM **MARQUEZII** Card. **var. ARGENTINENSE** Backeb.

A greyish-green, globular plant about 10cm in diameter, 4–5cm high. The eight to ten ribs are divided into prominent warts and the areoles are whitish, bearing seven to nine reddish-brown or brownish-grey radial spines to 2.5cm long and one or two centrals not exceeding the radials in size. Flowers are white, to 5cm long and across, and are day flowering in mid-summer. Needs partial shade; normal cactus compost; minimum temperature 10°C (50°F). *Argentina (Salta).*

   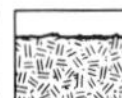 

GYMNOCALYCIUM **MARSONERI** (Fric) Y. Ito

A small greyish-green, somewhat flattened, globular species with about 15 notched ribs. Areoles are yellowish brown, bearing seven brownish radial spines up to 3cm in length, but no centrals. The flowers, yellowish white to white, 3.5cm long and 3–4.5cm across, are day flowering in mid-summer. Requires slight shade; normal cactus compost; minimum temperature 10°C (50°F). *Argentina (Salta).*

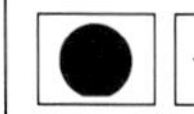    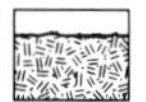 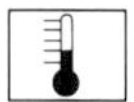

GYMNOCALYCIUM **MAZANENSE** Backeb.
Syn: *Echinocactus mazanensis* Backeb.

A globular, dull-greenish plant (shown on left of picture) 7–10cm in diameter with 14–18 rounded ribs divided into warts 1.5–2cm apart. Woolly areoles bear nine to twelve brownish, later greyish, spines 2–3.5cm long and spreading or recurving. The flowers are pinkish, about 4cm across. Summer flowering, they are diurnal and require partial shade; normal cactus compost; minimum temperature 10°C (50°F). Also depicted is *G. saglionis* (right). *Argentina (near Mazan).*

   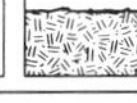  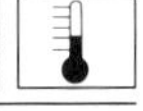

GYMNOCALYCIUM **MIHANOVICHII var. ALBIFLORUS** Werd.

A rather larger plant than the species, up to about 10cm in diameter, it has five to six radial spines with usually one central. The flowers are variable, rose pink or (as depicted) *fma. albiflora* has pale cream or white flowers. Flowering and cultivation requirements are the same as for the species. *Paraguay.*

    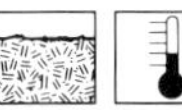

GYMNOCALYCIUM **MIHANOVICHII cv. 'Hibotan'**

A freak form of the variety due to a lack of chlorophyll when the seed was germinated. Its survival depends entirely upon its being grafted on to robust stock such as *Hylocereus*. Regardless of its 'peculiar existence', it nevertheless is able to produce attractive pink flowers. Requirements are the same as for the species.

GYMNOCALYCIUM **MIHANOVICHII var. FRIEDRICHII** (Fric & Gürke) Br. & R.

The stems are globular, greyish green or reddish green, and about 6cm in diameter. There are usually eight ribs, somewhat cross-banded. Areoles are white, bearing five to six radial spines up to 1cm long. Flowering in early summer, the blooms, which are diurnal, are bright pink or yellowish, with greenish outer segments, 4–5cm long and across. Requires slight shade; normal cactus compost; minimum temperature 10°C (50°F). *Paraguay (Bahia Negra).*

   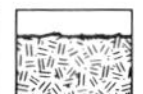 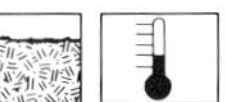

GYMNOCALYCIUM **MIHANOVICHII var. FRIEDRICHII Cristate 'Nishiki'**

Malformity occurs frequently with this species. The normal stem colouring often develops in conjunction with the reddish growth, the coloration of which is due to a lack of chlorophyll. Requirements are the same as for the species.

    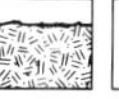

GYMNOCALYCIUM **MOSTII** (Gürke) Br. & R.

A somewhat globular plant, depressed at the top, it is up to 6 or 7cm tall, 12–13 cm in diameter, and deep green in colour. There are 11–14 ribs, deeply notched into tubercles with prominent 'chins'. The areoles have seven radial spines 5mm to 2.5cm long and one straight central. Summer flowering, and diurnal, the reddish flowers are about 8cm across. Requires a bright position; normal cactus compost; minimum temperature 10°C (50°F). *Argentina (Cordoba).*

    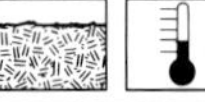

GYMNOCALYCIUM **NIDULANS** Backeb.

A dull brownish-green, solitary species about 10cm in diameter with about 17 notched ribs. The areoles are yellowish grey with six to seven greyish radial spines, and occasionally one central. Flowers are pinkish white with a somewhat darker throat and are about 5cm long. They are day flowering, in mid-summer. Requires normal cactus compost; very slight shade; minimum temperature 10°C (50°F). *Argentina (Mendoza).*

   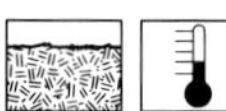

GYMNOCALYCIUM **OCCULTUM** Fric

The actual title is rather obscure – according to Borg it has a close relationship with *G. bodenbenderianum* and *G. stellatum.* This is featured in its habitat; the brownish-greenish stem is somewhat flattened and globular, with about 11 broad ribs, and three to five greyish radial spines. The flower is unknown. Culture is the same as for the majority of other species of the genus. *Argentina (Catamarca).*

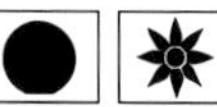   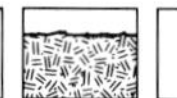 

GYMNOCALYCIUM **MULTIFLORUM** (Hook.) Br. & R.

This species has slightly bluish-green stems to 9cm high, 12cm wide and freely clustering. There are 10–15 ribs with areoles bearing seven to ten yellowish or reddish radial spines up to 3cm long, but no centrals. The flowers are a pale pinkish white, to about 4cm long, and are day flowering in mid-summer. Requires slight shade; normal cactus compost; minimum temperature 10°C (50°F). Also showing is the yellow-flowering *Gymnocalycium andreae* (Böed.) Backeb. (see above). *Argentina (Cordoba).*

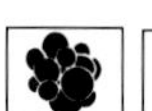    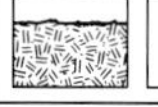

GYMNOCALYCIUM **NIGRIAREOLATUM** Backeb.

Globular, bluish-green plants about 15cm in diameter with usually 10 broad ribs. The areoles are felted and yellowish brown; they bear seven to eight pinkish-grey spines about 3cm in length. The ivory-white flowers have pale greenish outer segments; they are mid-summer flowering, and diurnal. Requires normal cactus compost; slight shade; minimum temperature 10°C (50°F). *Argentina (Catamarca).*

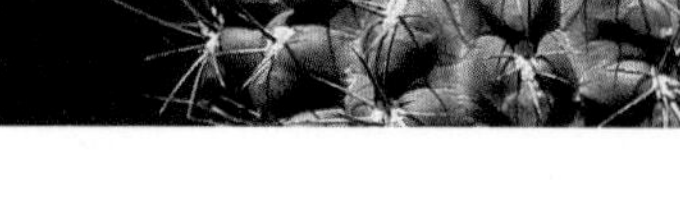

GYMNOCALYCIUM **PLATENSE** (Speg.) Br. & R.

Stems are green to bluish green, 8–10cm high and up to 10cm wide, with 12–14 ribs divided into obtuse warts. There is a prominent chin below each of the grey woolly areoles. These have five to seven radial spines, which are white, reddish at the base, and varying in size to about 1.5cm long; there are no centrals. Flowers are white, with a reddish throat, and the outer segments bluish green externally. They are day flowering in mid-summer. Requires very light shade; normal cactus compost; minimum temperature 10°C (50°F). *Argentina (Buenos Aires).*

     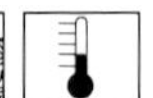

GYMNOCALYCIUM **PUGIONACANTHUM** Backeb.

A globular, solitary species about 10cm in diameter with about 10 broad ribs. The areoles bear six to seven curved spines 1–2cm in length. Flowers are about 4cm long, 4.5cm across, with creamy-white inner petals, reddish at the base, and greenish outer petals. They appear by day in mid-summer. Needs a bright position not in direct sun; normal cactus compost; minimum temperature 10°C (50°F). *Argentina (Catamarca).*

GYMNOCALYCIUM **QUEHLIANUM** (Haage) Berger var.

This is one of several varieties which differ in certain features from the species. The greyish-green, globular plant has about 15 prominent ribs and about seven widely spreading pale brownish radial spines. The lilac-pink flowers bloom by day in mid-summer. Requires normal cactus compost; slight shade; minimum temperature 10°C (50°F). *Argentina (Cordoba).*

GYMNOCALYCIUM **QUEHLIANUM** (Haage) Berger

A very variable species, it is a dull greyish green, sometimes tinged reddish brown, about 7cm in diameter. It has about 11 ribs divided into roundish warts and two to five horn-coloured spines, all radials, up to 1cm long. Flowers are white, sometimes with a small reddish throat, 5–7cm long, and are day flowering in mid-summer. Needs fairly bright light; normal cactus compost; minimum temperature 10°C (50°F). *Argentina (Cordoba).*

GYMNOCALYCIUM **cv. 'Reinelt'**

A product of Frank Reinelt of the USA who strove to cross-pollinate so as to produce very attractive plants, both in spination and flower. The parentage of this hybrid is not recorded. Culture is the same as for other *Gymnocalycium* species.

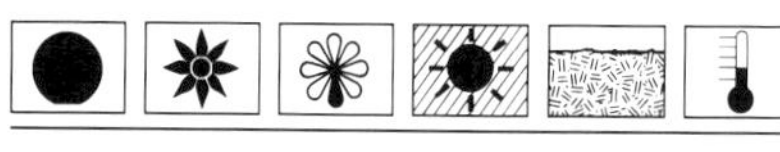

GYMNOCALYCIUM **RIOJENSE** Fric

A brownish-green or dull-greenish globular plant about 8cm high, 10cm wide with about 15 broad ribs. The areoles are 1.2cm apart, bearing five to seven pale brownish-yellow spines up to about 2cm long. The flowers are about 3.5cm across and are diurnal, flowering in summer. They have reddish sepals and whitish petals with a reddish midstripe. Requires very light shade; normal cactus compost; minimum temperature 10°C (50°F). *Argentina (La Rioja).*

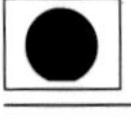    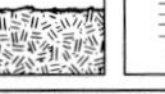 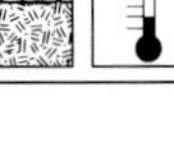

GYMNOCALYCIUM **SAGLIONIS** (Cels) Br. & R.

A large, rather flattened globular plant up to about 30cm in diameter. There are 10–30 or more ribs with prominent rounded tubercles and areoles bearing seven to fifteen brown and yellowish radial spines and about three centrals, all up to about 4cm long. Flowering in mid-summer, the plant is diurnal; flowers are a pale pinkish white, about 3.5cm long. Requires slight shade; normal cactus compost; minimum temperature 10°C (50°F). *Argentina (Salta, Tucuman, Catamarca).*

GYMNOCALYCIUM **SCHICKENDANTZII** (Weber) Br. & R.

A very dark olive-green, globular plant to about 10cm in diameter. It has seven to fourteen ribs, bearing five to seven reddish to horn-coloured radial spines up to 3cm in length. The flowers are white to reddish, olive green externally, and about 5cm long. Late summer flowering, the plant is diurnal. Needs a fairly sunny position; normal cactus compost; minimum temperature 10°C (50°F). *Argentina (Cordoba, Salta).*

    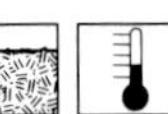

GYMNOCALYCIUM **SCHICKENDANTZII var. DELAETII** (K. Sch.) Backeb.

A roundish, bright-green variety divided into roundish warts. The areoles bear about seven horn-coloured radial spines and red flowers. Requirements are the same as for the species. *Argentina (Salta).*

GYMNOCALYCIUM **SCHROEDERIANUM var. OSTEN**

A globular plant, dark green in colour, with 12 or more ribs divided into warts. The areoles are brownish and bear five to seven yellowish radial spines which are slightly reddish at their base. The greenish-white flowers, about 7cm long, are diurnal, flowering in mid-summer. Needs protection from the midday sun; normal cactus compost; minimum temperature 10°C (50°F). *Uruguay.*

    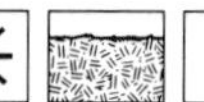

GYMNOCALYCIUM **VATTERI** Buin.

The stems are olive green to about 4cm high, 9cm in diameter, with eight to 16 broad ribs about 2.5cm high. The greyish areoles have one to three (up to five) yellowish-brown, adpressed spines. Flowering diurnally in summer, the flowers are white, sometimes with a reddish centre, and about 5cm long, 4cm across. Requires good light; normal cactus compost; minimum temperature 10°C (50°F). *Argentina (Cordoba).*

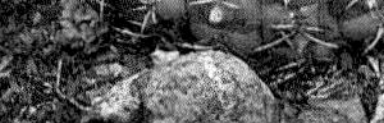

GYMNOCALYCIUM **SPEGAZZINII** Br. & R.

This solitary, globular species is very popular. Bluish green or greyish green to brownish in colour, it is up to about 18cm in diameter. There are 10–15 ribs and the yellowish-grey areoles bear reddish-brown to greyish spines, five to seven somewhat curved radials to 5.5cm long, and occasionally one central. Flowers are white or pinkish white with a reddish throat and 6–7cm long, and are day flowering in mid-summer. Needs slight shade; normal cactus compost; minimum temperature 10°C (50°F). *Argentina (Salta).*

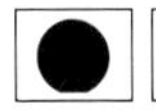    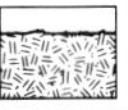 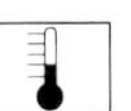

GYMNOCALYCIUM **TRIACANTHUM** Backeb.

A brownish or greyish-green globular species with about 12 flattish rounded ribs. The spines are yellowish grey, usually three in number, occasionally up to five. Flowers are white, 3.5cm long, and day flowering in summer. Needs good light; normal cactus compost; minimum temperature 10°C (50°F). *Argentina.*

  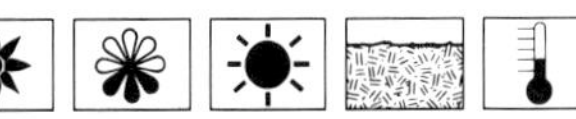 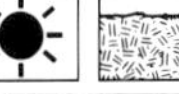

GYMNOCALYCIUM **WEISSIANUM** Backeb.

A variable species, greyish green and more or less globular to 9cm high, 14cm wide. It has about 19 ribs with slightly woolly areoles bearing bright, greyish-white spines consisting of six to eight radials to 3cm long and one central. The flowers are pale reddish brown with a darker throat. Flowering in mid-summer, it is diurnal. Requires slight shade; normal cactus compost; minimum temperature 10°C (50°F). *Argentina (Mazan).*

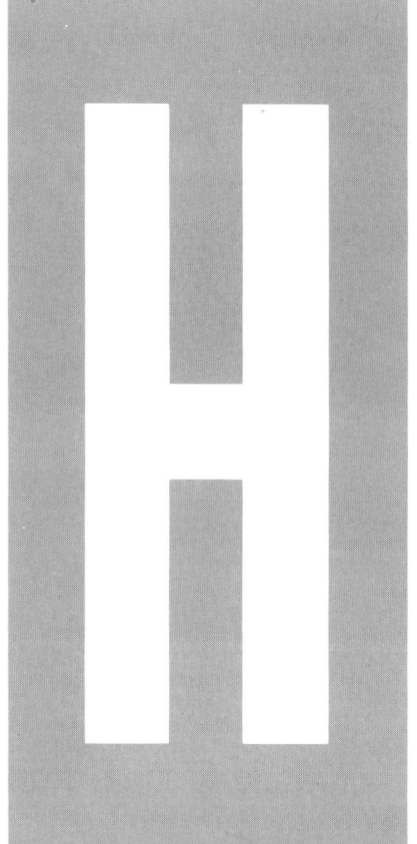

HAAGEOCEREUS **ACRANTHUS** (Vaup.) Werd. & Backeb.
Syn: *Cereus acranthus* Vaup.; *Binghamia acrantha* Br. & R.

A tall plant, it has thick clustering stems with 10–14 thick, slightly notched, low ribs. The areoles are closely set, bearing many yellow radial spines and one or two more brownish centrals up to 2cm in length. Flowering at night in summer, the blooms are pale pinkish or greenish white, 6–8cm long. Needs bright light; normal cactus compost; minimum temperature 10°C (50°F). *Peru.*

HAAGEOCEREUS **AUREISPINUS** Rauh & Backeb.

Bright-green columnar plants, 80cm tall, 6–8cm in diameter, with 18–20 ribs. The yellowish areoles bear 30–40 radial spines to 1cm long and one or two brownish-yellow centrals to 4cm. Flowers nocturnally in summer from near the tip of the stems. They are pure white, 6–7cm long and 3cm in diameter, the tube scaly and woolly. Large globular fruits follow flowering, up to 5cm long, and wine red. Careful watering is necessary, keep dry in winter. Requires a bright position; normal cactus compost; minimum temperature 13°C (55°F). *Peru (Canta).*

   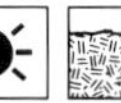 

HAAGEOCEREUS **ACANTHOCLADUS** Rauh & Backeb.
Syn: *Haageocereus multangularis* (Haw.) Ritter

A dark-green columnar plant to 70cm high, 6cm in diameter, with about 18 ribs. The areoles are large, woolly and fairly closely set, with many yellowish radial spines to 1.5cm in length, and one or two more centrally placed to about 5cm long. Flowers nocturnally, in summer, about 10cm long including the long green scaly tube, with white inner petals and reddish-tipped outer petals. Needs sun; normal cactus compost; minimum temperature 10°C (50°F). *Central Peru.*

  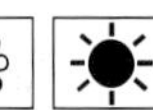 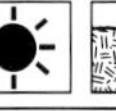 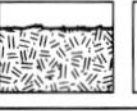 

HAAGEOCEREUS **CHOSICENSIS** (Werd. & Backeb.) Backeb.

A dark-green, columnar plant up to 1.5m tall, 6–10cm in diameter, with 18–26 ribs. Areoles are yellowish white bearing about 30 or more yellowish-white, sometimes reddish radial spines and bristles, and one to four centrals up to 2cm in length. Flowering in summer, it is nocturnal. The flowers are variable, being mostly carmine red, but sometimes white, 6–7.5cm long with a brownish-red scaly tube. Needs sun; a porous cactus compost; minimum temperature 13°C (55°F). *Central Peru (Chosica).*

     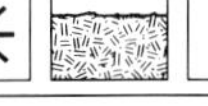  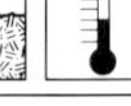 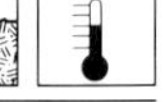

HAAGEOCEREUS **REPENS** Rauh & Backeb.

A trailing, cylindrical-stemmed plant. The greyish-green stems are up to about 2m long, 8cm thick with about 19 ribs and dark-yellowish areoles. Spines are dull yellow; there are about 40 radials to 1cm long and one or two brighter yellow centrals 1.5cm in length. The flowers, nocturnal and appearing in mid-summer, are pure white and up to 7cm long, 3.5cm wide. Needs sun; an enriched mineral-based compost; minimum temperature 13°C (55°F). *Northern Peru (Trujillo).*

 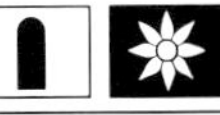    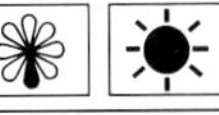 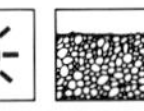 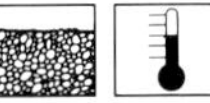  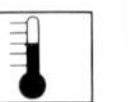

HAAGEOCEREUS **SETOSUS** (Akers) Backeb.

Ritter considers this a variety of *H. multangularis* (Willd.) Ritter. Erect, columnar plants 1–3m tall. The dull-green stems, about 6cm in diameter, have 20–21 ribs and pale brownish areoles set fairly close together. Spines are yellow and numerous, and include many bristles which are fine, hair-like and flexible, about 2cm long, and often whitish. Summer flowering and nocturnal, the flowers are about 5cm long, deep scarlet, with a similarly coloured tube. Requires full sun; a porous cactus compost; minimum temperature 13°C (55°F). *Peru (South of Lima).*

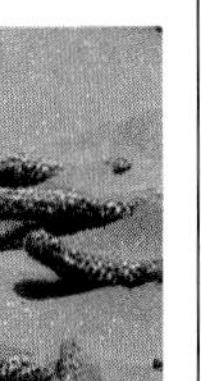

HAAGEOCEREUS **TENUIS** Ritter

A recent discovery of which little is known, this is a totally prostrate species from sandy desert regions. The stems are green, 15–30mm thick with 12–15 ribs and crenate margins. Areoles are 2mm wide, silver grey and set 4–7mm apart. Of the brownish or almost black spines, about 30 are radials 2–3mm long, and seven to ten are centrals up to 2cm in length. Flowers are unknown. Undoubtedly requires full sun; an enriched mineral compost; minimum temperature 13°C (55°F). *Peru (Lima).*

   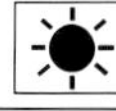 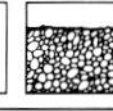 

HARRISIA **GRACILIS** (Mill.) Br. & R.

A rather sprawling plant, the dark-green stems often 5m or more long, 3.5cm thick. There are nine to eleven closely set ribs and white areoles, 2cm apart, bearing 10–16 black-tipped white spines up to 2.5cm long. Flowers are nocturnal in late summer appearing from the upper areoles. They are about 20cm long, white with pale-brownish outer petals. Requires slight shade; normal cactus compost; minimum temperature 15°C (59°F). *Jamaica.*

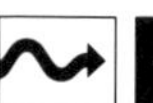    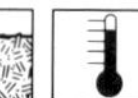

HAAGEOCEREUS **VERSICOLOR** (Werd. & Backeb.) Backeb.

A truly desert species, it is columnar, 1–2m tall, with dark-green stems 5–6cm in diameter, and 16–22 ribs. The round areoles are brown, bearing spines in a variety of colours – reddish, brown or yellowish. There are 25–30 radial spines about 5mm long and one or two centrals up to 4cm in length. Flowers are white, green externally, about 8cm long, 6cm across when fully open; they are nocturnal, in summer. Needs full sun; an enriched mineral compost; minimum temperature 13°C (55°F). *Northern Peru.*

   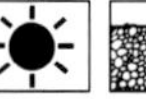  

HARRISIA **GUELICHII** (Speg.) Br. & R.
Syn: *Eriocereus guelichii* Berger

A slender-stemmed trailing or sprawling species with pale green stems 2–4cm thick. It has three to four prominent angular ribs with shallow grooves between them. Areoles are greyish, 2–6cm apart, bearing reddish, later becoming grey, spines tipped black or dark brown which consist of four to five radials up to 5mm long and one central, about 2.5cm in length. A nocturnal species flowering in early summer, the flowers are white, greenish externally, and 25cm long. Needs a sunny position; normal cactus compost; minimum temperature 10°C (50°F). *Argentina.*

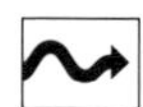     

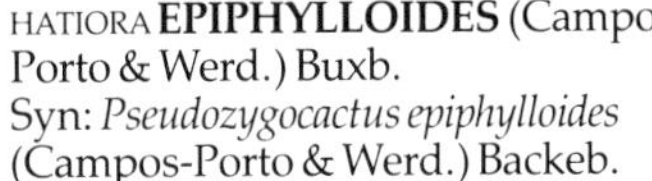

HATIORA **EPIPHYLLOIDES** (Campos-Porto & Werd.) Buxb.
Syn: *Pseudozygocactus epiphylloides* (Campos-Porto & Werd.) Backeb.

A choice rare epiphyte with long, jointed, pendent stems. Each joint is up to 2.5cm long, 1cm wide, bright green with minute spineless areoles. The flowers are yellowish, about 1cm long, and are day flowering in spring. Difficult in cultivation, it is best grafted on robust stock. Requires partial shade; normal cactus compost; minimum temperature 13°C (55°F). *Brazil (Sao Paulo, Rio de Janeiro).*

   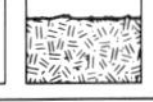 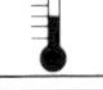

▲

▲

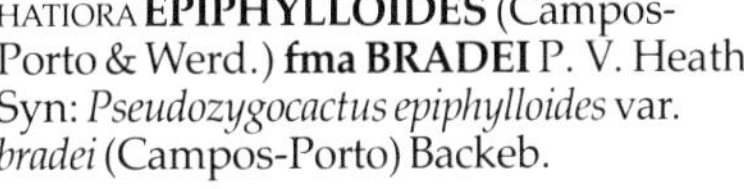

HATIORA **EPIPHYLLOIDES** (Campos-Porto & Werd.) **fma BRADEI** P. V. Heath
Syn: *Pseudozygocactus epiphylloides* var. *bradei* (Campos-Porto) Backeb.

An epiphyte from forest regions. The pendant segmented branches are 60cm or more long. Each joint or segment is 5–6mm wide, 1–1.5cm long, somewhat hatchet-shaped, and dull to bright green. Day flowering in spring, the flowers are pale yellowish, 1.5–2cm in diameter. It is not too easy in cultivation and is best grafted. Requires shade; normal cactus compost; minimum temperature 13°C (55°F). *Brazil (Serra Bocaina).*

   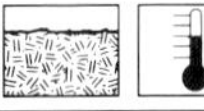

HATIORA **HERMINIAE** (Campos-Porto & Cast.) Backeb. ex Barthlott
Syn: *Hariota herminiae* Backeb.

An epiphytic species with dull greyish-green stems, more or less cylindrical in shape and about 5mm thick. It has small, short joints 2–5cm long with blunted tips and a very few pale-brownish areoles, these rarely having one or two minute bristles. The flowers are rose pink, to 2cm long, 2.5cm broad, and appear by day in late spring. The plant is best grafted. Needs filtered light; normal cactus compost; minimum temperature 13°C (55°F). *Brazil (Campos do Jordao).*

   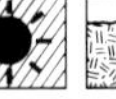 

HATIORA **SALICORNIOIDES** (Haw.) Br. & R.

A pale to deep-green semi-erect, bushy plant up to 40cm high, freely branching. In its habitat it is epiphytic or saxicolous. The joints are bottle-shaped, arranged in whorls of two to five, and 1–3cm long, 4–7mm thick. Flowering in spring, it is diurnal. The flowers occur on the tips of the newer areoles, and are golden yellow, about 1.2cm long, 1cm wide when fully open. Needs slight shade; normal cactus compost; minimum temperature 10°C (50°F). *Brazil (Rio de Janeiro, Minas Gerais).*

    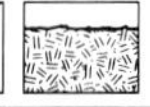 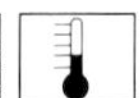

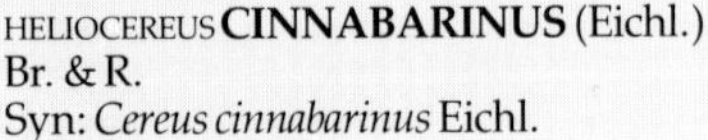

HELIOCEREUS **CINNABARINUS** (Eichl.) Br. & R.
Syn: *Cereus cinnabarinus* Eichl.

A trailing, clambering plant with three-angled, dark-green stems 40–60cm long, 2–3cm thick with rather serrated angles. Areoles are prominent with a few short, bristly yellowish-brown spines about 6mm in length. Flowering by day in mid-summer, the flowers are 8–9cm across fully expanded and up to 15cm long, with greenish-red outer petals and inner petals a glossy cinnabar red. Requires bright light but not full sun; normal cactus compost; minimum temperature 10°C (50°F). *Guatemala.*

   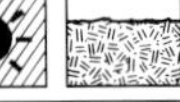 

HELIOCEREUS **SPECIOSUS** (Cav.) Br. & R.
Syn: *Cactus speciosus* Cav.

This species is either erect or trailing, rarely epiphytic. Stems are up to 1m long, 2–3cm thick, and dark green, the growing points more reddish green. There are three to five ribs with slightly serrated margins. The areoles are whitish with five to eight yellowish or pale brownish spines 1–1.5cm long. Flowers by day in early summer, the flowers are 12–15cm long, carmine red with a bluish sheen on the inner petals, borne on a green tube 8cm long. Requires half-shade; a rich, slightly acid soil; minimum temperature 10°C (50°F). *Central Mexico.*

    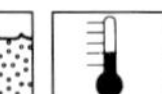 

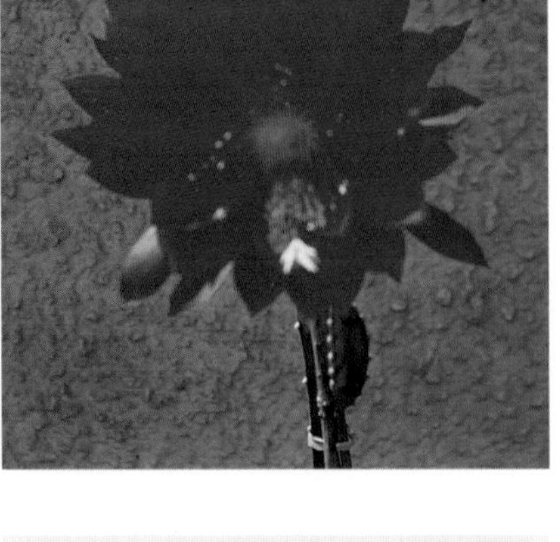

HELIOCEREUS **SPECIOSUS var. SERRATUS** Weingt.
Syn: *Heliocereus serratus* Weingt.

Erect, dull-green three to four-angled stems, prominently serrated. In general, the stems are considerably shorter than those of the species. The areoles are pale brown with a few very small yellowish spines, often absent. Flowering by day in summer, each bloom is 8–10cm across, with purplish-red inner petals, and reddish outer petals, the petals out-numbering those of the species or other varieties. Requires semi-shade; normal cactus compost; minimum temperature 13°C (55°F). *Guatemala.*

       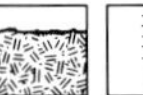 

HELIOCEREUS **Sp. nova**

An undescribed plant discovered by the late Charles Lankester many years ago, and rarely encountered in cultivation. The stems are more or less erect, brownish green, and three-angled, and the areoles are set 1–3cm apart with brownish wool and three to four fine spines to 1cm long. Flowers appear from the tips of the stems in summer, remaining open for two or three days, both night and day. The bright scarlet-red blooms are somewhat trumpet shaped, 8–9cm long and across. Requires slight shade; normal cactus compost; minimum temperature 13°C (55°F). *Guatemala, ?Costa Rica.*

   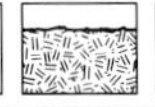

HELIOCEREUS **SPECIOSUS var. AMECAMENSIS** (Heese) Weingt.
Syn: *Heliocereus amecamensis* (Heese) Br. & R.

A very localized plant in its habitat with pendant stems similar to the species. The large, white flowers make an impressive display in mid-summer during the day; the flowers are about 14cm long from the tips of the stems. Requires semi-shade; an enriched porous compost; minimum temperature 13°C (55°F). *Mexico (Amecameca).*

    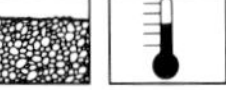

HELIOCEREUS **SPECIOSUS var. SUPERBUS** Ehrenb.
Syn: *Heliocereus superbus* (Ehrenb.) Berger

Very similar in growth habit to the species, but the stems are three- to seven-angled. Areoles are brownish with a few spines which often quickly fall. The flowers are about 15cm across when fully expanded and are a rich glossy purplish red, with red outer petals. They are diurnal, in summer. Needs filtered light; normal cactus compost; minimum temperature 10°C (50°F). *Central Mexico.*

HILDEWINTERA **AUREISPINA** (Ritter) Ritter
Syn: *Winteria aureispina* Ritter; *Winterocereus aureispinus* (Ritter) Backeb.; *Loxanthocereus auriespinus* (Ritter) Buxb.; *Cleistocactus aureispinus* (Ritter) D. R. Hunt

This is a columnar, branching, spreading and trailing plant with green stems up to 1.5cm long, 2.5cm thick, and 16–17 ribs. The areoles bear about 50 yellow spines 4mm to 1cm in length. Flowering in summer, by day. Each bloom is 4–6cm long, 5cm across, and various shades with a reddish midstripe to the petals. Requires sun; normal cactus compost; minimum temperature 10°C (50°F). *Bolivia (Florida).*

HOMALOCEPHALA **TEXENSIS** (Hopff.) Br. & R.
Syn: *Echinocactus texensis* Hopff.

A rather flattened, globular plant of greyish green, 10–15cm high, 20–30cm broad and densely woolly in the crown. It has 13–27 ribs with woolly areoles set well apart bearing six to seven reddish radial spines to 2cm long, and one thick central to 6cm or more long. Flowers are diurnal, in summer; bell-shaped and pale reddish pink with a satiny effect, they are 5–6cm long and across. Requires bright sun; enriched mineral, open compost; minimum temperature 10°C (50°F). *USA (Texas, New Mexico) Northern Mexico.*

    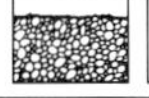 

HYLOCEREUS **BROXENSIS** Br. & R.

A sturdy climbing forest plant with long, somewhat jointed stems to over 3m in length. The stems are three-angled, and a dull greyish green, 3–4cm thick, the ribs persistently undulating with horny and brownish margins. Areoles are set at intervals of 2–3cm along the margins, each with about 10 brownish spines 5–6mm in length. Flowers appear in summer, and are nocturnal; they are about 25cm long with white inner petals arranged in series and yellowish outer segments. Needs semi-shade; normal cactus compost; minimum temperature 15°C (59°F). *Habitat unknown.*

    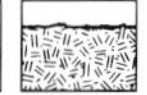 

HYLOCEREUS **CALCARATUS** (Weber) Br. & R.
Syn: *Cereus calcaratus* Weber

A semi-epiphytic, tall climbing species with elongated, three-angled, bright-green stems 4–6cm broad. The margins of the ribs are divided into prominent rounded lobes with small areoles set immediately above each. These are spineless or with one or more short white bristles. Flowers appear in mid-summer, and are nocturnal, about 18cm long with white or creamy-white inner petals and greenish-white outer petals. Requires semi-shade; rich acid compost; minimum temperature 15°C (59°F). *Costa Rica.*

HYLOCEREUS **GUATEMALENSIS** (Eichl.) Br. & R.
Syn: *Cereus trigonus guatemalensis* Eichl.; *Cereus guatemalensis* Berger

A forest species, the stems are three-angled, bluish or greyish green, to 4m long, 2–7cm broad. Ribs are horny-edged with areoles about 2cm apart bearing two to four conical spines 2mm long. Flowers are nocturnal in summer; highly perfumed, about 30cm long, 20cm or more across. The inner segments are white, the outer rose pink. Requires filtered light; acid compost; minimum temperature 15°C (59°F). *Guatemala, San Salvador.*

   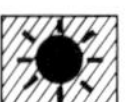  

HYLOCEREUS **OCAMPONIS** (Salm-Dyck) Br. & R.
Syn: *Cereus ocamponis* Salm-Dyck

A forest climbing plant with stems up to about 3m in length. These are glaucous green with slightly wavy margins, and usually three-angled, to 6cm in diameter. The areoles are brownish red with five to eight yellowish spines up to 1.5cm long. Flowering in mid-summer, the blooms are nocturnal, 30cm long with wide inner segments of pure white and narrower outer segments of pale yellowish green. Requires partial shade; normal cactus compost; minimum temperature 15°C (59°F). *Mexico.*

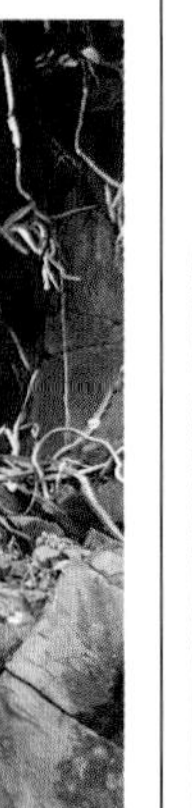

HYLOCEREUS **EXTENSUS** (Salm-Dyck) Br. & R.
Syn: *Cereus extensus* Salm-Dyck

A triangular-stemmed clambering epiphyte. The stems are green with aerial roots, branching freely, the three-angled joints 1.5–2.5cm wide. Areoles are small and woolly with two to four brown spines about 1mm long. The diurnal, early summer flowers are fragrant, about 15cm long with a green tube 8cm long. Inner petals are pinkish white, the outer ones greenish yellow edged with red. Requires partial shade; acid compost; minimum temperature 18°C (64°F). *Windward Islands and Trinidad.*

   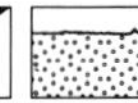 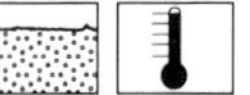

HYLOCEREUS **NAPOLEONIS** (Graham) Br. & R.
Syn: *Cereus napoleonis* Graham

A clambering, climbing species, invariably epiphytic, even on other cacti! The green, three-angled stems have margins somewhat rounded with areoles bearing small clusters of brown spines up to 8mm long. It is diurnal, flowering in mid-summer, and is fragrant. The flowers are 20cm long with a tube 8cm long, green with red scales. Inner segments are pure white, the outer ones slender and yellow. Needs a bright position; acid compost; minimum temperature 18°C (64°F). *Windward Islands (St. Vincent).*

   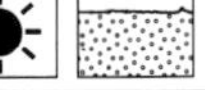 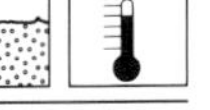

HYLOCEREUS **UNDATUS** (Haw.) Br. & R.
Syn: *Cereus undatus* Haw.; *Hylocereus tricostatus* Br. & R.

A widely cultivated species with stems divided into joints and freely branching. Climbs by means of aerial roots; the joints are triangular, 5–6cm in diameter. Areoles are set at intervals along the 'winged' margins with a few short, dark spines. Flowers, nocturnal in summer, are up to 30cm long; the inner segments are white, the outer ones yellowish green. Requires a bright position; normal cactus compost; minimum temperature 13°C (55°F). *Habitat unknown but probably West Indies.*

JASMINOCEREUS

JASMINOCEREUS **THOUARSII** (Weber) Backeb.

Columnar to about 8m high, branching from above the base. The branches are a dull greyish green, about 14cm in diameter and consisting of prominent 'joints' indicating the growth of successive seasons. There are 18–22 ribs, about 1cm high, set with brownish areoles. These each bear about 10 spines, blackish, becoming grey, up to 5cm. Flowers are nocturnal, in summer, 5–10cm long with an elongated reddish-brown or yellowish tube, woolly and scaly externally. Needs sun; normal cactus compost; minimum temperature 13°C (55°F). *Galapagos Islands.*

    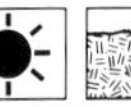 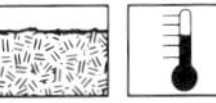

LASIOCEREUS

LASIOCEREUS **RUPICOLA** Ritter

Tree-like columnar plants, 3–4m high in their habitat, and freely branching. The branches are dark green, 4.5–7cm thick with 18–21 ribs divided into large warts. Areoles are fairly close set, bearing 18–20 or more pale yellow radial spines up to 1cm long and 10–12 similarly coloured centrals up to 3cm in length. Flowering at night in mid-summer, the flowers are white, 5cm long, with black-tipped outer segments. Requires sun; normal cactus compost; minimum temperature 13°C (55°F). *Peru (Cajamarca).*

  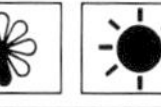 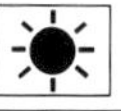 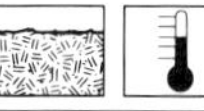

LEOCEREUS

LEOCEREUS **BAHIENSIS** Br. & R.

Tall, erect columnar plants, rarely branching, up to 2m high, 1–1.5cm in diameter. Dark green, they have 12–14 low ribs and close-set areoles which are round and white. There are numerous yellow spines, mainly spreading and very short except for the few centrals which are up to 3cm long. Flowering in summer, the blooms are nocturnal arising from the side of the stems. They are about 4cm long, with white inner petals, and greenish outer petals. Requires sun; normal cactus compost; minimum temperature 13°C (55°F). *Brazil (Bahia).*

    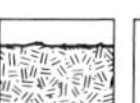 

LEOCEREUS **ESTEVESII** Braun

Very closely related to *L. bahiensis,* coming from the region of Piaui, but a taller plant reaching to over 2m. It has about 12 ribs, with longer yellowish, bristly spines. The nocturnal summer flowers are more or less terminal; tubular in shape, they are greenish externally, with white inner petals. The centre plant shows *L. bahiensis* var. *exiguospinus* Braun & Esteves. Needs full sun; normal cactus compost; minimum temperature 13°C (55°F). *Brazil (Bahia).*

    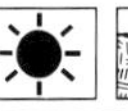  

LEPISMIUM **CRUCIFORME var. CAVERNOSUM** (Lindbg.) Backeb.
Syn: *Lepismium cavernosum* Lingbg.

A sparsely branched species; the joints are acutely three-angled or flat, 15–25cm long and up to 3cm wide, and deeply notched. The areoles have prominent tufts of whitish wool and pale-greyish bristles. Flowers are white, with greenish outer petals, about 1.3cm long. Requirements are the same as for the species. *Brazil (Rio de Janeiro, Minas Gerais).*

LEPISMIUM **CRUCIFORME** (Vellozo) Miquel

A most variable species, a number of varieties having botanical titles. The stems are green with reddish margins and are mainly three-angled, up to 2cm wide and 30-60cm in length. They have prominently notched edges, each notch set with a white areole. Flowers are solitary, 1–1.5cm long, and whitish; they are diurnal, appearing in spring. Requires shade; normal cactus compost; minimum temperature 13°C (55°F). *Brazil, Argentina, Paraguay.*

     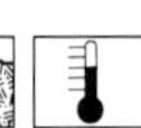

LEPISMIUM **CRUCIFORME var. ANCEPS** (Weber) Backeb.
Syn: *Rhipsalis anceps* Weber

A much-branching plant with mainly flat, lanceolate stems. These are dark purplish green, the margins notched with tufts of whitish wool in the areoles. Flowers, which are diurnal, are purplish white, appearing in late spring, and there are carmine-red fruits. Requirements are the same as for the species. *Brazil (Sao Paulo).*

      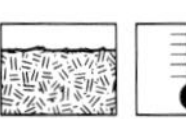 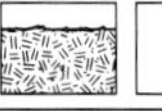

LEPISMIUM **CRUCIFORME var. KNIGHTII** (Pfeiff.) Boom

Similar to the species in all respects, except for the flowers which are glistening white with well-recurved petals. Requirements as for the species. *Brazil.*

    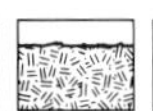 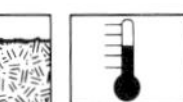

LEPISMIUM **CRUCIFORME var. MYOSURUS** (Salm-Dyck) Backeb.
Syn: *Lepismium myosurus* Pfeiff.

The three- to four-angled stems are 10–25cm long, 5mm to 1.2cm wide, narrowing to pointed tips, and greyish green in colour. Flowers are pinkish lilac, and about 3cm long. Requirements as for the species. *Brazil (Rio de Janeiro, Santa Catharina).*

   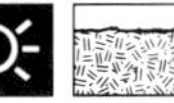 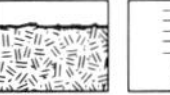 

LEPISMIUM **DISSIMILE** Lindbg.
Syn: *Rhipsalis dissimilis* K. Sch.

A somewhat bushy species with more or less erect cylindrical, slightly angular stems. These are about 5–7mm thick, 15cm or a little more long, and pale to dark green, branching in whorls. The very small areoles are arranged spirally, and are without wool or bristles on the upper joints. Flowers are reddish in bud, opening white and pink, and are 6mm to 1cm long. They bloom by day in spring. Requires semi-shade; normal cactus compost; minimum temperature 10°C (50°F). *Brazil (Sao Paulo).*

    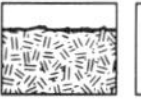 

LEPISMIUM **HOULLETIANUM** (Lem.) Barthlott
Syn: *Rhipsalis houlletiana* Lem.

A much-branched species, epiphytic in nature, but responding well to pot culture. The stems are either cylindrical and erect, about 2mm thick, or leaf-like, flat and lance-shaped, 30–40cm in length and 3–5cm broad with prominent toothed edges, pale to greyish green. Flowers from marginal areoles in late spring, diurnal; white or pale yellowish, up to 2cm long and bell-shaped, producing reddish fruits. Requires filtered light; normal cactus compost; minimum temperature 10°C (50°F). *Brazil (Minas Gerais).*

   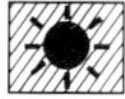  

LEPISMIUM **LORENTZIANUM** (Griseb.) Barthlott
Syn: *Rhipsalis lorentziana* Griseb.

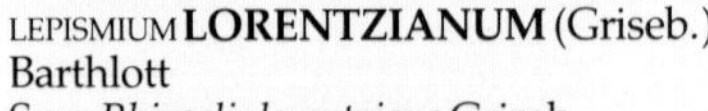

A freely branching epiphyte with flattened or three-angled fresh-green stems 10–30cm long, 2–4cm broad, with prominent midribs. Areoles are whitish, set in the notched margins. The yellowish-white flowers are small, appearing in daytime in late spring, and there are purple-black fruits. Needs semi-shade; normal cactus compost; minimum temperature 10°C (50°F). *Argentina (Salta).*

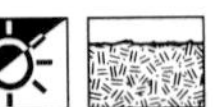

LEPISMIUM **WARMINGIANUM** (K. Sch.) Barthlott
Syn: *Rhipsalis warmingiana* K. Sch.

A branching epiphyte with dark-green, reddish-edged stems 10–40cm long and about 2cm broad. These are flat or three-angled with crenate margins. The areoles are slightly woolly, bearing white flowers about 1cm long, 2cm wide when fully open. These appear in late spring, early summer, and are diurnal. The fruits are blackish purple. Requires slight shade; normal cactus compost; minimum temperature 10°C (50°F). *Brazil (Minas Gerais).*

LEUCHTENBERGIA **PRINCIPIS** Hook.

Plants reach up to 70cm tall, becoming woody with age. There is a thick, fleshy stem from which arise large, bluish-green tubercles, 10–12cm long and triangular. At the tips of the tubercles are large greyish areoles bearing eight to fourteen radial and one or two central spines, twisted and papery and about 10cm long. Flowers are diurnal in mid-summer from the tips of young tubercles; glossy yellow and up to 8cm long, 5–6cm across. Needs full sun; enriched calcareous compost; minimum temperature 10°C (50°F). *Mexico (Northern and Central).*

LEPISMIUM **PARADOXUM** (Salm-Dyck) Backeb.
Syn: *Rhipsalis paradoxa* Salm-Dyck

An epiphyte with long, jointed stems with acute angles, twisted into shorter joints at intervals of 2–6cm with a whitish areole at the top of each angle. Flowers, which are diurnal, occur in late spring; they are white, and about 2cm long. The fruits are white, turning reddish. Requires partial shade; normal cactus compost; minimum temperature 10°C (50°F). *Brazil (Sao Paulo).*

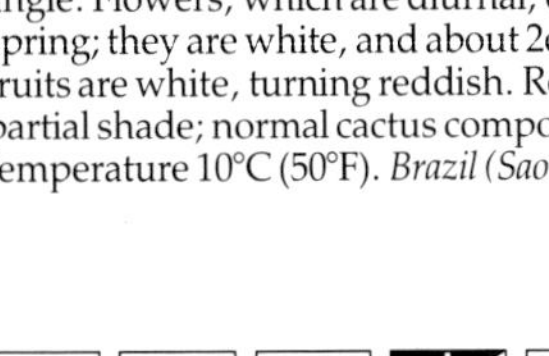

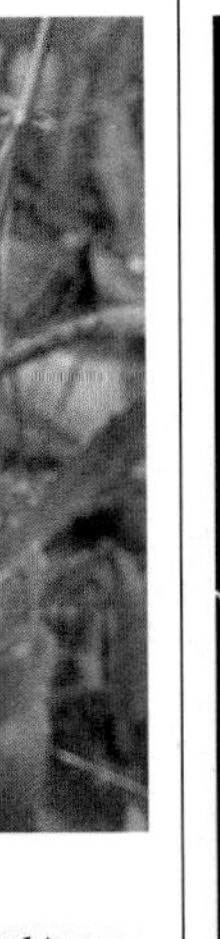

LOBIVIA **BACKEBERGII** (Werd.) Backeb.
Syn: *Echinopsis backebergii* Werd.

The pale green plant is solitary or offsetting, globular or oval, and 4–5cm in diameter, with about 15 spirally notched ribs. Areoles are slightly woolly and arranged about 1cm apart with three to seven brownish, spreading radial spines, often curved or hooked, and 5mm–5cm long; there are no centrals. Flowers are diurnal in summer, borne laterally; they are carmine red, and 4.5–5.5cm long. Requires a very bright position; normal cactus compost; minimum temperature 7°C (45°F). *Bolivia (La Paz, 3500m alt.)*

LOBIVIA **CHRYSANTHA** Werd.

A high-altitude, greyish-green, globular plant with about 13 ribs: in its habitat it is often sunken into the ground. The woolly areoles are greyish, bearing five to eight radial spines; these are initially reddish, later turning greyish, and up to about 2cm long. Flowers are bright yellow with a reddish-purple throat, and are fragrant, appearing by day in summer. Requires slightly calcareous compost; sunny position; minimum temperature 7°C (45°F). *Argentina, Bolivia.*

LOBIVIA **FAMATIMENSIS** (Speg.) Br. & R.
Syn: *Echinocactus famatimensis* Speg.

A most variable species with flowers ranging from white to deep red. Several varietal titles are recorded: that depicted is var. *nigricans* which has somewhat oval stems, mostly solitary. It is 4–5cm in diameter with 18–24 low ribs and closely set white areoles. There are eight to fourteen whitish spines about 4mm long. The flowers are yellow to scarlet, about 5cm long and somewhat trumpet-shaped. They are diurnal, in summer. Requires a sunny location; normal cactus compost; minimum temperature 7°C (45°F). *Argentina (La Rioja, San Juan).*

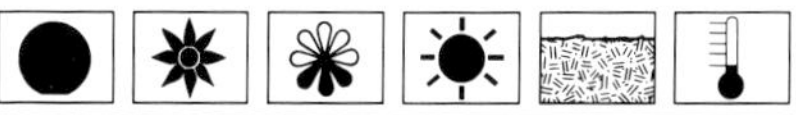

LOBIVIA **CAESPITOSA** Br. & R. **var. MINIATIFLORA** Ritter

A more or less globular plant 3–6cm high, 2–4cm thick with 10–13 bumpy ribs. The spines are very fine and slender, consisting of three to eight or more radials, and four to eight centrals from 1–5cm long. Day flowering in summer, the blooms are 5–6cm long, with yellowish red inner petals, red externally. Needs bright light; normal cactus compost; minimum temperature 10°C (50°F). *Bolivia (La Paz).*

LOBIVIA **CORBULA** (Herrera) Br. & R.
Syn: *Mammillaria corbula* Herrera

A globular plant, freely offsetting to form clusters of pale green stems each with 12–18 acute ribs arrayed with hatchet-like notches bearing white woolly areoles. The spines are brownish yellow, seven to twelve of them slightly curved radials to 5cm in length and rarely one curved central. The flowers open about midday in summer; they are about 3cm long borne on a long tube, with deep orange inner petals and carmine-red outer ones. Requires full sun; normal cactus compost; minimum temperature 7°C (45°F). *Peru (Cuzco).*

LOBIVIA **FAMATIMENSIS var. HAEMATANTHA** (Backeb. ex Wessn.) Backeb.

A brownish-green, short oval-shaped variety with 15 or more ribs, short spines and blood-red flowers. Requirements are the same as for the species. *Argentina.*

LOBIVIA **FEROX** Br. & R.
Syn: *Psedolobivia ferox* (Br. & R.) Backeb.; *Lobivia longispina* Br. & R.

Globular plants to 20cm high and in diameter with 15–25 or more ribs. The spines are at first brown, later greyish, of which eight to twelve are radials and about three are centrals, up to about 10cm long. Flowers are white, and bloom by day in summer. Requires a sunny position; an enriched mineral-based compost; minimum temperature 7°C (45°F). *Bolivia.*

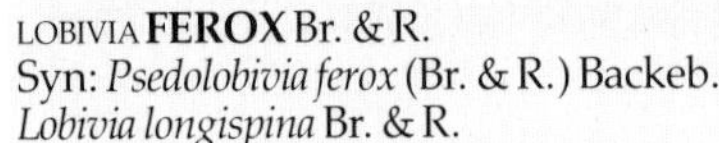

LOBIVIA **JAJOIANA** Backeb.
Syn: *Lobivia chrysantha* (Werd.) Backeb. ssp. *jajoiana* Rausch ex Rowley

These plants are solitary, rarely offsetting. The stem is oval or cylindrical, 5–6cm thick, deep or greyish green with 10–18 tuberculate ribs. There are eight to ten reddish-white radial spines about 1cm long and one pale brown central to 2.5cm in length. Flowers are diurnal in summer, varying considerably in size and colour from yellow through to deep red. They are 5–6cm in diameter and are often scented. Requires partial shade; normal cactus compost; minimum temperature 10°C (50°F). *Argentina.*

LOBIVIA **JAJOIANA** Backeb. **var. GLAUCA** Rausch
Syn: *Lobivia glauca* Rausch

Probably only a colour form of the species; the stem is very similar, and so is the spination. The almost completely deep rose-pink flowers perhaps justify a separate specific title as proposed by Rausch. Requirements are as for the species. *Bolivia.*

LOBIVIA **MARSONERI** (Werd.) Backeb.

The stems are greyish green, about 8cm high and thick, freely offsetting. There are about 20 ribs which are straight with close-set areoles, and the spines are yellowish grey to brownish: eight to twelve radials up to 3cm long and two to five centrals, usually hooked. The golden-yellow to red flowers are about 5cm long, 6cm across, and are fragrant, appearing by day, in summer. Requires filtered light or partial shade; normal cactus compost; minimum temperature 10°C (50°F). *Northern Argentina.*

LOBIVIA **OLIGOTRICHA** Card.
Syn: *Lobivia cinnabarina* (Hook.) Br. & R. var. *oligotricha* (Card.) Rausch

Bright-green, globular plants around 8cm high and in diameter. There are about 18 ribs with areoles set approximately 8mm apart, bearing about 15 spines, some to 1.5cm in length. The flowers are bright red, 3cm long, 2.5cm across; flowering in summer, they are diurnal. Requires sun; normal cactus compost; minimum temperature 10°C (50°F). *Bolivia (Cochabamba).*

LOBIVIA **SILVESTRII** (Speg.) Rowley
Syn: *Chamaecereus silvestrii* (Speg.) Br. & R.

The popular Peanut Cactus. A somewhat dwarf species with pale-green stems rarely more than 15cm long, 1.5–2.5cm thick, branching and offsetting freely. The seven to ten ribs bear 10–15 whitish, bristly spines, 2mm long. Flowers appear in early summer, and are diurnal; they are bright scarlet, 4–7cm long. Requires slight shade; normal cactus compost; minimum temperature 7°C (45°F), even lower if kept completely dry and in a bright location in winter. *Argentina (Tucuman).*

    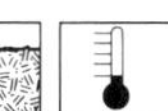

LOBIVIA **SUBLIMIFLORA** Backeb.
Syn: *Lobivia rebutiodes* var. *sublimiflora* (Backeb.) Backeb.

A somewhat globose, dark-green to violet plant with 12–20 ribs. The whitish spines are appressed; there are about 10, including one central longer than the others. Flowers, about 6cm long and wide, vary in colour from yellow, orange and red to almost purple; they appear by day in summer. Requires a bright position; an enriched mineral-based compost; minimum temperature 7°C (45°F). *Argentina (Salta).*

    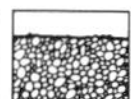 

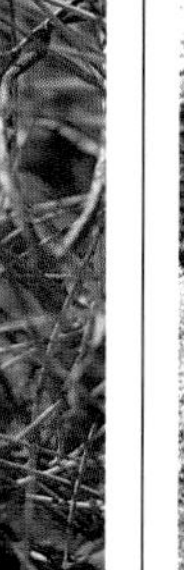

LOBIVIA **RAPHIDACANTHA** Backeb.

This species is currently considered synonymous with *Lobivia pentlandii* (Hook.) Br. & R. A more or less globular plant 6–8cm diameter, dark green in colour with about 16 spirally arranged ribs. Areoles bear five or more greyish radial spines of unequal length, ranging from 6mm to 1.5cm, with usually one prominent central to 7cm long. Flowers open in late afternoon in early summer; they are funnel-shaped, up to 5.5cm long and across, and pinkish purple in colour. Requires slight shade; normal cactus compost; minimum temperature 13°C (55°F). *Northern Bolivia, Peru (Puna).*

LOBIVIA **STILOWIANA** Backeb.

A high-altitude species. Plants are globular, dark green, about 6cm high, 5cm diameter with about 23 ribs and prominent warts. There are five to seven greyish radial spines 5mm to over 1cm long, and one central about 1.7cm in length. The flowers are cinnamon carmine, about 4cm long and across, and appear by day in summer. Needs a slightly shaded position; an enriched mineral compost; minimum temperature 7°C (45°F). *Argentina (Tucuman).*

LOBIVIA **TARATENSIS** Card.

Plants may be solitary or grouped. Each stem is up to 7cm high, 12cm thick and is green to greyish green with 15–30 ribs divided into hatchet-like tubercles to 1cm high. The 10–14 spines are yellowish, becoming greyish, from 4mm to 3cm in length. Flowers are magenta, up to 3.5cm long, 3cm across, and are diurnal, in early summer. Requires slight shade; normal cactus compost; minimum temperature 10°C (50°F). *Bolivia (Tarata).*

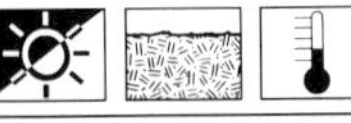

LOBIVIA **TIEGELIANA** Wessn.

A bright-green globular plant about 6cm in diameter with about 18 ribs. Areoles have four to six paired brownish-yellow radial spines with reddish-brown tips about 1cm in length and one to three brown-pointed centrals. Mid-summer flowering, it is diurnal. The flowers are reddish violet, 2.5cm long, about 4cm across. Needs good light; normal cactus compost; minimum temperature 10°C (50°F). *Bolivia (Tarija).*

▲

× LOBIVOPSIS **'Dainty Bess'** Johnson

A very attractive hybrid developed in the USA between a species of *Lobivia* and *Echinopsis*. It is diurnal, flowering in early summer. Needs a very bright position, essential in order to produce the abundance of flowers peculiar to this cultivar; normal cactus compost; minimum temperature 10°C (50°F).

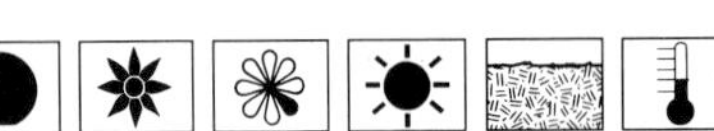

× LOBIVOPSIS **'Helena'** Innes

An attractive hybrid between *Lobivia cinnabarina* × *Echinopsis multiplex* developed in the UK about 1965. Flowering by day in early summer, the pale to salmon-pink flowers provide a display for several weeks, these appearing in succession. Requires fairly bright sun; normal cactus compost; minimum temperature 10°C (50°F).

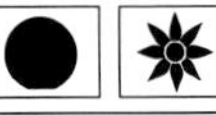

× LOBIVOPSIS **'Orange Glory'** Johnson

A Paramount Hybrid produced in the USA by Harry Johnson and originally featured in 1957. A clustering plant, it is diurnal and flowers in late spring and summer. The orange blooms are 6–7cm in diameter. Requires full sun; normal cactus compost; minimum temperature 10°C (50°F).

× LOBIVOPSIS **'Stars & Stripes'** Johnson

An outstanding Paramount Hybrid first featured in 1961. The many-petalled flowers of warm rose with a darker deep-rose centre area to the inner segments have made this an outstanding plant. Flowering in early summer, it is diurnal. Requires full sun; normal cactus compost; minimum temperature 10°C (50°F).

× LOBIVOPSIS **'Sussex Hybrids'** Innes & Hewitt

A group of hybrids produced in the UK, including 'Sussex Charm' (yellow), 'Sussex Dawn' (pink and red), 'Sussex Blend' (pale pink) and *Echinopsis oxygona* (Link) Zucc. (white), a parent of many hybrids. They are diurnal, flowering in early summer. Require slight shade; normal cactus compost; minimum temperature 10°C (50°F).

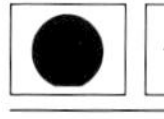   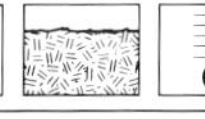  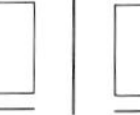

LOPHOCEREUS **GATESII** M. E. Jon.

A greyish-green, columnar, branching species, in its habitat up to 3m tall, and 9cm thick. It has 10–15 ribs with close-set areoles bearing eight to ten greyish radial spines and two centrals up to 1.5cm long. Flowering by night in mid-summer, the flowers are around 3cm long and wide, and are pinkish red. Requires bright light; slightly calcareous cactus compost; minimum temperature 10°C (50°F). *Mexico (Baja).*

LOPHOCEREUS **SCHOTTII** (Engelm.) Br. & R.
Syn: *Pachycereus schottii* (Engelm.) D. R. Hunt

Columnar 1–5m long, branching from base, erect or straggling. The stems are dull green, about 6cm thick, with four to twelve ribs and large, woolly areoles about 1cm apart. There are four to seven spines, blackish, 1cm long. Flowers are nocturnal, in summer from a terminal pseudocephalium. They are red, greenish externally and 3–4cm long. Needs slight shade; calcareous cactus compost; minimum temperature 10°C (50°F). *Mexico (Sonora, Baja).*

   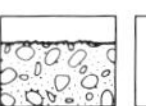 

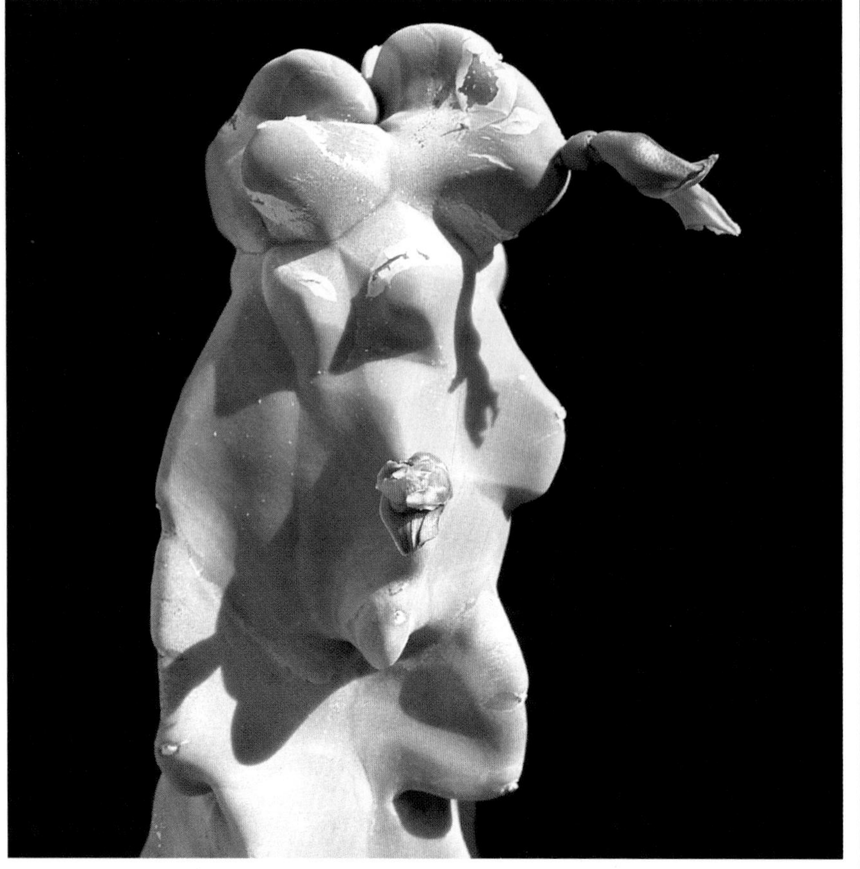

LOPHOPHORA **WILLIAMSII var. CAESPITOSA** Hort.

This is a clump-forming variety created by offsets developing from the base. Requirements are the same as for the species.

LOPHOCEREUS **SCHOTTII** (Engelm.) Br. & R. **var. MONSTROSUS**

So called 'deformities' in growth often produce most unusual features. This variety has very irregular ribs and spineless areoles and has earned the title of 'Totem Pole'. It flourishes on its own roots, and subsequent new branches rarely differ from the 'mother' plant. Requirements are the same as for the species.

LOPHOPHORA **WILLIAMSII** (Lem. ex Salm-Dyck) Coult.
Syn: *Echinocactus williamsii* Lem.; *Lophophora lewinii* Thompson

Bluish-green, globular with a flattened surface, 5–8cm wide. There are seven to ten low ribs, indistinctly tubercled with white-felted spineless areoles. Flowers are diurnal, lasting for two or three days in summer, pink or white, 1.2–2.5cm across. The plant contains narcotics. Requires a sunny position; a slightly calcareous cactus compost; minimum temperature 7°C (45°F). *USA (Texas), Mexico (Northern areas).*

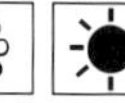

LOPHOPHORA **WILLIAMSII var. DIFFUSA**

A flat, globular, solitary plant to about 13cm in diameter. It is bluish green or greyish blue with about 13 low, tubercled ribs and well-spaced small, white-felted spineless areoles. The white flowers are about 2cm in diameter, and appear in daytime in summer. Requirements are the same as for the species. *Mexico (Quoretaro).*

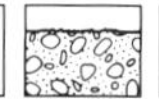

LOXANTHOCEREUS

LOXANTHOCEREUS **CAMANAENSIS** Rauh & Backeb.

This plant is likely to be reclassified within another genus. A low-growing, branching species with stems about 20cm long, 4cm thick and 13–14 ribs. Areoles are set about 1cm apart, bearing six to ten silvery-grey to greyish-brown needle-like radial spines about 5mm long, and one or two centrals to 3cm in length. Flowers are zygomorphic, orange-red, and about 8cm long; flowering in summer, they are diurnal. Requires a sunny position; normal cactus compost; minimum temperature 13°C (55°F). *Southern Peru.*

    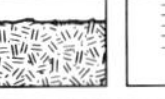 

LOXANTHOCEREUS **GRANDITESSELLATUS** Rauh & Backeb.

This plant is likely to be reclassified, possibly within the genus *Cleistocactus.* A long cylindrical-stemmed species about 2m in length, 5cm thick with six to seven notched ribs. The white woolly areoles are round, bearing purplish-brown spines consisting of six to eight radials up to 1cm long, and one, rarely two, centrals to 5cm. The red flowers are somewhat tubular, 5–6cm or more long, and are day flowering in summer. Needs a bright position; normal cactus compost; minimum temperature 13°C (55°F). *Central Peru.*

   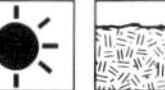 

LYMANBENSONIA

LYMANBENSONIA **MICRANTHA** Kimnach
Syn: *Acanthorhipsalis micrantha* Br. & R.; *Rhipsalis asperula* Vaup.

A somewhat sprawling plant, becoming quite shrubby. The two-to three-angled stems are 20cm or more long, and the areoles have three to ten spines up to 1cm in length. Flowers are bell-shaped to tubular, 2.7cm long, and purplish red in colour, appearing by day in early summer. Requires a bright position; normal cactus compost; minimum temperature 13°C (55°F). *Peru.*

MAIHUENIA

MAIHUENIA **POEPPIGII** (Otto) Weber
Syn: *Opuntia poeppigii* Otto

A low-growing, clustering species composed of many short cylindrical joints about 6cm long, 1–1.5cm thick. It has fleshy green leaves about 5mm long, and areoles with usually three to four very short spines, except for one which may be 2cm long. A summer, day flowering plant, the blooms are yellow, up to 3cm long. It is winter-hardy in Europe or North America, tolerating zero temperatures, but it must be planted in very porous, enriched compost, preferably on sloping ground. Needs good light. *Chile (Talca).*

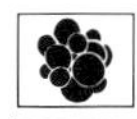    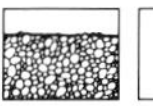 

MAIHUENIOPSIS **DARWINII var. HICKENII** (Br. & R.) Kiesl.
Syn: *Opuntia hickenii* Br. & R.

A low-growing bushy species, densely branched. Each oval joint is 2–4cm long and up to 2cm thick. The areoles are brownish yellow with tufts of yellowish glochids. Spines are whitish to brownish, about 5cm or more in length, and usually up to five per areole, but are occasionally absent. Summer flowering, the yellow flowers are diurnal. Needs full sun; enriched mineral-based compost; minimum temperature 7°C (45°F). *Argentina (Rio Negro).*

   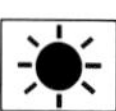 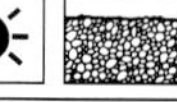 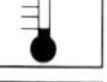

▲

TEPHROCACTUS **GLOMERATUS** (Haw.) Backeb.

About 10cm high, each joint 2–3.5cm long and thick, dull green. White areoles with deep-set brown glochids, one to three flat spines from the upper areoles, 1–3cm long and about 3mm broad. The flowers are whitish, 3–3.5cm across, by day in summer. Backeberg also records a variety *longispina* which could be the plant shown, found in San Juan. Requires full sun; enriched mineral-based compost; minimum temperature 10°C (50°F). *Argentina.*

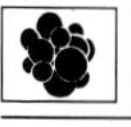    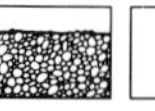

▼

MAMMILLARIA **ALBESCENS** Tiegel
Syn: *Dolichothele albescens* (Tiegel) Backeb.

Possibly a variety of *M. camptotricha* Dams. A green clustering species, each globular stem has prominent tubercles up to 2cm long bearing four to six golden-yellow spines 8mm–1.5cm in length. Day flowering in early summer, the flowers are 2cm long, 1.8cm across when expanded, with greenish-white sepals and white petals. Requires bright light; normal cactus compost; minimum temperature 7°C (45°F). *Mexico (Queretaro).*

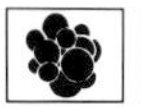    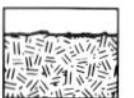 

MAMMILLARIA **ALBIARMATA** Böed.

A solitary plant, globular with a slightly flattened crown, the stems are green, up to 4cm broad, 1.5cm high. There are 20–25 whitish spines, 2–5mm long, all radials. Flowers are diurnal, appearing in summer; they are 2cm long and across, the creamy-white petals having a pale-brownish median line. Requires a sunny position; normal cactus compost; minimum temperature 10°C (50°F). *Mexico (Coahuila near Saltillo).*

MAMMILLARIA **ALBILANATA** Backeb.

Backeberg's *M. fuauxiana* is now considered synonymous. Globular plants, usually solitary but likely to offset with age. The greenish stem, up to 15cm high, 8cm in diameter, is densely covered with whitish wool and spines; the 15–20 radials are 2–4mm long and the two to four centrals 2–3mm in length with a brownish tip. Flowering is in summer, and diurnal. The blooms are quite small, rich carmine and about 7mm long. Needs full sun; very porous cactus compost with a little lime added; minimum temperature 10°C (50°F). *Mexico (Guerrero).*

    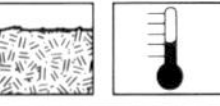

MAMMILLARIA **ARMILLATA** K. Brand.

A narrowly columnar plant, solitary or clustering, it is about 30cm high, 4.5cm wide, and dull green. There are nine to fifteen whitish or yellowish radial spines up to 1.2cm long and one to four centrals to 2cm in length. The flowers, which are diurnal, are pale pink or creamy white, 1.2cm long, 2cm across, appearing in mid-summer. Requires a bright, sunny position; normal cactus compost; minimum temperature 10°C (50°F). *Mexico (Baja).*

MAMMILLARIA **ALBICOMA** Böed.

A very attractive clustering species, each greenish stem is up to 5cm high, 3cm wide. The spines are numerous, white and hair-like, and totally cover the plants; of these there are 30–40 or more radials and one to four centrals, all to about 1cm in length, the centrals often with reddish tips. Flowers are greenish yellow to creamy white and about 1.5cm long, blooming by day in summer. Requires a position in good light, not necessarily full sun; normal cactus compost; minimum temperature 10°C (50°F). *Mexico (Tamaulipas).*

   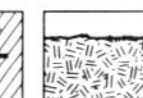 

MAMMILLARIA **ANNIANA** Glass & Foster

A small, solitary, globular plant only discovered in 1979. The rich-green stem, 1–5cm high, 1.5–5cm in diameter, has tubercles arranged in eight to thirteen spirals. Areoles are yellowish white, bearing about 14 pale yellowish-white radial spines to 1cm long, and five to nine golden-yellow centrals to 1.2cm in length. Flowers are diurnal, in summer, pale yellow or greenish yellow and up to 6mm wide when fully open. Needs a bright position, which is essential; normal cactus compost; minimum temperature 10°C (50°F). *Mexico (Tamaulipas).*

    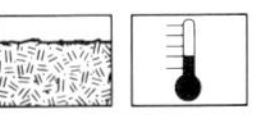

MAMMILLARIA **AUREILANATA** Backeb.

A solitary, globular plant, dark green in colour, up to 7.5cm tall and broad. The areoles have whitish, almost silky spines appearing rather woolly, of which 25–30 are radials to 1.5cm in length; there are no centrals. It flowers during daylight in summer. Requires very bright light; normal cactus compost; minimum temperature 10°C (50°F). *Mexico (San Luis Potosi).*

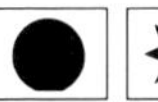   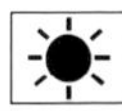 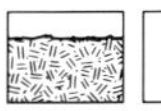 

MAMMILLARIA **BACKEBERGIANA var. ERNESTII** (Fittkau) Glass & Foster
Syn: *Mammillaria ernestii* Fittkau

A globular plant, occasionally offsetting, to about 6cm thick. It has dark-green tubercles tipped with areoles bearing seven to eight yellowish radial spines with brownish tips and one upward-pointing brownish central, all varying from 5mm to 1cm long. The purplish-red flowers are about 1.8cm long set around the crown of the plant. It is day flowering in summer. Requires bright light; normal cactus compost; minimum temperature 10°C (50°F). *Mexico (Federal State).*

▲

MAMMILLARIA **BARBATA** Engelm.

Globular plants, often clustering. Each stem is apple green, 3–5cm in diameter, with numerous, wide-spreading, slender spines consisting of 50–60 white radials, often with brownish tips, 6–8mm long, and one or two brown hooked centrals to 1.5cm in length. A summer, day-flowering species, the flowers are pale straw-coloured and 1.5–2cm long. Requires a sunny location; normal cactus compost; minimum temperature 7°C (45°F). *Mexico (Chihuahua).*

MAMMILLARIA **BALSASOIDES** Craig
Syn: *Mammillaria beneckei*

Closely allied to, possibly synonymous with, *M. beneckei* Ehrenb. It is a solitary, globular plant about 7cm in diameter with a few long bristles in the axils of the tubercles. The radial spines are white, 10–11 in number, and about 6mm long; there are four centrals to 9mm in length. Day flowering, in summer, the flowers are 4cm across, orange with green outer segments. Needs fairly bright light; normal cactus compost; minimum temperature 10°C (50°F). *Mexico (Guerrero).*

MAMMILLARIA **BAUMII** Böed.
Syn: *Dolichothele baumii* (Böed.) Werd. & Buxb.

An attractive white-spined clustering species with slightly elongating stems up to 8cm high, 3–6cm wide. It has prominent tubercles, and initially white woolly axils. Areoles bear 30–35 white, thread-like radial spines 1cm long and five to six pale-yellowish centrals to 1.8cm. Flowers are diurnal in summer, bright yellow, they are 2.5–3cm long and across when fully open. Requires slight shade; normal cactus compost; minimum temperature 10°C (50°F). *Mexico (Tamaulipas).*

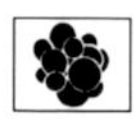     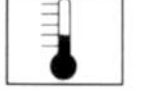

MAMMILLARIA **BENECKEI** Ehrenb.
Syn: *Dolichothele beneckei* (Ehrenb.) Backeb.; *Oehmea nelsonii* (Br. & R.) Buxb.

M. guiengolensis Bravo is considered synonymous. Stems are globular to elongating and clustering; they are covered with yellowish-green tubercles and are slightly woolly in the axils. There are 12–15 white radial spines with blackish tips, and usually two to six darker centrals with one hooked. Flowers are diurnal in early to mid-summer; these are bright yellow, 3–4cm across. Requires bright light; normal cactus compost; minimum temperature 10°C (50°F). *Mexico (Guerrero).*

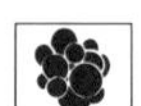    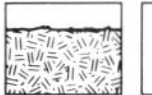 

MAMMILLARIA **BLOSSFELDIANA** Böed.
Syn: *Mammillaria shurliana* Gat.

A globular, solitary species about 4cm in diameter. It is dark green with close-set areoles bearing 15–20 yellowish, black-tipped radial spines 5–7mm long and three to four black centrals 1cm in length, one being hooked. Flowers are diurnal, in early summer, and are about 3.5cm long, 2cm across, pale pinkish with a deep carmine-red centre stripe. Requires bright light; normal cactus compost; minimum temperature 13°C (55°F). *Mexico (Baja).*

     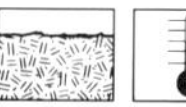 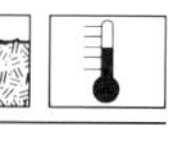

MAMMILLARIA **BOCASANA** Poselg.

A dark bluish-green, freely clustering globular species, each stem is 4–5cm in diameter. Tubercles are fairly close-set up to 1cm long, the axils having many thin white hairs. Areoles produce 25–30 fine, white, spreading radial spines to 2cm long and one or two yellowish-brown centrals of similar length, one hooked. Flowers are diurnal, in summer, yellowish white with a reddish median line and petals that are often tipped red. Requires very slight shade; normal cactus compost with a little lime added; minimum temperature 10°C (50°F). *Mexico (San Luis Potosi).*

MAMMILLARIA **BOCASANA** Poselg. **var. MULTILANATA** hort.

This is similar in most respects to the species, but the dense wool gives it particular significance. Requirements are the same as for the species. *Mexico (San Luis Potosi).*

MAMMILLARIA **BOMBYCINA** Quehl.

Globular plants to about 7cm high, 5–6cm in diameter, forming large clumps. They have somewhat cone-shaped tubercles and dense white wool in the axils. Areoles bear 30–40 whitish, thin radial spines 8mm in length and four yellowish or reddish-brown centrals up to 1cm long, the lower one being hooked, 2cm in length. Flowers are reddish purple, about 1.5cm long and wide, appearing by day in mid-summer. Requires full sun; normal cactus compost; minimum temperature 10°C (50°F). *Mexico (San Luis Potosi, Coahuila).*

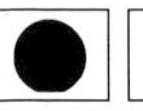

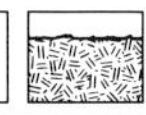

MAMMILLARIA **BOOLII** Linds.

A very small globular, solitary species to 3.5cm high, 3cm in diameter. It has roundish tubercles, woolly axils and areoles with about 20 whitish radial spines 1.5cm long, and one brown, hooked central to 2cm in length. Day flowering in summer, the flowers are pinkish red and about 2.5cm or little more long and across. Requires a very bright position; normal cactus compost with a little lime added; minimum temperature 13°C (55°F). *Mexico (Sonora, San Carlos Bay).*

MAMMILLARIA **CAMPTOTRICHA** Dams.
Syn: *Dolichothele camptotricha* (Dams) Tiegel

A globular plant which clusters freely, about 7cm in diameter. The type species has about four to eight bristly, yellowish radial spines over 2.5cm long but no centrals. That depicted is a peculiar form with much shorter spines. Flowers are white, about 2cm long, 1cm across; they are diurnal, in spring and summer. Requires full sun; normal cactus compost; minimum temperature 10°C (50°F). *Mexico (Queretaro).*

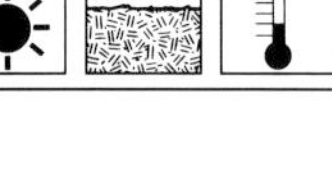

MAMMILLARIA **CAMPTOTRICHA**
cv. 'Mme Marnier' Glass & Foster

This is just one of a number of forms of this quite variable species, and the varietal title cannot be upheld. It is only a name used in certain catalogues in describing this very attractive plant.

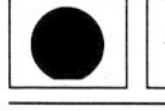

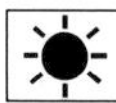
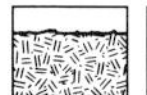

MAMMILLARIA **CANDIDA** Scheidw.
Syn: *Mammillaria ortiz-rubiona* (Bravo) Werd.

The plants are solitary or clustering, globular becoming elongated, and 6–12cm thick. There are bluish-green tubercles and the axils have four to seven white bristles. Round, woolly areoles carry 50 white, spreading radial spines and six to twelve pinkish-white centrals, 5–9mm long. Day-flowering in summer, and are about 2cm long, rose pink with white margins. Slight shade; normal cactus compost; minimum temperature 10°C (50°F). *Mexico (San Luis Potosi).*

   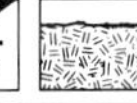 

MAMMILLARIA **CAPENSIS** (Gates) Craig

A slightly clustering species. The stems are olive green, up to 25cm long, 3–5cm thick. The 13 radial spines are white at the base, reddish black at the tips, and 8mm to 1.5cm long, and there is one hooked central, similarly coloured, to 2cm in length. Flowers are pink or whitish, 2cm long and across, appearing by day in summer. Needs sun; normal cactus compost; minimum temperature 13°C (55°F). *Mexico (Baja).*

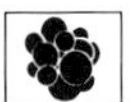    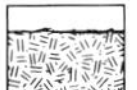 

MAMMILLARIA **CARMENAE** Castan.

A globular, clustering species. Each body is 3–4cm in diameter, often elongating to 5–6cm tall, with wool and bristles in the axils. The whitish areoles have numerous white or yellowish radial spines up to 5mm long, but no centrals. Day flowering in mid-summer, the whitish blooms are about 1cm long and across. Requires a bright location; normal cactus compost; minimum temperature 10°C (50°F). *Mexico (Tamaulipas).*

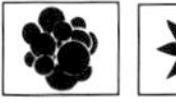     

MAMMILLARIA **CARNEA** Zucc. ex Pfeiff.

A globular species, becoming elongated, either solitary or clustering. It has angular tubercles and yellow, woolly axils. There are four to five pinkish-brown, often black-tipped spines, varying in length from 8mm to 2cm. Flowers are diurnal in summer. These are pale pink with a darker median line on the petals, 1.5–2cm long, 1.2–1.5cm across, and are followed by a brilliant display of red fruits (shown here). Requires full sun; normal cactus compost; minimum temperature 10°C (50°F). *Mexico (Hidalgo, Guerrero, Puebla and Oaxaca).*

MAMMILLARIA **CARRETII** Rebut ex K. Sch.
Syn: *Mammillaria saffordii* (Br. & R.) Bravo

A small roundish species, becoming slightly elongated, usually solitary, but sometimes offsetting from the base. The tubercles are tipped with areoles producing 14–15 yellowish radial spines up to 1.3cm long and one brown, hooked central to 1.6cm in length. Flowers, diurnal in summer, are white or pale yellowish with a faint pink central stripe. They are slightly scented, and up to 2.5cm long, 1.5cm across. Requires bright light; normal cactus compost; minimum temperature 10°C (50°F). *Mexico (Nuevo Leon).*

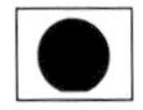    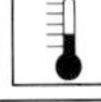

▲

MAMMILLARIA **CHIONOCEPHALA** Purp.
Syn: *Mammillaria ritterana* Böed.

A solitary, globular plant, later developing offsets to form clusters. The bluish-green stems are up to 12cm high and wide, with four-edged tubercles and thick white woolly axils. There are 22 24 white radial spines about 8mm long, and two to six white or brownish centrals to 6mm in length, tipped black and hooked. The flowers are white to pale pink with a reddish median line on the petals; by day in summer. Requires full sun; normal cactus compost with lime added; minimum temperature 10°C (50°F). *Mexico (Coahuila, Durango).*

MAMMILLARIA **CHICA** Reppenhagen
Syn: *Mammillaria aguirrei* nomen nudum

Bright-green globular plants, rarely clustering, 4–5cm high and 3–4cm thick. The tubercles are cylindrical, the axils slightly woolly. Areoles bear 35–50 whitish radial spines 3–5mm long and there are one or two similarly coloured centrals tipped dark brown and hooked, 5–6mm long. Day flowering in mid-summer, the flowers are reddish white, sometimes more yellowish with a reddish median line, and about 1.5cm long. Requires sun; normal cactus compost; minimum temperature 10°C (50°F). *Mexico (Queretaro).*

MAMMILLARIA **COLLINA** Purp.

Possibly a synonym of *M. haageana* Pfeiff. A greyish-green globular species up to 13cm diameter, having a rather flattened top, with cylindrical tubercles and axils scarcely woolly. Areoles have 16–18 straight, white radial spines 4mm long, and one or two white, brown-tipped centrals to 8mm in length. Flowers are pinkish red, 1.5–2cm long, and are diurnal in summer. Requires full sun; normal cactus compost; minimum temperature 10°C (50°F). *Mexico (Puebla).*

MAMMILLARIA **COLLINSII** (Br. & R.) Orc.

A group-forming species, each globular head is about 6cm diameter, greenish brown to purplish with woolly and bristly axils. The areoles bear yellowish spines: about seven radials 5–7mm long with brownish tips, and one long central to 1.2cm. Flowering in daytime in early to mid-summer, the flowers are yellowish with a pink centre stripe, and about 1.5cm long and wide. Requires full sun; normal cactus compost with a little lime added; minimum temperature 13°C (55°F). *Mexico (Oaxaca).*

MAMMILLARIA **COMPRESSA** DC.
Syn: *Mammillaria sietziana* Mart.

A most variable species. The more or less globular plant readily offsets to form large clusters, each head about 8cm wide. The prominent tubercles have white woolly, bristly axils and areoles bearing two to six white or pale-brownish radial spines 2–7mm long. Flowers are diurnal in summer, and are deep purplish red, up to 1.5cm long and across. Requires full sun; normal cactus compost; minimum temperature 10°C (50°F). *Mexico (San Luis Potosi, Queretaro).*

MAMMILLARIA **CRUCIGERA** Mart.

A partially elongating, clustering species. Each head is about 4cm across, dark brownish green with close-set tubercles, and has white woolly axils and areoles bearing 24 or more minute white radial spines 2mm long with four to five yellowish centrals of similar length. Flowering is in summer, and is diurnal; the flowers are very small, pinkish purple. Careful watering is essential. Requires full sun; normal cactus compost with lime added; minimum temperature 13°C (55°F). *Mexico (Oaxaca, Puebla, Hidalgo, San Luis Potosi).*

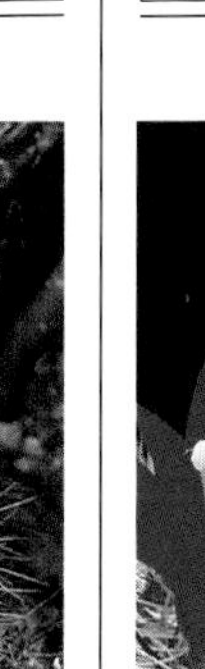

MAMMILLARIA **DECIPIENS** Scheidw.
Syn: *Dolichothele decipiens* (Scheidw.) Tiegel

A dark greyish-green globular, clustering species with tubercles about 1cm long, and woolly axils with about four bristles. The areoles bear seven to eight pale yellowish or whitish radial spines 1cm long and one or two yellowish, brownish-tipped centrals up to 1.8cm in length. Flowers are diurnal, in summer; they are 1.5–2cm long, white with a pinkish-red median line. Requires bright light; normal cactus compost; minimum temperature 10°C (50°F). *Mexico (San Luis Potosi).*

MAMMILLARIA **DEHERDTIANA** Farwig

A solitary, globose species, with a compressed crown, up to 2.5cm high, 4.5cm wide with woolly axils. The white areoles carry 33–36 pale-yellowish or white radial spines 3–6mm long and one to six dark reddish-brown centrals 3–7mm long, often absent. Flowering in early to mid-summer, diurnal; pale pinkish violet with a darker centre stripe and tip to the petals, about 5cm diameter, and on a tube 2cm in length. Requires a sunny position; normal cactus compost; minimum temperature 13°C (55°F). *Mexico (Oaxaca).*

MAMMILLARIA **DEHERDTIANA var. DODSONII** (Bravo) Glass & Foster
Syn: *Mammillaria dodsonii* Bravo

A high-altitude plant, similar in shape and size to the species. Areoles bear 20–21 whitish, curved radial spines to 1.8cm long and three to five brownish centrals 1–2cm in length. Flowers are diurnal; they are a deeper rose violet, fading to a lighter shade, but with a prominent protruding white style. Requirements are the same as for the species. *Mexico (Oaxaca).*

MAMMILLARIA **DENSISPINA** (Coult.) Orc.
Syn: *Cactus densispina* Coult.

A globular, solitary plant. The tubercles are conical, the axils only woolly for a time, and the areoles bear about 25 yellow or brown radial spines to 1.3cm long and reddish-brown centrals to 2cm in length. Flowering by day, early to mid-summer, with sulphur-yellow inner petals, the outer ones sometimes reddish; they are about 1cm long, 2cm across. Requires a sunny position; normal cactus compost; minimum temperature 10°C (50°F). *Mexico (San Luis Potosi, Queretaro).*

MAMMILLARIA **DUOFORMIS** Craig & Dawson

Somewhat cylindrical, often clustering; 3–4cm thick, and up to 9cm high. The tubercles are conical, the axils with few bristles, while the areoles bear 18–20 whitish, radial spines up to 7mm long and four blackish-brown centrals to 1.2cm in length. Flowers appear by day in summer, red, about 1.5cm long, 1.2cm across. Requires very bright light; normal cactus compost with a little lime; minimum temperature 10°C (50°F). *Mexico (Puebla to Oaxaca).*

MAMMILLARIA **ECHINARIA** DC.

A clustering species which is closely allied to both *M. elongata* and *M. gracilis* and possibly synonymous or a variety of one or the other. The stems, up to about 10cm tall, 3–4cm thick, are armed with many yellowish radial spines and three to five centrals, the latter being up to 1.5cm long. Flowers are a pale yellow, about 1cm long and across, and appear by day in summer. Requires full sun; normal cactus compost; minimum temperature 10°C (50°F). *Mexico (Hidalgo).*

MAMMILLARIA **DISCOLOR** Haw.

Globular or slightly cylindrical pale bluish-green plants, solitary or clustering, 4–7cm high and 4–5cm wide. The tubercles are conical, the axils without wool or bristles. Areoles have 16–20 white radial spines to 1cm long, and five to eight yellowish centrals, sometimes brownish, of similar length. Flowers are diurnal, in summer; about 2cm long, 1.5cm across, yellow with a reddish centre line on the outer petals, sometimes pink with a deeper median line. Requires full sun; normal cactus compost; minimum temperature 10°C (50°F). *Mexico (Puebla).*

MAMMILLARIA **DUWEI** Rogozinski & P. J. Braun

Closely allied to *M. nana* Backeb. The plants are solitary, up to 1.5cm tall, 2–2.5cm in diameter, and fresh green in colour, with cylindrical tubercles and woolly, bristly axils. Areoles have 30–40 fine, hairy whitish radial spines and one or two centrals 4–6mm in length. Day flowering in summer, the flowers are pale yellowish, about 1.5cm in diameter. Needs a sunny position; normal cactus compost; minimum temperature 10°C (50°F). *Mexico (San Luis Potosi, Guanajuato).*

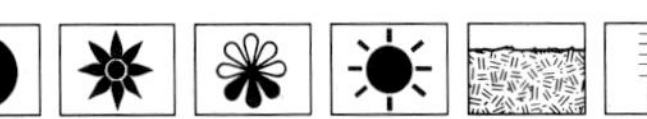

MAMMILLARIA **EICHLAMII** Quehl.

A freely clustering species. Each head is yellowish green, about 15cm high, 4–6cm thick, with slightly angular, conical tubercles and whitish or yellowish woolly axils. The areoles bear seven to eight whitish radial spines tipped with black and 3–5mm long, and one yellowish central tipped with red and up to 1cm in length. Flowers are creamy yellow with a dark reddish line down the centre of the outer petals, and are day flowering in early summer. Requires full sun; normal cactus compost; minimum temperature 13°C (55°F). *Mexico (Chiapas), Guatemala.*

MAMMILLARIA **ELEGANS** DC.
Syn: *Mammillaria dealbata* Otto

Synonymous with *M. haageana*. A solitary plant, offsetting in maturity. Globular to cylindrical stems, pale green with a woolly, spiny crown, 5–10cm tall, 5–8cm thick. Close-set tubercles with whitish woolly areoles bearing 25–30 white radial spines 5–6mm long and one or two brown-tipped white centrals to 1cm in length. Day flowering in mid-summer. Carmine red 1.5cm long and 8mm across, followed by red fruits containing brown seeds. Requires full sun; normal cactus compost; minimum temperature 10°C (50°F). *Mexico (Puebla, Hidalgo).*

   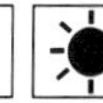  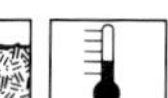

MAMMILLARIA **ELONGATA** DC.

One of the most variable species within the genus. A densely clustering plant, each stem is 1–3cm thick and 6–15cm long, and considerably longer in its habitat. The areoles bear about 20 more or less yellow radial spines, although whitish, reddish or brownish spines can occur. There may be one to three central spines or they may be absent. All are 8mm–1cm long. Flowers are whitish to yellowish, about 1.5cm long, and are diurnal in mid-summer. Best in a bright sunny position; normal cactus compost; kept completely dry autumn and winter; minimum temperature 10°C (50°F). *Mexico (Hidalgo).*

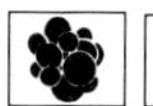   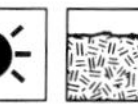 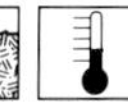

MAMMILLARIA **ELONGATA** DC.

The variously coloured spine formations of this species provide very bright displays. The spines, which range from yellow to brown and are often yellow with differing coloured tips, have given rise to a number of varietal titles within the species. Spines mostly number 15 to 20 from each areole. Bright light is most essential. *Mexico (Hidalgo, Queretaro).*

    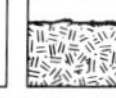 

MAMMILLARIA **ELONGATA** DC. **fma. CRISTATA**

Very occasionally an abnormal growth develops. Unfortunately this gives no guarantee that further such growths will offset from it. Always provide a very bright position.

   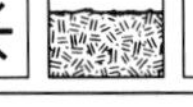 

MAMMILLARIA **ERECTACANTHA** Förster

A globular, solitary species with a dark-green body 9–12cm thick. The areoles are of white wool when young, bearing nine to fifteen yellowish-white, brown-tipped radial spines up to 6mm long and one brown, black-tipped central 6–8mm in length. A day flowering plant in mid-summer, it requires full sun; normal cactus compost; minimum temperature 13°C (55°F). *Mexico (Hidalgo etc.).*

   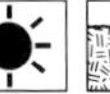  

▲

▲

MAMMILLARIA **ERYTHROSPERMA** Böed.
Syn: *Mammillaria multiformis* (Br. & R.) Böed.

A clustering species of small globular or slightly elongating stems of dull green. The tubercles are cylindrical and the axils have no wool, but bristles only. Whitish areoles bear 15–20 white radial spines, yellowish at the base and 8–10mm long and one to three hooked yellow centrals with brown tips, about 1cm in length. A summer flowering plant, the flowers are carmine with pinkish edges to the petals, 1.5cm long and wide, and are diurnal. Requires a very bright position; normal cactus compost; minimum temperature 10°C (50°F). *Mexico (San Luis Potosi).*

   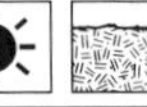 

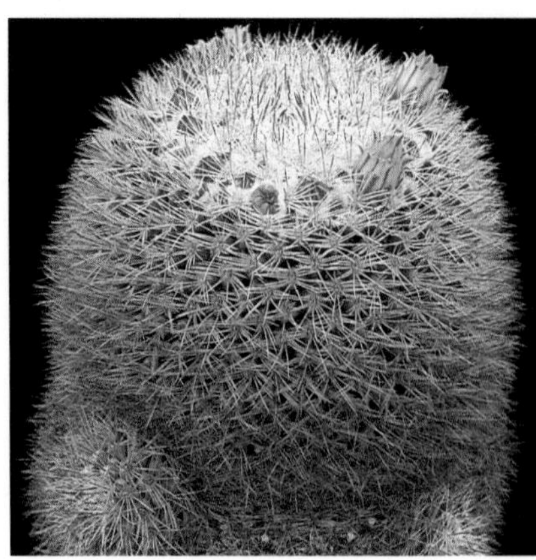

MAMMILLARIA **EVERMANNIANA** (Br. & R.) Orc.

A greyish-green, mostly solitary species, globular, and 5–7cm in diameter. Any offsetting occurs from around the base. The tubercles are conical with whitish wool and bristles in the axils. Areoles carry 12–15 whitish, thin radial spines to 1cm long and two to three centrals of similar length and colour, all tipped with brown. Flowers are diurnal in summer. These are yellow with a reddish-purplish median line 1–1.5cm long, 1cm across. Requires full sun; normal cactus compost; minimum temperature 13°C (55°F). *Mexico (Cerralbo Island).*

MAMMILLARIA **FITTKAUI** Glass & Foster

A freely clustering plant, each pale-green stem is about 5cm thick. The tubercles are conical and the axils are without wool or bristles. The whitish areoles have seven to nine white radial spines 6–7mm long, occasionally minutely brownish-tipped, and there are four brown central spines with a whitish base, three straight, one hooked. The flowers, day flowering in mid-summer, are white to pale pink with a deeper pinkish median line, and are 1.5cm long, 1cm across. Requires bright light; a permeable, enriched mineral compost; minimum temperature 13°C (55°F). *Mexico (Jalisco).*

MAMMILLARIA **FORMOSA** Galeoti ex Scheidw.

A dull-green globular to elongated plant, solitary at first but later offsetting, and up to 8cm in diameter. It has short pyramidal tubercles and white woolly axils. The areoles bear 20–25 short, thin radial spines 3–6mm long and four to six pinkish centrals with black tips, up to 8mm. Summer flowering and diurnal, the flowers are about 1.5cm long and wide, pinkish purple with pale pink edges. Requires full sun; normal cactus compost; minimum temperature 10°C (50°F). *Mexico (San Luis Potosi, Hidalgo).*

MAMMILLARIA **GAUMERI** (Br. & R.) Orc.

A dullish-green, globular or short-cylindrical plant, 10–12cm tall. The tubercles are slightly angular, with bare axils, and the areoles carry 10–12 or more brownish-tipped, white radial spines 5–7mm long, and one long brown central to 1cm. Summer-flowering, and diurnal, the flowers are greenish white or pink, 1–1.4cm long, 6–8mm across. Needs good light, which is essential; normal cactus compost; minimum temperature 13°C (55°F). *Mexico (Yucatan).*

    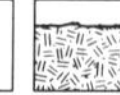 

MAMMILLARIA **GARESSII** Cowper

Closely allied to *M. barbata* Engelm. A small clustering plant with each stem 3–8cm high, 2.5–5cm wide. There are 16–22 whitish-pink radial spines which usually have minute blackish dots, and are about 4–8mm long, and one or two hooked central spines tipped pinkish orange, up to 1.5cm in length. Flowers are white or pink with greenish outer segments, 2.5cm long, 1.5cm across, and are diurnal, appearing in summer. Requires slight shade; normal cactus compost; minimum temperature 10°C (50°F). *Mexico (Chihuahua).*

     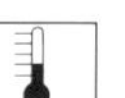

MAMMILLARIA **GLAREOSA** Böed
Syn: *Mammillaria dawsonii* (Houghton) Craig

A round plant with a flattened top, 4–6cm in diameter, and dark green. The tubercles are prominently four-angled, the axils slightly woolly, and the areoles bear nine to ten whitish or brownish radial spines up to 6mm long, with one brown central of similar length. Flowers are a pale greenish yellow with a reddish-brown median line on the outer petals, each 1–1.2cm long and across. They bloom by day in summer. Requires full sun; normal cactus compost; minimum temperature 10°C (50°F). *Mexico (Baja).*

    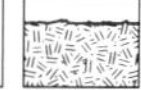 

MAMMILLARIA **GLASSII** R. Foster

Small globular plants which form clusters. Each head scarcely exceeds 2–3cm in diameter, and there are many whitish, hair-like bristles proceeding from the axils, which with the spines densely cover the whole plant. The areoles carry 50–60 white, hairy radial spines up to 1.5cm long and six to eight smaller sub-centrals with one slightly hooked brown central. Flowers are a very pale pink, 1.4cm long, to 5mm across, appearing by day in summer. Requires partial shade; a permeable, enriched mineral compost; minimum temperature 13°C (55°F). *Mexico (Nuevo Leon).*

   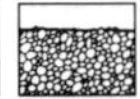 

MAMMILLARIA **GLASSII var. NOMINIS-DULCIS** Lau

A newly introduced variety of the species with whitish radial spines and brownish-purple centrals. The flowers are a deep purplish red with darker centre stripe, about 1.3cm long, 1.5cm across. Requirements are the same as for the species. *Mexico (Nuevo Leon).*

       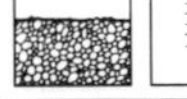

MAMMILLARIA **GRUSONII** Rünge

A large globular plant up to about 25cm in diameter. Dull greenish in colour, it has four-angled tubercles and axils which are woolly at first, this quickly dispersing. The areoles carry about 14 straight, reddish-brown radial spines which become white with age, 6–8mm long, and two to three similar centrals of equal length. Flowering in summer, the blooms are diurnal, pale yellow or pinkish with a deeper pinkish median stripe, about 2.5cm long and across. Requires full sun; normal cactus compost; minimum temperature 10°C (50°F). *Mexico (Coahuila).*

     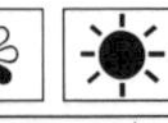 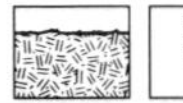  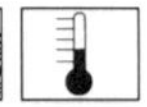

MAMMILLARIA **GLASSII var. ASCENSIONIS** (Reppenhagen) Glass & Foster
Syn: *Mammillaria ascensionis* Reppenhagen

Small globular plants 2–3cm in diameter, forming quite large clusters. In most respects it is similar to the species, but the whitish to pale pink flowers are decidedly larger. Requirements are the same as for the species. *Mexico (Nuevo Leon).*

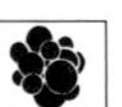    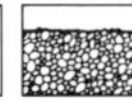 

MAMMILLARIA **GUELZOWIANA** Werd.
Syn: *Krainzia guelzowiana* (Werd.) Backeb.

A choice globular species, clustering with age. Each head is about 7cm tall, 6cm thick and there is no wool or bristles in the axils. Radial spines are white, very fine and hair-like, 60–80 to an areole and about 1.5cm long. There are one to three reddish or yellowish centrals, often hooked, and 1.1–1.6cm long. Flowers are diurnal in summer, very large – up to 5cm long, 6cm across, and brilliant carmine pink. Requires very careful, almost meagre watering; full sun; normal cactus compost; minimum temperature 13°C (55°F). *Mexico (Durango).*

MAMMILLARIA **GUILLAUMINIANA** Backeb.

A globular species up to 5.5cm high, 3–5cm in diameter, and clustering freely. The stems are dark or dull greenish with conical tubercles, and bare axils. Areoles bear 30 or more white radial spines 6–7mm long, and four to five centrals of similar length, one of which is hooked, with a reddish-brownish tip. Day flowering in summer, the flowers are about 1cm long and wide, with pink inner petals, and white outer petals with a deep pinkish median line. Requires bright light; normal cactus compost; minimum temperature 13°C (55°F). *Mexico (Durango).*

    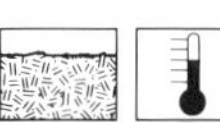 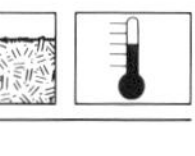

MAMMILLARIA **HALEI** K. Brandegee
Syn: *Cochemiea halei* (K. Brandegee) Walt.

The stems are 30–50cm tall, 5–7.5cm thick, and form clusters. The tubercles are short with woolly axils and the areoles bear 10–20 pale-brownish radial spines up to 1.5cm long and three to four centrals to 3.5cm which are always straight. Flowers appear in early to mid-summer, and are diurnal; rich scarlet, they are 2.5–5cm long. Needs full sun; normal cactus compost; minimum temperature 13°C (55°F). *Mexico (Baja, Magdalena Isl.).*

    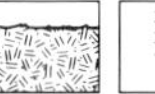 

MAMMILLARIA **GUERRERONIS** (Bravo) Böed.

Stems are cylindrical, quickly forming clusters. They are 40–60cm tall in habitat, and about 6cm in diameter, dull greyish green with conical tubercles and white woolly axils with 15–20 bristles. There are 20–30 white or pinkish radial spines up to 1cm long, and four brown-tipped centrals to 1.5cm in length, occasionally hooked. Flowers are red; they are diurnal, appearing in summer. Requires full sun; normal cactus compost; minimum temperature 13°C (55°F). *Mexico (Guerrero).*

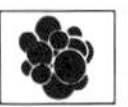    

MAMMILLARIA **HAHNIANA** Werd.

Green globular plants which become group-forming, 9–20cm high, 10–12cm thick, coated completely with long white hairs, spines and bristles. There are conical tubercles and white bristly axils, and the areoles bear 20–30 white, hair-like radial spines up to 1.5cm long and one to three or more white centrals with often darker tips, to 8mm in length. The flowers are carmine red, 1.5–2cm long and wide, and are diurnal, appearing in summer. Requires full sun; normal cactus compost with lime added; minimum temperature 10°C (50°F). *Mexico (Queretaro, Guanajuato).*

MAMMILLARIA **HEIDIAE** Krainz

Small globular plants about 3cm high, 5.5cm wide, soon clustering. The tubercles are cylindrical with axils having one to five white bristles 1cm long. There are about 16–24 white radial spines about 1cm long and one or two centrals which are slightly longer and hooked, and are yellow with brown tips. Flowers occur in summer, and are diurnal; they are yellowish green and up to 3cm long, 2.5cm in diameter. Requires sun; normal cactus compost; minimum temperature 10°C (50°F). *Mexico (Puebla).*

 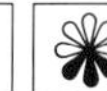   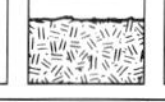 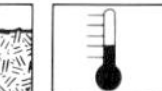

MAMMILLARIA **HERNANDEZII** Glass & Foster

A small, somewhat globose plant 2.5–4.5cm in diameter. The pyramidal-shaped tubercles are arranged spirally around the stems, and have woolly axils. Areoles bear 17–25 white radial spines 1.2–2.2mm long. Flowering in summer, the plant is diurnal, with cerise to pale magenta blooms about 2cm long and wide. Requires bright light; normal cactus compost; minimum temperature 13°C (55°F). *Mexico (Oaxaca).*

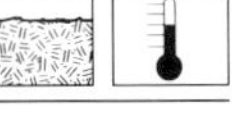

MAMMILLARIA **HEYDERI** Mühlpf.

Dull green and mostly solitary, this is a more or less globular plant with stems 10cm high, 8–10cm wide. The tubercles are small and pyramid-shaped with woolly axils when young. There are 15–22 white radial spines with brown tips, very bristly and 5–8mm long, and one brown central about 6mm in length. Day flowering in summer, the flowers are about 2cm long, creamy white; red fruits. Requires sun; normal cactus compost; minimum temperature 10°C (50°F). *USA (Texas), Mexico (Northern areas).*

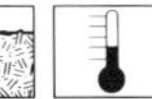

MAMMILLARIA **HUMBOLDTII** Ehrenb.

A solitary, rarely clustering species with more or less globular stems about 5cm in diameter. The tubercles are very small with bristly, woolly axils. Areoles have up to 80 or even more white radial spines, 4–6mm long, but no centrals. Summer flowering, it is diurnal; the flowers are purplish red, about 1.5cm long and wide. Careful watering is essential. Requires full sun; normal cactus compost with a little lime added; minimum temperature 13°C (55°F). *Mexico (Hidalgo).*

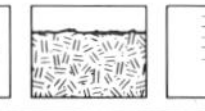

MAMMILLARIA **HERRERAE** Werd.

The plants are solitary or clustering, globular, and 2–3cm thick. The small tubercles are densely covered with numerous white or pale-grey radial spines about 1.5mm long: there are more than 100 to each small areole. Day flowering in summer, the flowers are pale pink to reddish violet, 2–2.5cm long, and up to 3cm in diameter. Careful watering is essential. Requires full sun; a porous enriched cactus compost; minimum temperature 13°C (55°F). *Mexico (San Luis Potosi, Querataro).*

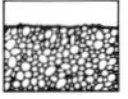

MAMMILLARIA **JALISCANA** (Br. & R.) Böed.

A choice globular species 5–6cm in diameter and dull green in colour with cylindrical tubercles and bare axils. The areoles have about 30 white radial spines about 8mm long and four to eight reddish-brown, sometimes almost black centrals up to 9mm in length, the lowest being hooked. Flowers are pink to pale purple, about 1cm in diameter, and are fragrant. These are diurnal, appearing in summer. Requires full sun; normal cactus compost; minimum temperature 10°C (50°F). *Mexico (Guadalajara).*

MAMMILLARIA **KARWINSKIANA** Mart.
Syn: *Mammillaria confusa* (Br. & R.) Orc.; *Mammillaria nejapensis* Craig & Dawson

More or less round or semi-cylindrical plants which cluster from the base, each head being 7–9cm in diameter. Tubercles are pyramidal with wool and bristles in the axils. Spines are brownish to greyish, made up of three to six radials and occasionally one central. Flowers are white with a red median line, 2cm long, 1.5cm across, and appear by day in summer. Requires sun; normal cactus compost; minimum temperature 10°C (50°F). *Mexico (Oaxaca).*

    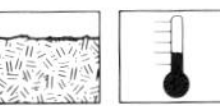

MAMMILLARIA **KRAEHENBUEHLII** Krainz

A clustering species with somewhat rounded individual stems about 3–12cm long, 3.5cm wide. The tubercles are rather angular, and the axils are without bristles or wool. It has 18–24 whitish radial spines with brown tips, 3–8mm long, usually one central of similar colouring and slightly longer. Flowers, which are carmine red, about 1.8cm long, are day flowering in summer. Requires very slight shade; normal cactus compost with lime added; minimum temperature 13°C (55°F). *Mexico (Oaxaca).*

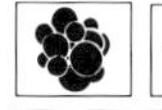    

MAMMILLARIA **JOHNSTONII** Br. & R.

Bluish-green, globular plants about 12cm in diameter, and 20cm high. Tubercles are four-edged, the axils bare. The areoles bear 10–16 or more brown-tipped white radial spines 6–9mm long and two or more dark-brown or blackish central spines 1–2.5cm in length. Flowers are diurnal, occurring in mid-summer, and are about 2cm long and across, white and pale yellowish with a dark median stripe on the outer petals. Requires bright light; normal cactus compost with a little lime added; minimum temperature 10°C (50°F). *Mexico (Sonora, San Carlos Bay).*

   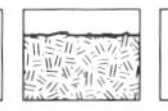 

MAMMILLARIA **KNIPPELIANA** Quehl.

A solitary, globular plant, very rarely clustering. The stems are 5–7cm tall to 5cm wide with white wool and bristles in the axils. There are four to six white spines with red-brown tips, all radials, and up to 3cm long. Flowering in summer, it is diurnal; the blooms are yellowish, with reddish tips and markings to the petals and about 1.5cm long, 1cm wide. Needs bright light; normal cactus compost; minimum temperature 10°C (50°F). *Mexico (Morelos).*

MAMMILLARIA **LASIACANTHA** Engelm.
Syn: *Mammillaria lasiacantha* var. *denudata* Engelm.

A miniature plant with a grey-green globular stem about 4cm in diameter, and covered with soft spines. Tubercles are very small with bare axils. The areoles bear 40–80 hair-like spines in several rows, each 2mm long. Flowers are white with a distinctive red centre stripe to the petals, and about 1.2cm long; they are day flowering, in summer. Requires sun; normal cactus compost plus lime; minimum temperature 10°C (50°F). *Mexico (Northern States), USA (Texas).*

 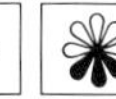   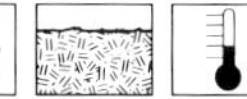

MAMMILLARIA **LAUI** D. R. Hunt

A comparatively recent introduction discovered by Alfred Lau. It is a variable species with roundish stems 4–5cm high and in diameter, frequently clustering, especially in its habitat. The varying forms are suitably named: fma. *laui* has slightly woolly axils, and areoles bearing numerous white, bristle-like radial and central spines, with the centrals usually brown-tipped. Flowers are pinkish purple, about 1cm across, and appear by day, in summer. A high-altitude form requiring sun; normal cactus compost; minimum temperature 13°C (55°F). *Mexico (Tamaulipas).*

 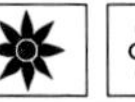    

MAMMILLARIA **LAUI** D. R. Hunt **fma SUBDUCTA**

This is in most respects similar to fma. *laui*, but it comes from lower altitudes up to about 800m. The spines are yellowish or brown and 7–10mm in length, but not as numerous as that described. Flowers, rather bell-shaped, are a slightly paler pinkish purple of similar size. Requirements are the same as for the species.

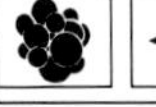    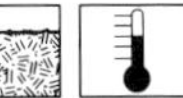

MAMMILLARIA **LENTA** Brandegee

A small globular plant, sometimes clustering. Each stem is 1–2cm high, 4–5cm across, with slender tubercles, conical to 8mm long, and axils with short wool and often one bristle. Areoles bear 30–40 clear-white to pale-yellowish radial spines 3–7mm long, but no centrals. The flowers are white with a pale-purple median line to the petals and about 2cm long, 2.5cm across: they are day flowering, in summer. Requires bright light; normal cactus compost; minimum temperature 10°C (50°F). *Mexico (Coahuila).*

    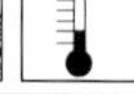

MAMMILLARIA **LAUI** D. R. Hunt **fma DASYACANTHA**

A very high-altitude plant to 1700m. It has fine, hair-like white spines 6–9mm long, the radials and centrals inter-mingling to form a complete covering to the plant. Flowers are almost magenta. Requirements are the same as for the species.

    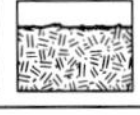 

MAMMILLARIA **LONGIFLORA** (Br. & R.) Berger
Syn: *Krainzia longiflora* (Br. & R.) Backeb.

A globular, clustering species. Each stem is about 8–9cm in diameter, dark green with long tubercles and slightly felted axils. Radial spines are white or pale yellow, 1–1.3cm long, and there are four yellowish or brown centrals of similar length, one of which is hooked. Day flowering in summer, the flowers are in shades of pink with a deeper shade centre line, and up to 4.5cm long, 4cm across. Requires careful watering; sun; normal cactus compost; minimum temperature 10°C (50°F). *Mexico (Durango).*

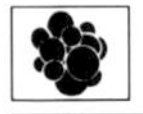    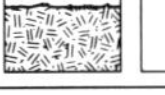 

MAMMILLARIA **LONGIMAMMA** DC.
Syn: *Dolichothele longimamma* (DC.) Br. & R.

Plants are globular, solitary or clustering, bright green. Each stem is 10cm or more in diameter and the tubercles are long, from 2.5–7cm, with slightly felted or bare axils. Areoles have nine to ten fine, white to pale-yellowish radial spines 1.2–1.8cm long and occasionally a single pale-brown central up to 2.5cm in length. Flowers are bright yellow, up to 6cm long and across, in early summer, and are diurnal. Requires good light; normal cactus compost; minimum temperature 10°C (50°F). *Mexico (Hidalgo).*

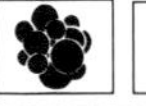    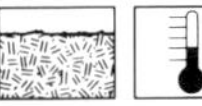 

MAMMILLARIA **MAGNETICOLA** Meyran

Very closely resembles *M. vetula* Mart. It is a small globular, clustering species, about 4cm in diameter, bright green with blunt conical tubercles. Spines are white: 25–30 radials at first, later increasing to 50, and there are four to seven centrals, often more brownish. Flowers are diurnal, and pale yellowish, about 1.5cm across, appearing in summer. Requires bright light; normal cactus compost; minimum temperature 7°C (45°F). *Mexico (Hidalgo).*

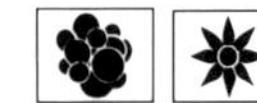 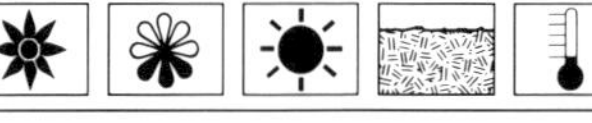

MAMMILLARIA **LONGIFLORA fma STAMPFERI** (Reppenhagen) D. R. Hunt
Syn: *Mammillaria stampferi* Reppenhagen

A high-altitude variant from the same locality. It is similar to the species but has larger tubercles and shorter central spines. The flowers are a soft pale pink and appear by day in summer. Requirements are the same as for the species.

    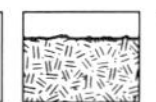 

MAMMILLARIA **LONGIMAMMA var. UBERIFORMIS** (Zucc.) D. R. Hunt
Syn: *Dolichothele uberiformis* (Zucc.) Br. & R.

Similar to the species, but a smaller plant. The tubercles are 3.5cm long and there are fewer spines, three to six radials up to 1.6cm long and no centrals. Flowers are similar to those of the species, about 3.5cm across, and cultivation requirements are the same. *Mexico (Hidalgo).*

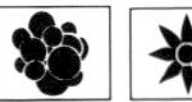 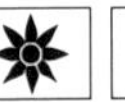  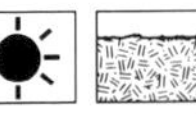 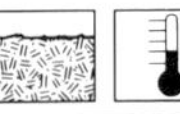

MAMMILLARIA **MAGNIFICA** Buchenau

A globular, becoming elongated, species which clusters from the base. The greyish-green stems are often 20 to 40cm tall, 7–9cm diameter. Axils have white wool and 8–15 bristles and the spines vary in colour: there are 18–24 white to yellowish radials, 3–8mm long and four to eight bright yellowish-brown centrals, the lower one hooked and 3.5–5.5cm long. Flowers appear by day, in summer, and are reddish purple, 2cm long, 1.2cm across. Requires full sun; normal cactus compost; minimum temperature 10°C (50°F). *Mexico (Puebla).*

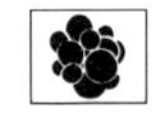 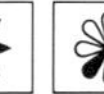  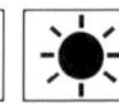 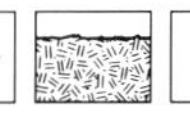 

MAMMILLARIA **MAINIAE** Brandegee

Usually a clustering plant, sometimes solitary, globular or slightly elongated to 10cm high. Tubercles are conical, the axils bare. The areoles have 10–15 yellowish, brown-tipped, radial spines 6mm–1.2cm long and one to three centrals, brown with a darker tip, one of which is hooked and up to 1.5cm long. Flowers are white with a wide red centre stripe; they are 2cm long, 2.5cm across, and are diurnal, appearing in summer. Requires slight shade; normal cactus compost; minimum temperature 7°C (45°F). *Mexico (Sonora).*

MAMMILLARIA **MATUDA** Bravo

The plants are solitary or clustering, each head slightly cylindrical up to 20cm or more high, and 3cm thick. The tubercles are conical with bare axils and there are 18–20 white radial spines with a yellowish base, 2–3mm long, and one pinkish-white central with a reddish tip, 5mm in length. Summer flowering by day, the flowers are purplish brown, about 1.2cm long, the inner petals more pale reddish. Requires bright light; normal cactus compost; minimum temperature 13°C (55°F). *Mexico (Guerrero, Mexico State).*

MAMMILLARIA **MELALEUCA** Karw. ex Salm-Dyck
Syn: *Dolichothele melaleuca* (Karw.) Craig

A globose species 8–10cm wide, occasionally offsetting to form clusters. Tubercles are conical to cylindrical and about 1cm long, 7mm thick with bare axils, and there are six to nine radial spines up to 1.5cm long, the upper ones brown, the lower ones white, and one brown central of similar length, often absent. Flowering diurnally in mid-summer, the bright yellow blooms are 2–3cm long and across. Requires sun; normal cactus compost; minimum temperature 13°C (55°F). *Mexico (Tamaulipas).*

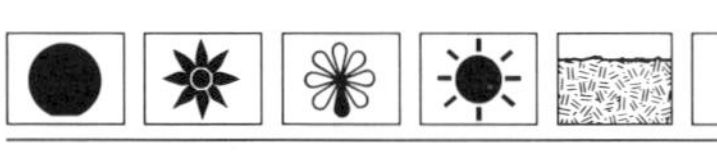

MAMMILLARIA **MARKSIANA** Krainz

A globular plant, generally solitary, but occasionally offsetting. Stems are 5cm high, 8cm thick, and covered with four-angled pyramidal tubercles. The areoles are of yellow wool, more so towards the top, and have eight to ten yellowish radial spines 5–8mm long, and one central 8mm in length. Flowering in summer, the plant is diurnal and the flowers yellow or greenish yellow, up to 1.5cm long and across. Requires good light; normal cactus compost; minimum temperature 10°C (50°F). *Mexico (Sinaloa).*

MAMMILLARIA **MAZATLANENSIS** (Rebut) K. Sch. & Gürke

Principally clustering plants, each greyish-green stem is about 12cm high, 4cm thick. The tubercles are rather cone-shaped, and the axils have one or two short bristles. Areoles carry 12–13 thin, white radial spines to 1cm long and three or four reddish-brown centrals up to 1.5cm in length. The bright carmine-red flowers occur in summer, and are diurnal, and about 4cm long. Requires slight shade; normal cactus compost; minimum temperature 10°C (50°F). *Mexico (Mazatlan in Sinaloa).*

MAMMILLARIA **MERCADENSIS** Patoni

Dull greyish-green globular plants, offsetting from the base. Each head is about 5cm thick with more or less cone-shaped tubercles and bare axils. Areoles bear 25–30 white radial spines 5–8mm in length and four to seven reddish centrals 1.5–2.5cm long. Day flowering in early summer, the pale-pink flowers are 1.5–2cm long and wide. Requires full sun; normal cactus compost; minimum temperature 10°C (50°F). *Mexico (Durango).*

MAMMILLARIA **MICROCARPA** Engelm.

The pale-green plants are cylindrical to 15cm high, 3.5–4.5cm wide, and usually clustering, with conical tubercles and bare axils. The areoles carry 18–30 whitish radial spines up to 1.2cm long and one to three reddish-brown, almost black centrals up to 1.8cm in length, one of which is hooked. Summer flowering, and diurnal, the flowers are rose pink, 2.5cm long, 2.8cm across. Requires full sun; normal cactus compost with a little lime added; minimum temperature 10°C (50°F). *Mexico (Sonora, Chihuahua), USA (Arizona).*

MAMMILLARIA **MICROCARPA var. GRAHAMII** (Engelm.) L. Benson
Syn: *Mammillaria grahamii* Engelm.

A globular plant, only rarely offsetting. It is dark green, 5–10cm high, 4.5–11.5cm thick, with small cone-shaped tubercles and bare axils. Spines are pale brownish or whitish, of which 20–35 are radials 6–8mm in length and two to four are centrals, one of which is hooked, 1.2–2.5cm long; these are mostly brownish-tipped. Flowers, diurnal in summer, are pale pink, rarely white, and up to 2.5cm across. Requirements are the same as for the species. *Mexico (Sonora, Chihuahua), USA (Arizona).*

   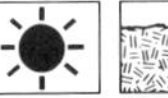 

MAMMILLARIA **MICROCARPA var. OLIVIAE** (Orc.) L. Benson
Syn: *Mammillaria oliviae* Orc.

Very similar to the species, readily clustering, but spines are generally paler, the centrals shorter. The pinkish purple flowers have paler edges to the petals, but the colouring can, however, be variable. Requirements are the same as for the species. *Mexico (Sonora), USA (Arizona).*

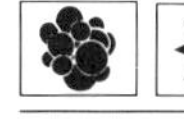     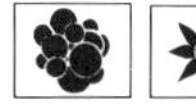  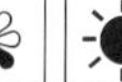  

MAMMILLARIA **MICROTHELE** Mühlpf.

Backeberg gives the habitat as Oaxaca, Mexico. A small greyish-green, clustering species with tubercles about 7mm long. Spines are white, densely covering the whole body of the plant, made up of 22–24 radials, 3–4mm long, and two centrals 2mm in length. It is summer flowering, and diurnal; the blooms are white, and up to 1.5cm long. Needs sun; slightly calcareous cactus compost; minimum temperature 10°C (50°F). *Mexico (East San Luis Potosi).*

    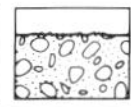 

MAMMILLARIA **MIEGEANA** W. H. Earle

A usually solitary species 8–10cm in diameter, and a dull dark green. The tubercles are closely set, with bare axils except in the crown. Areoles bear 10–11 slightly curved, greyish-white radial spines 8–9mm long, and two, rarely three, brown straight centrals 7–8mm in length. Summer flowering, and diurnal, the flowers are pinkish red or an even deeper shade, particularly towards the centre of the petals; they are about 2cm long and often slightly more across. Requires sun; normal cactus compost; minimum temperature 10°C (50°F). *Mexico (Sonora).*

  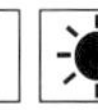   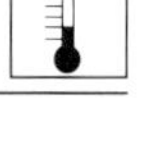

MAMMILLARIA **MOELLERIANA** Böed.

A bright-green globular plant, usually solitary, about 6cm in diameter with somewhat ovoid tubercles and bare axils. Areoles bear 35–40 whitish radial spines 7–9mm long and eight to ten centrals 2cm or more long, the lower two hooked; these are reddish brown, yellowish near the base. Flowering in early to mid-summer, the blooms are diurnal, 1.5cm long and broad, and creamy yellow with a deeper yellow median stripe or pale pink with a deeper centre line. Requires bright sunshine; normal cactus compost; minimum temperature 10°C (50°F). *Mexico (Durango).*

   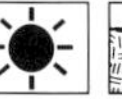 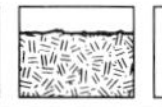 

MAMMILLARIA **MOLLENDORFFIANA** Shurly

A more or less solitary plant, globular becoming elongated to 30cm high, 7–8cm thick. The tubercles are cylindrical, the axils woolly and bristly. Areoles have 24–28 white radial spines up to 5mm long and four to six pale-brownish centrals with darker tips, up to 1.4cm in length. Flowers are about 1cm long, 8mm across, and are purplish red, appearing by day in mid-summer. Requires bright light; normal cactus compost; minimum temperature 10°C (50°F). *Mexico (Hidalgo).*

    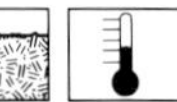

MAMMILLARIA **MOVENSIS** Craig

A greyish-green, somewhat globular species up to about 5cm high, 10cm in diameter with conical tubercles and dense whitish-wool axils. Areoles bear 10–13 more or less pale-brownish radial spines 3mm to 1.5cm long and one to four more reddish-brown centrals 5mm to 2cm in length. Flowers are purplish pink, appearing in summer, and are diurnal. Needs good light; normal cactus compost; minimum temperature 10°C (50°F). *Mexico (Movas).*

▲

▲

MAMMILLARIA **MUEHLENPFORDTII** Först.
Syn: *Mammillaria neopotisina* Craig

A globular, clustering species. Each head is up to 10cm high, 8cm wide, and is dark green, with pyramidal-shaped tubercles and white, woolly and bristly axils. The areoles are white and woolly, with 40–50 white radial spines 2–6mm long and four yellowish centrals varying from 5mm to 3.5cm in length. Flowering is in mid-summer; the small deep-pink flowers are diurnal and 1–1.5cm long, 1cm wide. Requires full sun; normal cactus compost; minimum temperature 13°C (55°F). *Mexico (Queretaro, San Luis Potosi).*

    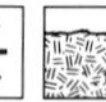 

MAMMILLARIA **MULTIDIGITATA** Radley ex Lindsay

A clump-forming species with stems often to 20cm long, 2–5cm thick. The tubercles are conical and the axils slightly woolly. Areoles bear 15–25 white radial spines 6–8mm long and usually four white, brown-tipped centrals, up to 8mm in length. Day flowering in summer, the flowers are white with a greenish midstripe on the outer petals, and up to 1.5cm long and across. Needs bright light; normal cactus compost; minimum temperature 10°C (50°F). *Mexico (Baja).*

▲

MAMMILLARIA **NANA** Backeb.

Fresh-green, solitary plants about 1.5cm high, 2.5cm in diameter. The tubercles are cylindrical, and the axils have wool and bristles. The whitish areoles bear about 35 white radial spines and one or two brownish centrals up to 5mm long. Flowers appear in early to mid-summer; these are creamy white or pale yellow, 1.5cm wide, about 1cm long, and are diurnal. Requires full sun; normal cactus compost with a little lime added; minimum temperature 10°C (50°F). *Mexico (San Luis Potosi).*

▼

MAMMILLARIA **MYSTAX** Mart.

Plants are solitary or clustering. The greyish-green stems are 15cm high, 10cm in diameter, with four-edged tubercles and white wool and bristles in the axils. Areoles bear five to six or more white, brown-tipped, radial spines 4–8mm long and three to four purplish, becoming grey, centrals mostly 1.5–2cm long, but one up to 7cm in length. The plants are day flowering in summer, with 2.5cm long, 2cm across, purplish-pink blooms, often with paler inner petals. Requires full sun; normal cactus compost; minimum temperature 10°C (50°F). *Mexico (Hidalgo, Oaxaca).*

MAMMILLARIA **NAPINA** Purp.

A globular or clustering species, each head is about 5cm in diameter and darkish green, with cone-shaped tubercles and slightly woolly or bare axils. There are 10–12 whitish or pale-yellow spines 8–9mm long, all radiating; there are no centrals. Flowering in summer, it is diurnal, with rose-pink to pale carmine flowers, the inner petals slightly paler, and up to 4cm across. Requires sun; normal cactus compost; minimum temperature 10°C (50°F). *Mexico (Puebla near Tehuacan).*

MAMMILLARIA **NEJAPENSIS** Craig & Dawson

Considered by some authorities to be synonymous with *M. karwinskiana*. A branching plant with individual stems 15cm high, 7.5cm thick. It has conical tubercles and dense woolly and bristly axils. All the spines are radial, whitish with brown tips and three to five in number, 2–5mm long with often one much longer to about 5cm. Day flowering, in summer, flowers are a dull white with a reddish median line to the petals, about 2cm long, 1.5cm across. Requires a sunny position; normal cactus compost; minimum temperature 13°C (55°F). *Mexico (Oaxaca).*

    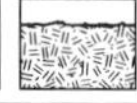 

MAMMILLARIA **NIVOSA** Link
Syn: *Mammillaria flavescens* (DC.) Haw.

Generally globular with stems up to 18cm in diameter in its habitat, but cultivated plants are 6–8cm thick. Tubercles are cone-shaped with white woolly axils. Areoles are white and often densely woolly, bearing eight to ten yellow to brownish radial spines – sometimes up to 14, and to 1.5cm long, with one slightly longer central to 2cm. Flowers are diurnal, occurring in early to mid-summer; they are creamy yellow and up to 2cm long. Requires a bright sunny position; normal cactus compost; minimum temperature 13°C (55°F). *West Indies.*

  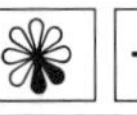  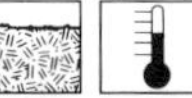 

MAMMILLARIA **NUNEZII** (Br. & R.) Orc.

A globular to cylindrical-shaped plant up to 15cm high, 6–8cm thick, and dull greenish in colour. The tubercles are cone-shaped, and there are bristles in the axils. There are 25–30 white radial spines 7mm long, and one to five slightly longer reddish-tipped centrals. Flowers are purplish pink, about 1.5cm long and across, and appear by day in summer. Requires full sun; normal cactus compost; minimum temperature 10°C (50°F). *Mexico (Guerrero).*

   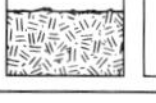 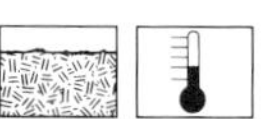

MAMMILLARIA **OBCONELLA** Scheidw.
Syn: *Mammillaria tetracantha* (Salm-Dyck) Br. & R.

The plants are rounded or elongated, later clustering. Each dark-green stem is up to 25cm tall, 15cm thick, and has four-edged or rounded tubercles and dense white woolly axils. The brownish-yellow spines are mainly centrals up to 2.5cm long; only rarely are there one or two very thin radials. Day flowering in summer, the blooms are carmine red with pinkish edges, about 2cm long, 1.5cm across. Requires a sunny position; normal cactus compost; minimum temperature 10°C (50°F). *Mexico (Hidalgo).*

        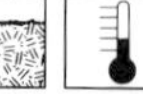

MAMMILLARIA **OTEROI** Glass & Foster

A dull-green, clustering species with stems 2–3cm high, 3–4cm thick. It has cylindrical tubercles and woolly axils with a few hair-like bristles. The large, white areoles bear 12–14 white radial spines tipped with pale brown, 6–8mm long, and one longer hooked central, up to 1.1cm, and white, with a reddish-brown tip. Flowers are whitish, each petal having a prominent centre stripe of reddish brown. They are 1.5cm long and across, day flowering in summer. Requires slight shade; normal cactus compost; minimum temperature 13°C (55°F). *Mexico (Oaxaca).*

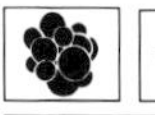     

MAMMILLARIA **PAINTERI** Rose

A small globular species 2cm or more in diameter, though often up to 5cm in cultivation. It is dull green, with somewhat cylindrical-shaped tubercles, and bare axils. The areoles carry about 25 white radial spines 5mm long and four to five dark-brown centrals, one hooked, about 1cm in length. Flowers are greenish-white, 5cm long and across; they are summer flowering, and diurnal. Requires full sun; normal cactus compost; minimum temperature 10°C (50°F). *Mexico (Queretaro).*

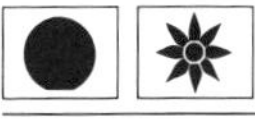    

MAMMILLARIA **PARKINSONII** Ehrenb.

An unusual species, comprising globular stems which divide dichotomously, each about 10cm thick, clustering to form clumps of 40–50 heads or more. The tubercles are pyramidal, with wool and bristles in the axils. The areoles bear 30–35 white radial spines 3–7mm long and two to five white, brown-tipped centrals, one hooked, to 3.5cm in length. Flowering by day in mid-summer, creamy white or pinkish with a dark-pink median line, about 1.5cm long and across. Requires full sun; normal cactus compost with a little lime; minimum temperature 13°C (55°F). *Mexico (Hidalgo, Queretaro).*

MAMMILLARIA **PECTINIFERA** Weber
Syn: *Solisia pectinata* (Stein) Br. & R.

A popular species with globular stems about 8cm high, 6cm thick, rarely offsetting from the base. The tubercles are axe-shaped, and the axils bare. The elongating areoles carry about 40 silvery-white radial spines arranged like a comb, each 2mm long; there are no centrals. It is day flowering in early to mid-summer, producing pale-pink flowers with a pale-purplish median line, 2cm long, opening to 2.5cm across. Requires slight shade; normal cactus compost with a little lime added; minimum temperature 10°C (50°F). *Mexico (Puebla).*

    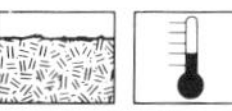 

MAMMILLARIA **PENNISPINOSA** Krainz

A globular, solitary species, only clustering with age. Individual stems are 3–4cm tall and thick with slightly cylindrical-shaped tubercles and bare axils, only slightly felted as young plants. There are 16–20 pubescent, greyish white radial spines up to 8mm long, and one to three reddish centrals about 1cm long, one of them hooked. A day flowering plant in summer, the flowers are pale yellowish or pinkish white with a pinkish median line, about 1.5cm long and 1.2cm wide. Requires a very bright position; normal cactus compost; minimum temperature 10°C (50°F). *Mexico (Durango).*

   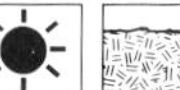 

MAMMILLARIA **PENNISPINOSA var. NAZASENSIS** Glass & Foster

Very similar to the species in size and particular characteristics. The difference is mainly in the spines which are not as pubescent and are yellow in colour. Requirements are the same as for the species. *Mexico (Durango, Coahuila).*

MAMMILLARIA **PETROPHILA** K. Brand.

A solitary, later clustering species, the grey-green stems are up to 15cm thick. Tubercles are cone-shaped, and the axils have brownish-yellow wool and bristles. White areoles bear eight to ten brownish-black radial spines 1–1.5cm in length and one longer, similarly coloured central up to 2cm long. Flowers are greenish yellow with a slightly deeper shade in the centre of the petals, and are 2cm long and across. Summer flowering, they are diurnal. Requires full sun; normal cactus compost; minimum temperature 10°C (50°F). *Mexico (Baja).*

    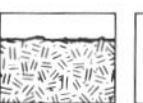 

MAMMILLARIA **PETTERSONII** Hildm.

A large, roundish plant 15cm or more in diameter, with large tubercles spirally arranged. These are three-edged, 1cm long and wide, and there are white woolly axils. The 10–12 radial spines are variable in colour, being white, or yellowish brown, often with black tips, and 2–9mm long. There are four similarly coloured centrals, up to 2cm in length. Flowers, which are diurnal and summer flowering, are deep pink with an almost magenta mid-stripe, 2.5cm long and across. Requires bright sun; normal cactus compost; minimum temperature 13°C (55°F). *Mexico (Guanajuato).*

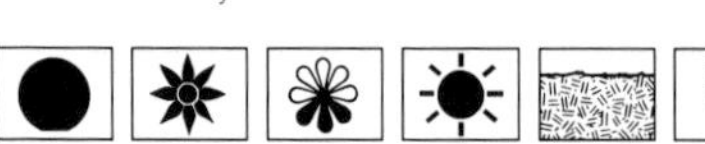

MAMMILLARIA **PILCAYENSIS** Bravo

This is also spelt "pitcayensis" in error. A dark-green, cylindrical-shaped plant up to 24cm high, 4–5cm thick, with somewhat conical tubercles. Axils are woolly and bristly and the radial and central spines are very similar, all whitish, tipped reddish or pale brown, and 5–6mm long. Flowering in summer, the flowers are diurnal and about 2cm long, reddish purple. Requires bright light; normal cactus compost; minimum temperature 10°C (50°F). *Mexico (Guerrero).*

MAMMILLARIA **PILISPINA** Purp.

Somewhat globular plants eventually forming clusters. Each head is dark green and about 4cm thick, with cylindrical tubercles and woolly axils with fine bristles. Areoles bear white, pubescent, thin white spines made up of four to five radials 6–7mm long and one central to 7mm. Flowers are creamy white with a deep-pink midstripe, 1.5cm long and 1cm across; they are summer flowering and diurnal. Requires bright light; normal cactus compost plus a little lime; minimum temperature 13°C (55°F). *Mexico (San Luis Potosi).*

MAMMILLARIA **PLUMOSA** Weber

Globular plants, clustering freely. Each stem is about 7cm in diameter with white woolly axils; the cylindrical tubercles are hidden by the general white woolly covering and spines. There are about 40 radial spines 3–7mm long, all white and feathery. The flowers are greenish white or pale yellowish with a darker median stripe, about 1.5cm long and wide, and are diurnal, appearing in summer. Careful watering is essential, but best around the plant, not over it. Requires full sun; a normal cactus compost with lime added; minimum temperature 10°C (50°F). *Mexico (Coahuila).*

MAMMILLARIA **PLUMOSA** Weber

The more rounded stem form is usually referred to as the "golf-ball variety". It nevertheless gradually clusters, but tends to retain its almost globular shape.

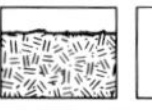

▲

MAMMILLARIA **PONDII** Greene
Syn: *Cochemiea pondii* (Greene) Walt.

A rather cylindrical-shaped plant up to 30cm high, 3–4cm wide, frequently offsetting. It has whitish wool and bristles in the axils and 15–30 whitish or pale-brownish radial spines up to 1cm long. There are four to six or more centrals, 2.5–3cm long and pale yellowish with brown tips, one of them hooked. Flowers appear in mid-summer and are diurnal. These are bright scarlet, about 5cm long. Requires full sun; normal cactus compost; minimum temperature 13°C (55°F). *Mexico (Baja, Cedros Isl.).*

MAMMILLARIA **POSELGERI** Hildm.
Syn: *Cochemiea poselgeri* (Hildm) Br. & R.

Somewhat cylindrical plants to 2m long in their habitat, rarely exceeding 4cm thick. Bluish or greyish green in colour, they frequently branch from the base to form clusters. Axils are woolly, occasionally with a few bristles. The areoles bear about eight white, brown-tipped radial spines to 1cm long, and one hooked central similar in colour, up to about 2cm long. Mid-summer flowering, the plant is diurnal with bright scarlet flowers 3cm long. Requires full sun; normal cactus compost; minimum temperature 13°C (55°F). *Mexico (Baja).*

    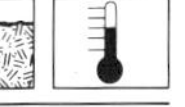

MAMMILLARIA **PROLIFERA** (Mill.) Haw.

A dull-green, dense clustering species. Individual stems are 8–9cm long, 4–5cm thick, with roundish, conical tubercles and fine white hairy axils. Areoles bear 20–40 white radial spines up to 1cm or more in length and five to twelve white, yellowish or pale-reddish centrals 4–9mm long. Summer flowering, and diurnal, the flowers are creamy yellow with a brown or reddish median stripe, 1–1.8cm long. Requires full sun; normal cactus compost; minimum temperature 13°C (55°F). *USA (Texas), West Indies.*

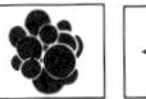    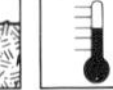 

MAMMILLARIA **REKOI var. LEPTACANTHA LAU** (BR. & R.) Vaup.
Syn: *Mammillaria pullihamata* Backeb.

A globular to elongated species up to 12cm tall, 5–6cm wide, offsetting from the base. The fresh-green stems have cone-shaped tubercles and axils with white wool and bristles. There are about 20 whitish radial spines 4–6mm long and four brown central spines 1–1.5cm long, the lower one hooked. Flowers are reddish purple, about 1.5cm long, and appear by day in summer. Requires bright light; normal cactus compost; minimum temperature 10°C (50°F). *Mexico (Oaxaca).*

MAMMILLARIA **REPPENHAGENII**
D. R. Hunt

A globose or elongating species, occasionally offsetting, up to about 6cm in diameter. The crown of the stems is covered in dense white wool. Areoles have about 22 white radial spines, 2–3mm long and two to five brownish, later becoming greyish, centrals, about 8mm in length. Day flowering in summer, the flowers are carmine red, with the edges of the petals slightly paler, 1–1.2cm long and across. Requires full sun; normal cactus compost with a little lime added; minimum temperature 10°C (50°F). *Mexico (Colima, Michoacan).*

MAMMILLARIA **RHODANTHA var. RUBRA**
K. Sch.

Similar to the species, but more cylindrical. The spines are dark brown, the bright purplish-pink flowers forming in profusion around the crown of the plant. Requirements are the same as for the species. *Mexico (Hidalgo, Queretaro).*

MAMMILLARIA **SABOAE** Glass

A solitary or clustering species, each dark-green globular stem is 1–2cm high and wide. It has somewhat pyramid-shaped tubercles and bare axils. The spines, all radials, are 2mm long and white, yellowish near the base. Flowers occur in daytime in summer; they are rose pink and around 4cm long and across. Requires bright light; normal cactus compost; minimum temperature 10°C (50°F). A very attractive cristate form occasionally occurs; this stem formation is best maintained by grafting on to *Cereus* stock. *Mexico (Chihuahua).*

MAMMILLARIA **RHODANTHA** Link & Otto

Mostly solitary, globular plants up to 30cm tall, 10cm thick with rather cone-shaped tubercles and white, woolly axils. Areoles have 16–24 white or yellowish radial spines 6mm–1cm in length and four to seven often curved centrals, 1–1.5cm long. Flowers occur in summer and are diurnal, purple pink, 2cm long and about 1cm across. Requires bright light; normal cactus compost; minimum temperature 10°C (50°F). *Mexico (Hidalgo, Queretaro).*

MAMMILLARIA **RUBROGRANDIS**
Reppenhagen & Lau

A dull-green globular plant, usually solitary, and up to 10cm high, 18cm broad. It has four-angled tubercles and axils at first woolly, later bare, as are also the areoles. These have 11–13 pale to dark-brown radial spines 4mm to 1.2cm long, and one to four centrals 1–2cm in length. Day flowering in early summer, the blooms are funnel-shaped, about 4cm long and wide, and bright carmine. Requires slight shade; normal cactus compost; minimum temperature 10°C (50°F). *Mexico (Tamaulipas).*

MAMMILLARIA **SABOAE var. GOLDII** (Glass & Foster) Glass & Foster
Syn: *Mammillaria goldii* Glass & Foster

Very similar to the species except that there are 35–45 radial spines and they are glassy white, 2–3mm long. Flowers are dark lavender pink, about 3.5cm long and across. Requirements are the same as for the species. *Mexico (Sonora).*

    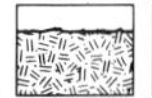 

MAMMILLARIA **SABOAE var. HAUDEANA** (Lau & Wagner) Glass & Foster
Syn: *Mammillaria haudeana* Lau & Wagner

Similar to the species. The greenish stem is 2–4cm in size, and it has 18–27 spines, slightly recurved to 6mm in length. Flowers are dark lilac pink, 6.5cm across when fully expanded. Requirements are similar to those for the species. *Mexico (Sonora).*

MAMMILLARIA **SCHIEDEANA var. DUMETORIUM** (Purp.) Glass & Foster
Syn: *Mammillaria dumetorum* Purp.

Plants are solitary or clustering. Individual stems are globular with flattish tops, 5–6cm in diameter, and up to 10cm high. Tubercles are somewhat cone-shaped, and the axils have long white woolly hairs. All spines are radial; 70–80 or more in number, they are very fine, hair-like, golden yellow and 2–5mm long. There is also var. *dumetorum* (Purp.) Glass & Foster, with stiff, glassier spines. Flowering is by day in summer and autumn and the flowers are about 2cm long, yellowish white, often with a deeper shade median line. Requires sun; slightly calcareous cactus compost; minimum temperature 10°C (50°F). *Mexico (Hidalgo).*

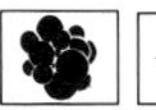    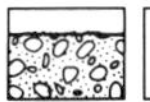

MAMMILLARIA **SCHUMANNII** Hildm.
Syn: *Bartschella schumannii* (Hildm.) Br. & R.

The stems are globular to elongating, 4–5cm high, 3cm thick, and clustering freely. Tubercles are four-angled at the base with woolly axils which become bare with age. The white, brownish-tipped spines consist of nine to fifteen radials, 6mm–1.2cm long, and one to four centrals 1–1.5cm long, one of them hooked. Day flowering in summer, the flowers are pale purplish, with the petal edges more pinkish, and 3–4cm across. Requires sun; normal compost; minimum temperature 13°C (55°F). *Mexico (Baja).*

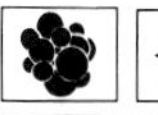    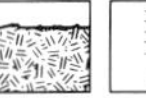 

MAMMILLARIA **SCHWARZII** Shurly

A rapidly clustering species, the globular stems are 2–3.5cm in diameter. Tubercles are more or less cylindrical, and the axils have several white bristles about 5mm long. Areoles bear 35–40 fine white radial spines to 8mm long and eight to nine white, brown-tipped centrals about 6mm long, one of them hooked. Flowers occur in summer and are diurnal; they are about 1.5cm long, 1.2cm across, whitish or pale yellowish, with a red or pink median line to the petals. Requires bright light; normal cactus compost; minimum temperature 13°C (55°F). *Mexico (Northern Guanajuato).*

    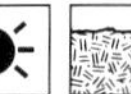 

MAMMILLARIA **SCRIPPSIANA** Br. & R.

A bluish-green, clump-forming species, each globular stem is about 6cm high, with oval tubercles and dense white woolly axils and areoles. These have eight to ten pinkish-red radial spines 6–8mm long and two brown centrals up to 1cm in length. Day flowering in summer, the pinkish-yellow to purplish-pink flowers are about 1.5cm across. Requires bright light; normal cactus compost; minimum temperature 10°C (50°F). *Mexico (Jalisco).*

MAMMILLARIA **SEMPERVIVI** DC.
Syn: *Mammillaria pseudocrucigera* Craig

A globular plant which 'reluctantly' offsets. The stems are dark green and 7–8cm in diameter, with slender pyramidal tubercles and dense wool in the axils. Areoles bear three to seven white radial spines about 3mm long, and two, rarely four, reddish or yellowish centrals to 4mm in length. Flowers, which are whitish or yellowish pink with a reddish median stripe in the petals, are summer flowering, and diurnal. Requires sun; normal cactus compost; minimum temperature 10°C (50°F). *Mexico (Hidalgo).*

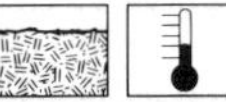

MAMMILLARIA **SENILIS** (Lodd.) Salm-Dyck
Syn: *Mamillopsis senilis* (Lodd.) Weber

These are globular to oval plants, eventually clustering. Each light-green stem is 10–15cm long, 6cm wide, with white, woolly and bristly axils. There are 30–40 pure white or yellowish-white radial spines up to 1.4cm long and five to six centrals up to 2cm long, one hooked. These are white with yellow or very pale-brownish tips. Flowers appear in early summer, and are diurnal, violet red in colour and 6cm long, 4–5cm across borne on a long tube. The plant must be kept totally dry in the rest period. Requires sun; a porous, enriched mineral compost; minimum temperature 7°C (45°F). *Mexico (Chihuahua, Durango, Oaxaca).*

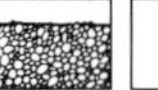

▲

▲

MAMMILLARIA **SETISPINA** (Coult.) Engelm. ex K. Brand.
Syn: *Cochemiea setispina* Coult.

A clustering plant with stems up to 30cm high, 3–6cm thick. Both axils and areoles have white wool and the spines are white with black tips. There are 10–12 radials 1–3.5cm long and one to four centrals 2–5cm in length, the lowest often hooked and curved. Flowers are scarlet, up to 5cm long, the stigma and anthers exserted; they are diurnal, and summer flowering. Needs good light; normal cactus compost; minimum temperature 13°C (55°F). *Mexico (Baja).*

   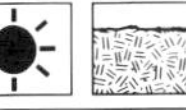 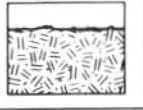

MAMMILLARIA **SOLISIOIDES** Backeb.

A bright-green globular species 4–6cm diameter, rarely offsetting. The tubercles are short cone-shaped, with bare axils. It has about 25 white radial spines, 5mm or a little longer, arranged in a comb-like formation; there are no centrals. Flowers are diurnal, appearing in spring or summer. Yellowish white, they are about 2cm long, 2.5cm across. Requires very careful watering at all times; bright light; normal cactus compost; minimum temperature 13°C (55°F). *Mexico (Puebla).*

   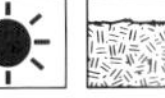 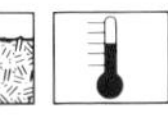

MAMMILLARIA **SPHACELATA** Mart.

A bright-green species, solitary becoming clustering, cylindrical in shape, up to 20cm tall, 2–3cm thick. The tubercles are cone-shaped, and the axils are woolly and bristly. The 10–15 white radial spines are 5–8mm long, with tips sometimes speckled red, and there are one to four centrals, white with brown tips, 4–8mm in length. The flowers are dark purplish red, about 1.5cm long, 8mm across; these are diurnal, appearing in summer. Requires sun; normal cactus compost; minimum temperature 10°C (50°F). *Mexico (Puebla, Oaxaca).*

  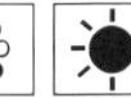 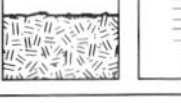

MAMMILLARIA **SPHAERICA** Dietr.
Syn: *Dolichothele sphaerica* (Dietr.) Br. & R.

A dense clustering species; each stem is about 5cm diameter with long tubercles about 1.5cm in length, and axils either bare or with a little wool. Spines are whitish or pale yellowish, made up of nine to fifteen radials 6–8mm long and one central 3–6mm in length. Flowers appear in summer, and are diurnal; bright yellow, they are 6–7cm across. Requires bright light; normal cactus compost; minimum temperature 10°C (50°F). *Mexico (Tamaulipas), USA (Texas).*

MAMMILLARIA **SPINOSISSIMA** Lem.

Oval-shaped, bluish-green plants up to 20cm high, 6–7cm thick. They have oval, cone-like tubercles and white woolly and bristly axils. The areoles bear 20–30 white, yellowish or brownish radial spines to 1cm in length and seven to fifteen whitish or yellowish centrals, one sometimes hooked, about 2cm long. Summer flowering plants, they are diurnal, with the flowers set in a ring around the top of the stems. Each is about 1.5cm long and wide, and is purplish pink. Requires full sun; normal cactus compost; minimum temperature 10°C (50°F). *Mexico (Morelos, Hidalgo, Puebla, Guerrero).*

MAMMILLARIA **STANDLEYI** (Br. & R.) Orc.

A dark-green globular species which tends to remain solitary. It is 10–15cm diameter with cone-shaped tubercles and white woolly, bristly axils. Areoles have 16–19 brown-tipped white radial spines 4 to 8mm long, and four brownish, bristly centrals 8mm or more long. The purplish flowers, about 1.2cm long and wide, appear in summer, and are day flowering. Requires slight shade; normal cactus compost; minimum temperature 10°C (50°F). *Mexico (Sonora, near Alamos).*

    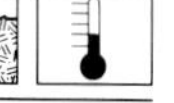

MAMMILLARIA **SWINGLEI** (Br. & R.) Böed.

Globular to columnar plants and clustering. The dark-green stems are 10–20cm tall, 3–5cm in diameter, with somewhat conical tubercles and axils with only a few bristles. The black-tipped whitish radial spines are 11–18 in number and up to 1.4cm long and there are one to four brownish-black centrals to 1.5cm in length. Flowers are white or creamy white with a brownish-green centre stripe, about 3cm long and across; these are diurnal, in summer. Requires sun or very light shade; normal cactus compost; minimum temperature 10°C (50°F). *Mexico (Sonora).*

 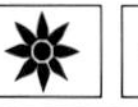  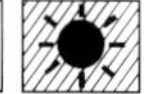 

MAMMILLARIA **TAYLORIORUM** Glass & Foster

The stem is globular, solitary or clustering, up to 25cm high, 10–11cm wide. It has conical tubercles, and the axils are woolly when young, then sparse with one or two bristles. There are about 12 brownish-tipped white radial spines about 9mm long and two or three or possibly four to five centrals similar to the radials. Summer flowering and diurnal, the flowers are 1.5cm long, 1.2cm across, pinkish with white edges to the petals. Requires full sun; normal cactus compost; minimum temperature 10°C (50°F). *Mexico (San Pedro Nolaso Isl., Sonora).*

   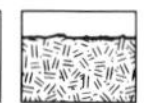 

MAMMILLARIA **SURCULOSA** Böed.
Syn: *Dolichothele surculosa* (Böed.) Buxb.

A bright-green, clustering species with stems up to 4cm high, 3cm thick. It has cylindrical tubercles up to 8mm long, and bare axils. There are 12–15 white, stiff radial spines to 1cm long and one hooked, yellowish-brown central to 2cm long. The flowers are bright yellow, about 1.8cm long, with inner petals tipped orange-red; these are diurnal, appearing in summer. Requires good light; normal cactus compost; minimum temperature 10°C (50°F). *Mexico (San Luis Potosi, Tamaulipas).*

    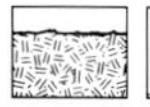 

MAMMILLARIA **TEGELBERGIANA** Linds.

A dull-green globular species, offsetting with age, 7–8cm high and 6cm in diameter. The tubercles are conical, and the axils have white wool. There are 18–24 white radial spines 2–4mm long and four to six white to pale-yellow, brown-tipped centrals, about 7mm long. Flowering is by day in early to mid-summer; the flowers are purplish pink, 1.2–1.4cm long. Requires very slight shade; normal cactus compost; minimum temperature 13°C (55°F). *Mexico (Baja).*

   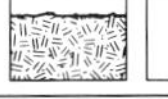  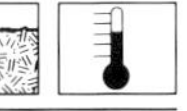

MAMMILLARIA **THERESAE** Cutak

Dark-green solitary plants, rarely clustering. They are oval-shaped, 4cm tall and 2–3cm wide, with oval tubercles and axils with little wool. The sparsely woolly areoles bear 22–30 white, feathery radial spines; there are no centrals. Flowering in summer, and diurnal, the rich violet-purple flowers are about 3.5cm wide, 3.5–4.5cm long. Requires full sun; normal cactus compost; minimum temperature 13°C (55°F). *Mexico (Durango).*

    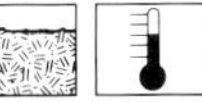

MAMMILLARIA **VETULA** Mart.

M. magneticola Meyran is possibly synonymous. Round, about 4cm in diameter, quickly clustering. Stems are a fresh green with conical tubercles, the axils occasionally woolly. There are about 30 white bristle-like radial spines, 1–1.2cm long. The central spines are reddish or yellowish, and about 1cm long, normally one or two, but frequently four or more. Flowers are yellow, about 1.5cm long, 1.2cm across, and appear by day in summer. Requires bright light; normal cactus compost plus a little lime; minimum temperature 10°C (50°F). *Mexico (Hidalgo).*

    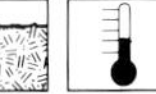

MAMMILLARIA **TETRANCISTRA** Engelm.
Syn: *Phellosperma tetrancistra* (Engelm.) Br. & R.

These vary from about 5cm to 25cm tall, and 5–10cm in diameter, with roundish tubercles, and axils with bristles and little wool. There are 30–60 whitish or purplish brown radial spines 5–10mm long, and one to four, brown or black centrals to 1.4cm long, hooked or straight. Flowers are lavender pink, edged white, and 2.5cm long, 2.5–3.5cm across: they are diurnal, in summer. Requires sun; normal cactus compost; minimum temperature 10°C (50°F). *USA (Southern States), Mexico (Baja, Sonora).*

    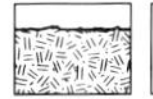 

MAMMILLARIA **UNCINATA** Zucc. ex Pfeiff.

A bluish-green globular, solitary plant, 8cm high, 10cm in diameter. It has somewhat rounded, pyramid-shaped tubercles and axils with white wool, especially in the younger plants. There are four to seven black-tipped white radial spines 5–6mm long and one to three pinkish centrals with brownish tips, 1.2cm long and slightly hooked. Day flowering summer plants, flowers are reddish white with a brown centre stripe to the petals, 1.5–2cm long and 1.8cm across. Needs slight shade; normal cactus compost; minimum temperature 10°C (50°F). *Mexico (Hidalgo, Guanajuato, San Luis Potosi).*

   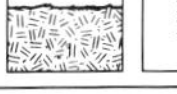

MAMMILLARIA **VIPERINA** Purp.

Closely related to *M. sphacelata* Mart. The stems are very slender, 15–20cm long, 1.5–2cm thick, and bright green. The tubercles are somewhat cylindrical in shape, and the axils often woolly and bristly. Radial spines, of which there are 25–30, vary from pale yellowish to brown, and are about 5mm or little more long; there are no centrals. Day flowering in summer, the flowers are about 1cm long, and bright carmine red. Requires full sun; normal cactus compost; minimum temperature 10°C (50°F). *Mexico (Tamaulipas).*

   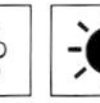 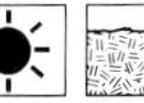 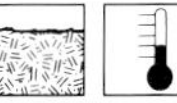

MAMMILLARIA **VOBURNENSIS** Scheer

Also spelt *M. woburnensis.* A clump-forming species with individual stems up to 20cm tall, 8cm in diameter. The angular tubercles are dark green and reddish, with woolly and bristly axils. There are eight to nine white radial spines, 4–5mm long, and one to three central spines, white becoming brownish, 7mm to over 1cm long. Summer flowering, and diurnal, the flowers are about 2cm long and are yellow, tinged with red. Needs bright light; normal cactus compost; minimum temperature 13°C (55°F). *Guatemala.*

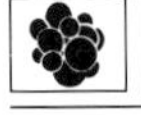    

MAMMILLARIA **WIESINGERI** Böed.

A bright-green, globular species, slightly flattened on the top, up to 4cm high, 8cm diameter. It has slender pyramid-shaped tubercles, and sometimes bristly axils. The 18–20 radial spines are glassy white, very thin, and 5–6mm long; the four, sometimes five or six, central spines are reddish brown, and 5–6mm long. Summer flowering, and diurnal, the flowers are rose pink with a darker median line, 1.2cm long and across. Requires a fairly sunny position; normal cactus compost; minimum temperature 10°C (50°F). *Mexico (Hidalgo).*

     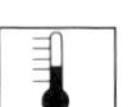

MAMMILLARIA **WINTERAE** Böed.
Syn: *Mammillaria zahniana* Böed. & Ritter

The plants are solitary, globular, 20–30cm wide. The bluish-green stems have four-angled tubercles, about 1.5cm long and wide, with white woolly axils. Areoles bear four central spines, grey or reddish, with brownish tips, sideways pointing up to 1.5cm, the upper and lower around 3cm. Summer flowering, diurnal, the flowers are 3cm long, yellow or whitish yellow with a reddish centre stripe to the outer petals. Requires very bright light; normal cactus compost; minimum temperature 10°C (50°F). *Mexico (Nuevo Leon).*

MAMMILLARIA **WEINGARTIANA** Böed.

Globular, clustering plants, each medium-green stem 4–5cm in diameter. The tubercles are somewhat conical, the axils bare. Areoles bear 20–28 white radial spines, 6–8mm long and there are one to three centrals, one hooked, which are dark brown, about 1.2cm long. Flowering in mid-summer, and diurnal, the flowers are greenish yellow or pale pinkish with a pale reddish-brown median line to the petals. Requires full sun; normal cactus compost; minimum temperature 13°C (55°F). *Mexico (Nuevo Leon).*

MAMMILLARIA **WILCOXII** Br. & R.

Seemingly close to *M. wrightii* as var. *wilcoxii* Toumey ex K. Sch. Very similar to *M. wrightii* with stems up to 10cm high. It has about 20 white, brown-tipped radial spines up to 1.5cm long and one to three longer centrals up to 3cm in length. Day flowering in summer, the flowers are about 3.5cm long, 4cm across, and more or less a pale pinkish purple or yellow. Needs good light; normal cactus compost; minimum temperature 10°C (50°F). *USA (Arizona).*

   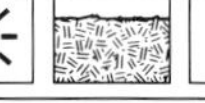

MAMMILLARIA **WRIGHTII** Engelm.

A short columnar plant, 5–7cm in diameter. Stems are solitary, only rarely offsetting. The tubercles are somewhat cylindrical, about 1cm long, with bare axils. There are 10–20 white radial spines up to 1cm or more long and one to three hooked brown centrals, up to 1.5cm long. Day flowering, in summer, the flowers are 2.5cm or more long and across and are purple or magenta with pinkish edges. Needs sun; normal cactus compost; minimum temperature 10°C (50°F). *USA (New Mexico, Texas, Arizona).*

MAMMILLARIA **YAQUENSIS** Craig

Stems are cylindrical up to 7cm high, 1.5cm thick and clustering freely. They are reddish green, with small conical tubercles and slightly felted axils. Areoles bear 18 white, brown-tipped radial spines, 5–6mm long, and one reddish-brown central 1.7cm long, tipped blackish brown. Flowers are diurnal in summer. These are pale pink with a deeper pink median line, about 2cm long and wide. Requires sun; a porous, enriched mineral compost; minimum temperature 10°C (50°F). *Mexico (Sonora).*

MAMMILLARIA **ZEILMANNIANA** Böed.

A well-known, popular species. The dark-green globular stems are up to 6cm tall, 4.5cm wide, readily clustering, with somewhat oval cylindrical tubercles and bare axils. The 15–18 radial spines are white, almost hair-like, and up to 1cm long; there are four reddish-brown central spines, one hooked, about 8mm long. Flowers are about 2cm long, reddish violet, pinkish or white; they appear by day in early to late summer. Requires sun; normal cactus compost; minimum temperature 10°C (50°F). *Mexico (Guanajuato).*

MAMMILLARIA **ZACATECASENSIS** Shurly

A dark-green, solitary globular plant 5–10cm high and about 7cm thick. The tubercles are cylindrical, the axils bare. Areoles bear 20–25 pale-yellowish radial spines 3–5mm long and three to four centrals, yellow with reddish tips, the upper two or three about 1cm long, the lower hooked to 1.5cm. Flowering in summer, and diurnal, the flowers are white or pale pink with a deeper pink median line and throat, up to 1.8cm long and 1.5cm wide. Requires bright light; normal cactus compost; minimum temperature 13°C (55°F). *Mexico (Zacatecas).*

MAMMILLARIA **ZEPHYRANTHOIDES** Scheidw.
Syn: *Dolichothele zephyranthoides* (Scheidw.) Backeb.

Solitary, globular up to 8cm high, 10cm thick, and dull green. The tubercles are conical, up to 2.5cm long, the axils bare. There are 12–18 hair-like whitish radial spines to 1cm long with one yellowish-brown central to 1.4cm, hooked. Flowering in summer, it is diurnal, white to yellow flowers with a red centre stripe, to 4cm long and across. Requires sun; normal cactus compost; minimum temperature 13°C (55°F). *Mexico (Oaxaca, Puebla, Hidalgo, Queretaro).*

   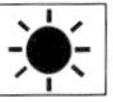  

MATUCANA **AURANTIACA** (Vaup.) Buxb.
Syn: *Submatucana aurantiaca* (Vaup.) Backeb.; *Borzicactus aurantiacus* (Vaup.) Kimnach & P. C. Hutch.

Dark-green, globular about 15cm high and in diameter. It has 16 ribs with elliptical-shaped areoles bearing yellow to reddish-brown spines, consisting of up to 30 radials to 2.5cm in length, and two to four up to 4.5cm. Diurnal flowering in late summer, slightly zygomorphic; up to 9cm long, 5–7cm across, they are orange-yellow, reddish near the throat. Requires bright light; normal cactus compost; minimum temperature 10°C (50°F). *Peru (Cajamarca).*

    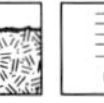 

MATUCANA **KRAHNII** (Donald) Bregman
Syn: *Borzicactus krahnii* Donald

A greyish-green, more or less globular, clustering species, with about 18 ribs divided into prominent, broadly conical tubercles. The areoles are white with dark-brownish spines, about eight radials and one to four centrals, 5mm to about 1cm long, some later reaching 6–8cm in length. Day flowering, the flowers, which are slightly zygomorphic, appear in mid-summer. They are deep reddish lilac, 7–8cm long, to 7cm across. Needs sun; normal cactus compost; minimum temperature 18°C (64°F). *Peru (Amazonas).*

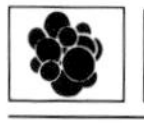   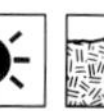 

MATUCANA **AUREIFLORA** Ritter
Syn: *Submatucana aureiflora* Backeb.; *Borzicactus aureiflorus* (Ritter) Donald

A variable species. The globular plant has a somewhat flattened top, about 12cm in diameter with 11–28 dark greyish-green tubercled ribs. Greyish-white felted areoles bear yellowish-brown spines, deeper brown at the base, of which 8–13 are radials 7mm to 1.8cm in length, and one or two are centrals up to 2.5cm. It is summer flowering, and diurnal; flowers are symmetrical, golden yellow and 3–4.5cm long. Requires sun; normal cactus compost; minimum temperature 10°C (50°F). *Peru (Cajamarca).*

   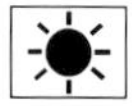 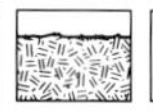 

MATUCANA **MADISONIORUM** (P. C. Hutch.) Rowley
Syn: *Submatucana madisoniorum* (P. C. Hutch.) Backeb.; *Borzicactus madisoniorum* P. C. Hutch.

A globular species 8cm wide, 10cm high, dull greyish or bluish green. Seven to twelve ribs with small blackish areoles about 3mm wide. The reddish-orange flowers, diurnal in mid-summer, are 6–10cm long to 5cm across. Older plants discharge black brown seeds from globose fruits. Requires slight shade; normal cactus compost; minimum temperature 18°C (64°F). *Peru (Amazonas).*

MATUCANA **MYRIACANTHA** (Vaup.) Buxb.
Syn: *Borzicactus myriacantha* (Vaup.) Donald; *Submatucana myriacantha* (Vaup.) Backeb.

Globular, up to 8cm high, 10cm in diameter with about 26 ribs and small felted areoles. The bristly spines are yellow, later brownish or grey, of which 20–30 are radials 6mm to 1.5cm or more long and about 10 are centrals 2.5cm long. Summer flowering, diurnal; flowers are yellow to pale rose, about 6cm long. Needs a bright position; normal cactus compost; minimum temperature 18°C (64°F). *Peru (Amazonas).*

MATUCANA **OREODOXA** (Ritter) Slaba
Syn: *Eomatucana oreodoxa* Ritter; *Borzicactus oreodoxa* (Ritter) Donald

Globular, bright greyish-green plants, sometimes offsetting to form clusters, about 10cm in diameter. It has seven to twelve bumpy ribs and very small areoles bear four to twelve yellowish-brown spines which later turn grey, from 7mm to 3–4cm in length. The flowers are symmetrical, reddish orange with a paler throat, and 4–6cm long; they are diurnal, appearing in summer. Needs bright light; normal cactus compost; minimum temperature 13°C (55°F). *Peru (Ancash).*

MATUCANA **PAUCICOSTATA** Ritter
Syn: *Submatucana paucicostata* (Ritter) Backeb.

Plants with rather elongated stems up to 14cm high, 7cm wide, with seven to twelve ribs and low, cone-shaped tubercles. The spines, at first yellowish brown, later grey, consist of four to eight radials 5mm to 3cm or more long and sometimes one central. Flowers are slightly zygomorphic, about 6cm long, and dark vermilion often edged with violet. Appearing in summer, they are diurnal. Requires good light; normal cactus compost; minimum temperature 10°C (50°F). *Peru (Ancash).*

MATUCANA **POLZII** Diers, Donald & Zecher

A globular species, freely ceaspitose. The stems are grass green, about 4cm tall, 6cm wide with nine to sixteen ribs. Areoles bear many golden, needle-like spines to about 1.5cm in length. It is day flowering in summer and the flowers, which are slightly zygomorphic, are crimson, and 7cm long, 5cm across. Requires bright light; normal cactus compost; minimum temperature 10°C (50°F). *Peru (Huanuco).*

    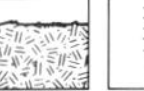

MATUCANA **RITTERI** Buin.
Syn: *Submatucana ritteri* (Buin.) Backeb.; *Borzicactus ritteri* (Buin.) Donald

Flattened globular plant to about 14cm in diameter. Has about 12–22 ribs and longish areoles. The dark-brown, almost black spines are slightly curved. Seven to ten or more radials 1–3cm long and one or two or more centrals 2–4cm in length. Flowers are bright vermilion or orange, about 9cm long, opening to around 5cm in diameter in summer, diurnal. Requires bright light; normal cactus compost; minimum temperature 10°C (50°F). *Peru (La Libertad).*

  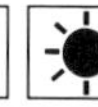 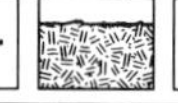  

BORZICACTUS **VIOLACEUS** P. C. Hutch

This title is apparently invalid. The plant appears to be one of the several forms of *M. myriacantha*, particularly in respect to flower colour, this being the original colouring referred to in the initial description by Vaupel. Requirements are the same as for *M. myriacantha. Peru.*

   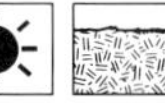 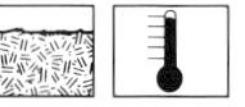

MELOCACTUS **AMETHYSTINUS** Buin. & Bred.
Syn: *Melocactus salinensis* (HU 173) n.

A globular species about 12cm high, 17cm in diameter. It has nine to thirteen or more ribs with horn-coloured spines, about eight of them radials and one prominent central. The cephalium is of white wool with reddish-brown bristles and the carmine-red flowers are followed by similarly coloured fruits. It is day flowering in summer. Requires normal cactus compost; a bright sunny position; minimum temperature 18°C (64°F). *Brazil (Minas Gerais).*

    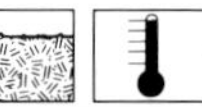 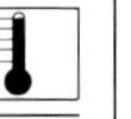

MELOCACTUS **AZUREUS** Buin. & Bred.

A large, greyish blue-green globular species up to about 14cm in diameter. It has nine to eleven deeply furrowed prominent ribs. The spines are greyish brown or whitish, consisting of about seven radials, mostly slightly curved, and one straight central. The cephalium is white-haired with red bristles, and bears carmine-red flowers about 1.5cm long in summer; these are diurnal. Requires bright sunny conditions; normal cactus compost; minimum temperature 16°C (61°F). *Brazil (Bahia).*

 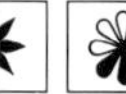 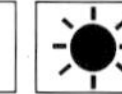 

MELOCACTUS **BAHIENSIS** (Br. & R.) Werd.

Dull, dark-green globular plants to about 15cm diameter, with 10–12 straight ribs. There are seven to ten brownish-grey radial spines and one, rarely up to four, centrals to about 2cm long. The cephalium is densely bristly with white woolly hairs and bears rose-pink flowers, and often some of a deeper shade, up to 2cm long; these are diurnal, in summer. Requires full sun; enriched mineral cactus compost; minimum temperature 16°C (61°F). *Brazil (Bahia).*

MELOCACTUS **BROADWAYI** (Br. & R.) Backeb.

Barrel-shaped to about 20cm high, 7–10cm diameter. Pale green, they have 14–18 ribs with narrow furrows between. There are eight to ten yellowish-brown radial spines 1–1.5cm long and one, rarely two to three, centrals slightly longer. The cephalium, of dense white wool and brown bristles, is up to 6cm diameter and 2–3cm high. Flowers are pale purplish, about 1cm across, and are diurnal, in summer. Requires full sun; enriched mineral compost; minimum temperature 16°C (61°F). *West Indies (Windward Islands, Tobago).*

   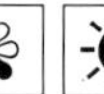 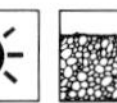  

MELOCACTUS **CAESIUS** Wendl.

A bluish-green globular plant 10–20cm high, 14cm thick. It has 10–15 deeply furrowed ribs. The areoles are set about 2cm apart, bearing six radial spines to 2cm long and one central of similar length; these are reddish brown when young, later pale yellowish. There is a white woolly cephalium and brownish bristles which criss-cross, about 6cm wide, and the flowers, diurnal in summer, are dark pink and about 2cm wide. Requires sun; normal cactus compost; minimum temperature 18°C (64°F). *Venezuela, Trinidad.*

MELOCACTUS **ERYTHRACANTHUS** Buin. & Bred.

The plants are globular to conical and up to about 12cm in diameter, dark green, with 11–12 prominent ribs. The large areoles bear seven yellowish-brown radial spines and four longer centrals, all more or less curved and generally 1.5–3cm long, but the lowest is about 5cm in length. Flowering by day, in summer, the flowers are lilac red, about 2cm long and tubular, protruding through the white woolly cephalium. Needs full sun; normal cactus compost; minimum temperature 18°C (64°F). *Brazil (Bahia).*

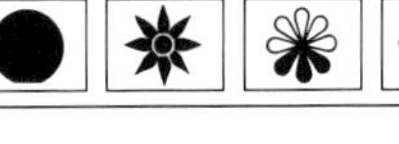

MELOCACTUS **LANSSENSIANUS** Braun

A slightly flattened globular plant, bluish green in colour, about 20cm in diameter. It has about 14 broadly spaced ribs with areoles bearing six to seven brownish-grey radial spines and one central. The rather low cephalium is of white and brownish wool and the flowers, day flowering in summer, are dark pink. Requires normal cactus compost; full sun; minimum temperature 18°C (64°F). *Brazil (Pernambuco).*

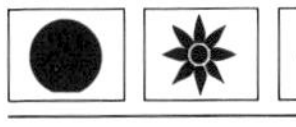

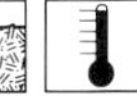

MELOCACTUS **ERNESTII** Vaup.
Syn: *Melocactus uebelmannii* Buin.

A bright-green globular plant 18–20cm high and diameter, with 10–12 curved ribs and a woolly cephalium with dark-red bristles. There are 10–15 reddish-brown spines, the upper ones 1–3cm, a downward-pointing one to 15cm, and the others 4–9cm in length. Day flowering, in summer, the flowers are violet pink, and up to 2cm long, 1cm wide. Requires sun; normal cactus compost; minimum temperature 18°C (64°F). *Brazil (Bahia).*

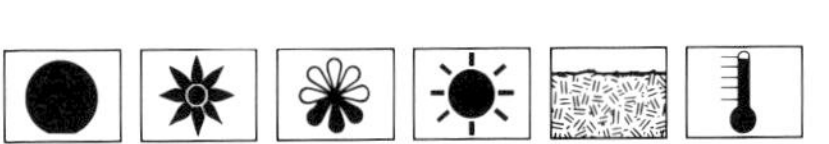

MELOCACTUS **ESTEVESII** Braun

Discovered north of the Amazon River near the border with Venezuela, this is a dull-green, slightly elongated globular species with about 12–14 ribs and many brownish-red, twisted spines. The almost dome-shaped cephalium is of white wool with fine reddish-yellow bristles protruding. The flowers are carmine, appearing by day in summer, followed by typical melocactus seeds. Requires bright light; normal cactus compost; minimum temperature 18°C (64°F). *Brazil (Roraima).*

MELOCACTUS **LEVITESTATUS** Buin. & Bred.

Large globular plants to 30cm high, 20cm diameter with 14–15 ribs. The areoles bear pinkish spines – about 10 radials to 2.5cm long, and two upward-pointing centrals about 2.5cm in length. The cephalium is of white wool and brownish bristles. Flowers are tubular, lilac-violet red, and about 2cm long; they are day flowering in summer. Requires normal cactus compost; full sun; minimum temperature 18°C (64°F). *Brazil (Bahia).*

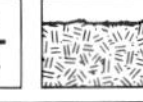

MELOCACTUS **MATANZANUS** Leon

A globular, pale-green plant to 9cm high, 8–9cm thick. It has eight to nine straight ribs; often more develop towards the top of the plant. The spines are brownish white or greyish, consisting of seven to eight radials 1–1.5cm long, and one central to 2cm in length. Densely covered with reddish-brown bristles, the cephalium is 5–6cm wide, to 9cm high, and the flowers are pink, about 1.7cm long, diurnal after midday in summer. Requires full sun; normal cactus compost; minimum temperature 16°C (61°F). *Cuba.*

     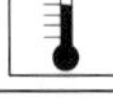

MELOCACTUS **OAXACENSIS** (Br. & R.) Backeb.

A dull-green more or less globular plant, to 15cm diameter. It has 11–15 deeply furrowed ribs with areoles set about 2cm apart. There are eight to twelve reddish-brown radial spines to 2cm long, and one longer central. The cephalium is 2–5cm high, with dense brown bristles and a whitish woolly top. Flowers are dark rose and about 1.8cm long; they are diurnal, in summer. Requires bright sun; slightly calcareous cactus compost; minimum temperature 16°C (61°F). *Mexico (Oaxaca).*

   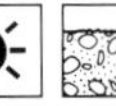  

MELOCACTUS **OREAS ssp. CREMNOPHILUS** (Buin. & Bred.) Braun
Syn: *Melocactus cremnophilus* Buin. & Bred.

A green to dark-green species about 12cm high and up to 14cm diameter with 11–13 ribs. The slightly sunken areoles bear eight to nine reddish-brown, darker-tipped radial spines 4–6cm long and four centrals up to 3cm in length. The cephalium, up to about 12cm high, consists of greyish wool and a few bristles. Flowers are carmine red, about 1.6cm long, and appear by day in summer. Requires bright light, which is essential; normal cactus compost; minimum temperature 18°C (64°F). *Brazil (Bahia).*

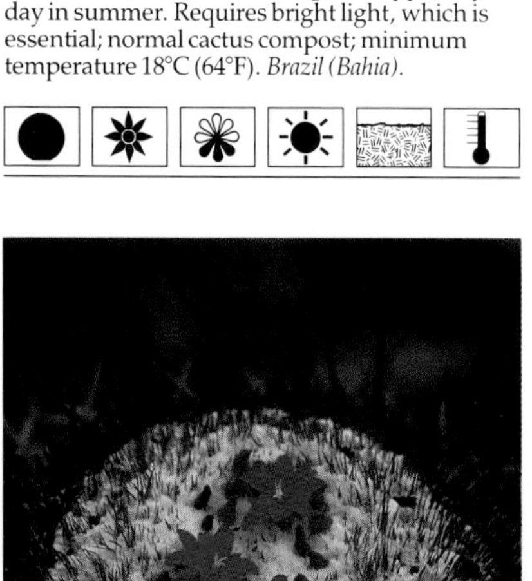

MELOCACTUS **PERUVIANUS var. CANETENSIS** Rauh & Backeb.

A globular plant about 15cm diameter with a dense red spiny and white woolly cephalium to 10cm high and wide. It has about 16 ribs, with areoles having about 10 yellowish-brown to reddish spines from 1–4cm in length. Flowering in summer, it is diurnal; the flowers are a rich carmine red about 1.5cm in diameter. Needs full sun; normal cactus compost; minimum temperature 18°C (64°F). *Peru (Canete).*

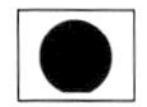    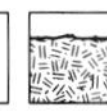 

MELOCACTUS **PERUVIANUS** Vaup. **var. LURINENSIS** Rauh & Backeb.

A greyish-green more or less round plant 10cm high and in diameter. It has 12–15 ribs with areoles about 1.5–2cm apart and yellowish-brown spines, about 10 radials to 1.5cm long and one central slightly longer. The cephalium consists of blackish-brown bristles and white hairy wool. Flowers are carmine red, about 9mm across, and are diurnal in summer. Requires sun; normal cactus compost; minimum temperature 16°C (61°F). *Peru.*

MELOCACTUS **WARASII** Pereira & Bueneker

One of the largest species within the genus: plants have been discovered over 1m tall. The greyish-green or bluish-green elongated stem has 12 prominent ribs, brownish-grey spination and a brownish-red cephalium. The flowers are reddish pink, and are day flowering in summer. Needs full sun; normal cactus compost; minimum temperature 18°C (64°F). *Brazil (Western Bahia).*

MICRANTHOCEREUS **AURI-AZUREUS** Buin. & Bred.

A clustering columnar plant of bluish green densely covered with yellowish spines. The stems reach over 1m in length, 6–7cm in diameter and have 15–18 ribs. The numerous radial spines are 1–1.3cm long, and there are about six centrals 3–8cm in length. Flowers are cylindrical, overall 2.5cm long, with lilac-pink inner petals. They are night flowering in summer. Needs full sun; normal cactus compost; minimum temperature 13°C (55°F). *Brazil (Minas Gerais).*

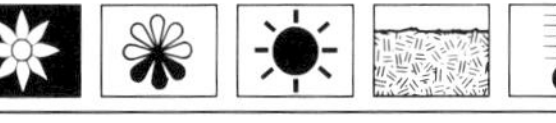

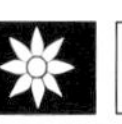

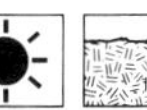
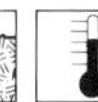

MELOCACTUS **RORAIMENSIS** Braun & Esteves

A very recent discovery in the Amazonian jungle during 1989. This species is a bright-green globular plant with about 16 straight ribs, seven to eight greyish radial spines and one or two centrals. The cephalium consists of white wool and brown bristles, and the flowers are reddish; they are day flowering in summer. Needs very bright light; normal cactus compost; minimum temperature 18°C (64°F). *Brazil (Roraima).*

MELOCACTUS **ZEHNTNERI ssp. CANESCENS** (Ritter) Braun
Syn: *Melocactus canescens* Ritter

A somewhat short, cylindrical plant, often globular, with about 15 ribs. There are about seven brownish-grey radial spines and one central and the cephalium consists of white wool and reddish bristles. Day flowering, in summer, the blooms are carmine. Requires normal cactus compost; sunny location; minimum temperature 18°C (64°F). *Brazil (Bahia).*

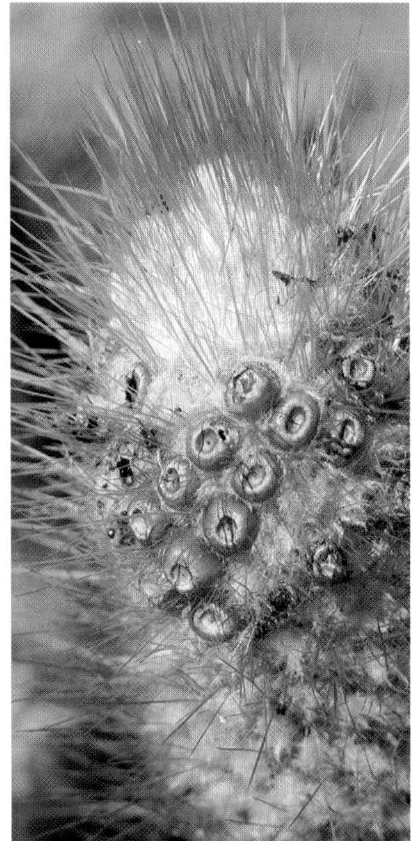

MICRANTHOCEREUS **STRECKERI** van Heek & van Criekinge

A fairly recent discovery from Seabra. The plant is of long columnar growth, with dull-bluish-green stems and many close-set ribs, yellowish-brown spines and lateral cephalium. Night flowering in summer, the blooms are almost purple, many appearing at one time from the yellowish bristly cephalium. Needs full sun; normal cactus compost; minimum temperature 13°C (55°F). *Brazil (Bahia).*

    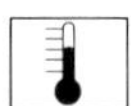

MICRANTHOCEREUS **DENSIFLORUS** Buin. & Bred.

Columnar, clustering from the base, 30–50cm high, 4.5–5cm thick, and bluish green. The 15 ribs have close-set areoles, woolly when young. The yellow spines consist of fine radials 6–8mm long and about eight centrals, 7–8mm long. The cephalium is composed of yellowish wool and long yellowish to reddish-brown spines and bristles. Flowers from the cephalium in summer, nocturnal, somewhat cylindrical, 1.5cm long, 5–6mm wide. Requires sun; normal cactus compost; minimum temperature 13°C (55°F). *Brazil (Bahia).*

     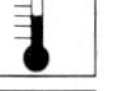

MICRANTHOCEREUS **POLYANTHUS** (Werd.) Backeb.

A columnar, branching species up to 1.25m tall. The bluish-green branches, 5–6cm in diameter, have 15–20 ribs and the yellowish-white areoles bear 20–30 yellowish radial spines 5mm to 1.2cm in length and three or more yellowish-brown centrals up to 3cm long. Flowers appear from a pseudocephalium almost at the tip of the stems in summer. They are nocturnal, and are usually profuse, rose red with often paler inner petals, and about 1.8cm long. Requires bright light; normal cactus compost; minimum temperature 13°C (55°F). *Brazil (Bahia).*

   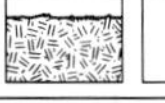

MICRANTHOCEREUS **VIOLACIFLORUS** Buin.

A bushy, columnar plant to about 1m high with stems up to 4cm in diameter. It has 14–16 ribs, with whitish or brownish hairy areoles. There are 20–25 or more radial spines and one central; these are reddish-brown, about 2.5cm in length. Flowers are borne laterally from a pseudocephalium of white to brownish wool in summer, and are nocturnal. They are 2–2.5cm long, with bluish-violet inner segments and are orange violet externally. Requires sun; normal cactus compost; minimum temperature 18°C (64°F). *Brazil (Minas Gerais).*

MILA **CAESPITOSA** Br. & R.

A short cylindrical-stemmed, group forming species. Individual stems are 10–15cm tall, green or greyish-green, and 2–3cm thick with about 10 ribs. Areoles bear about 20 or more yellowish or brownish-tipped white spines up to 1cm long and one to three centrals up to 3cm. It is day flowering in summer; the flowers are yellowish or reddish yellow, and about 1.5cm long, 3cm wide. Requires full sun; enriched mineral-based compost; minimum temperature 10°C (50°F). *Peru.*

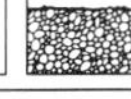
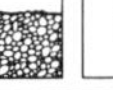

MILA **NEALEANA** Backeb.

A pale-green, clustering species with stems 30–45cm long, 3cm thick, often prostrate. It has 11–13 ribs resolved into tubercles. The white or yellowish areoles are felted and bear 12–30 fine bristly, brown-tipped white radial spines and one to six centrals, one downward pointing and up to 2cm in length. Day flowering in summer, the flowers are pale to bright yellow, and 3.5cm long, 2.5cm across. Requires full sun; normal cactus compost; minimum temperature 10°C (50°F). *Peru.*

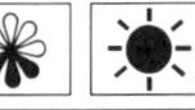
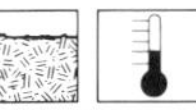

MIRABELLA **MINENSIS** Ritter

This appears to belong more properly to *Monvillea.* It is a bluish-green columnar plant of semi-prostrate habit with three to five ribs and areoles about 5mm in diameter set at intervals of 1.5–3.5cm and bearing three to six spines about 2.5cm long. The flowers have a somewhat hairy receptacle, and are whitish; they appear by night in summer. Requires bright light; slightly calcareous cactus compost; minimum temperature 13°C (55°F). *Brazil (Minas Gerais).*

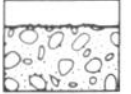

MILA **FORTALEZENSIS** Rauh & Backeb.

A greyish-green, somewhat globular plant, often forming clusters. Individual stems are up to 10cm long with 11–13 ribs. The round, yellowish areoles have nine to twelve bristle-like radial spines and up to four centrals up to 1cm long. Flowering in summer, the plant is diurnal. The satiny-yellow flowers are about 3.5cm long, 2.5cm across. Requires bright sun; normal cactus compost; minimum temperature 10°C (50°F). *Peru.*

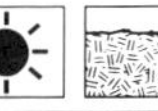
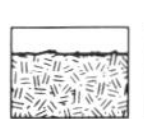

▲

▲

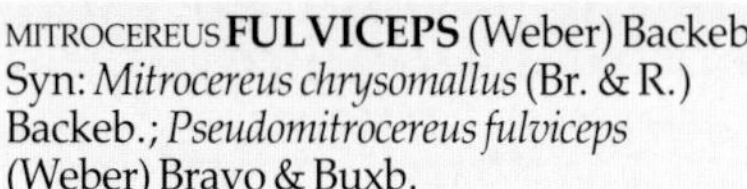

MITROCEREUS **FULVICEPS** (Weber) Backeb.
Syn: *Mitrocereus chrysomallus* (Br. & R.) Backeb.; *Pseudomitrocereus fulviceps* (Weber) Bravo & Buxb.

Columnar up to 18m tall, branching from the base. The stems are 12–30cm across, with 11–14 ribs, with large brownish areoles about 2cm apart. The spines are brown, later grey. Eight to twelve are radials, to 2cm long, usually three centrals, one up to 13cm in length. Summer-flowering, at night; flowers are about 8cm long and creamy white. Needs a bright sunny position; normal cactus compost; minimum temperature 13°C (55°F). *Mexico (Puebla, Oaxaca).*

    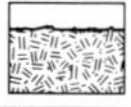 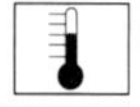

MITROCEREUS **RUFICEPS** (Weber) Backeb.
Syn: *Neobuxbaumia macrocephala* Daws.

Tall, tree-like plants reaching 15m high in their habitat, and branching from the main stem which is about 40cm in diameter. There are about 26 ribs with areoles bearing eight to ten reddish radial spines about 1cm long, and one to three centrals 4–5cm long, all eventually turning greyish. Flowers, which occur in summer and are nocturnal, are produced from the top of the branches; they are pinkish white and bell-shaped, about 5cm long. Requires full sun; normal cactus compost; minimum temperature 13°C (55°F). *Mexico (Puebla, Tehuacan).*

  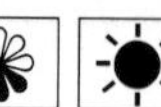 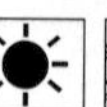 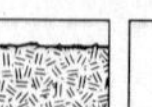

MONVILLEA **CAMPINENSIS** (Backeb. & Voll.) Backeb.
Syn: *Praecereus campinensis* Backeb. & Voll

A tall, slender, semi-erect columnar species reaching to about 5m tall; the bluish-green branches are about 6cm wide. It has seven to nine ribs with grey-felted areoles and seven to eleven grey spines up to 1.5cm long. Flowering by night in summer, the blooms are greenish white, about 10cm long, 6cm across. Requires free watering in summer; slight shade; normal cactus compost; minimum temperature 10°C (50°F). *Brazil (São Paulo).*

MONVILLEA

MONVILLEA **SPEGAZZINII** (Weber) Br. & R.
Syn: *Cereus spegazzinii* Weber

A bushy, semi-climbing or trailing plant with dark bluish-green, greyish marbled stems up to 3m long and 2cm thick. The three to five ribs have areoles set on prominences 2–4cm apart carrying three to five black radial spines up to 5mm long and rarely one longer central, also black. Flowering at night in mid-summer, the flowers are pinkish-white with white inner petals and reddish-pink outer segments, up to 13cm long. Fruits red. Needs a bright position; normal cactus compost; minimum temperature 10°C (50°F). *Paraguay.*

   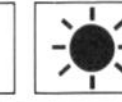 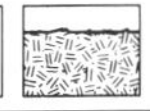 

× MYRTGEROCACTUS

× MYRTGEROCACTUS **LINDSAYI** Moran

Considered a hybrid of *Myrtillocactus cochal* and *Bergerocactus emoryi*. This is an interesting hybrid plant up to 2.5m tall. It is dark green and densely covered with golden-yellowish brown spines. Stems are up to 5cm in diameter with 11–13 ribs and areoles bearing numerous spines, 1–3cm long. The flowers, diurnal in mid-summer, are yellow, 3cm long and wide. Requires full sun; normal cactus compost; minimum temperature 13°C (55°F). *Mexico (Baja).*

    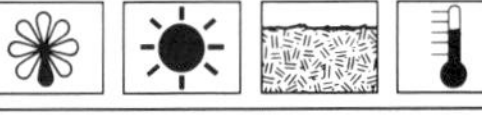  

× MYRTILLENOCEREUS

× MYRTILLENOCEREUS **HYBRIDUS**

The inter-generic title established by Rowley is that of an unnamed natural hybrid discovered by Charles Glass, a result of *Stenocereus dumortieri* crossed with *Myrtillocactus geometrizens*. The tall, erect bluish-green stems have six to seven prominent ribs with greyish areoles bearing a few brownish radial spines and one or more longer centrals. Flowers appear by day in early summer; they have pale rose-pink reflexed petals and a prominent yellowish style and stamens. Requires full sun; normal cactus compost; minimum temperature in winter 10°C (50°F). *Southern Mexico.*

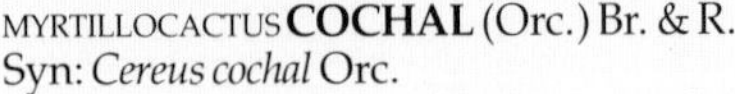

MYRTILLOCACTUS **COCHAL** (Orc.) Br. & R.
Syn: *Cereus cochal* Orc.

A branching species with a short trunk, 1–3m tall, the trunk 15cm or more in diameter, generally bluish-green in colour. It has six to eight shallow-grooved ribs with five greyish or black radial spines about 8mm long, and sometimes one central to 2cm. Flowers are both diurnal and nocturnal, and bloom in early summer. They are about 2.5cm long and across, white tinged with green or purple. Requires a bright sunny position; normal cactus compost; minimum temperature 10°C (50°F). *Mexico (Sonora, Baja).*

MYRTILLOCACTUS **GEOMETRIZANS** (Mart.) Cons.
Syn: *Cereus geometrizans* Mart.

A tree-like species up to 4m high with a central stem branching from just above ground level. The stem and branches are bluish to dull green and there are five to six smooth and rounded ribs with large areoles bearing a few short brownish or black radial spines 5mm or more long, and one central 2.5–5cm or more in length. Flowers whitish, diurnal, produced in early summer from upper areoles and are up to 3.5cm across. Requirements are the same as for *M. cochal*. *Mexico (central) to Guatemala.*

    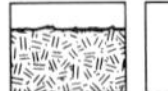 

MYRTILLOCACTUS **SCHENCKII** (Purp.) Br. & R.
Syn: *Cereus schenckii* Purp.

A tree-like species up to 4–5m high with a very short trunk and deep-green ascending branches to about 10cm thick. It has seven to eight ribs and close-set, black areoles with six to eight small blackish radials, and one longer brownish central up to 5cm in length. Flowering in summer, the flowers are diurnal, with whitish inner petals, and brownish white externally, about 4cm across. Requires full sun; normal cactus compost; minimum temperature 13°C (55°F). *Mexico (Puebla, Oaxaca).*

   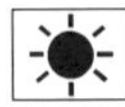 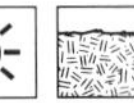

NEOBINGHAMIA **MIRABILIS** Rauh & Backeb.

Columnar up to 1.20m high, about 10cm thick, branching from the base. The 22 brownish-green ribs are edged with areoles bearing about 50 thin, reddish-brown radial spines about 2cm long and one or two similar centrals, rather longer. Flowers appear from the often irregularly zoned cephaliums, which are clusters of white wool. The blooms are trumpet-shaped, with red inner petals and purple sepals, about 6cm long, nocturnal, in mid-summer. Requires sun; normal cactus compost; minimum temperature 13°C (55°F). *Peru (Olmos).*

    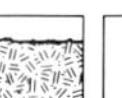 

NEOBINGHAMIA **VILLIGERA** Rauh & Backeb.

Dark-green columnar plants to over 1m high, 10cm in diameter, with 20 straight ribs. The yellowish-brown, fairly close-set areoles bear about 80 very fine short yellowish radial spines and one or two longer centrals, one of which is often 4cm long. Night flowering in summer, the flowers are produced from a white densely woolly cephalium near the tips of the stems. The greenish-white blooms are 6.5cm long, 4cm across. Needs sun; normal cactus compost; minimum temperature 13°C (55°F). *Peru (Churin).*

    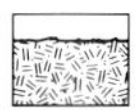 

NEOBINGHAMIA **CLIMAXANTHA** (Werd.) Backeb.

A bright-green columnar plant with erect growth to about 1m high, 6–8cm in diameter. It has between 19–27 ribs with brownish areoles bearing 50–70 fine bristly, yellowish-brown radial spines 5–8mm long and one to three centrals to 2cm in length. Flowers appear in summer from a white woolly pseudocephalium and are nocturnal. These are 3–4cm long, with white inner petals and rose-pink outer petals. Requires full sun; normal cactus compost; minimum temperature 13°C (55°F). *Peru (Eulalia).*

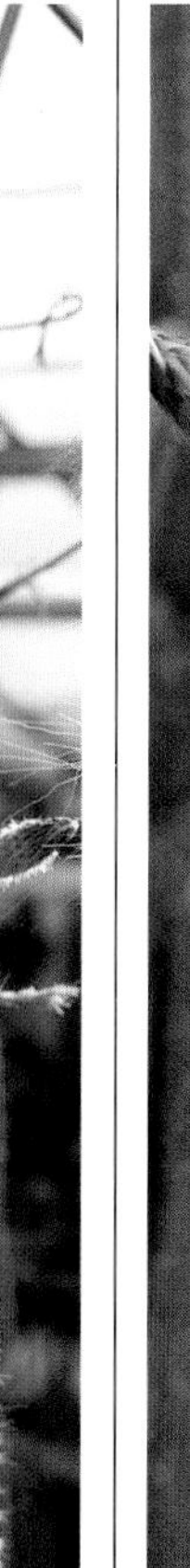

NEOBUXBAUMIA **EUPHORBIOIDES** (Haw.) Buxb.
Syn: *Rooksbya euphorbioides* (Haw.) Backeb.; *Cereus euphorbioides* Haw.

Tall columnar plants eventually reaching 3–5m, very erect, and about 9cm thick. There are eight to ten acute and straight ribs with equally placed white-felted areoles. These bear one to five almost black spines, 1–3cm long. The nocturnal flowers appear in early summer, and are borne laterally. Bell-shaped, they are reddish pink and 8–10cm long. Requires bright light; a porous, enriched cactus compost; minimum temperature 10°C (50°F). *Mexico (Tamaulipas).*

   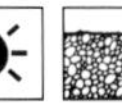 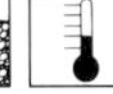

NEOBUXBAUMIA **POLYLOPHA** (DC.) Backeb.
Syn: *Cephalocereus polylopha* (DC.) Br. & R.; *Cereus polylophus* DC.

A tall, solitary, pale green, columnar plant reaching to 13m in the wild and about 35cm thick. It has 20–50 somewhat rounded ribs with small, white-felted areoles. The spines are yellow: seven to nine radials, 1–2cm long, one central to 7cm long and yellowish bristles. Flowers at night in summer in shades of red, 4–5cm long, about 3cm across. Requires a sunny position; normal cactus compost; minimum temperature 10°C (50°F). *Mexico (Hidalgo).*

NEOBUXBAUMIA **TETETZO** (Weber) Backeb.
Syn: *Pilocereus tetetzo* Weber

Tall, erect, columnar and tree-like plants to 15m tall with greyish-green stems 30cm in diameter. There are 13–20 somewhat rounded ribs with regularly placed round, brownish areoles bearing blackish spines, of which 8–13 are radials to 1.5cm long, and there is one central about 5cm in length. Nocturnal flowering in summer; flowers are almost terminal, whitish, and about 6cm long. Needs full sun, which is essential; normal cactus compost; minimum temperature 13°C (55°F). *Mexico (Puebla to Oaxaca).*

   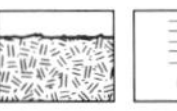 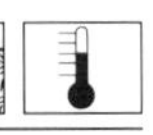

▲

▲

NEODAWSONIA **APICICEPHALIUM** (Dawson) Backeb.

An impressive columnar, tree-like species 1–3m tall with bluish-green stems about 10cm in diameter. It has 22–27 ribs with elliptical areoles bearing fine, bristly, greyish-white spines, nine to twelve radials 2–3cm long and two to six centrals 2–4cm long. Flowers appear from the small terminal cephalium which is white and densely woolly. Each flower is 5–6cm long, about 3cm across, rose-pink with yellowish suffusions; they are nocturnal, in summer. Requires full sun; normal cactus compost; minimum temperature 13°C (55°F). *Mexico (Oaxaca).*

    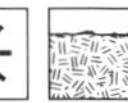 

NEODAWSONIA **TOTOLAPENSIS** Bravo & T. MacDoug.

A tall, elegant plant up to about 8m high, 12–15cm thick, greyish or brownish green. There are about 28 ribs with round, greyish-white areoles bearing 10–13 whitish radial spines up to 1.3cm long and three to six slightly longer centrals. Flowers are nocturnal in early summer borne in a terminal cephalium which is later grown through, leaving raised sections along the stems. The blooms are rose pink, 3.5cm long. Requires bright light; normal cactus compost; minimum temperature 13°C (55°F). *Mexico (Oaxaca).*

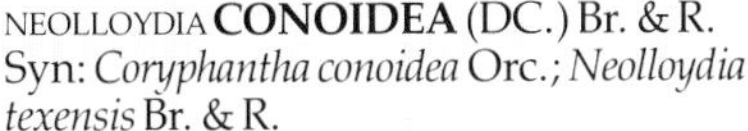

NEOLLOYDIA **CONOIDEA** (DC.) Br. & R.
Syn: *Coryphantha conoidea* Orc.; *Neolloydia texensis* Br. & R.

Globular to cylindrical, freely branching. The stems are 7–10cm tall, 7cm thick with oval tubercles and woolly axils. Spines are white to greyish-black; about 16 are radials to 1cm long, there are three to five centrals to 3cm. Flowers are diurnal in summer, reddish violet, about 6cm across. The pinkish-lilac form, earlier named *N. texensis*, is sometimes considered a separate species. Requires a sunny position; an enriched mineral, porous compost; minimum temperature 10°C (50°F). *USA (Texas), Mexico.*

  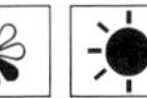 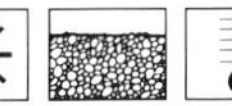

NEOLLOYDIA **CONOIDEA var. CERATITES** (Quehl) Kladiwa & Fittkau
Syn: *Neolloydia ceratites* (Quehl) Br. & R.; *Coryphantha ceratites* Berger

Stems are similar to those of the species, greyish green with four-edged tubercles and woolly axils. The spines are greyish, sometimes tipped black; about 15 are spreading radials to 1.5cm long, and three to six are centrals to 3cm in length. It flowers by day in summer; the flowers are purple and 3–3.5cm long. Requirements are the same as for the species. *Mexico.*

    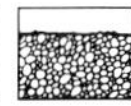 

NEOLLOYDIA **CONOIDEA var. GRANDIFLORA** (Otto) Kladiwa & Fittkau
Syn: *Neolloydia grandiflora* (Otto) Br. & R.; *Coryphantha grandiflora* Berger

Similar to the species, but the cylindrical or globular stem has closer-set tubercles and denser white woolly axils, especially when young. The spines are white with darker tips, consisting of about 25 radials to 6mm long and one or two brownish-black centrals to 3cm in length, often absent. Flowers, diurnal in summer, are rich purple-pink and 3–3.8cm long. Requirements as for the species. *Mexico (Tamaulipas).*

   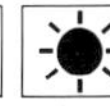 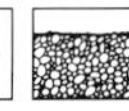 

NEOLLOYDIA **CONOIDEA var. MATEHUALENSIS** (Backeb.) Kladiwa & Fittkau
Syn: *Neolloydia matehualensis* Backeb.

Up to about 15cm tall, the plant is cylindrical and greyish green with prominent tubercles and white-felted axils. There are 10–12 greyish-white or pale yellowish radial spines about 1cm long, and one or two centrals up to 2cm in length. Flowers are purplish, up to 3cm long, and appear by day in summer. Requirements are the same as for the species. *Mexico (San Luis Potosi).*

NEOPORTERIA **ANDREAEANA** (Backeb.) Donald & Rowley
Syn: *Neochilenia andreaeana* Backeb.

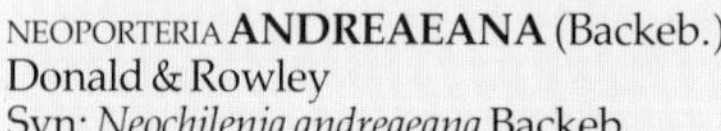

A greyish-green, oval plant to about 15cm high, 5cm in diameter, with about 14 ribs. The areoles bear about eight whitish-grey radial spines and four to five dark reddish-brown centrals about 2.2cm in length. Flowers have yellowish inner petals and are brownish red externally, 3cm long, 3.7cm across; they are day flowering in late summer. Requires a bright position; normal cactus compost; minimum temperature 10°C (50°F). *Chile.*

NEOPORTERIA **CRISPA** (Ritter) Donald & Rowley
Syn: *Pyrrhocactus crispus* (Ritter) Backeb.; *Horridicactus crispus* (Ritter) Backeb.

A dark grey-green globular species about 7cm in diameter arising from a tuberous root-stock. It has 13–16 ribs with whitish areoles bearing black or greyish spines, six to ten radials 2–5cm long and two to four central spines 4–8cm in length. Late summer or autumn flowering, diurnal, the flowers are reddish with a red midstripe to the inner petals, about 3.5cm long. Needs bright light; normal cactus compost; minimum temperature 10°C (50°F). *Chile (Freirina).*

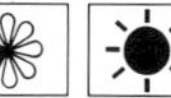
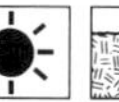

NEOPORTERIA **ERIOCEPHALA** (Backeb.) Donald & Rowley
Syn: *Neochilenia eriocephala* Backeb.; *Neochilenia floccosa* (Ritter) Backeb.

A green tuberous-rooted plant to 30cm high, 6cm thick. It has about 13 prominent ribs nearly 1cm high and many small tubercles. The areoles are whitish and bear black or greyish erect spines, eight to ten radials 7mm to about 2cm long and one or two or more centrals 1–2.5cm in length. Day flowering in late summer, the flowers are pale yellow, and about 3.5cm long. Needs very good light; normal cactus compost; minimum temperature 10°C (50°F). *Chile.*

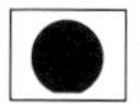

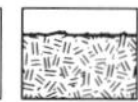

NEOPORTERIA **LINDLEYI** (Först.) Donald & Rowley
Syn: *Islaya paucispina* Rauh & Backeb.

A greenish-grey globular plant about 8cm in diameter with 12–16 ribs. The areoles bear five to eight pale-reddish radial spines to 1.5cm long and one brownish-red central about 3cm in length. It is day flowering, in late summer; the flowers are bright yellow, 1.5cm long. Requires a bright position; normal cactus compost; minimum temperature 10°C (50°F). *Southern Peru.*

NEOPORTERIA **NIDUS** (Phil.) Backeb. **var. GEROCEPHALA** (Y. Ito) Ritter
Syn: *Neoporteria gerocephala* Y. Ito

A somewhat globular or slightly elongated plant about 5cm in diameter, to 10cm tall. It is dark greyish in colour with about 20 whitish or nearly black spines, often up to 5cm in length, which densely cover the whole stem. Day flowering in late summer, the flowers are a rich magenta, 4–6cm long, 4–5cm across. Needs a sunny position; normal cactus compost; minimum temperature 10°C (50°F). *Chile.*

NEOPORTERIA **PLANICEPS** Ritter

Also known as *N. Laniceps* Ritter. A more or less globular species up to 20cm tall, 40cm thick, with 13–17 somewhat bumpy ribs. The areoles are white, set about 5mm apart, and bearing about 50 hairlike spines including, usually, two brownish centrals 2–4cm long. Flowers are carmine red, 2.5–3cm long; these are diurnal, in late summer. Needs good light; normal cactus compost; minimum temperature 13°C (55°F). *Northern Chile.*

NEOPORTERIA **MEGLIOLII** (Rausch) Donald
Syn: *Pyrrhocactus megliolii* Rausch

A greyish bluish-green globular species which is most variable, especially in its habitat. There are about nine to twenty broad, round ribs, usually slightly notched, and the areoles carry many erect or twisting, greyish or greyish-brown spines. Flowers, which occur by day in late summer, are pinkish white or often a deeper shade. Requires a sunny position; normal cactus compost; minimum temperature 10°C (50°F). *Argentina (Marayes, San Juan).*

NEOPORTERIA **OCCULTA** (Phil.) Br. & R.
Syn: *Neochilenia occulta* (Phil.) Backeb.

Small globular plants 1.3–2.5cm in diameter, yellowish brown to almost blackish in colour, with eight to ten prominently tuberculate ribs. The areoles are whitish, bearing six to ten radial spines up to 8mm long, and one central about 1.5cm in length; all tend to fall with age. Flowers are diurnal, appearing in summer. They are pale yellow, very pale brownish at the base of the petals, and about 2.5cm long, 2cm across. Requires a bright position; normal cactus compost; minimum temperature 10°C (50°F). *Chile (Copiapo).*

NEOPORTERIA **SANJUANENSIS** (Speg.) Donald & Rowley
Syn: *Pyrrhocactus sanjuanensis* (Speg.) Backeb.

A dark-green, slightly elongating, globular species with 13 ribs. The areoles are large, with grey, reddish-grey or brownish spines, of which nine to fifteen are radials, three to seven centrals. Flowers are funnel-shaped and white to yellow; they are day flowering, appearing in late summer. Needs full sun; normal cactus compost; minimum temperature 10°C (50°F). *Argentina (San Juan).*

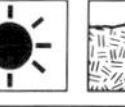

NEOPORTERIA **SETIFLORA** (Backeb.) Donald & Rowley
Syn: *Pyrrhocactus setiflorus* Backeb.

A globular, bluish-green plant with about 15 ribs. The large, brownish-white felted areoles bear about eight to ten reddish-grey radial spines and about four centrals up to 2.5cm long. Flowers are 3cm long, a pale yellow often with orange shading, and appear by day in late summer. Requires slight shade; normal cactus compost; minimum temperature 10°C (50°F). *Argentina (Mendoza).*

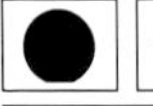 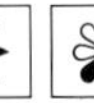  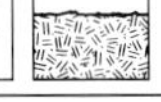  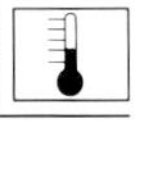

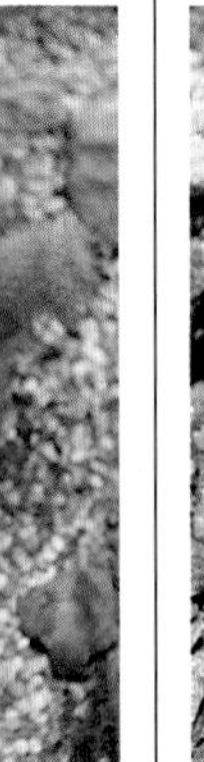

NEOPORTERIA **SUBGIBBOSA** (Haw.) Br. & R. **fma LITORALIS** (Ritter) Donald & Rowley
Syn: *Neoporteria litoralis* Ritter

A green, more or less globular plant 8–10cm in diameter with 14–21 ribs. The white or yellow-felted areoles are oval with about 30 hair-like radial spines up to 2cm long, and eight to twelve centrals up to 3cm, the colour varying from yellowish white to almost black. Flowers are diurnal, occurring in late summer; they are carmine pink, and up to nearly 3cm long. Requires a bright position; cactus compost; minimum temperature 10°C (50°F). *Chile.*

  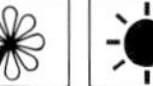 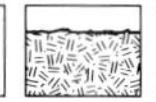 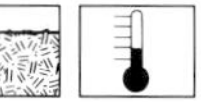

NEOPORTERIA **UMADEAVE** (Frič) Donald & Rowley

Previously included within *Pyrrhocactus.* A dull-green, globular species up to 25cm tall, 11cm thick, with 18–25 humped ribs. There are 30–35 spines, ranging from white to black, and 3–4cm long. Flowers are pale yellow, 3–3.5cm long, and occur diurnally in late summer. Needs bright light; normal cactus compost; minimum temperature 10°C (50°F). *Northern Argentina (Jujuy).*

NEOPORTERIA **UMADEAVE var. MARAYESENSIS** (Backeb.) Donald & Rowley
Syn: *Pyrrhocactus umadeave var. marayesensis* Backeb.

A fairly bright-green plant, somewhat globular in shape and completely covered with blackish blue-greyish spines mostly tending to be upward-pointing. The flowers, appearing by day in late summer, are white, pinkish externally. Requires a sunny position; normal cactus compost; minimum temperature 10°C (50°F). *Northern Argentina (Marayes).*

   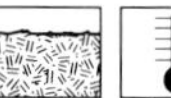 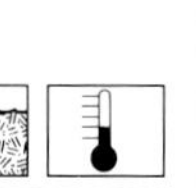

NEOPORTERIA **VILLICUMENSIS** (Rausch) Donald
Syn: *Pyrrhocactus villicumensis* Rausch

Small greyish-green globular plants with eight to twelve rounded ribs. The areoles, which are slightly white-felted, bear about eight dark-greyish or greyish-black radial spines and one or two, rarely more, centrals. Flowers are pinkish brown, darker coloured externally, but it is a variable species. It is day flowering, in late summer. Needs sun; normal cactus compost; minimum temperature 10°C (50°F). *Argentina (San Juan, Villicun).*

   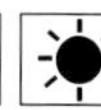  

NEORAIMONDIA **GIGANTEA** (Werd. & Backeb.) Backeb.

Currently known as *N. arequipensis* var. *gigantea* Backeb. or *N. peruviana* (L.) Ritter. Columnar, grouping, up to 8m high. It is bright green, branching from the base, with four to five straight ribs, the slightly rounded edges having large, protruding, round, brown areoles. There are 12 or more greyish-black spines from each areole, unequal in length, usually two or three are 12cm or more long. Flowers are diurnal, in summer, up to 4cm long, purplish rose. Requires sun; normal cactus compost; minimum temperature 15°C (59°F). *Northern Peru.*

   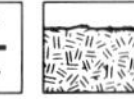 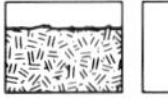

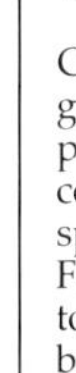

NEORAIMONDIA **ROSEIFLORA** (Werd. & Backeb.) Backeb.
Syn: *Neoraimondia arequipensis* var. *roseiflora* (Backeb.) Ritter

Columnar, up to about 2m tall with a thick greyish-green stem with five ribs. These have prominent warts tipped with large areoles consisting of tufts of brownish bristles. The spines are greyish-white, 10cm or more long. Flowers are pinkish-red with purplish centre line to the petals and 4–5cm long, including the brown-felted tube: they occur by day, in summer. Needs bright light; cactus compost; minimum temperature 13°C (59°F). *Peru (Chosica).*

    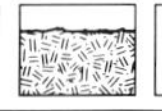

NEOWERDERMANNIA **VORWERKII** Frič.
Syn: *Weingartia vorwerkii* (Frič.) Backeb.

A dark greyish-green globular species 6–8cm in diameter with 16 or more tuberculate ribs. Areoles are in the depressions between the tubercles, and there are about ten brownish spines up to 1.5cm long and one more central spine which is often hooked. Flowers are white or pale lilac pink, and are 2–2.5cm long and wide; they are day flowering, in summer. The plant must be kept completely dry in winter. Requires a sunny position; an enriched mineral compost; minimum temperature 7°C (45°F). *Northern Argentina, Northern Bolivia.*

    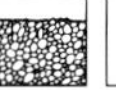 

NOPALXOCHIA

NOPALXOCHIA **HORICHII** Kimnach

An epiphytic species from forest regions. The stems are initially erect but become pendulous and the branches are about 60cm long, trigonous becoming flat to 4cm wide. The margins are serrate with wool and a few fine bristles in the serrations. Flowers are funnel-shaped, about 17cm long, 13cm across, rosy pink to magenta and with a long protruding yellowish style. They are day flowering, in early summer. Needs filtered light; normal cactus compost; minimum temperature 13°C (55°F). *Costa Rica.*

NOPALXOCHIA **MACDOUGALLII** (Alex.) Marsh.
Syn: *Lobeira macdougallii* Alex.

A rare epiphyte with long, fleshy, flat stems up to 25cm long and about 5cm broad. The margins are prominently crenated with inset areoles which are spineless. Flowering in daytime in early summer, the lilac-rose flowers are narrowly trumpet-shaped, about 5mm long, and with a stoutish style, six to nine stamens and white stigma lobes. A choice, rare species requiring filtered light; slightly acid, porous compost; minimum temperature 15°C (59°F). *Mexico (Chiapas).*

   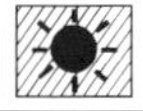 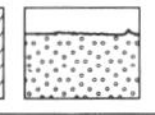 

NOPALXOCHIA **PHYLLANTHOIDES** (DC.) Br. & R.
Syn: *Cereus phyllanthoides* DC.

A slender, branching epiphytic cactus with soft, strap-like branches 30–45cm or more long. It is bright green in colour, with crenate margins and very small brownish, spineless areoles. A late spring, day flowering species, the flowers are in shades of pink, 7–9cm long on a tube about 2cm in length. It makes an ideal houseplant. Careful watering is necessary, and it requires filtered light; normal cactus compost; minimum temperature 10°C (50°F). *Mexico (Puebla).*

   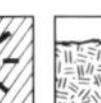 

NOTOCACTUS

NOTOCACTUS **CORYNODES** (Otto ex Pfeiff.) Krainz
Syn: *Wigginsia corynodes* (Otto ex Pfeiff.) D. M. Porter

A semi-globular, elongating species up to 20cm high, 10cm in diameter. Dark green, it has a densely woolly crown and 13–16 notched ribs with areoles 1–2cm apart. The spines are yellowish, darker at the tips; seven to twelve are radials to 2cm long, and there is one longer central. Flowering in summer, it is diurnal, with bright yellow flowers up to 5cm across. Requires full sun; normal cactus compost; minimum temperature 10°C (50°F). *Argentina, Uruguay.*

NOTOCACTUS **FLORICOMUS** (Arech.) Berger **var. VELENOVSKII** (Frič ex Backeb.) Krainz
Syn: *Notocactus velenovskii* Frič

A dark glossy green, more or less globular plant about 8cm high, 10–15cm in diameter. It has about 20 notched ribs and the areoles bear many glassy-white radial spines, often tipped reddish, about 1cm long with usually one similarly coloured long central. Day flowering in summer, the flowers are a glossy golden yellow, 5–6cm in diameter. Needs full sun; normal cactus compost; minimum temperature 10°C (50°F). *Uruguay.*

NOTOCACTUS **POLYACANTHUS** (Link & Otto) Theunissen
Syn: *Wigginsia polyacantha* Ritter

Dark-green, somewhat globular plants up to 10cm in diameter with about 17 notched ribs. The areoles are whitish, set about 1cm apart, and bear six to eight whitish radial spines up to 1cm long with usually one longer central. Early-summer flowering and diurnal, the flowers are canary yellow with prominent reddish stigma lobes, and are 1.5–2cm in diameter. Requires sun; normal cactus compost; minimum temperature 10°C (50°F). *Southern Brazil.*

NOTOCACTUS **PURPUREUS** Ritter

A dark-green globular, later elongating species up to 14cm in diameter. It has 14–19 notched ribs and the white areoles are set 5–8mm apart. These bear about 15 whitish radial spines 6mm to 1.4cm long and four to six yellowish-brown centrals to 2cm in length. Flowering in mid-summer, it is diurnal; the flowers are 4cm long, pinkish purple, with wide-spreading white stigma lobes. Requires a sunny position; normal cactus compost; minimum temperature 10°C (50°F). *Brazil (Rio Grande do Sul).*

NOTOCACTUS **MINIMUS** Frič & Krzgr.

A small cylindrical or globose plant with 12–15 narrow ribs. The areoles bear 15–17 stiff, bristly, glassy-white radial spines and three to four slightly brownish centrals, varying from 5 to 6mm in length. The flowers are yellow, about 4cm in diameter and 2.7cm long, and appear by day, in summer. Requires fairly good and bright light; normal cactus compost; minimum temperature 10°C (50°F). *Uruguay.*

NOTOCACTUS **PROLIFERA** (Ritter) Theunissen
Syn: *Wigginsia prolifera* Ritter

A greyish-green globular plant 4–8cm in diameter. It has 13–17 ribs with crenate edges. The areoles are 3–5mm in diameter and carry brownish spines, six to nine radials 1–2cm long and one, or often up to four, centrals 2–3cm in length. Flowers are yellow, about 3cm long and across; they appear in summer, and are diurnal. Needs bright sun; normal cactus compost; minimum temperature 10°C (50°F). *Brazil (Rio Grande do Sul).*

NOTOCACTUS **TEPHRACANTHUS** (Link & Otto) Krainz
Syn: *Malacorcarpus tephracantha* (Link & Otto) K. Sch.

A dark-green, slightly flattened globular plant up to 15cm in diameter, with 16–18 slightly notched ribs. Areoles are about 1–1.5cm apart, bearing five to seven pale yellowish-brown radial spines and usually one central of unequal length up to 2.5cm. It flowers by day, in summer, the flowers a bright canary yellow, up to 5cm long and wide. Requires bright light; normal cactus compost; minimum temperature 10°C (50°F). *Brazil, Argentina, Uruguay.*

NOTOCACTUS

▲

▲

NOTOCACTUS **UEBELMANNIANUS** Buin.

A dark-green globular species, somewhat flattened on the upper surface, and about 17cm in diameter. It has 12–16 prominent thick ribs and large, white areoles with six to eight greyish-white radial spines 1–3cm in length. Mid-summer flowering, it is diurnal; the flowers are glossy red, and about 4.5cm long and wide. Needs bright light; normal cactus compost; minimum temperature 10°C (50°F). *Brazil (Rio Grande do Sul).*

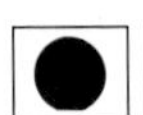    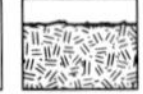 

NYCTOCEREUS

NYCTOCEREUS **CHONTALENSIS** Alex.

A creeping, trailing plant with stems to 1m or more in length, and branching freely. The stems are yellowish or pale green and about 5cm thick with four to six angular ribs. The spines are brownish, varying from 5mm to 1cm in length, of which five to seven are radials, and one to four are centrals. Flowers are nocturnal, appearing in early summer; they are whitish, 6–8cm long, and sweetly scented. Requires a position in slight shade; normal cactus compost; minimum temperature 13°C (55°F). *Mexico (Oaxaca).*

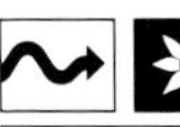    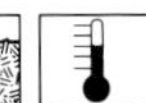

NYCTOCEREUS **SERPENTINUS** (Lagasca & Rodr.) Br. & R.
Syn: *Peniocereus serpentinus* (Lagasca & Rodr.) N. P. Taylor

Stems are erect or slightly pendant, often trailing; they are 5–6m in length, 2–5cm thick, with 10–13 slightly rounded ribs. There are about 12 whitish or brownish spines 1–3cm long. Night flowering in summer, the flowers are white, pinkish externally, and 15–20cm long. Needs slight shade; normal cactus compost; minimum temperature 13°C (55°F). *Mexico (probably Eastern).*

OBREGONIA

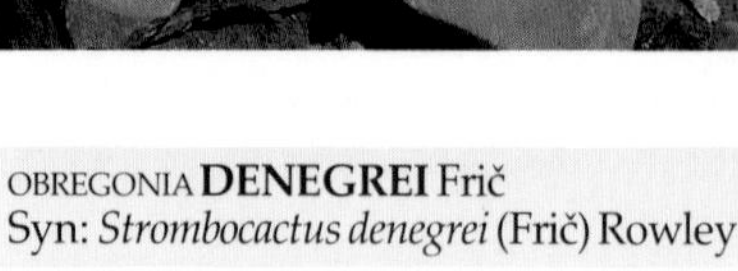

OBREGONIA **DENEGREI** Frič
Syn: *Strombocactus denegrei* (Frič) Rowley

A globular plant with a thick taproot. The stems, 8–12cm in diameter, are covered with greyish-green or brownish-green flat, leaf-like tubercles which are spirally arranged, and are about 1.5cm long, 2.5cm wide at the base. Areoles appear at the tips of the tubercles bearing a few bristly spines which soon fall. Flowers form in centre of plant; these are white, 2–4cm across and are diurnal, appearing in summer. Requires full sun; normal cactus compost; minimum temperature 10°C (50°F). *Mexico (Tamaulipas).*

    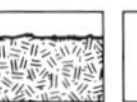 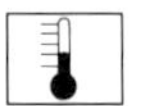

OPUNTIA **ALBISAETACENS** Backeb.

A low-growing plant with somewhat cylindrical or longish, flattened joints 4cm or more long, 2.5cm broad. These are covered with soft whitish, bristle-like spines, about 10 from each areole and about 6cm long, curved and spreading in all directions. Flowers are reddish purple and 4–5cm across: they are diurnal, in summer. Needs good light; normal cactus compost; minimum temperature 10°C (50°F). *Bolivia (Tupiza).*

OPUNTIA **ALCAHES** Weber

A branching, spiny shrub up to about 1m high. It has more or less dark-green cylindrical joints 6–15cm long to 5cm thick with prominent tubercles. The areoles are whitish, bearing yellow glochids, with five to twelve whitish-yellow spines 2–3cm in length. Day flowering in mid-summer, the flowers are greenish-yellow with reddish edges to the petals and 3–3.5cm long. Needs a bright sunny position, which is essential; normal cactus compost; minimum temperature 10°C (50°F). *Mexico (Baja).*

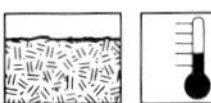

OPUNTIA **ARBUSCULA** Engelm.

A shrub-like plant 1–2m tall. It has spreading branches with joints 5–15cm long, 1–1.2cm thick and low, inconspicuous tubercles up to 3cm long. There are one to four reddish spines, 1–4cm long, in sheaths of pale brown from each areole. Flowers, 2–3.5cm in diameter, are yellowish green and are diurnal, occurring in early summer. Requires full sun; normal cactus compost; minimum temperature 7°C (45°F). *USA (Arizona), Mexico (Sonora).*

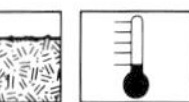

OPUNTIA **ARECHAVALETAI** Speg.

A shrubby, erect, much branching plant 1–3m tall. The bright-green joints are oblong or obovate and flat, and 25–30cm long. It has quite small brown areoles with one to three spreading white spines up to 9cm in length. Flowers are yellow, with white stamens and style; they are diurnal, coming in mid-summer. Needs a sunny location; normal cactus compost; minimum temperature 10°C (50°F). *Argentina, Uruguay.*

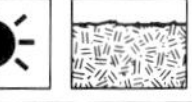

OPUNTIA **ARGENTINA** Griseb.

A tree-like plant up to 15m tall in its habitat. It has a thick, cylindrical, fresh-green trunk 6–8cm thick and cylindrical branches bearing flat oblong joints 5–12cm long with one, rarely more, slender spine up to 1cm in length. Flowering by day in mid-summer, the flowers are greenish yellow and 3–4cm in diameter. Its fruits are red, differing in this respect from the similar *O. brasiliensis* Haw. which has yellowish fruits. Requires full sun; normal cactus compost; minimum temperature 10°C (50°F). *Northern Argentina.*

OPUNTIA **ARMATA** Backeb.

A dull-green, low-growing, spreading plant with joints about 3.5cm long, 1.5–2cm wide. The areoles are small but prominent, and reddish brown with tufts of minute reddish-brown glochids. There are about nine white spines, often with darker tips, varying from 5mm to 2cm in length. Flowers are possibly yellow, and appear by day in mid-summer. Needs good light; a slightly calcareous compost; minimum temperature 10°C (50°F). *Northern Argentina.*

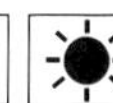
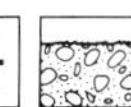
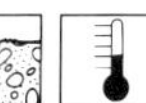

OPUNTIA **AZUREA** Rose

A low, bushy species borne on a short stem. The bluish-green joints are more or less oval in shape, thick and fleshy, and 10–15cm long. Areoles, set about 2cm apart, bear brown glochids and one to three brownish-black reflexed spines 2–3cm in length. It is day flowering in summer; the flowers are deep yellow with reddish bases to the petals, and about 4cm long. Requires sun; normal cactus compost; minimum temperature 13°C (55°F). *Mexico (Zacatecas).*

▲

OPUNTIA **BRACHYCLADA** (Griffiths) Munz
Syn: *Opuntia brachyclada* Griffiths

A low-growing, spreading plant with small greyish-green joints 5–8cm long, 2.5–4cm wide. They bear many small brownish areoles with brown glochids which are spineless. Flowers are a deep red, cup-shaped and 5–8cm in diameter; they appear by day, in summer. A choice, quite rare plant. Requires full sun; a normal cactus compost with a little lime added; minimum temperature 7°C (45°F). *USA (California).*

▼

OPUNTIA **BASILARIS** Engelm. & Bigelow

A bush species up to about 1m high. The joints are almost oval, bluish green or a pale reddish green and 10–20cm long, with a velvety appearance. The areoles are brownish with reddish-brown glochids and sometimes one short spine. Day flowering in early summer, the flowers are reddish purple, 6–8cm long and across. Requires a very bright position; a porous enriched mineral compost; minimum temperature 7°C (45°F). *Northern Mexico, USA (Arizona, Nevada).*

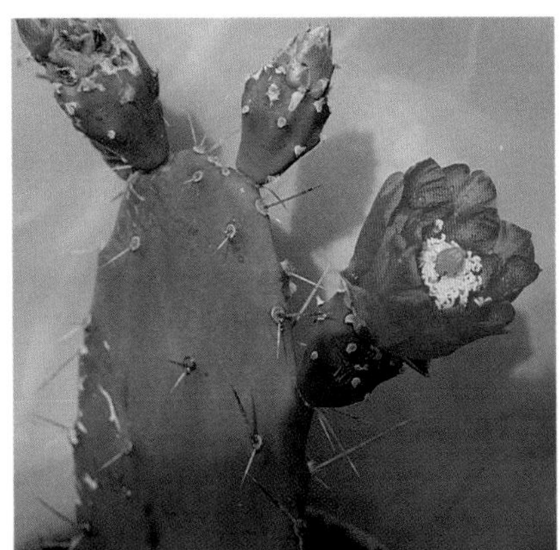

OPUNTIA **BERGERIANA** Weber

A tree-like species attaining 2–3m in height. The joints are pale to fresh green, 10–25cm long, 5–10cm wide, with greyish areoles and yellowish glochids. There are two to three spines which are yellowish passing to grey, and 2–4cm long. It flowers freely in summer, and is diurnal, with bright red blooms up to 6cm diameter. Easy to cultivate, it requires full sun; normal cactus compost; minimum temperature 7°C (45°F). *Habitat unknown.*

OPUNTIA **BIGELOWII** Engelm.
Syn: *Cylindroipuntia bigelowii* (Engelm.) F. Knuth

An erect shrubby species up to about 1m high. The light-green joints are cylindrical up to 15cm long, 5cm thick. Areoles are white with yellow glochids and there are many pale-yellow spines, six to ten radials up to 1.5cm long, and six to ten slightly longer centrals. Flowers are purple, about 4cm long and across, and are diurnal, appearing in summer. Requires full sun; a normal cactus compost; minimum temperature 10°C (50°F). *USA (California, Arizona), Northern Mexico (Baja).*

  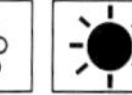   

OPUNTIA **BURRAGEANA** Br. & R.

A low spiny shrub up to about 1m tall. The dull-green joints are 1–2cm thick and each is about 15cm long and more or less cylindrical. The brown areoles are closely set, and bear short yellow glochids and numerous bright yellow spines about 2cm long. It is summer flowering and diurnal; the flowers are reddish, green at the base, and 3–4cm in diameter. Requires bright sun; normal cactus compost; minimum temperature 10°C (50°F). *Mexico (Baja).*

      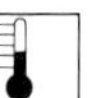

OPUNTIA **CHLOROTICA** Engelm. & Bigelow

A bushy, somewhat tree-like species up to 1m or more tall. The joints are a pale bluish-green, 12–20cm long, 12–16cm broad with round, greyish areoles. These have yellow glochids and one to six pale yellowish spines which become almost black with age and are 2–4cm long. Flowers are diurnal, occurring in summer, and are yellow, flushed reddish externally, and about 5cm long, 7cm broad. Requires full sun; normal cactus compost; minimum temperature 7°C (45°F). *Mexico (Sonora, Baja), USA (California, Nevada, New Mexico).*

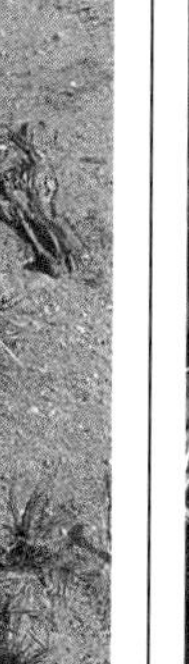

OPUNTIA **BRADTIANA** K. Brand.
Syn: *Grusonia bradtiana* Br. & R.

A low, bushy plant, semi-erect or sprawling, consisting of elliptical or cylindrical greyish-green joints. It has eight to nine ribs with areoles set about 1cm apart bearing glochids which soon fall, as do the small leaves. The spines are yellowish white, of which 12 or more are radials up to 2cm long, and four to five are centrals to 5cm. Summer flowering, the bright yellow flowers appear by day and are 3–4cm across. Needs a sunny position; normal cactus compost; minimum temperature 10°C (50°F). *Mexico (Coahuila).*

OPUNTIA **CANTERAI** Arech.

A tree-like species about 1m or little more high. It has slender oblong joints up to 20cm long, 4–6cm broad. The brownish-violet areoles bear up to two whitish, often brown-tipped spines 1–2cm long, but are sometimes spineless. Flowering in late summer, the plant is diurnal, with the blooms lasting several days. The orange flowers are 1.5 to 4cm in diameter. Requires bright light; normal cactus compost; minimum temperature 13°C (55°F). *Uruguay.*

OPUNTIA **CHOLLA** Weber
Syn: *Cylindropuntia cholla* (Weber) F. Knuth

A shrub-like plant 1–3m tall in its habitat. The dull-green joints are cylindrical to oval, 25cm long and 4–5cm thick. The areoles have yellow glochids and numerous yellowish radial spines 1cm or more long and one longer central. Flowering by day in mid-summer, the flowers are rose pink and 3–4cm in diameter. Requires sun; normal cactus compost; minimum temperature 10°C (50°F). *Mexico (Baja).*

OPUNTIA **CLAVARIOIDES** Pfeiff.
Syn: *Puna clavarioides* Keisl.

A low bushy, straggling species with greyish-brown joints which are cylindrical, flattish or fan-shaped. The close-set areoles have four to ten short, white, fine spines. Flowers are brownish yellow and about 6.5cm long, 5cm across, appearing by day in mid-summer. Needs slight shade; normal cactus compost; minimum temperature 10°C (50°F). *Chile, Argentina.*

OPUNTIA **COCHINELIFERA** Mill.
Syn: *Nopalea cochenillifera* (L.) Salm-Dyck (specific title variously spelt)

A tree-like species 3–4m high with glossy green, obovate-elongated joints 8–25cm long, 5–12cm wide. The areoles are set far apart with a few yellow glochids; they are either spineless or have two to four spines 8mm to 1.5cm long. A summer flowering plant, and diurnal, the flowers are 6–7cm long and reddish pink. Requires a bright location; normal cactus compost; minimum temperature 13°C (55°F). *Tropical Central America.*

OPUNTIA **COMPRESSA** (Salisb.) Macbr.

A clump-forming species with dull to greyish-green more or less orbicular joints 10–17cm long, 6–12cm broad. It has brown areoles and glochids, and only one spine to an areole; these are 2.5–4cm long, and greyish. It is a summertime plant, day flowering, with bright yellow flowers 4–6cm in diameter. Requires sun; normal cactus compost; minimum temperature 7°C (45°F). *USA (Southern States).*

OPUNTIA **CLAVATA** Engelm.
Syn: *Corynopuntia clavata* (Engelm.) Knuth

A clump-forming species with stems up to 7cm long, 2–3cm thick. It is more or less oval in shape with close-set areoles and pale yellow glochids. The spines are white, with about 10 radials up to 1.5cm long, and four to eight centrals up to 3cm. Summer flowering, it is diurnal, with golden-yellow flowers about 4cm long. Requires bright sun; slightly calcareous cactus compost; minimum temperature 7°C (45°F). *USA (New Mexico).*

    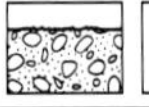 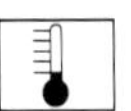

OPUNTIA **COLUBRINA** (Cast.) Backeb.

A rarely encountered, slender cylindrical plant to 1m high with dull-green, almost bluish-green joints 6–18cm long and about 1cm thick. It has a few areoles bearing minute whitish glochids and one to three bristly whitish spines 5–8mm long. The flowers are citron yellow, about 5.5cm in diameter, and are followed by purplish-red fruits. They bloom in mid-summer, and are diurnal. Requires sparse shade; normal cactus compost; minimum temperature 13°C (55°F). *Argentina (Formosa).*

  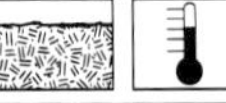

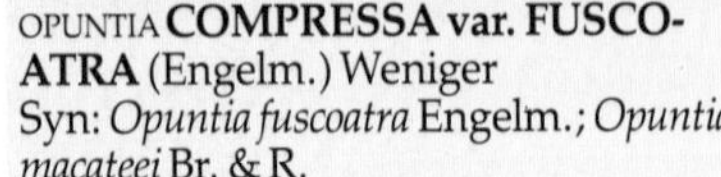

OPUNTIA **COMPRESSA var. FUSCO-ATRA** (Engelm.) Weniger
Syn: *Opuntia fuscoatra* Engelm.; *Opuntia macateei* Br. & R.

This is a more or less prostrate plant with bright-green to bluish-green joints up to about 10cm long, 7–8cm wide, and somewhat club-shaped. The areoles have clusters of reddish-brown glochids and one to three yellowish, becoming greyish, spines 6mm to 5cm in length. It flowers in mid-summer and is diurnal, with sulphur-yellow flowers, to about 10cm in diameter. Requires full sun; normal cactus compost; minimum temperature 7°C (45°F). *USA (Texas).*

   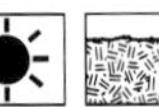 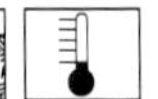

OPUNTIA **DILLENII** (Ker.) Haw.
Syn: *Opuntia horrida* Salm-Dyck.

A densely branched, often rather sprawling bush with dark-green obovate joints 20–25cm long bearing large areoles with yellow glochids. Spines vary considerably; they are sometimes absent, or there may be several, up to 10, yellowish ones 1–4cm long. These may be either straight, twisted or decidedly curved. The flowers are pale yellow and up to 8cm long, flowering by day in late summer. Requires full sun; very porous enriched mineral compost; minimum temperature 13°C (55°F). *West Indies, Tropical South America, USA (Florida), Mexico.*

    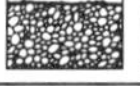 

OPUNTIA **DISCOLOR** Br. & R.

A semi-prostrate plant with very dark green joints 5–15cm long, 1–2.5cm thick, and almost cylindrical in shape. It has dark brown areoles with brown glochids. There are usually two or three greyish-brown spines, 1–3cm in length. Flowers are bright yellow, about 3cm across, and bloom by day in summer. Needs good, bright light; normal cactus compost; minimum temperature 10°C (50°F). *Argentina.*

   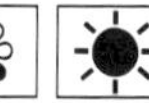 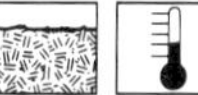 

OPUNTIA **ECHIOS** How.
Syn: *Opuntia galapageia* var. *echios* (How.) Backeb.

Tree-like plants up to 8m high and much branched. The joints are bright green, ovoid to elliptical, and up to 30cm long with woolly areoles and yellow glochids. The plant has yellowish-brown spines 11–13cm long, some of them spreading, others downward pointing, and golden-yellow flowers about 7cm long which are diurnal, in summer. Requires bright sun and warmth, which are essential; normal cactus compost; minimum temperature 15°C (59°F). *Galapagos Islands.*

        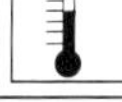 

OPUNTIA **ELATA** Link & Otto

A fairly tall, bushy species with bright green, smooth elongated joints 15–25cm in length and up to 15cm wide. The white woolly areoles are set well apart. Spines are often absent, but there is usually one about 3cm long on younger growth, and older joints are more spiny. Flowering in late summer, it is diurnal. The flowers are pale orange-yellow with prominent yellowish white stamens. Needs good light; normal cactus compost; minimum temperature 10°C (50°F). *Paraguay.*

    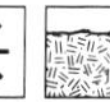 

OPUNTIA **ENGELMANNII** Salm-Dyck

A most variable species, medium to bluish green, and up to about 1.5m high. The joints are broadly oval, 20–30cm long. Areoles with brownish wool bear brownish glochids and have from one to several yellowish or greyish spines up to 2cm long. The flowers are diurnal, appearing in early summer, and are a clear sulphur yellow and up to about 5cm diameter. Requires full sun; normal cactus compost; minimum temperature 10°C (50°F). *Widespread in Mexico & Southern USA States.*

OPUNTIA **ENGELMANNII var. LINGUIFORMIS** (Griffiths) Weniger
Syn: *Opuntia linguiformis* Griffiths; *Opuntia lindheimeri var. linguiformis* (Griffiths) L. Benson

An upright or sprawling plant. The pale-green, elongated joints are 20–40cm long, about 10cm wide, and the areoles are brown with yellowish glochids. They have one to five yellowish spines, 1–2cm long. Mid-summer flowering, and diurnal, the flowers are yellow or orange, often on same plant, and about 7cm in diameter. Requirements are the same as for the species. *USA (Texas).*

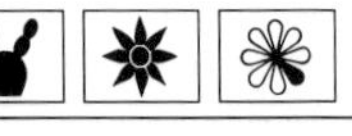

OPUNTIA **ERECTOCLADA** Backeb.

A clump-forming species, the dark-green joints are about 5cm long, 4cm wide, and narrowly oblong and flat. Areoles have reddish-brown glochids and spines, usually two to four per areole. The flowers are bright carmine, about 4cm diameter, and are day flowering in summer. Requires slight shade; normal cactus compost; minimum temperature 10°C (50°F). *Argentina.*

OPUNTIA **ENGELMANNII var. ACICULATA** (Griffiths) Weniger
Syn: *Opuntia aciculata* Griffiths; *Opuntia lindheimeri var. aciculata* Bravo

In its manner of growth this is similar to the species: the joints are 13–20cm long, dark green with areoles bearing dense tufts of reddish-brown glochids. They have one to three brownish spines, occasionally more, 3–5.5cm long. Flowering in early summer, it is diurnal; the flowers are reddish magenta or orange, rarely yellow, and 8–10cm in diameter. Requirements are the same as for the species. *USA (Texas), Mexico (Nuevo Leon).*

OPUNTIA **ENGELMANNII var. TEXANA** (Griffiths) Weniger

In general, this is very similar to the species. The areoles are scarcely woolly and set well apart, with few glochids and one to three or more slender pale yellowish spines, 2–3cm long, especially from the upper areoles. Flowers are yellow, 8–10cm in diameter, and appear by day in mid-summer. Requirements are the same as for the species. *USA (Texas), Northern Mexico.*

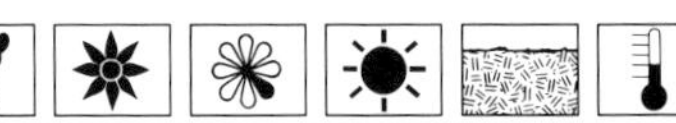

OPUNTIA **ERINACEA** Engelm. & Bigelow
Syn: *Opuntia hystricina* var. *bensonii* Backeb.

A clump-forming plant with bluish-green, more or less oblong joints 5–15cm long, 4–6cm wide. It has fairly close-set areoles armed with yellowish glochids and many whitish spines up to 5cm in length. Day flowering in mid-summer, the flowers are about 6cm broad, and usually deep red. Requires sun; slightly calcareous cactus compost; minimum temperature 7°C (45°F). *USA (Southern States).*

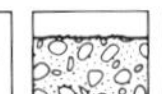

OPUNTIA **ERINACEA var. URSINA**
(Weber) Parish
Syn: *Opuntia hystricina* var. *ursina* (Weber) Backeb.

Generally similar to the species in respect of the joints, the principal feature being the numerous greyish-white long spines which are very flexuous and curving, and are 8–10cm long. The flowers are yellowish, about 8cm broad, and appear by day in early summer. Requires a sunny position; normal cactus compost with lime chippings added; minimum temperature 7°C (45°F). *USA (Arizona, California, Nevada, Utah).*

OPUNTIA **ERINACEA var. UTAHENSIS**
(Engelm.) L. Benson
Syn: *Opuntia erinacea* var. *rhodantha* L. Benson

Similar to the species: the joints are obovate, 5–9cm long, 5–8cm broad, with numerous greyish-white spines in the upper areoles, 2.5–5cm long, straight or recurving. Flowering by day in early summer, the flowers are red, and about 8cm across. Requires full sun; normal cactus compost with lime chippings added; minimum temperature 7°C (45°F). *USA (Northern Arizona, California, New Mexico).*

   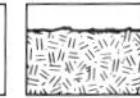 

▲

OPUNTIA **ESTEVESII** Braun

A very recently introduced species of which little is known in cultivation. It is named for the discoverer, Esteves Pereira. The large greyish to bluish-green joints have numerous areoles arranged in rows, bearing minute brown or blackish spines. Flowers are unknown, but presumably they are diurnal in summer, requiring bright light; normal cactus compost; minimum temperature 10°C (50°F). *Brazil (Bahia).*

     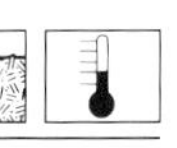

OPUNTIA **EXALTATA** Berger
Syn: *Austrocylindropuntia exaltata* (Berger) Backeb.

Closely allied to *O. subulata*, this is a tree-like species up to nearly 6m tall in its habitat, having more or less cylindrical leaves about 7cm long. The greyish-green stems and joints are cylindrical, with areoles bearing a few spines initially, later up to 12 or more; these are darkish yellow to reddish brown. Flowering by day in summer, the flowers are more or less brick red, 6cm or more across. Fruits red. Needs sun; normal cactus compost; minimum temperature 13°C (55°F). *Ecuador, Peru, Bolivia.*

   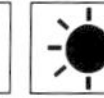 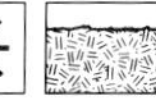 

OPUNTIA **FALCATA** (F. Knuth)
Syn: *Consolea falcata* (Ekm. & Werd.) F. Knuth

Tree-like plants up to about 1.5m high, with dark glossy-green joints to 35cm long, 9cm broad. The flattened surfaces are marked with somewhat obscure prominences. Areoles, which are whitish, bear two to eight pale brownish or yellowish spines 1cm or more long; these are rough and needle-like. The reddish flowers, 3–5cm across, appear in summer, and are diurnal. Requires light shade; normal cactus compost; minimum temperature 13°C (55°F). *Haiti.*

   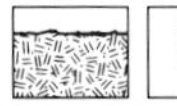 

OPUNTIA **FICUS-INDICA** (L.) Mill.

Probably the most common member of the *Cactaceae* having been cultivated and naturalized in many parts of the world. It is a tree-like plant 3m or more tall, the greyish-green joints 20–40cm long, 10–20cm broad with whitish areoles and yellow glochids. Usually spineless, more occasionally there are one or two thick, straight spines. Flowering in the daytime in summer, the flowers are yellow, and about 6.5cm long. Requires full sun; normal cactus compost; minimum temperature 10°C (50°F). *Tropical America.*

   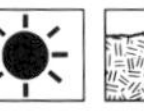 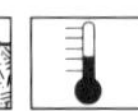

OPUNTIA **FULGIDA** Engelm.
Syn: *Cylindropuntia fulgida* F. Knuth

A tree-like plant 1–3m high with a thick cylindrical stem, branching above. The joints are greyish-green, 10–20cm long and 4cm thick. The small areoles bear pale yellowish glochids with about 10 brownish or yellowish spines with white sheaths, 2.5–3.5cm long. Flowering by day in mid-summer, the flowers are rose pink and about 3cm across. Needs full sun; slightly calcareous cactus compost; minimum temperature 10°C (50°F). *USA (Arizona), Mexico (Sonora).*

    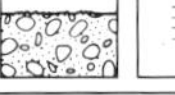 

OPUNTIA **GOSSELINIANA** Weber

A glaucous-green, densely bushy species up to 1m high with more or less orbiculate joints 8–18cm wide, slightly less long, and up to 1cm thick. Areoles carry tufts of yellowish-brown glochids and one to five twisting, flexuous whitish spines 2–5cm long with one up to 10cm. Summer flowering, and diurnal, the flowers are 6–9cm across, deep yellow with pale reddish bases to the petals. Requires full sun; normal cactus compost; minimum temperature 10°C (50°F). *Mexico (Baja, Sonora).*

  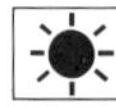       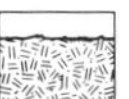 

OPUNTIA (Micropuntia)
GRACILICYLINDRICA Wiegand & Backeb.

A small, slender species, often with a short stem and fairly long cylindrical joints up to 20cm long, 6–9mm wide. The areoles are minute, white felted, and bearing 16 or more fine, white radial spines 3–6mm long and one central slightly longer. It flowers by day in early summer with rose-pink flowers 3–4cm wide. Requires good light, which is essential; slightly calcareous compost; minimum temperature 10°C (50°F). *USA (Nevada).*

    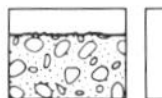 

OPUNTIA **HYSTRICINA** Engelm. & Bigelow

A low-growing, clump-forming species with almost circular dark-green joints 8–13cm long, 6–10cm broad. The areoles are close–set with pale-brown glochids and six to fifteen spines which are brownish, becoming grey, and 1–8cm long. It is day flowering in summer; the flowers are generally bright yellow and 5–8cm in diameter. Needs a sunny position; normal cactus compost; minimum temperature 7°C (45°F). *USA (Nevada, Arizona, New Mexico).*

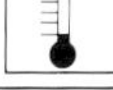

OPUNTIA **IMBRICATA var. ARBORESCENS** (Engelm.) Weniger
Syn: *Opuntia arborescens* Engelm.

A bushy or low tree-like plant, 1–3m high, but the size can be most variable. Joints are more or less cylindrical, ranging from 5 to 15cm or more long, 2cm or a little more thick, covered with elongating tubercles, 5–6mm high. The areoles have few glochids and two to ten pale-brownish spines 1.2–4cm long, and the flowers are pinkish or lavender coloured and up to 7cm across. Requirements are the same as for the species. *USA (New Mexico, Northern Mexico).*

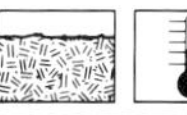

OPUNTIA **IMBRICATA var. VIRIDIFLORA** (Br. & R.) Weniger
Syn: *Opuntia viridiflora* Br. & R.

A bush-like species 30–60cm high, generally more dwarfed in cultivation. It has joints from 5–7cm long, to 2cm thick, more or less cylindrical and covered with tubercles. The greyish areoles bear tufts of yellowish glochids and five to seven spines up to 2cm long. Flowers are greenish, tinged reddish, and are 4–5cm long. Requirements are the same as for the species. *USA (New Mexico).*

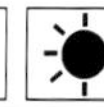

OPUNTIA **IMBRICATA** Haw.
Syn: *Opuntia decipiens* DC.

A green to bluish-green, low species about 3m high, much branched. The joints are 7–20cm long, 3–4cm thick, with prominent tubercles and large yellowish areoles with few glochids. It has 10–30 spines to an areole; reddish or whitish and 1–2.5cm long. Flowers, diurnal in summer, are variable: they may be purplish, reddish, or yellowish and are mainly 4–8cm across. That shown is associated with *O. decipiens*. Requires full sun; normal cactus compost; minimum temperature 10°C (50°F). *USA (Southern States) to Central Mexico.*

OPUNTIA **IMBRICATA var. LLOYDII** (Rose) Bravo

Somewhat similar to O. *imbricata* var. 'Arborescens', with rather longer joints about 2.5cm thick and five to ten greyish-white spines, 6–9mm or slightly more long. Summer flowering, it is diurnal with dull-purplish blooms, 3–4cm in diameter. Requirements are the same as for the species. *Central Mexico.*

OPUNTIA **INAMOENA** K. Sch.

A low-growing species rarely exceeding 60cm high. The joints are brownish green or bluish green and 8–16cm long, 5–7cm wide, often to 3cm thick. The small areoles have whitish glochids, which are usually spineless. Summer flowering, it is diurnal with brick-red flowers 3–3.5cm long, 4cm across. Needs a bright position, which is essential; normal cactus compost; minimum temperature 13°C (55°F). *Brazil (Pernambuco).*

OPUNTIA **INARMATA Backeb.**
Syn: *Austrocylindropuntia inarmata* Backeb.

A low-growing, clump-forming species, olive-green in colour with oblong joints 3–5cm long, 1.5–2cm broad. It has large white areoles bearing a few bristles which quickly fall, and minute glassy-white glochids which are more or less spineless. Day flowering, in late summer, the flowers are a bright deep red, about 4cm in diameter, with a stigma with blackish-violet lobes. Requires full sun; normal cactus compost; minimum temperature 13°C (55°F). *Bolivia.*

OPUNTIA **IPATIANA** Card.

Very closely allied to *O. salmiana*, this is a low-growing plant 30–40cm high. The main stem is green, often slightly purplish, and about 1.5cm thick with cylindrical branches 7–8cm in length. The white areoles set at 7mm intervals have pale yellowish glochids and five to nine brownish-white spines, some soon falling, others 1–2cm long. Summer flowering, and diurnal, the flowers are a pale orange-pink, about 3.5cm long. Needs a bright position; normal cactus compost; minimum temperature 13°C (55°F). *Bolivia (Santa Cruz).*

OPUNTIA **KLEINIAE** DC. **var. TETRACANTHA** (Toumey) Earle
Syn: *Opuntia tetracantha* (Toumey) F. Knuth

A bushy plant to over 1m in height. The branches are about 30cm long, 1.5cm thick, with prominent tubercles to 2cm long. The brown areoles bear three to six, usually four, brownish spines, up to 5cm long. Flowers appear by day, in summer, and are orangy red or yellowish green suffused with purple and 3–3.5cm in diameter. Needs full sun; slightly calcareous compost; minimum temperature 7°C (45°F). *USA (Arizona).*

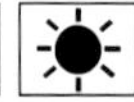
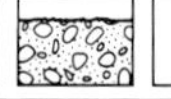
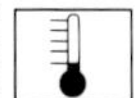

OPUNTIA **INVICTA** Brandegee

A bushy plant rarely more than 50cm tall. It has dark-green short cylindrical joints 8–10cm long, 6–7cm thick with long, low-set tubercles. The areoles are white with a few white glochids and about 20 straight and curving spines up to 3cm in length, which are red at first then becoming greyish. It flowers by day in mid-summer; the blooms are bright yellow, about 5cm across. Requires full sun; normal cactus compost; minimum temperature 13°C (55°F). *Mexico (Baja).*

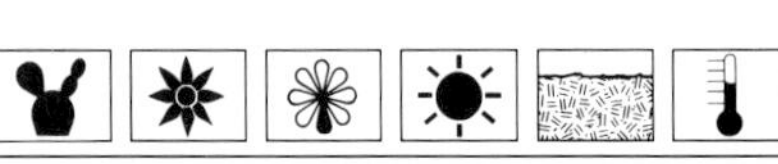

OPUNTIA **KISKA-LORO** Speg.

A semi-prostrate, spreading species with glossy green, flat joints up to 30cm long, 4.5cm broad, and more or less lance-shaped. There are a few small, whitish areoles with one or two pale spines, up to 4cm long. It is diurnal, flowering in late summer with rich orange blooms, 4–5cm across. Needs bright light; normal cactus compost; minimum temperature 10°C (50°F). *Argentina (Catamarca).*

OPUNTIA **LANCEOLATA** Haw.

A tree-like plant to over 2m high. The bright-green joints are lanceolate and up to 30cm long, 8cm broad, with areoles bearing yellowish-brown glochids and one or two whitish spines up to 1cm long which soon fall. Flowering by day in early summer, the flowers are sulphur yellow with green outer segments, 5cm broad, 6.5cm long. Requires full sun; normal cactus compost; minimum temperature 15°C (59°F). *West Indies, South America.*

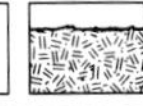

OPUNTIA **LEPTOCAULIS** DC.

A most variable bushy plant to over 1m high. The joints are green, 5mm or a little more thick, and slightly warty. The areoles bear tufts of yellowish glochids and one to three brownish spines 2–5cm in length. Flowers are yellowish, about 2cm long, and appear by day in mid-summer. Requires a bright position; normal cactus compost; minimum temperature 7°C (45°F). *Mexico, USA (Texas, New Mexico, Arizona).*

  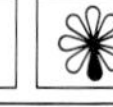     

OPUNTIA **MACROCENTRA** Engelm.

A bushy plant up to nearly 1m tall. The joints are dark, almost bluish green, oblong or nearly rounded, and 10–20cm long, about 15cm wide. Areoles are greyish with brown glochids and one to three brown to blackish slender erect spines 4.5–6.5cm long. Flowers are yellow with a red centre, about 5cm long, 7cm across, appearing in summer, and are diurnal. Needs a very sunny position; normal cactus compost; minimum temperature 7°C (45°F). *USA (Texas, Arizona), Northern Mexico.*

 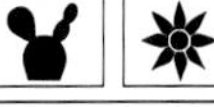      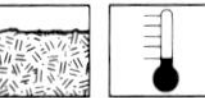 

OPUNTIA **MARENAE** S. H. Parsons
Syn: *Marenopuntia marenae* (S. H. Parsons) Backeb.

A low-growing spiny species with long, slender dark-green or brownish-green joints 5–15cm long, 1–2cm thick. Areoles are whitish-yellow with a few minute glochids and eight to nine spreading spines, including one or two much longer, about 1.5cm in length. Flowering by day in mid-summer, the flowers are yellowish with pinkish outer segments, and 4–5.5cm in diameter. Requires a sunny position; slightly calcareous cactus compost; minimum temperature 10°C (50°F). *Mexico (Sonora).*

OPUNTIA **LEUCOTRICHA** DC.

A tree-like plant which attains 3–4m in height in the wild and branches freely. Joints are somewhat oval in shape, up to 25cm long, 12cm wide, and covered with dense whitish-grey velvety hairs. The close-set areoles are white with yellowish glochids and one to three prominent white spines 5–8cm long. Flowering in mid-summer, and diurnal, the flowers are a rich yellow, with a red style and green stigma lobes, and are 6–8cm across. Needs sun; an enriched mineral compost; minimum temperature 10°C (50°F). *Central Mexico.*

    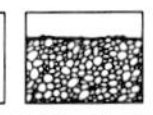 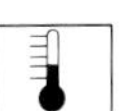 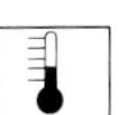

OPUNTIA **MICRODASYS** (Lehm.) Pfeiff. **var. ALBISPINA** Fobe

An erect, bushy plant with broadly oval yellowish-green joints 6–12cm long. These are thickly dotted with areoles bearing numerous minute white glochids, which are generally spineless. The flowers, appearing by day in summer, are bright yellow, 4–5cm long and in diameter. Requires slight shade; normal cactus compost; minimum temperature 10°C (50°F). *Central Mexico.*

   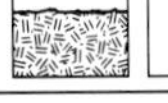 

OPUNTIA **MICRODASYS var. RUFIDA** K. Sch.
Syn: *Opuntia rufida* Engelm.

Plants are up to about 50cm tall with dark greyish-green, more or less oval joints, 5–8cm long. Areoles are reddish-brown with similar-coloured glochids, and are spineless. Yellow or orange-yellow flowers appear in summer, and are diurnal. Requirements are the same as for O. *microdasys* var. *albispina*.

 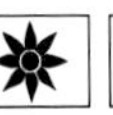  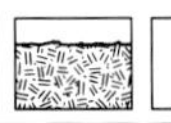 

OPUNTIA **MICRODASYS var. PALLIDA** Hort.

Similar to O. *microdasys* var. *albispina* except that the areoles and glochids are yellow and the joints rather longer and more slender. Flowers are similar. Requirements are the same as for var. *albispina*.

   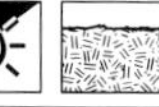 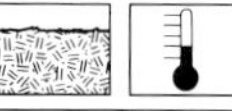 

OPUNTIA **MIQUELII** Monv.
Syn: *Austrocylindropuntia miquelii* (Monv.) Backeb.

Cylindrical-stemmed plants up to about 1m tall, mainly branching from the base and forming large clumps. The bluish-green stems are about 6cm thick, and have prominent tubercles. Areoles have brownish glochids and around 10 greyish-white spines, some up to 10cm long. Day flowering in summer, the flowers are white or pinkish-white, rarely yellow, and 4–8cm long. Needs good light; normal cactus compost; minimum temperature 10°C (50°F). *Chile (Atacama).*

   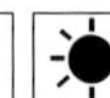 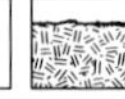 

OPUNTIA **MOELLERI** Berger

A low-growing plant up to about 15cm high with oval or conical joints 6–9cm long and about 5cm thick. These have prominent tubercles and whitish areoles with similar-coloured glochids. The spines are brownish grey, of which seven to eight are radials to about 8mm long and there are one to five centrals to 1.6cm. Day flowering, in early summer, the flowers are yellow, about 2.5cm across. Requires full sun, which is essential; normal cactus compost; minimum temperature 13°C (55°F). *Mexico (Coahuila).*

    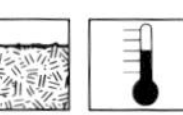

OPUNTIA **ORBICULATA** Salm-Dyck
Syn: *Opuntia crinifera* Pfeiff.

A tall, shrubby plant up to 2m high with oval or roundish joints 15–25cm long, 10–15cm broad, and glaucous or pale bluish green in colour. The areoles are greyish, with reddish-yellow glochids and about six yellowish, becoming greyish-white, spines up to 4cm in length. Numerous whitish hairs are very apparent on the surface of the joints. The yellow flowers, about 10cm across, appear by day in summer. Needs sun; normal cactus compost; minimum temperature 7°C (45°F). *Northern Mexico.*

OPUNTIA **MORTOLENSIS** (Br. & R.) F. Knuth

An erect, shrub-like, dark-green plant to about 60cm tall, the several branches 15–45cm long, and up to 1cm thick. The white woolly areoles each have usually one to three greyish-white spines, often up to 4cm in length. Flowering by day in summer, the greenish-yellow flowers are about 2.5cm long and across. Needs a sunny position; normal cactus compost; minimum temperature 10°C (50°F). *Mexico.*

   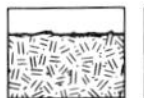 

OPUNTIA **PACHYPUS** K. Sch.
Syn: *Austrocylindropuntia pachypus* (K. Sch.) Backeb.

An erect, mostly solitary plant up to 1m high and about 8cm thick. It has closely set, flattish tubercles and large, white areoles, bearing yellow glochids and 20–30 whitish spines, varying from 5mm to 2cm in length. Summer flowering, it is diurnal; the flowers are scarlet, 7cm long and across. A rare species needing good light; normal cactus compost; minimum temperature 13°C (55°F). *Peru (Chosica).*

 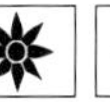   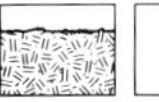 

OPUNTIA **PALMADORA** Br. & R.

A dense shrub-like plant up to about 3m high with a centre trunk about 9cm thick. The joints are thin, narrowing to about 10–15cm long, 4–7cm wide with whitish areoles and a few brownish glochids. Spines are yellowish, one to four or more in number, and up to 3cm long. Flowering by day in early summer, the flowers are brick red, with petals standing erect, and are 3–5cm long. Requires light shade; normal cactus compost; minimum temperature 13°C (55°F). *Brazil (Bahia).*

   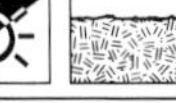 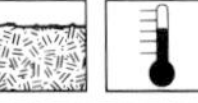 

OPUNTIA **PICARDOI** Marn.-Lap.

A low-growing, spreading species with pale to dark-green somewhat oval joints, about 7cm long, 3–4cm broad. Areoles are yellowish brown with up to 10 white spines 3–5mm in length, and minute golden-yellow glochids. Flowering in mid-summer, the flowers are diurnal, bright red, and 4cm in diameter. Requires a bright sunny position; slightly calcareous cactus compost; minimum temperature 13°C (55°F). *Argentina (Salta).*

      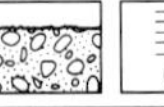  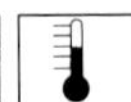 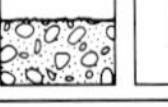  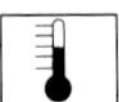

OPUNTIA **PUBERULA** Pfeiff.

Probably a natural hybrid of *O. microdasys*. This is a bushy plant up to 1m tall with broadly oval greenish joints to 12cm long, 8cm wide and large yellow areoles with tufts of yellow glochids. Mostly spineless, but occasionally there are three or more yellowish spines about 1cm long. Mid-summer flowering, it is diurnal, with pale yellow flowers, about 4cm across. Requires a sunny position; normal cactus compost; minimum temperature 10°C (50°F). *Mexico.*

       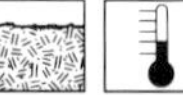

OPUNTIA **PARAGUAYENSIS** K. Sch.

A semi-erect, bushy plant with dark-green oblong joints, 18–21cm long, 8–15cm wide. The prominent areoles, about 4mm long, are yellowish white with yellowish glochids. Spines are usually absent, though there is occasionally one to 1cm long. Flowering by day in mid-summer, the flowers are orange-yellow and about 8cm across when fully open. Needs very bright light; normal cactus compost; minimum temperature 13°C (55°F). *Paraguay, Argentina.*

OPUNTIA **PILIFERA** Weber

A tree-like species, in its habitat up to 4m high. The pale-greenish joints are usually oblong, 12–30cm long, 7–12cm broad. Areoles are grey with yellowish-red glochids and fine curly hairs and carry two to nine whitish, slender spines 1–1.5cm long. Day flowering, in summer, the flowers are dark red and about 6cm in diameter. Needs a bright position; normal cactus compost; minimum temperature 10°C (50°F). *Mexico (Puebla).*

OPUNTIA **PULCHELLA** Engelm.

A clump-forming species arising from a glochid-covered tuber 5–8cm in diameter. The joints are variable, but are mostly cylindrical or clavate and covered with low tubercles, up to about 10cm long but more frequently not exceeding 5–6cm. The areoles have yellow glochids and whitish or greyish spines of which eight to fifteen are radials 2–4mm long, and there is one central, 2.5cm in length. The plant is summer flowering and diurnal, with purple to rose flowers about 5cm broad. Requires sun; normal cactus compost; minimum temperature 10°C (50°F). *USA (Arizona, Nevada).*

   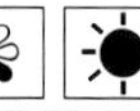 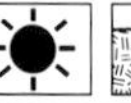 

OPUNTIA **PYCNANTHA** Engelm.

A fairly low-growing species with dark-green oval joints 12.5–15cm long, about 12.5cm broad. These are slightly pubescent and covered with closely set brown areoles bearing tufts of brownish-yellow glochids. The brownish spines are reflexed, 2–3cm long. Flowers, greenish yellow and 4–4.5cm across, appear in summer and are diurnal. Requires a sunny position; normal cactus compost; minimum temperature 13°C (55°F). *Mexico (Baja).*

         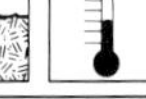  

OPUNTIA **QUIMILO** K. Sch.

A shrub-like plant up to 4m high in the wild. The greyish-green joints are more or less elliptical and are up to 50cm long, 25cm broad and 2–3cm thick. Large areoles bear initially one stiff white spine 7–15cm long and later somewhat shorter, often twisted spines. Flowers are bright red, about 7cm across, and appear by day in mid-summer. Needs sun; normal cactus compost; minimum temperature 10°C (50°F). *Northern Argentina.*

OPUNTIA **ROBUSTA** Wendl.

A variable species, generally tree-like and up to 5m high in the wild. The greyish-green joints are often broader than long, thick, smooth, and up to 30cm broad. Areoles are brown with small reddish glochids, the upper areoles having a few thick, yellowish spines, becoming whitish, 1–5cm long. Flowers are yellow, about 7cm across, and appear by day, in summer. Requires bright light; normal cactus compost; minimum temperature 10°C (50°F). *Central Mexico.*

   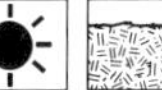 

OPUNTIA **PYCNANTHA var. MARGARITANA** Coult.

Very similar to the species but with pale glochids and more numerous whitish spines, up to about 1cm in length. Occasionally a cristated growth develops (as illustrated). Flowers are sulphur yellow, about 4–5cm diameter. Requirements are the same as for the species. *Mexico (Santa Margarita Island).*

OPUNTIA **RAMOSISSIMA** Engelm.

A bushy or arborescent species, rarely more than 60cm high. The greyish-green joints are slender, 5–10cm long, spreading to form dense, spiny clumps. The joints are 5–6mm thick with a 'woody' core, covered with flattened tubercles with apical areoles. Usually there is only one developing spine to over 5cm long, which often quickly falls. Flowers in summer, diurnal, about 4cm long, 1–2cm in diameter. The greenish-yellow petals are tinged with lavender. Requires full sun; normal cactus compost; minimum temperature 10°C (50°F). *USA (California, Nevada).*

   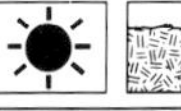 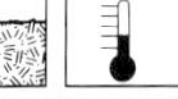

OPUNTIA **SALMIANA** Parm.
Syn: *Austrocylindropuntia salmiana* (Parm.) Backeb.

Cylindrical-stemmed, 50–75cm tall, with branches 25cm or more long and about 1cm in diameter. These are glaucous green, reddish or purplish. The areoles are very small and whitish, with tufts of glochids, spineless or with about three yellowish spines about 4mm in length. Flowers in late summer, diurnal, yellow and about 3.5cm across. Requires a sunny position, normal cactus compost; minimum temperature 13°C (55°F). *Brazil, Paraguay, Argentina.*

  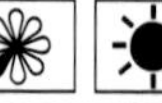 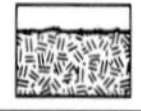 

OPUNTIA **SAXATILIS** (Ritter) Braun & Esteves **var. POMOSA** Braun

A somewhat low-growing, semi-prostrate species with greyish-green joints 10–12cm long, 5–7cm broad and 1cm thick. The areoles are white with usually two to three pale brownish-white spines to about 1cm long. Flowers are bright yellow, about 3cm long, and appear by day in mid-summer. Needs bright light; normal cactus compost; minimum temperature 10°C (50°F). *Brazil (Minas Gerais).*

    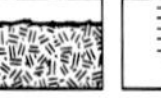 

OPUNTIA **SCHICKENDANTZII** Weber

A rather slender greyish-green species eventually reaching 1–2m tall. Flattened cylindrical joints are up to 20cm long, 1.5–2.5cm thick and have small whitish areoles bearing whitish glochids and one or two white spines up to 2cm long. The flowers are yellow, about 4cm across, diurnal and summer flowering. Needs bright light; normal cactus compost; minimum temperature 10°C (50°F). *Argentina (Tucuman, Salta).*

OPUNTIA **SCHOTTII** Engelm.
Syn: *Corynopuntia schottii* (Engelm.) F. Knuth

A low-growing, spreading plant rarely exceeding 20cm high. It has erect, oval joints, 4–7cm long and up to 2cm thick, with prominent tubercles 1.5cm long. The areoles are white with white glochids and six to eight white radial spines to 2cm long with four pale brownish centrals up to 4cm in length. Summer flowering, and diurnal, the flowers are bright yellow, 3cm in diameter. Needs bright light; normal cactus compost; minimum temperature 10°C (50°F). *USA (Texas), Northern Mexico.*

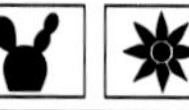      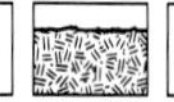  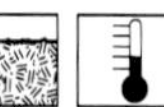

OPUNTIA **SPEGAZZINII** Weber
Syn: *Opuntia albiflora* K. Sch.; *Austrocylindropuntia salmiana var. albiflora* (K. Sch.) Backeb.

A cylindrical-stemmed, branching species up to 1m high. The smooth, glaucous-green branches are about 30cm long, 1–2cm thick, and the small, white areoles have white glochids and two to five whitish spines, about 8mm long. Flowering by day in late summer, the blooms are white, about 2cm diameter. Requires a bright position; normal cactus compost; minimum temperature 13°C (55°F). *Argentina.*

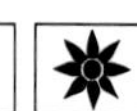  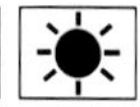  

OPUNTIA **SUBULATA** (Müehlf.) Engelm.
Syn: *Austrocylindropuntia subulata* (Müehlf.) Backeb.

Erect, 2–4m high, 6–10cm thick, generally branching. The stems and joints are regularly covered with more or less oblong tubercles. Semi-cylindrical leaves form towards the upper portion of the stems, about 10cm long, often persisting. The areoles have a few yellowish glochids and one or two pale yellowish spines up to 8cm long. Reddish flowers appear by day, in summer, 2cm or more wide. Requires bright light; normal cactus compost; minimum temperature 10°C (50°F). *Peru, Argentina, Chile?*

    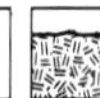 

OPUNTIA **STENOPETALA** Engelm.

A semi-prostrate plant with pale greyish-green joints 10–20cm long, obovate or almost round. The brown areoles are set far apart with brownish glochids and there are two to four brownish-red spines which become greyish, and are up to 5cm long. Flowers are bright flame red, 4cm in diameter when fully open; they appear by day in summer. The oval fruits which follow are spineless or almost so, and a deep rose pink. Requires full sun; normal cactus compost; minimum temperature 10°C (50°F). *Central Mexico.*

OPUNTIA **STENOPETALA var. RIVIEREANA** Backeb.

Very similar to the species but with larger joints 22cm long, 14cm broad and 3cm thick. The areoles are whitish with brownish glochids and one or two spines to 3cm long. Flowers are orange-red, 4cm long, 2cm in diameter when fully open; they are summer flowering, and diurnal. Requirements are the same as for the species. *Central Mexico.*

  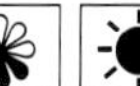 

OPUNTIA **SULPHUREA** G. Don
Syn: *Opuntia maculacantha* Forst.

A low-growing spreading, straggling plant with pale-green, oval-shaped joints 10–20cm long. The small areoles bear yellowish-red glochids and two to eight mostly twisted, stiff spines which initially are reddish, and later turn greyish white with brownish tips. Sulphur-yellow flowers, 4cm long, appear by day, in summer. Requires sun; normal cactus compost; minimum temperature 10°C (50°F). *Argentina (Santiago).*

     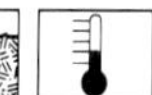

OPUNTIA **TUNICATA** Link & Otto
Syn: *Cylindropuntia tunicata* (Lehm.) F. Knuth

A bushy, erect plant to about 50cm high, freely branching in whorls. The glaucous-green stems and joints are 6–12cm long, about 4cm thick, with prominent white areoles and yellow glochids. The six to ten pale yellow spines, 4–5cm long, are barbed. Day flowering in early summer, the flowers are yellowish green and about 5cm in diameter when fully open. Requires bright sun; slightly calcareous cactus compost; minimum temperature 10°C (50°F). *Mexico, possibly also South America.*

   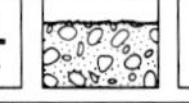 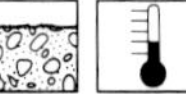 

OPUNTIA **VERSICOLOR** Engelm.
Syn: *Cylindropuntia versicolor* F. Knuth

Tree-like, 2m or more high, with a short trunk and longer branches. These have dullish green, tuberculate joints 10–25cm long, 2–4cm thick, often turning purplish, and a few cylindrical leaves, which soon fall. The areoles and glochids are reddish brown; there are seven to twelve brown spines, about 1.5cm long. Flowers, about 5cm in diameter, are red, rose purple, brown or greenish yellow, appearing by day in summer. Requires a sunny position, normal cactus compost; minimum temperature 10°C (50°F). *USA (Arizona), Northern Mexico.*

   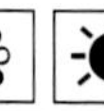 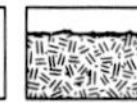 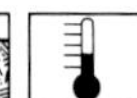

OPUNTIA **VIOLACEA** Engelm.

This plant, up to about 1m tall, is almost tree-like with green obovate joints which are always tinged bluish green or reddish purple, and are 10–15cm long and often up to 1cm thick. It has reddish-brown areoles and glochids with three dark-brown spines up to 6cm long on the top margin of each joint. The flowers bloom by day in summer. Each flower is 6–9cm in diameter and is bright yellow with a red throat. Requires a sunny location; normal cactus compost; minimum temperature 10°C (50°F). *USA (Arizona, New Mexico).*

    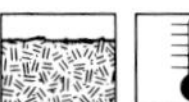 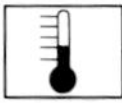

OPUNTIA **VERSCHAFFELTII** Weber
Syn: *Austrocylindropuntia verschaffeltii* (Cels) Backeb.

A low-growing, cylindrical-stemmed plant. The dull-green stems are 10–15cm long, 1–1.5cm thick, and slightly tuberculate, bearing cylindrical leaves 1–5cm in length, these often persisting. The areoles are whitish with yellow glochids and sometimes one to three very fine, hair-like spines up to 6cm in length. Flowering by day in late summer, the flowers are red, about 4cm in diameter. Requires a bright position; normal cactus compost; minimum temperature 10°C (50°F). *Bolivia.*

    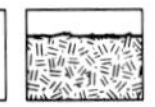 

▲

OPUNTIA **VESTITA** Salm-Dyck
Syn: *Austrocylindropuntia vestita* (Salm-Dyck) Backeb.

The plants are semi-erect or sprawling with cylindrical pale-green, warty joints up to 50cm long, 2–3cm thick. Areoles have white glochids, the upper ones bearing leaves about 1cm long. There are four to eight spines up to 2cm long inter-mingling with numerous fine white hairs which envelop the stems. The flowers are dark red, about 4cm wide; these are diurnal, in summer. Requires slight shade; slightly calcareous compost; minimum temperature 10°C (50°F). *Bolivia (La Paz).*

    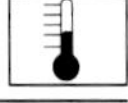

▶

OPUNTIA **VITELLINIFLORA** Ritter

A prostrate species with glossy-green joints, more or less oblong in shape and 12–22 cm long, 3–7cm wide, to 1cm thick. There are well-spaced, grey felted areoles 1mm in diameter and the spines are pale brownish, one to three in number and 5mm to 2cm in length. Day flowering in late summer, the flowers are orange-red, about 6cm long and 4cm across. Requires slight shade; normal cactus compost; minimum temperature 10°C (50°F). *Bolivia (Florida).*

    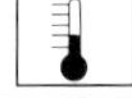

OPUNTIA **WHIPPLEI** Engelm. & Bigelow

A straggly, bushy plant up to 1m or more high. The joints are a dull green, 5–30cm long, 2cm thick, with tubercles about 1cm long and wide. The whitish areoles have a few glochids, and there are six to ten pinkish or brownish spines with whitish sheaths, 2.5–5cm long and strongly barbed. Flowering in summer, and diurnal, the blooms are pale yellow and about 3cm in diameter. Requires sun; normal cactus compost; minimum temperature 10°C (50°F). *USA (Arizona, New Mexico, Nevada, Utah).*

OREOCEREUS **CELSIANUS** (Lem.) Ricco.
Syn: *Pilocereus celsianus* Lem.

Should possibly be included within *Borzicactus*. The stems are erect, columnar and over 2m tall, 8–12cm thick, branching from the base, with about 10–25 rounded ribs. The large, white woolly areoles are about 1.5cm apart, the spines are yellowish to reddish brown, seven to nine are radials about 2cm long and one to four are centrals. Flowers by day in summer, 7–9cm long, pale purplish-pink inner petals, brownish-red externally. Requires bright sun; normal cactus compost; minimum temperature best at 10°C (50°F). *Bolivia, Argentina.*

    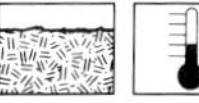

OREOCEREUS **CELSIANUS var. FOSSULATUS** (Backeb.). Krainz
Syn: *Oreocereus fossulatus* (Lab.) Backeb.

This is somewhat similar to the species with nine to fourteen ribs. The areoles, arranged 3cm apart, bear longer, honey-yellow spines and many hairs. The flowers are red or brownish-red, about 9cm or slightly longer, and appear by day, in summer. Needs bright sunshine; normal cactus compost; minimum temperature best at 10°C (50°F). *Peru, Bolivia.*

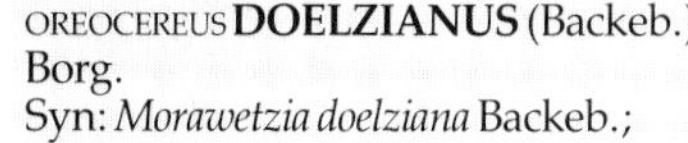

OREOCEREUS **DOELZIANUS** (Backeb.) Borg.
Syn: *Morawetzia doelziana* Backeb.; *Morawetzia sericata* Ritter

The olive-green stems are about 1m tall, 4–8cm thick, with nine or more ribs. Grey silky areoles are set about 1.5cm apart bearing 10–16 radial spines up to 1.5cm long, and four centrals to 4cm in length. Flowers appear by day in summer from the dense white woolly and bristly cephalium; carmine with a bluish suffusion on the inner petals and about 10cm in length. Needs bright sun; normal cactus compost; minimum temperature 10°C (50°F). *Central Peru.*

 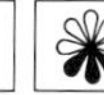   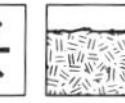 

OREOCEREUS **HENDRIKSENIANUS** Backeb.

Stems to about 1m high, branching from the base, and 6–10cm thick with about 10 rounded, deep-green ribs. The areoles, set about 2cm apart, bear seven to nine reddish radials up to 2cm long and one to four reddish-brown centrals to 5cm in length. There are dense, white woolly hairs from the tips of the stems. Flowers in mid-summer, diurnal; the flowers are carmine red, about 7cm long. That shown is possibly var. *densilanatus* Rauh & Backeb. Needs sun; normal cactus compost; minimum temperature 10°C (50°F) advisable. *Southern Peru.*

  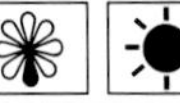 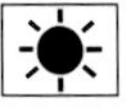 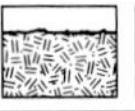 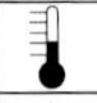

OREOCEREUS **TROLLII** (Kupper) Backeb.
Syn: *Oreocereus celsianus var. trollii* Kupper

A low-growing columnar plant about 50cm tall, branching from the base. The pale green stems are 6–9cm thick, with 15 or more notched ribs. Areoles are set about 2cm apart with a mass of white or greyish-white woolly hairs around the stem. The spines are yellow, reddish or brown, made up of 10–15 radials, and one or more centrals, all varying in size up to 2cm or more long. Flowers are pink to carmine, about 4cm long, by day, in mid-summer. Needs full sun; normal cactus compost; minimum temperature 10°C (50°F). *Bolivia, Argentina.*

   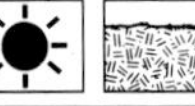 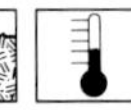

OROYA **NEOPERUVIANA** Backeb.

A dull-green, somewhat globular plant up to 40cm high, 25cm in diameter, with 34–35 or more ribs. The areoles bear many dull-yellowish spines with brown bases, of which there are 20–30 radials to 1.5cm in length, and one to five centrals. Flowers are pale to carmine red with a yellow centre, and are 2–2.5cm long; they appear by day, in summer. Requires bright light; normal cactus compost with additional humus added; minimum temperature 10°C (50°F). *Peru (Oroya).*

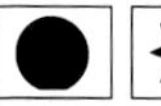    

OROYA **BORCHERSII** (Böed.) Backeb.

A fresh-green globular species (in centre of picture) up to about 30cm tall, 20cm or more in diameter, with up to 30 ribs. The brown areoles bear yellowish to reddish-brown spines which ultimately cover the body of the plant; there are 25–30 radials and one to three centrals, arranged like a comb, and 2–2.5cm or more long. Summer flowering, and diurnal, the flowers are about 2cm long, 1cm in diameter, and yellow to greenish yellow. Needs a bright position; an enriched cactus compost; minimum temperature 10°C (50°F). *Peru (Ancash).*

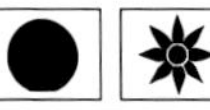  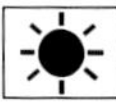 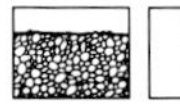

OROYA **PERUVIANA** (K. Sch.) Br. & R.

A bluish-green, rather flattened globular plant about 15cm wide, 10cm tall. It has 12–23 or more rounded ribs, notched into long tubercles, upon which are set the linear areoles nearly 1cm long. The radial spines, set in a comb-like arrangement, are yellowish brown and about 1cm long and there may be up to six central spines to 3cm in length. Flowers appear from the new central areoles in summer, and are diurnal. They are about 2.5cm long and bell-shaped, pale pink, yellowish at the base and reddish externally. Requires full sun; normal compost; minimum temperature 13°C (55°F). *Central Peru.*

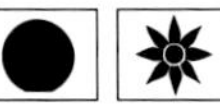 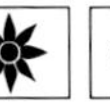  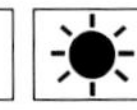 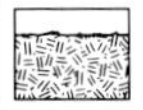 

ORTEGOCACTUS **MACDOUGALII** Alex.
Syn: *Neobesseya macdougalii* (Alex.) Kladiwa

A small globular species 3–4cm in diameter, pale greyish green, with large rhomboid tubercles about 1.2cm broad. The white woolly areoles bear black-tipped white or totally black spines consisting of seven to eight radials up to 1cm long and one central 4–5mm in length. It is day flowering in summer, producing greenish-yellow flowers about 3cm long, 2.5–4cm wide. Needs a bright position; an enriched cactus compost with a high mineral content; minimum temperature 15°C (59°F). *Mexico (Oaxaca).*

PACHYCEREUS **HOLLIANUS** (Weber) Buxb.
Syn: *Lemaireocereus hollianus* (Weber) Br. & R.

Columnar, 4–5m high, branching from the base. The branches are grey-green, 5–6cm thick with eight to ten ribs. Areoles are at intervals of 1–3cm with whitish-grey wool, bearing red spines which become grey. Twelve are radials to 2cm long and three to four are centrals to 10cm. Flowers are diurnal, in early summer, near or at the tips of the branches, white, about 10cm long. Needs a bright, sunny position; normal cactus compost with grit; minimum temperature 13°C (55°F). *Mexico (Puebla).*

   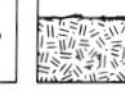 

PACHYCEREUS **PECTEN-ABORIGINUM** (Engelm.) Br. & R.

A deep-green tall, branching, columnar species up to about 8m in height and 30cm in diameter. It has 10–12 somewhat rounded ribs with large, greyish-white areoles set closely together and bearing eight to nine stiff, thick brownish radial spines and one or two centrals. Flowers are diurnal, appearing in summer, and are about 8.5cm long, white, and reddish externally. Requires full sun; normal cactus compost; minimum temperature 10°C (50°F). *Mexico (Northern, Central & Baja).*

   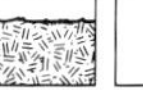 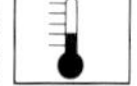

PACHYCEREUS **WEBERI** (Coult.) Backeb.
Syn: *Lemaireocereus weberi* (Coult.) Br. & R.

A giant tree-like, columnar plant up to about 10m tall, branching from well above the base with erect, almost bluish-green branches about 10cm or more thick. It has eight to ten ribs with elongated areoles 3–5cm apart and about nine reddish-brown or black radial spines 2–3cm long, and one flat central up to 10cm in length. The flowers are nocturnal, yellowish white and up to 10cm long, appearing in mid-summer. Requires sun and warmth; normal cactus compost; minimum temperature 13°C (55°F). *Mexico (Puebla, Oaxaca).*

   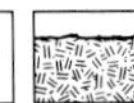 

X PACHYGEROCEREUS **ORCUTTII** (K. Brand.) Moran
Syn: *Cereus orcuttii* K. Brand.

An erect columnar plant up to about 3m high. The bright-green stems are 15cm thick, branching from the base, and there are 14–18 ribs with round greyish areoles set about 3cm apart bearing brownish spines. These consist of 12–20 spreading radials 1–2cm long and five centrals up to 7cm or slightly longer, and also spreading. Flowers, diurnal in summer, are about 4cm long and pale brownish. Requires full sun; normal cactus compost; minimum temperature 10°C (50°F). *Mexico (Baja).*

   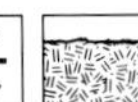 

PACHYCEREUS **PRINGLEI** (S. Wats.) Br. & R.

Tree-like, up to about 12m tall, the main trunk up to 60cm diameter. It has many erect, sturdy, greyish-green to dark-green branches and 10–16 rounded ribs closely set with large, oval, greyish areoles bearing reddish-grey spines. About 20 are radials to 2cm long, and one to three are centrals, slightly longer. Nocturnal flowers appear in summer; about 8cm long, and have white inner petals and greenish-red outer ones. Needs bright light; normal cactus compost; minimum temperature 10°C (50°F). Occasionally a crest-like growth occurs. *Mexico (Sonora, Baja).*

   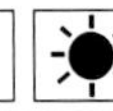 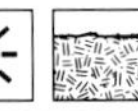 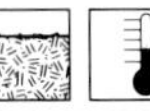 

▲

▲

PARODIA **AUREICENTRA** Backeb.

A dark-green globular plant about 15cm in diameter and densely covered with dark yellowish-brown spines. It has 13–15 ribs with white woolly areoles bearing about 40 radial spines and six to ten centrals, all up to 2cm or a little more in length. Flowers are a deep bright red, about 4cm across, and appear by day, in summer. Needs bright light; normal cactus compost; minimum temperature 10°C (50°F). *Argentina (Salta).*

     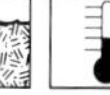

PARODIA **AUREISPINA** Backeb.

Fresh-green globular plants about 6.5cm diameter, with about 16 spiralling ribs divided into small tubercles. The areoles bear about 40 whitish radial spines about 8mm–1cm long and six yellowish-brown centrals 1.5–2cm in length, one of which is hooked at the tip. Flowering in mid-summer, the golden-yellow blooms are diurnal, and are about 3cm in diameter. Requires bright light; normal cactus compost; minimum temperature 10°C (50°F). *Argentina (Salta).*

   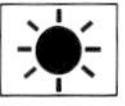 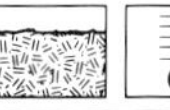 

PARODIA **AUREISPINA** (Backeb.) **var. SCOPAOIDES** (Backeb.) Brandt

This is similar to the species, about 6cm in diameter, to 10cm high. Deep green in colour, it has numerous small whitish radial spines and to four reddish centrals 1.5cm long. The flowers are orange-yellow, 3cm in diameter. Requirements are the same as for the species. *Argentina (Salta).*

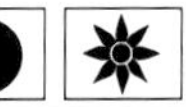 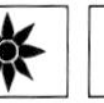   

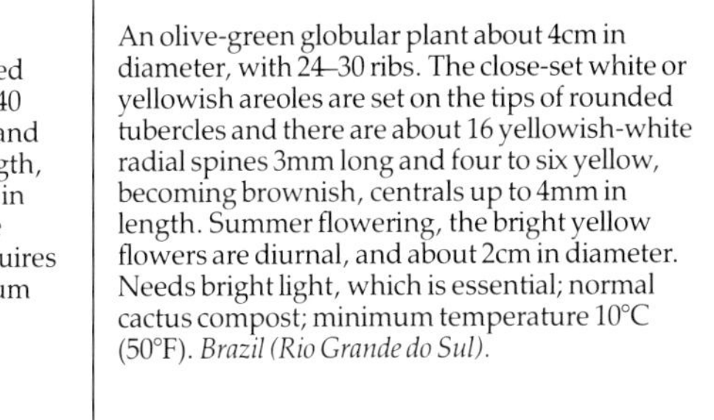

PARODIA **BREVIHAMATA** W. Haage

An olive-green globular plant about 4cm in diameter, with 24–30 ribs. The close-set white or yellowish areoles are set on the tips of rounded tubercles and there are about 16 yellowish-white radial spines 3mm long and four to six yellow, becoming brownish, centrals up to 4mm in length. Summer flowering, the bright yellow flowers are diurnal, and about 2cm in diameter. Needs bright light, which is essential; normal cactus compost; minimum temperature 10°C (50°F). *Brazil (Rio Grande do Sul).*

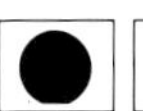    

PARODIA **BUENEKERI** Buin.

Deep-green globular plants about 5cm high, 6cm in diameter, with up to 20 ribs. The areoles are greyish white and bear about 13 whitish radial spines from 6mm to over 2cm in length, and five to six brownish centrals 3cm long. Mid-summer flowering and diurnal, the flowers are golden yellow, about 4cm long and across. Needs bright light, which is essential; normal cactus compost; minimum temperature 10°C (50°F). *Brazil (Rio Grande do Sul).*

    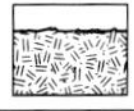 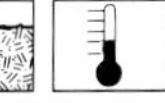

PARODIA **BUININGII** (Buxb.) N. P. Taylor
Syn: *Notocactus buiningii* Buxb.

A dark-green globular plant about 12cm in diameter, 8cm high, with 16 or more well-defined ribs. New areoles have white wool with a very few inconspicuous radial spines, but four dark-brown central spines with paler tips 1.2cm or more in length. The flowers are yellow, about 7cm long, and appear by day in summer. Requires very good light; normal cactus compost; minimum temperature 10°C (50°F). *Uruguay.*

PARODIA **CHRYSACANTHION** (K. Sch.) Backeb.
Syn: *Echinocactus chrysacanthion* K. Sch.

Pale-green globular plants about 10cm in diameter, 6–8cm high. They have about 24 ribs spirally arranged and divided into tubercles, and the yellowish-white areoles bear 30–40 fine yellow radial spines and one or more centrals 1–2.5cm in length. Flowering in mid-summer, the yellow blooms are diurnal and about 2cm long and across. Requires a sunny position; normal cactus compost; minimum temperature 10°C (50°F). *Argentina (Salta, Jujuy).*

PARODIA **CLAVICEPS** (Ritter) Brandt
Syn: *Eriocactus claviceps* Ritter; *Notocactus claviceps* (Ritter) Krainz

A dark-green, more or less cylindrical, club-shaped plant up to 50cm tall and about 12cm wide, with around 26 ribs. The areoles are whitish, carrying many somewhat drooping, soft yellowish spines up to 1cm in length. Mid-summer flowering and diurnal, the flowers are sulphur yellow and 4–5cm across. Requires a bright position; normal cactus compost; minimum temperature 10°C (50°F). *Paraguay, Brazil.*

PARODIA **COMARAPANA** Card.

Globular plants about 8cm in diameter and 5cm high with 18–20 bumpy ribs and grey-white areoles. The spines are brownish, of which there are 18–23 radials and three to four centrals, varying from 3mm to 2cm in length. Flowering in mid-summer, the flowers are diurnal, yellowish orange in colour and about 2.5cm long, to 1cm across. Requires bright light; normal cactus compost; minimum temperature 10°C (50°F). *Bolivia (Comarapa).*

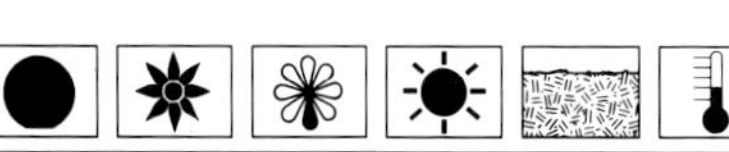

PARODIA **COMPRESSA** Ritter

A dark green, somewhat elongated, globular plant up to 15cm tall, 6cm in diameter, with 14–22 ribs. The white areoles carry six to nine radial spines 4mm to 1.2cm long and one to four yellowish-brown centrals about 8mm long. The flowers are red, 3cm long and about 2cm in diameter, and are day flowering in summer. Needs fairly bright light; normal cactus compost; minimum temperature 10°C (50°F). *Bolivia (Oropeza).*

PARODIA **CONCINNA** (Monv.) N. P. Taylor
Syn: *Notocactus concinnus* (Monv.) Berger

A dull-green, somewhat flattened globular plant up to 6cm high, 10cm wide, with 16–18 ribs. The whitish areoles bear 10–12 bristly yellow spines up to 7mm long and four yellowish-brown centrals to 2cm. Flowers are deep yellow, 7cm long, and appear by day in summer. Needs bright light; normal cactus compost; minimum temperature 10°C (50°F). *Brazil, Uruguay.*

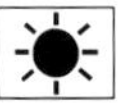

PARODIA **CRASSIGIBBA** (Ritter). N. P. Taylor
Syn: *Notocactus crassigibbus* Ritter

A dark-green, rather flattened globular species 5–18cm in diameter, with 10–15 ribs set with prominent chin-like protuberances. White woolly areoles bear seven to ten radial spines and usually one pale-brown central which becomes grey and is 2–3cm long. Day flowering in early summer, the flowers are sulphur yellow, 5–6cm across. Requires bright light; normal cactus compost; minimum temperature 10°C (50°F). *Brazil (Rio Grande do Sul).*

PARODIA **GROSSEI** (K. Sch.) Brandt
Syn: *Eriocactus schumannianus* (Nic.) Backeb.; *Notocactus schumannianus* (Nic.) Berger

Dark-green globular plants, 6–8cm wide becoming elongated to about 1m tall, the crown set at an angle, with about 30 prominent ribs. The areoles are brownish with four to seven or more yellowish-brown spines up to 2cm long. It is summer flowering, diurnal, with yellow flowers about 3.5cm long, 4cm in diameter. Needs bright light; normal cactus compost; minimum temperature 13°C (55°F). *Paraguay.*

PARODIA **ERINACEA** (Haw.) N. P. Taylor
Syn: *Wigginsia erinacea* (Haw.) D. M. Port.; *Malacocarpus erinaceus* (Lem.) Rumpl.

Dull-green globular plants up to about 15cm high and diameter with 15–20 somewhat spiralling ribs and areoles about 1cm apart. The spines are brown, becoming grey, of which there are six to eight radials up to 1cm long, and one central to 2.5cm. Flowers are funnel-shaped, yellow, and about 4cm long, 7cm across; they are day flowering, in summer. Needs bright light; normal cactus compost; minimum temperature 10°C (50°F). *Uruguay, Brazil, Argentina.*

PARODIA **GRAESSNERI** (K. Sch.) Brandt.
Syn: *Notocactus graessneri* (K. Sch.) Berger

A dark-green solitary, globular plant about 10cm high and wide, with 50–60 ribs divided into prominent tubercles. The areoles are whitish with about 60 yellow spines, mostly radials: there are only five to six centrals, up to 2cm long. Flowers are a pale yellowish green, about 1.8cm long, and appear by day in summer. Needs good light; normal cactus compost; minimum temperature 10°C (50°F). *Brazil (Rio Grande do Sul).*

PARODIA **HASELBERGII** (Haage Jr.) Brandt
Syn: *Notocactus haselbergii* (Haage Jr.) Berger; *Brasilicactus haselbergii* (Haage Jr.) Backeb.

A greyish-green, globular plant about 10cm wide with 30 or more ribs and the woolly crown set at an angle. The white areoles bear 20 or more yellowish-white radial spines up to 1cm in length, and three to five more yellowish centrals slightly longer. Summer flowering, and diurnal, the flowers are yellowish red or orange-red and about 1.5cm long. Needs bright light; normal cactus compost; minimum temperature 10°C (50°F). *Brazil (Rio Grande do Sul).*

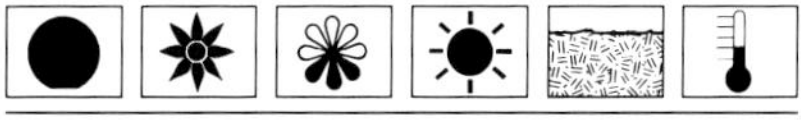

PARODIA **HERTERI** (Werd.) N. P. Taylor
Syn: *Notocactus herteri* Werd.

A pale-green plant with somewhat globular stems about 15cm in diameter, and about 22 prominently tubercled ribs. The tubercles are rather conical in shape and the brownish areoles have eight to eleven white, often brown-tipped, radial spines to 2cm long, and usually four dark brownish-red centrals of similar length. The flowers, appearing by day in summer, are purplish red with a paler, yellowish throat about 4cm long. Needs bright light; normal cactus compost; minimum temperature 10°C (50°F). *Uruguay.*

PARODIA **HETERACANTHA** Ritter

An elongating, bluish to greyish-green globular plant 4–8cm in diameter with many ribs, and densely covered with bristly spines. The areoles are of whitish-brown wool and the comparatively few radial spines are whitish, the centrals dark brown. Flowers are unknown. This still appears to be botanically undescribed and might well be associated with another species. *Argentina (Salta).*

PARODIA **HORSTII** (Ritter) N. P. Taylor
Syn: *Notacactus horstii* Ritter

A globular plant about 14cm in diameter with a spiny, white woolly crown. It has 12–16 ribs, and the areoles bear 10–15 white or slightly brownish radial spines 1–3cm in length and one to four brown, longer centrals. The plant is summer flowering by day, with flowers orange-red to vermilion, more yellowish internally, and 3–3.5cm long. Requires bright light; normal cactus compost; minimum temperature 13°C (55°F). *Brazil (Rio Grande do Sul).*

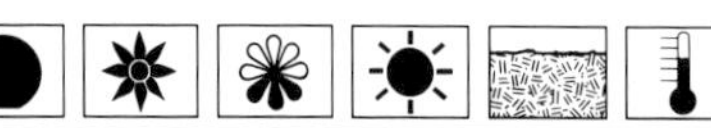

PARODIA **LAUI** Brandt

A dark-green globular species 6–9cm in diameter, with about 20 ribs. The areoles are white to brown, and there are numerous whitish appressed radial spines and one or two brownish centrals up to 1cm long. Flowers are dark red and up to 2.5cm long, about 1.5cm or a little more across; they appear in summer and are diurnal. Needs good light, which is essential; normal cactus compost; minimum temperature 10°C (50°F). *Bolivia.*

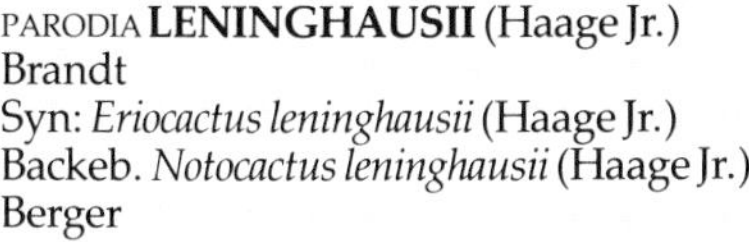

PARODIA **LENINGHAUSII** (Haage Jr.) Brandt
Syn: *Eriocactus leninghausii* (Haage Jr.) Backeb. *Notocactus leninghausii* (Haage Jr.) Berger

A globose later columnar species with the crown set at an angle. Up to 1m high, 10cm thick, and has about 30 ribs. The small, white areoles bear about 15 pale yellow radial spines and three to four deeper yellow centrals, up to 4cm in length. Day flowering in mid-summer, bright yellow, about 4cm long, 5cm across. Needs sun; normal cactus compost; minimum temperature 10°C (50°F). *Southern Brazil.*

PARODIA **MAGNIFICA** (Ritter) Brandt
Syn: *Notocactus magnificus* (Ritter) Krainz

Bluish-green, globular-stemmed plants, frequently offsetting to form clumps. The stems are up to 15cm in diameter with 11–15 ribs and grey-felted areoles. There are numerous whitish radial spines about 8mm long, and about 12 brownish centrals 1–2cm in length. Summer flowering, the plant is diurnal, with sulphur-yellow flowers about 5cm long and across. Needs bright light, which is essential; normal cactus compost; minimum temperature 10°C (50°F). *Brazil (Rio Grande do Sul).*

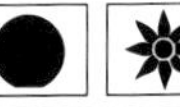    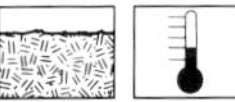

PARODIA **aff. MAIRANANA** Card.

Uncertainty exists as to the specific title. It has been stated to have a close relationship with *P. horstii*. The dark-green body with its woolly crown is 5–6cm in diameter with about 14–15 spiralled ribs. The brownish-red areoles bear seven to nine whitish radial spines and one to four brown centrals. Flowers are carmine red, 1–2cm long, and appear by day in summer. Needs bright light; normal cactus compost; minimum temperature 10°C (50°F). *Bolivia.*

PARODIA **MALYANA var. RUBRIFLORA** Brandt.

A bright-green globular plant with 24 or more slightly spiralled ribs. The whitish areoles bear over 20 greyish-brown, darker-tipped radial spines and two to three or more fine centrals of similar colouring. Flowers are bright red, funnel-shaped, and about 4cm long; they are day flowering, in summer. Needs bright light, which is essential; normal cactus compost; minimum temperature 10°C (50°F). *Argentina (Catamarca).*

    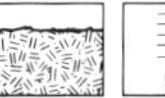 

PARODIA **MAMMULOSA** (Lem.) N. P. Taylor
Syn: *Notocactus mammulosus* (Lem.) Backeb.

A dark-green globular plant about 6cm in diameter and up to 10cm tall with 18–20 ribs. Areoles bear 10–13 or more yellowish-white radial spines 5mm long and three to four brown-tipped yellow centrals 1–1.4cm in length. Day flowering in summer, the flowers are bright yellow with a prominent reddish stigma, and about 4cm long. Requires good light; normal cactus compost; minimum temperature 10°C (50°F). *Argentina, Uruguay.*

PARODIA **MINUTA** Ritter

Closely allied to *P. gibbulosa*, this is a small, dark bluish-green species 4–5cm diameter, with 25 or more closely set ribs. The areoles are whitish, and bear seven to nine fine whitish radial spines and one to three brown, hooked centrals. Flowers are bright red, 2.5–3cm across, flowering by day in mid-summer. Needs sun; normal cactus compost; minimum temperature 10°C (50°F). *Bolivia (Valle Grande).*

     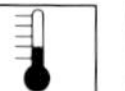

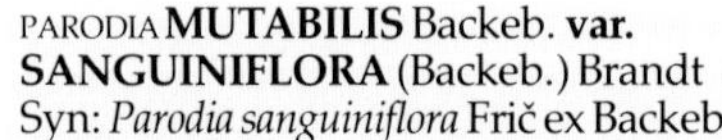

PARODIA **MUTABILIS** Backeb. **var. SANGUINIFLORA** (Backeb.) Brandt
Syn: *Parodia sanguiniflora* Frič ex Backeb.

A dark-green globular plant, 5–8cm in diameter, with 25 or more spirally arranged ribs divided into tubercles. The areoles are whitish and bear about 15 white radial spines 6–8mm long and four reddish-brown centrals around 2cm in length. Deep-red flowers, 3–4cm in diameter, appear in mid-summer, and are diurnal. Requires bright light; normal cactus compost; minimum temperature 10°C (50°F). *Argentina (Salta).*

   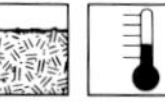

PARODIA **OTTONIS** (Lehm.) N. P. Taylor
Syn: *Notocactus ottonis* (Lehm.) Berger

A variable species with globular stems 5–11cm in diameter. It has six to thirteen ribs and a white woolly crown, and there are eight to fifteen yellow radial spines with three to four brownish centrals, all 1–2.5cm in length. Flowers are a deep yellow, 4–6cm long, blooming by day in summer. Needs full sun; normal cactus compost; minimum temperature 10°C (50°F). *Brazil, Uruguay, Argentina, Paraguay.*

PARODIA **MUTABILIS** Backeb.

A high-altitude, globular species about 8cm in diameter. It is glaucous green with a white woolly crown and ribs arranged in spirals. The white woolly areoles bear about 50 whitish radial spines and most usually four centrals, up to about 1.2cm long. Day flowering in summer, the flowers are bright golden yellow and 3–5cm across when fully open. Needs very bright light; normal cactus compost; minimum temperature 10°C (50°F). *Argentina (Salta).*

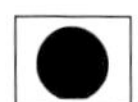    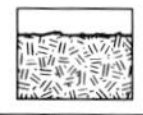 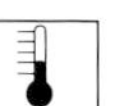

PARODIA **PENICILLATA** Fechs. & Steeg

A tall columnar plant up to 40cm high, 12cm thick. Mid-green in colour, it has about 17 spirally arranged ribs closely set with tubercles. The brownish woolly areoles carry around 40 yellowish radial spines of varying lengths and one central 3–5cm long. Flowers range from orange-yellow to vermilion, and are up to 5cm long, 4cm in diameter; they appear in summer, and are diurnal. Requires a sunny position; normal cactus compost; minimum temperature 10°C (50°F). *Argentina (Salta).*

PARODIA **PILTZIORUM** Weskamp

A dark greyish-green, slightly elongated globular species with 20 or more spiralling ribs with large brownish-wool areoles. Spines are pale yellowish brown or horn-coloured, consisting of 10–12 somewhat paler radials and usually four prominent centrals. The flowers are yellow, with outer segments having a brownish midstripe externally. They are day flowering, in summer. Needs bright light; normal cactus compost; minimum temperature 10°C (50°F). *Argentina (Salta).*

PARODIA **AFF. PSEUDOSTUEMERI** Backeb.

This bluish-green plant is about 25cm tall, 12cm in diameter, with 13 or more ribs. The areoles bear 20–25 greyish-white to pale-brownish radial spines and about four brownish centrals, all up to 1cm or slightly more in length. Flowers are orange-red, and about 2.5cm long; they are summer flowering, and diurnal. Needs a sunny position; normal cactus compost; minimum temperature 10°C (50°F). *Northern Argentina(?).*

PARODIA **RAUSCHII** Backeb.

Stems are green, about 25cm long and 15cm wide with about 13 ribs. The pale-brownish areoles carry about 20 yellowish radial spines up to 1.2cm long, and six yellowish centrals to 10cm in length. Flowers appear by day, in summer, orange-red to red or, rarely, white. Needs bright light, which is essential; normal cactus compost; minimum temperature 10°C (50°F). *Argentina (Salta).*

PARODIA **RECHENSIS** (Buin.) Brandt
Syn: *Notocactus rechensis* Buin.

A globular species, offsetting from the base to form clumps. The individual stems are bright green with about 20 ribs and whitish, becoming brownish, areoles. Spines are white or brownish-yellow: these consist of eight to twelve radials and one, sometimes more, central spine up to 1cm in length. Flowering in summer, the flowers are diurnal, and a bright golden yellow, 3cm or more broad when fully open. Requires sun; normal cactus compost; minimum temperature 10°C (50°F). *Brazil.*

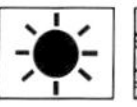
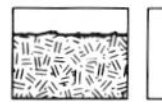
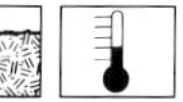

PARODIA **RIGIDA** Backeb.

A small globular plant about 4.5cm tall and in diameter, with 16–20 ribs. Whitish or pinkish-white spines are made up of seven to nine radials about 5mm long, and three to four centrals up to 8mm in length. The flowers, about 2cm long and across, are bright yellow with a white throat, and appear by day in summer. Requires bright sun; normal cactus compost; minimum temperature 10°C (50°F). *Northern Argentina.*

PARODIA **SAINT-PIEANA** Backeb.

A globular species 4–6cm in diameter, offsetting freely to form clusters. It has about 22 ribs spirally arranged and divided into conical tubercles. The yellowish-white areoles bear around 17 straight, very short yellowish or pale-brownish spines about 3mm long. Appearing in mid-summer, the flowers are diurnal, bright yellow in colour and about 2.5cm long and wide. Needs bright light; normal cactus compost; minimum temperature 10°C (50°F). *Argentina (Jujuy).*

PARODIA **SCOPA var. GLAUSERIANUS** Krainz

In most features this is similar to the species – the radial spines are bright yellow, the central spines orangy red or chestnut brown. Flowers and requirements are the same as for the species. *Uruguay.*

PARODIA **RUTILANS** (Dän.& Krainz) N. P. Taylor
Syn: *Notocactus rutilans* Dän. & Krainz

A rather roundish, bluish-green plant about 5cm in diameter with 18–24 spirally arranged ribs. The white woolly crown is slightly sunken. Areoles are of whitish wool and carry 14–16 brown-tipped white radial spines 5mm long and two slightly longer reddish-brown centrals. Summer flowering, and diurnal, the blooms are 3–4cm long, to 6cm across, and have pink tips to the petals, merging with a yellowish-white throat. Needs good light; normal cactus compost; minimum temperature 10°C (50°F). *Uruguay.*

   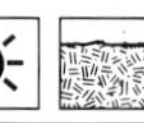 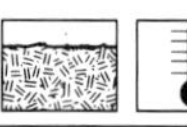

PARODIA **SCOPA** (Spreng.) N. P. Taylor
Syn: *Notocactus scopa* (Spreng.) Berger

A fresh-green, short cylindrical globose plant up to 25cm high, 10cm in diameter. It has a spiny, woolly crown and 30–35 ribs with areoles set about 8mm apart. There are about 40 white radial spines up to 7mm long and three to four reddish-brown central spines to 1cm. Summer flowering, and diurnal, the flowers are canary yellow, about 4cm in diameter. Requires bright light; normal cactus compost; minimum temperature 10°C (50°F). *Southern Brazil, Uruguay.*

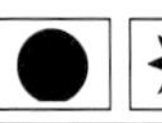   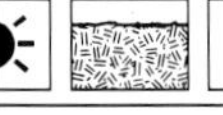

PARODIA **SETOSA** Backeb.

A bluish-green globular plant which becomes cylindrical and is up to 25cm high, 12cm in diameter. The crown is of dense white wool and there are about 35 ribs with areoles set on short but prominent tubercles. The whitish radial spines, numbering around 40, are 2cm long, and there are four reddish-brown central spines up to 1.2cm. Flowering in mid-summer, and diurnal, the flowers are carmine red, and up to 2cm in diameter. Needs fairly bright light; normal cactus compost; minimum temperature 10°C (50°F). *Argentina (Tumbaya).*

     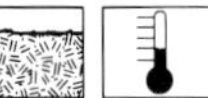

PARODIA **STUEMERI** (Werd.) Backeb.

Dull-green, somewhat globular plants to about 20cm high, 15cm diameter. There are 20 or more ribs, and the areoles bear about 25 whitish radial spines up to 2cm in length, and generally four brownish centrals to 2.5cm. Flowers are yellowish orange or reddish, 2–4cm long, and occur by day, in summer. Needs bright light; normal cactus compost; minimum temperature 10°C (50°F). *Argentina (Salta).*

PARODIA **SUBMAMMULOSUS** (Lem.) N. P. Taylor
Syn: *Notocactus submammulosus* (Lem.) Backeb.

A globular species 6–9cm in diameter, and dark greyish-green, with about 13–16 ribs divided into tubercles. The spines are yellowish-white, of which about six are radials to 1cm in length, and one or two are rather flattened centrals up to 2cm long. Flowers are yellow, about 4cm long, and day flowering, in summer. Needs bright light, which is essential; normal cactus compost; minimum temperature 10°C (50°F). *Uruguay, Argentina.*

PARODIA **UHLIGIANA** Backeb.

A more or less globular, grey-green species about 10cm in diameter, with a crown of dense white wool interspersed with reddish-brown spines. There are about 20 slightly spiralled ribs set with tubercles and the whitish areoles are 1cm long, bearing about 35 similarly coloured radial spines up to 1cm long and four or more dark-brown centrals, one of which is up to 5cm in length. Summer flowering, the flowers are diurnal, and are reddish brown or copper coloured, 2.5–3cm long. Requires a bright location; normal cactus compost; minimum temperature 10°C (50°F). *Argentina (Salta).*

PEDIOCACTUS **BRADYI** L. Benson

More or less globular plants 3.5–6cm long, 2.5–5cm wide with well-distributed tubercles. The areoles are whitish, bearing 14–15 white or pale-yellowish radial spines 3–6mm long; there are no centrals. Day flowering, in summer, the flowers are yellowish-white, up to 2cm or more long, 1.5–3cm across. Requires good light; normal cactus compost; minimum temperature 10°C (50°F). *USA (Arizona, Colorado).*

PEDIOCACTUS **DESPAINII** Welsh & Goodrich

Stems are sub-globose, up to 6cm high, 9.5cm wide with prominent tubercles 1cm long and wide. Areoles are elliptical, bearing nine to fifteen white radial spines 2–6mm long, but no centrals. The outer petals of the bronze-pink flowers have a purple midstripe, and the blooms are up to 2.5cm long and wide. They are summer flowering by day. Needs good light; slightly calcareous cactus compost; minimum temperature 10°C (50°F). *USA (Utah).*

PEDIOCACTUS **KNOWLTONII** L. Benson
Syn: *Pediocactus bradyi* L. Benson and var. *knowltonii* (L. Benson) Backeb.

A dark greenish-brown, globular plant up to 4–5cm tall, 3–4cm wide. The 12–18 ribs have wart-like tubercles and small areoles bearing 18–23 fine hair-like spines of whitish pink 1mm long, but no centrals. Day flowering, in summer, the flowers appear in the crown of the plant; they are very pale, almost creamy pink to rose, and about 1.5cm long. Requires extremely careful watering; good light; rich permeable compost; winter minimum temperature 7°C (45°F). *USA (Colorado, New Mexico).*

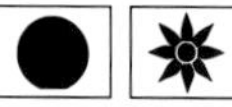     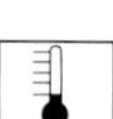

PEDIOCACTUS **PEEBLESIANUS var. FICKEISENIAE** (Backeb.) L. Benson
Syn: *Navajoa fickeisenii* Backeb.

Dark bluish-green globose plants to 7cm long, 5cm in diameter, covered with prominent wart-like tubercles. The areoles are yellowish, becoming grey, with straw-coloured spines, five to seven radials 3mm long and one slightly curved central about 3cm long. Flowers appear during the day in summer; yellow with a pale reddish centre band on the petals, they are about 1.7cm long, 3cm across. Requires sun; permeable mineral, enriched compost; minimum temperature 7°C (45°F). *USA (Northern Arizona).*

     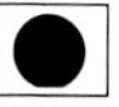

PEDIOCACTUS **SILERI** (Engelm.) L. Benson
Syn: *Utahia sileri* (Engelm.) Br. & R.

A somewhat oval plant up to 15cm tall, 12cm in diameter with about 12–14 spiralling ribs bearing prominent circular areoles. There are 11–15 white radial spines, up to 2cm long, and three to seven brownish-black centrals becoming almost white with age, about 3cm long. Flowers are diurnal in summer, and are yellowish, 2.5cm or a little more in diameter. A high-altitude plant, it requires bright light; porous mineral, humus-enriched compost, minimum temperature 7°C (45°F). *USA (Northern Arizona, Utah).*

  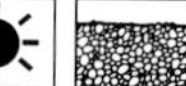 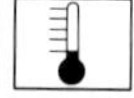

▼

PEDIOCACTUS **PARADINEI** B. W. Benson
Syn: *Pilocanthus paradinei* (B. W. Benson) B. W. Benson & Backeb.

A solitary plant with greenish-grey globular stems 3–5cm high, 6–8cm across. It has 12–15 ribs with wart-like tubercles bearing small circular areoles with hair-like white spines, about 20 radials and four to six centrals, 4–7cm long. The plant is day flowering, in summer, with cream-coloured flowers with a faint pinkish stripe and up to 2.5cm across. Requires careful watering at all times; bright light; porous enriched compost; minimum temperature 7°C (45°F). *USA (Navajoan Desert, altitude 1750m).*

PEDIOCACTUS **SIMPSONII** (Engelm.) Br. & R.
Syn: *Echinocactus simpsonii* Engelm.

Up to over 20cm tall, 15cm in diameter, the plant has 12 spiralling ribs, with tubercles bearing whitish areoles. These carry 15–25 whitish radial spines 1–2cm long and five to ten brown centrals to 2.5cm long. Flowers are pinkish rose, up to 2.5cm long, and are day flowering, in summer. Careful culture is required, and the plant is best grafted. Requires bright light; if on its own roots use permeable mineral compost enriched with leaf-mould; minimum temperature 7°C (45°F). *USA (High altitudes, Arizona).*

      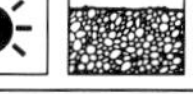   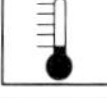

PEDIOCACTUS **WINKLERI** Heil

Usually solitary, sub-globose plants up to about 6.5cm high, 4cm wide, with prominent tubercles 4–7mm in diameter. The areoles are mainly woolly, bearing nine to fourteen white, somewhat pectinate radial spines up to 4mm long, but no centrals. Flowering in summer, and diurnal, the flowers are up to 2.2cm long and 3cm in diameter, peach-coloured with a reddish-brown midstripe to the outer segments. Needs good light; normal cactus compost; minimum temperature 10°C (50°F). *USA (Utah).*

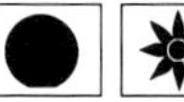  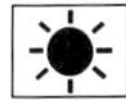 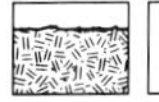 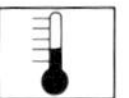

PELECYPHORA **ASELLIFORMIS** Ehrenb.

A small, somewhat globular plant 5–10cm high, 2–5cm in diameter, covered with greyish-green, spirally arranged tubercles which are flat and laterally compressed. The long, narrow areoles are at the tips of the tubercles and have numerous minute spines arranged like a comb. Flowers appear in summer in the crown of the plant during the day; they are reddish violet, 3–4cm across. Requires full sun; an enriched, permeable mineral compost; minimum temperature 13°C (55°F). *Mexico (San Luis Potosi).*

        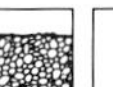  

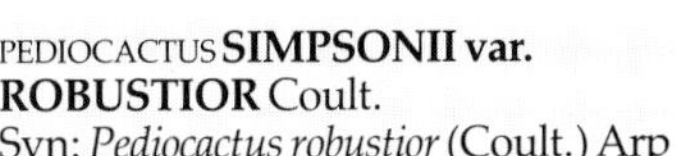

PEDIOCACTUS **SIMPSONII var. ROBUSTIOR** Coult.
Syn: *Pediocactus robustior* (Coult.) Arp

Very similar to the species, but occasionally clustering. It differs principally in the flower colour, which is pale yellow or white. Requirements are similar to those of the species. *USA (North Central Oregon).*

    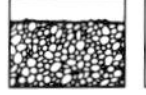 

PELECYPHORA **STROBILIFORMIS** (Werd.) Frič & Schelle
Syn: *Encephalocarpus strobiliformis* (Werd.) Berger

Probably better known under the original title. It is an almost globular, greyish-green plant, 4–7cm in diameter, and covered with numerous bract-like tubercles. Areoles on the inner side of the tubercles have minute spines and wool. Flowers reddish violet, 3–4cm wide, opening in daytime in summer. Keep totally dry in winter. Requires sun; enriched permeable compost; minimum temperature 10°C (50°F). *Mexico (Tamaulipas).*

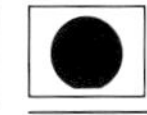    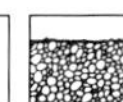 

PENIOCEREUS

PENIOCEREUS **JOHNSTONII** (Berger) Br. & R.
Syn: *Cereus johnstonii* Berger

This species has a large, fleshy tuberous rootstock with greyish-green, elongated slender stems three to five-angled, and often reaching up to 3m long. The areoles are very closely set with nine to twelve radial spines and one to three centrals, none exceeding 8mm in length. Fragrant and nocturnal, flowers have a slender tube up to 15cm long and white petals, appearing early summer. Requires a very bright position; normal cactus compost; minimum temperature 13°C (55°F). *Mexico (Baja).*

   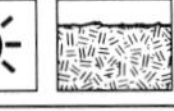 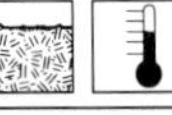

PENIOCEREUS **MARIANUS** (Gentry) Sanchez-Mejorada
Syn: *Wilcoxia mariana* Gentry

An erect or clambering species 1–6m long. The stems and branches are four to five-angled and are set with whitish areoles bearing seven to ten blackish-brown radial spines and one similarly coloured central. Flowering at night in summer, the flowers are 8–9cm long and tubular, the spreading outer petals white, tipped brownish-red, and inner petals white, about 2cm long. Needs warmth; good light; enriched porous cactus compost; minimum temperature 10°C (50°F). *Mexico (Sonora).*

   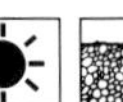 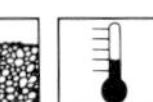

PERESKIA

PERESKIA **ACULEATA** Miller

A climbing, trailing plant with stems 8–10m in length to 1cm thick and dark-green leaves up to 9cm long, 4cm wide. The areoles have one to three spines, but no glochids. Flowers appear in late summer and are diurnal. They are up to about 4.5cm across and whitish yellow shading to pinkish at the base. Requires very bright light; normal cactus compost; minimum temperature 10°C (50°F). *USA (Florida), West Indies, Brazil, Paraguay.*

  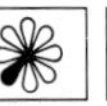 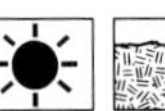 

PERESKIA **ACULEATA var. GODSEFFIANA** (Sand.) Knuth
Syn: *Pereskia aculeata cv. Godseffiana*

This differs from the species in that the young leaves are all peach-coloured, with the under-surface often slightly reddish. Cultivation requirements are the same as for the species.

    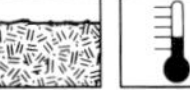

▲

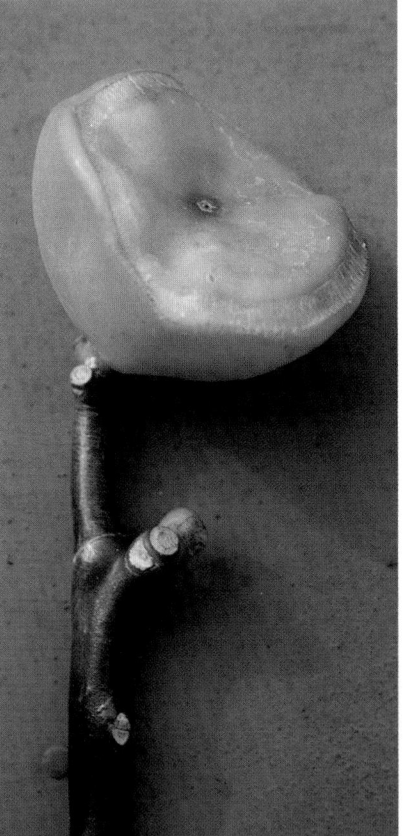

▲

PERESKIA **BLEO** (Knuth) DC.
Syn: *Cactus bleo* Knuth; *Rhodocactus bleo* (HBK.) Knuth

A shrub-like plant up to 7m high, with many branches, these initially red becoming green. Leaves are bright green, up to 20cm long, 5cm wide, and there are five to six spines to each areole, varying in length. Flowering in summer, and diurnal, the pinkish-red flowers are grouped two to four together in clusters, and are about 4cm across. Needs bright light; normal cactus compost; minimum temperature 18°C (64°F). The pale yellow fruits are also a feature of interest. *Colombia, Panama.*

     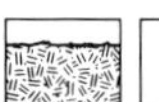 

PERESKIA **DIAZ-ROMEROANA** Card.

A bushy plant to 1.3m high, with horizontally spreading branches. Leaves are dark green and elliptical, about 2.5cm long, 1cm broad. Greyish-white areoles bear about five spines at first, increasing to about 12, yellowish or whitish, and 5mm up to 2cm in length. Flowers are wine red, about 1cm long, and appear by day, in summer. There has also been discovered a broader leafed form, otherwise similar in other respects. The small brownish-reddish fruits are only 5mm in diameter. Requires bright light; normal cactus compost; minimum temperature 13°C (55°F). *Bolivia (Cochabamba).*

     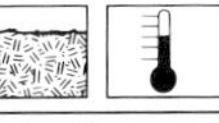

PERESKIA **GRANDIFOLIA** Haw. **var. GRANDIFOLIA**
Syn: *Rhodocactus grandifolius* (Haw.) Knuth; *Pereskia grandiflorus* hort.

An erect, shrubby species 2–5m high with thick spiny stems. Green fleshy leaves, 15–20cm long, 3–4cm broad. The areoles develop one or two blackish spines up to about 5cm in length. The flowers are borne in clusters, about 4cm in diameter. The details of the flower are especially fascinating, and so are the small, green pear-shaped fruits. Day flowering in summer, needs a very bright position; normal cactus compost; minimum temperature 13°C (55°F). *Brazil.*

    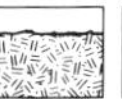

PERESKIA **GRANDIFOLIA** Haw. **var. VIOLACEA**

An unusual form of *P. grandifolia,* currently known under the Field Collecting No. HU226. It was discovered in Brazil in recent years and cultivated at the Botanic Gardens Berlin-Dahlem, Germany. Requirements are the same as for the species.

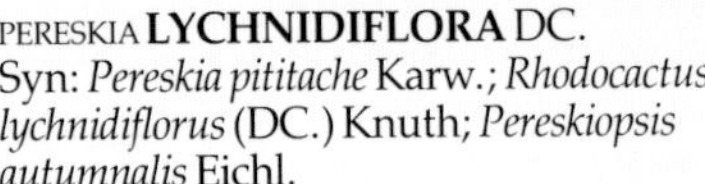

PERESKIA **LYCHNIDIFLORA** DC.
Syn: *Pereskia pititache* Karw.; *Rhodocactus lychnidiflorus* (DC.) Knuth; *Pereskiopsis autumnalis* Eichl.

A tree-like plant reaching up to more than 9m tall with many branches bearing pale-green leaves 4–7cm long, seen here growing amidst *Opuntia* species. The areoles are black with a few white hairs and one long spine 2–5cm in length. Flowers are yellowish orange, about 6cm in diameter, and appear by day, in summer. Requires full sun; normal cactus compost; minimum temperature 13°C (55°F). *Guatemala, Mexico.*

   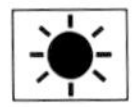 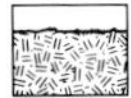 

PERESKIA **NEMOROSA** Rojas Acosta
Syn: *Pereskia amapola* Weber; *Pereskia argentina* Weber

Closely allied to *P. sacharosa* with which it is often confused. It is a shrubby plant, often tree-like, 6–8m high with smooth green branches. The more or less lance-shaped leaves are slightly fleshy and 8–12cm long, and the greyish-white areoles have up to three or more spines, the longest to 5cm. Flowers are produced in terminal clusters and are diurnal, blooming in summer, each flower about 8cm wide, white or pink. Requires good light; normal cactus compost; minimum temperature 13°C (55°F). There is significant development in young seedlings: this shows two-week-old plantlets in cultivation. *Paraguay, Argentina.*

PERESKIA **PORTULACIFOLIA** (L.) DC.
Syn: *Rhodocactus portulacifolius* (L.) Knuth

A tree-like plant up to 6m high. The branches are terete and very spiny; on younger growth the spines are usually solitary, but on older stems areoles have clusters of seven to nine, sometimes up to 2cm in length. The leaves are spatula-shaped and about 1cm long. Pinkish-red flowers bloom in summer, and are diurnal; they are about 3cm broad. Requires sun; slightly calcareous cactus compost; minimum temperature 18°C (64°F). *Dominican Republic, Haiti, Jamaica?*

PERESKIA **SACHAROSA** Griseb.
Syn: *Rhodocactus sacharosa* (Griseb.) Backeb.; *Pereskia saipinensis* Card.

A tall, tree-like plant 6–8m high with many erect branches. The dark-green leaves are lance-shaped, and 8–12cm long. Areoles are greyish-white and bear usually one to three reddish-brown spines up to 5cm in length, though older branches may have six or more. Flowering in summer, the rose-pink blooms are diurnal, 7–8cm wide, and are produced mostly in clusters. Requires slight shade; normal cactus compost; minimum temperature 13°C (55°F). *Paraguay, Argentina.*

   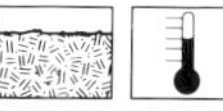 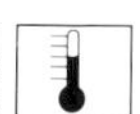

PERESKIA **WEBERIANA** K. Sch.

A shrubby species reaching 2–3m high, with many very slender branches only 3–5mm thick. Leaves are ovate to elliptical 3cm long, 2cm wide. The white woolly areoles bear one to six yellowish spines up to 2cm. White flowers, which are diurnal, are produced in clusters in summer, and are up to 1cm long, 2cm wide; some blooms change colour with age. Needs bright light; normal cactus compost; minimum temperature 13°C (55°F). *Bolivia.*

   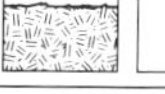

PERESKIA **QUISQUEYANA** Liogier

A shrub-like plant 3–4m high with widely spreading branches in its habitat. The shiny green leaves are about 1cm wide, varying from 1–4cm in length, and the spines are brownish, only two to three on young growth, but several developing later up to 5cm long. Pink flowers up to about 6cm in diameter appear in mid-summer, and are diurnal. Requires slight shade; normal cactus compost; minimum temperature 18°C (64°F). *Dominican Republic.*

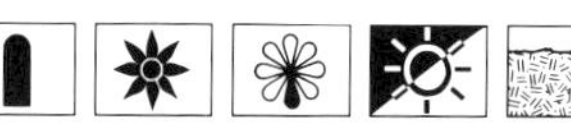

PERESKIA **STENANTHA** Ritter

A large bushy plant 3–6m high in its habitat, the main stem often up to 10cm or more thick. The fleshy leaves are about 6–10cm long, 4–7.5cm wide, and the areoles are 2–5mm wide. New growth has just one or two spines, with more developing later. These are brownish becoming whitish, and 2–6cm in length. Flowers, about 3.5cm long, are nocturnal, appearing in summer. The petals are pink-purple, 2–2.5cm long and 1–1.2cm wide. Requires good light; normal cactus compost; minimum temperature 13°C (55°F). *Brazil (Bahia).*

PERESKIA **ZINNIIFLORA** DC.
Syn: *Rhodocactus zinniaeflorus* (DC.) Knuth

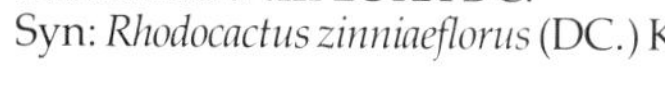

A large, shrubby species 1.5m or more high, often becoming tree-like. The oval to oblong leaves, 2–4cm long, about 2cm broad, are cuneate at the base. Areoles are oval in shape, with one or two brownish spines on young branches, and three to five on older stems, up to 1cm in length. Rose-red or purplish flowers, about 5cm in diameter, are diurnal, in summer. Requires slight shade; normal cactus compost; minimum temperature 13°C (55°F). *Mexico.*

   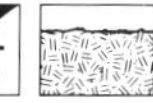 

PERESKIOPSIS

PERESKIOPSIS **GATESII** Baxter

A somewhat trailing, shrub-like plant with pale-green stems and branches, and leaves almost oval in shape. The areoles bear one or many dull-brown or grey spines up to 5cm in length, and the glochids are dark brown. The bright-yellow flowers are 2–3cm in diameter and appear by day, in summer. Requires slight shade; normal cactus compost; minimum temperature 13°C (55°F). *Mexico (Baja).*

   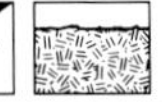 

PERESKIOPSIS **VELUTINA** Rose

A dark-green, bushy plant reaching to over 1m tall, slightly pubescent, and about 1cm thick. The elliptical leaves are also velvety, 2–6cm long, 1.5–2.5cm wide in the middle. Areoles have whitish hairs, minute glochids and whitish spines, often up to 1cm long and the flowers are bright yellow, 1–3cm long and wide, with widely spreading petals; they appear by day in summer. Requires bright light; normal cactus compost; minimum temperature best at 13°C (55°F). *Mexico (Queretaro).*

   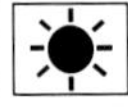  

PFEIFFERA

PFEIFFERA **IANTHOTHELE** (Monv.) Weber
Syn: *Lepismium ianthothele* (Monv.) Barthlott

An epiphyte on forest trees. Pendant in habit, the bright-green stems are usually four-angled and 30–50cm long, about 1.5cm wide. Areoles bear six to seven yellowish spines about 5mm long. Early summer flowering, in the day. Up to 2.5cm long, they are bell-shaped, with yellow inner petals and pinkish-purple outer ones, followed by pinkish fruits. Needs slight shade; normal cactus compost; minimum temperature 10°C (50°F). *Bolivia, Argentina.*

PILOSOCEREUS

PILOSOCEREUS **ALBISUMMUS** Braun & Esteves

A tall, columnar species of greyish to clear green with about 10 straight ribs, fairly close-set areoles and fine, pale-brownish spines. It has a cephalium of white wool and dark-brown bristles, through which appear silvery-white flowers which are night flowering, in summer. The cephalium becomes very pronounced as the flowering season approaches. Requires bright light; a calcareous cactus compost; minimum temperature 13°C (55°F). *Brazil (Minas Gerais).*

    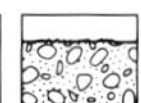 

PILOSOCEREUS **AURILANATUS** Ritter

A columnar plant 1–2m tall with glaucous-green stems 5–7cm thick. There are 14–18 ribs and large areoles bearing yellowish-brown spines, about 12 radials up to 1.5cm long and three to five centrals of similar length. The pseudocephalium is copiously covered with whitish yellow wool. White flowers appear at night, in summer, and are about 4cm long. Needs bright light, which is essential; normal cactus compost; minimum temperature 10°C (50°F). *Brazil (Minas Gerais).*

PILOSOCEREUS **BARBADENSIS** (Br. & R.) Byl. & Rowley

A tall, columnar plant, freely branching from the base. The stems are up to 6m high, 5–12cm thick, and have eight to nine ribs. Areoles bear about 10 yellowish-brown spines up to 4cm in length. Nocturnal flowering, in mid-summer, the flowers are a clear rose pink, 6cm long. Requires full sun; normal cactus compost; minimum temperature 18°C (64°F). *Barbados.*

PILOSOCEREUS **BRAUNII** Esteves

This species was discovered by Leopold Horst (pictured) in the early 1970s and named for the explorer and botanist Pierre Braun. It is a greyish-blue, columnar plant up to about 2m high, grouping from the base, and has 14–18 ribs with brown areoles and spines. There is a brown bristly, lateral cephalium through which appear the night-flowering whitish, trumpet-shaped flowers in summer. Needs an airy, sunny position; normal cactus compost; minimum temperature 10°C (50°F). *Brazil (Western Bahia).*

   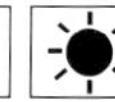  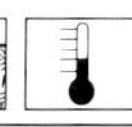

PILOSOCEREUS **CENEPEQUEI** Rizzini & Mattos

A blue or greyish-blue columnar plant, branching from the base. There are about 14 ribs with close-set areoles bearing short, brownish spines and long white hairs. White flowers appear laterally from the pseudocephalium, and are night flowering, in summer. Requires partial shade or out of direct sun; normal cactus compost; minimum temperature 10°C (50°F). *Brazil (North-eastern Minas Gerais).*

   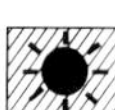 

PILOSOCEREUS **CINCINNOPETALUS** Braun & Esteves

Recorded as being the only species of this genus growing in the region. It was discovered by Esteves in the early 1970s, but remained unnamed until recently. It is a blue-stemmed columnar plant with 10–12 ribs and areoles bearing dark spines and wool, and a terminal cephalium of long white woolly hairs. Flowers are borne laterally; these are white, more or less funnel-shaped, and night flowering in summer. Requires a bright position; normal cactus compost; minimum temperature 13°C (55°F). *Brazil (South-western Goias).*

  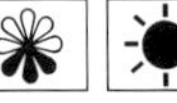   

PILOSOCEREUS **GLAUCOCHROUS** (Werd.) Byl. & Rowley
Syn: *Cephalocereus glaucochrous* (Werd.) Borg

An erect or semi-erect, bluish-green columnar species, sometimes branching from the base, and up to 4m long, 5–7cm thick. It has five to nine deep, notched ribs and white hairy areoles set about 1.5cm apart. These bear nine to twelve pale brownish-yellow radial spines up to 2cm long and three to four similarly coloured centrals up to 5cm in length. Summer flowering in the daytime, the flowers are about 5.5cm long, with pale pink or whitish inner petals and greenish-red outer segments. Requires full sun; an enriched mineral, open compost; minimum temperature 13°C (55°F). *Brazil (Bahia).*

PILOSOCEREUS **CRISTALINENSIS** Braun & Esteves

Named on account of its habitat – Cristalina, a locality within Goias. It is a dark-greyish or dull-green columnar plant with about 14 deeply furrowed ribs. The greyish-white areoles bear many fine radial spines of pale brown and deeper-coloured centrals. The cephalium terminal consists of dense wool and long yellowish-brown bristly spines. Reddish flower buds open at night, in summer. Requires a bright position; normal cactus compost; minimum temperature 13°C (55°F). *Brazil (Goias).*

PILOSOCEREUS **FLEXIBILISPINUS** Braun & Esteves

A fascinating species from the newly created (in 1988) State of Tocantins and the first of the genus to be found there. It is a greyish-blue columnar plant with 10–12 straight and prominent ribs and brownish areoles. The spines are yellowish brown; both radials and centrals are particularly long and flexible, hence its specific title. The flowers are very small and a deep olive green to brownish colour. Summer flowering, they are nocturnal. Requires slight shade; normal cactus compost; minimum temperature 13°C (55°F). *Brazil.*

   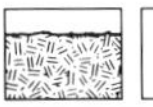

PILOSOCEREUS **LINDAIANUS** Braun & Esteves

A bluish-green columnar plant, rarely exceeding 1m in height. Although discovered nearly 20 years ago by Esteves, it has only recently been described and named after his wife. It has about 14 ribs with smallish areoles bearing brown, later more greyish spines. The cephalium is laterally developed, and the flowers are white, blooming at night, in summer. Requires bright light; normal cactus compost; minimum temperature 10°C (50°F).

PILOSOCEREUS **LINDAIANUS var. GRACILIS**

Very similar to the species but with more slender, bluish stems, and 10–12 ribs. The pseudocephalium is brownish and produces very pale pinkish-white flowers. It is night flowering, in summer. Requirements are the same as for the species. *Brazil.*

  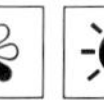 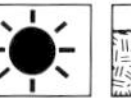 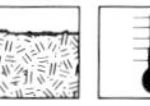 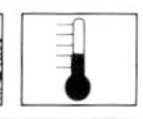

PILOSOCEREUS **LUETZELBURGII** (Vaup.) Byles & Rowley

Originally known as *Cereus lutzelburgii* Vaup, this is a branching, columnar plant to 1m high. Arising from the base, the dark-green branches have whitish wool and yellowish-brown spines. There are 13–16 ribs with white woolly and hairy areoles up to 2cm long. Spines are yellowish to grey, of which 15–18 are radials to 1.5cm long, and four to five are centrals to 3cm. The flowers, 5cm long, are olive green with white inner petals and are night flowering, in summer. Requires bright light; normal cactus compost; minimum temperature 10°C (50°F). *Brazil (Bahia).*

   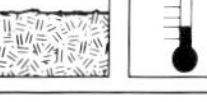

PILOSOCEREUS **MAGNIFICUS** (Buin. & Bred.) Ritter
Syn: *Pseudopilosocereus magnificus* Buin. & Bred.

A columnar plant 2–3m tall, with bluish stems 7–8cm thick, branching from the base. It has five to seven ribs with whitish areoles with pale to brownish-yellow spines, 10–14 radials 4mm to 1cm long, and six to eight centrals up to 2cm. The flowers are whitish, up to 5.5cm long, 3cm across, and are night flowering, in mid-summer. Requires a sunny position; normal cactus compost; minimum temperature 10°C (50°F). *Brazil (Minas Gerais).*

PILOSOCEREUS **NOBILIS** (Haw.) Byl. & Rowley

Pale-green columnar plants 4–6m high, 3–8cm thick, branching from the base to form thick clusters. The stems have five to seven prominent rounded ribs with yellowish areoles set about 2cm apart, which have a few yellowish hairs. Of the yellowish-brown spines, there are about nine radials 2–3cm long, and one to six centrals 4cm or more in length. Flowering in mid-summer, the plant is nocturnal, with reddish-pink flowers about 5cm long, 4cm across. Needs sun; normal cactus compost; minimum temperature 18°C (64°F). *West Indies (Windward Islands).*

   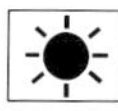 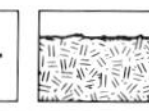 

PILOSOCEREUS **PURPUSII** (Br. & R.) Byl. & Rowley

A bright-green columnar plant, branching from the base, 3–4cm thick and often up to 3m in length. It has 12 ribs with closely set whitish areoles with long silky hairs. The spines are yellowish, becoming grey with age, and up to 3cm long. Flowers appear through the terminal white hairy cephalium, and are nocturnal in mid-summer; they are pale pinkish rose with white edges, and about 7cm long. Requires a sunny position; normal cactus compost; minimum temperature 10°C (50°F). *Mexico (Sinaloa, Sonora).*

    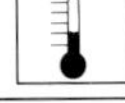

PILOSOCEREUS **PUSILLIBACCATUS** Braun & Esteves

A greyish-green columnar plant up to a little over 1m in height, 4.5cm thick. It has nine to eleven ribs with round to oval areoles of greyish felt. The spines are brownish yellow, later becoming grey to dark brown: there are 12–16 radials varying from 3mm to 2cm long, and one to three centrals up to 2cm in length. The flowers, nearly 5cm long, have pale greenish-white inner petals, and cream or pale-green outer segments. They are night flowering, in summer. Requires filtered light; normal cactus compost; minimum temperature 13°C (55°F). *Brazil (Maranhao).*

   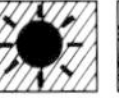  

PILOSOCEREUS **ROSAE** Braun

This species is named for Rosa Uebelmann, the wife of the Swiss cactus collector. It is a tall, blue-stemmed columnar plant, branching at or near the base. There are nine to ten very straight ribs with fairly close-set areoles and an orange-yellow pseudocephalium along just one rib. Spines are pale brownish or yellowish brown, and the flowers are funnel-shaped with clear white inner petals and pale olive-green outer segments. They open at night, in summer. Requires full sun; normal cactus compost; minimum temperature 13°C (55°F). *Brazil (Central Minas Gerais).*

   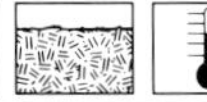

PILOSOCEREUS **ROYENII** (L.) Byl. & Rowley

A tree-like, columnar plant up to about 8m high with bluish-green branches 8cm or more thick. It has six to eleven ribs with brown areoles bearing whitish hairs and many yellow or reddish spines up to 6cm long but varying in length and colour. Flowering by day, in summer, the flowers are about 5cm long, white, and reddish externally. Needs full sun, which is essential; normal cactus compost; minimum temperature 18°C (65°F). *West Indies.*

PILOSOCEREUS **SCHOEBELII** Braun

An erect columnar species up to 4m tall, developing branches like a candelabra. The stems and branches are pale blue, 4–7cm thick, with 12 ribs and creamy-white areoles 5–6mm apart. Spines are pale brownish, later greyish black, 16–20 radial spines 4–9mm long, and four centrals up to 1.5cm. The pseudocephalium consists of a few tufts of whitish wool, and the whitish-green flowers are 5.5–6cm long, appearing at night, in summer. Needs full sun; normal cactus compost; minimum temperature 13°C (55°F). *Brazil (Northern Minas Gerais).*

   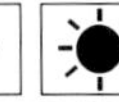 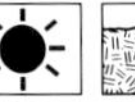  

PILOSOCEREUS **SUPERFLOCCOSUS** (Buin. & Bred.) Ritter
Syn: *Pseudopilosocereus superfloccosus* Buin. & Bred.

A tall plant to 4m, with greyish-green stems about 6cm thick. It has nine to sixteen ribs with whitish-yellow woolly areoles bearing yellowish to pale-grey spines consisting of radials to 1.5cm long, and seven centrals of similar length. Flowers from a white hairy cephalium. The 5cm long white blooms are nocturnal, in mid-summer. Needs full sun; normal cactus compost; minimum temperature 13°C (55°F). *Brazil (Western Bahia).*

     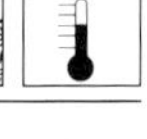

PILOSOCEREUS **SUPTHUTIANUS** Braun

A greyish-blue, shorter columnar species up to 1.5m high, sparsely branching from the base. Stems are about 5cm thick with 10–12 yellowish ribs, and later, brown areoles bearing yellowish to greyish spines consisting of 22–26 radials and eight to ten centrals. The woolly pseudocephalium is lateral on a few ribs with hairs up to 1.6cm long. The flowers, bell-shaped and 5–5.5cm long, are pinkish white, often brownish red, and occur at night, in summer. Needs a bright position, which is essential; normal cactus compost; minimum temperature 13°C (55°F). *Brazil (Central Minas Gerais).*

▲

PILOSOCEREUS **VILABOENSIS** (Diers & Esteves) Braun

Named after the original name of the city Goias – Vila Boa. A dark-green columnar species with about 15–16 ribs, whitish areoles and yellow or brownish spines. The pseudocephalium is not much in evidence; the fairly long, partly tubular flower has an olive-green, smooth tube with pale reddish tips to the scales and pure white inner petals. The flowers appear at night, in mid-summer. Needs a bright position; normal cactus compost; minimum temperature 13°C (55°F). *Brazil (Goias).*

     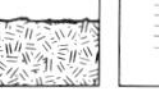

PILOSOCEREUS **WERDERMANNIANUS** (Buin. & Bred.) Ritter **var. DENSILANATUS** Ritter

Columnar plants with slender stems up to about 1.5m high, the bright-greyish stems branching from or near the base, and up to 5cm thick. There are 13–17 ribs, covered with white hairs. The areoles bear eight to twelve radial spines 4mm–1.2cm long, and four to eight centrals 5mm–3cm in length. The white flowers, 3.5–5cm long, are nocturnal, in mid-summer. Requires sun; slightly calcareous cactus compost; minimum temperature 13°C (55°F). *Brazil (Minas Gerais).*

    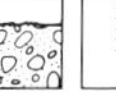 

POLASKIA **CHICHIPE** (Goss.) Backeb.
Syn: *Lemaireocereus chichipe* (Goss.) Br. & R.

A columnar plant, branching from the base, 4–5m high. The pale-green stems are 5–7cm thick, with seven to twelve acute ribs, 2cm deep, and areoles set about 1.5cm apart. Spines are greyish, initially almost blackish brown; six to seven are radials to 1cm long, and there is one central about 1.5cm. Flowering by day in summer, the flowers are creamy white or greenish yellow with a reddish midstripe and about 3cm long, 4cm across. Requires bright light; normal cactus compost; minimum temperature 13°C (55°F). *Mexico (Oaxaca, Puebla).*

   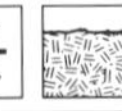  

PSEUDOACANTHOCEREUS
BOREOMINARUM Rizzini & Mattos

The generic title is considered obsolete by certain authorities, and it is now referred to *Acanthocereus*. It is a sprawling, slender-stemmed plant with three to four-angled stems and branches about 2.5cm thick. The areoles are brownish, set along the margins, with short pale brownish spines. Flowers have an elongated tube, 12–15cm long, and are white, appearing at night, in summer. Requires a sunny position; normal cactus compost; minimum temperature 13°C (55°F). *Brazil (North-eastern Minas Gerais).*

   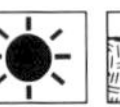 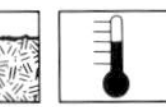

PSEUDOPILOSOCEREUS **AZUREUS** Buin. & Bred.
Syn: *Pilosocereus azureus* Ritter

Columnar plant 4–5m high, greyish-blue branches, 7–8cm thick. It has seven to ten ribs, with slightly crenate margins. 'V'-shaped furrow above each areole bears yellowish-brown spines consisting of 12–16 small radials and six to nine centrals. Flowers, which are white, are cylindrical, and about 5cm long. They are nocturnal, occurring in summer. Requires bright light; slightly calcareous cactus compost; minimum temperature 13°C (55°F). *Brazil.*

    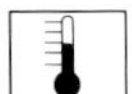

PSEUDOPILOSOCEREUS **ULEI** (K. Sch.) Buxb.
Syn: *Pilosocereus ulei* (K. Sch.) Byl. & Rowley

A columnar plant up to 7m high in its habitat. The branches are bluish, about 10cm wide with eight ribs. Large, woolly areoles with silvery hairs bear about 10 thin brown radial spines about 1.5cm long and one or two darker brown centrals up to 2cm in length. Flowers appear from a lateral cephalium consisting of wool and hairs. Flowering at night, in summer, the flowers are white and 4–5cm long. Requires sun; normal cactus compost; minimum temperature 13°C (55°F). *Brazil (Cabo Frio).*

   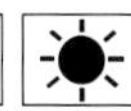  

PTEROCACTUS **FISCHERI** Br. & R.

The plant is up to about 15cm high, with green stems 1–2cm thick and more or less cylindrical in a series of joints set one above another. Spines arise from whitish areoles; about 12 are white radials to 6mm long and there are four brownish-yellow centrals 1–1.5cm in length. Day flowering in late summer, the flowers arise from the tips of the stems – white, tubeless, and 4cm or more in diameter. Requires very careful watering because of its large tuberous rootstock; sun; slightly calcareous cactus compost; minimum temperature 10°C (50°F). *Argentina (Patagonia).*

PTEROCACTUS **HICKENII** Br. & R.

A cylindrical-stemmed species with a tuberous rootstock. The greyish-brown or greenish-brown stems or joints are about 2cm thick, 2–3cm long, and are covered with stiff, pale-brownish spines 2–3cm long. The terminal flowers, about 4cm across, are yellowish with pink edges and are day flowering, in early summer. Needs full sun; normal cactus compost; minimum temperature 7°C (45°F). *Argentina (Mendoza).*

PTEROCACTUS **RETICULATUS** Kiesling

A clumping species arising from a tuberous rootstock with tubers about 20cm long, 10cm diameter! The cylindrical, jointed stems are 2–3cm long, 1–2cm thick and reddish grey with many very shallow 'warts' below each areole; these bear one to three minute whitish spines. Flowers are yellow and about 4cm across. They appear by day, in early summer. Requires full sun; normal cactus compost; minimum temperature 10°C (50°F). *Argentina (San Juan).*

PTEROCACTUS **GONJIANII** Kiesling

A recently recorded species with a tuberous rootstock. The stems are jointed, cylindrical, brownish or reddish green in colour and 5–6cm long. Areoles are arranged regularly, almost spirally, around the joints and bear very small whitish spines. Flowers are pinkish white, about 2.5–3cm across, and appear by day in early summer. Requires full sun; normal cactus compost; minimum temperature 10°C (50°F). *Argentina (San Juan).*

PTEROCACTUS **MEGLIOLII** Kiesling

A tuberous-rooted plant, the tubers are about 15cm long, 5–8cm thick. It has cylindrical jointed stems up to 5cm long and about 1cm thick with regularly spaced, whitish areoles bearing minute spines. Flowers are yellow, 3–4cm across, flowering by day in early summer. Needs full sun; slightly calcareous cactus compost; minimum temperature 10°C (50°F). *Argentina (San Juan).*

PTEROCACTUS **TUBEROSUS** (Pfeiff.) Br. & R.
Syn: *Pterocactus kuntzei* K. Sch.

Plants have a large tuberous root which accounts for the specific title. Many branches arise from this rootstock; these are brownish green, cylindrical, about 1cm thick and of lengths varying from 5–40cm. Small areoles occur at regular intervals bearing minute whitish hair-like spines. The flowers are yellow, 2–3cm across, and are day flowering, in summer. Requires full sun; normal cactus compost; minimum temperature 7°C (45°F). *Argentina (Mendoza).*

PTEROCEREUS **FOETIDUS** T. MacDoug. & Mir.

A dull-green, tree-like columnar plant up to about 8m high. It has many angular branches created by three to four prominent ribs about 7cm high. The greyish-white areoles have 10–20 widely spreading reddish spines about 4.5cm long. Appearing by day in early summer, the flowers are borne laterally; they are about 9.5cm long, greenish white, and open to about 4cm across. Requires bright light; an enriched cactus compost; minimum temperature 15°C (59°F). *Mexico (Chiapas).*

  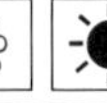 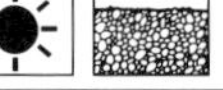 

PTEROCEREUS **GAUMERI** (Br. & R.)
Syn: *Anisocereus gaumeri* (Br. & R.) Backeb.

A long slender plant, greyish blue-green in colour, it is somewhat tree-like, to 7m high in its habitat. The stems have three to four almost wing-like thin ribs and the yellowish-brown areoles bear three to six brown spines 1–3cm in length. Flowers are borne laterally, appearing by day in early summer. They are about 5cm long, and are yellowish white to yellowish green. Needs bright light, which is essential; an enriched mineral compost; minimum temperature 15°C (59°F). *Mexico (Yucatan).*

  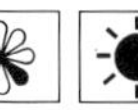  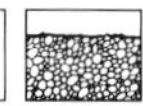 

PYGMAEOCEREUS **AKERSII** Johnson

This is very closely allied to *P. bylesianus* and is undoubtedly just a form or variety of that species. It differs principally in having a longer central spine. Requirements are the same as for *P. bylesianus. Peru.*

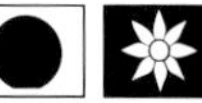   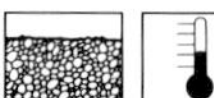

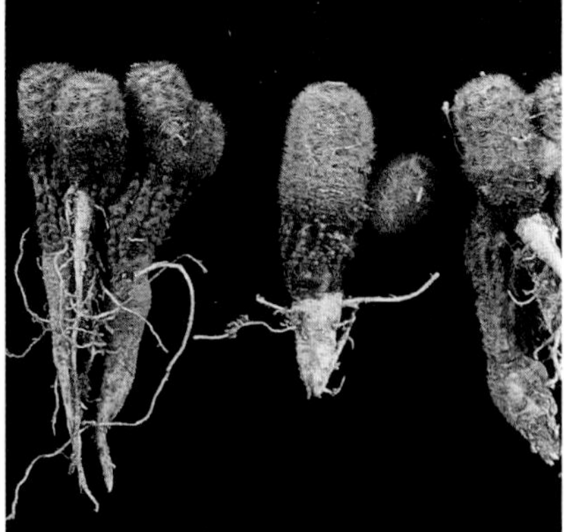

PYGMAEOCEREUS **BYLESIANUS** Andreae & Backeb.

Dark-green, semi-columnar or globular species, to 10cm high. 12–14 ribs with round, areoles bearing fine, greyish radial spines and one or two longer centrals 3–5mm long. Flowers at night in mid-summer, blooms 6cm long, with white inner petals and pale greenish outer ones. Requires careful cultivation because of the long fleshy taproot, as illustrated. Needs a bright position; a very porous enriched cactus compost; minimum temperature 10°C (50°F). *Southern Peru.*

    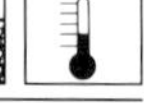

PYGMAEOCEREUS **BYLESIANUS** Andreae & Backeb.

This species, which has a close affinity to *P. rowleyanus* Backeb. and in all probability is synonymous, is often difficult in cultivation. By grafting on to robust stock success can be more readily achieved, the general growth often being slightly at variance with that of wild plants.

     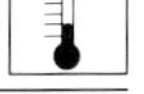

PYGMAEOCEREUS **DENSIACULEATUS** Backeb.

A small grouping species with stems about 1.7cm in diameter. It has about 18 ribs with close-set, round, light-brown areoles about 2mm apart. There are about 30 very fine pale reddish-brown spines, about 3mm long, more or less covering the whole body. Flowers are rose-pink, with outer segments a deeper pink; they are nocturnal flowering, in summer. Requires a sunny position; normal cactus compost; minimum temperature 10°C (50°F). *Peru*.

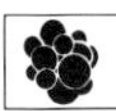    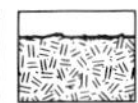 

PYGMAEOCEREUS **ROWLEYANUS** Backeb.

This was referred to *Arthrocereus* by Buxbaum, and is probably synonymous with *P. bylesianus*. It is a dark greyish-green short columnar to globular plant up to about 8cm high, 2cm in diameter. It has about 16–18 ribs with round, white areoles bearing many fine greyish-white radial spines up to 2mm long and one or more black central. Flowers are nocturnal, blooming in mid-summer. They are white, funnel-shaped and up to about 6cm in length, externally scaly. Requires good light; normal cactus compost; minimum temperature 10°C (50°F). *Peru*.

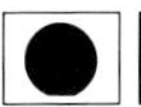    

QUIABENTIA **ZEHNTNERI** Br. & R.

A tall, bushy plant 2–3m high with slender, green, cylindrical stems and roundish or oval-shaped leaves 2–4cm long. The areoles are white-felted, bearing numerous short and fine whitish spines. Day flowering in summer, the flowers are a reddish pink and about 4cm long, opening to 8cm in diameter. Requires careful watering at all times; bright light; an enriched mineral compost; minimum temperature 13°C (55°F). *Brazil (Bahia)*.

    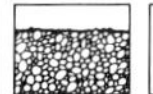 

RAUHOCEREUS **RIOSANIENSIS var. JAENENSIS** Rauh

Somewhat similar to the species, the main stem is about 20cm in diameter with about six ribs and fewer woolly areoles. Spines are dull grey with two to three radials to 1.5cm long and two centrals up to 2cm. Flowers, which are nocturnal, in summer, arise from the top of the stems; they are white, about 8cm long, 4cm across, and externally green, scaly and woolly. Requirements are the same as for the species. *Northern Peru (Jaen).*

REBUTIA **ALBIFLORA** Ritter & Buin.
Syn: *Aylostera albiflora* (Ritter & Buin.) Backeb.

A globular, clustering plant, the bright-green individual stems are often slightly elongated. It has 14–16 spirally arranged ribs and areoles with up to 15 fine whitish radial spines and about five centrals, 2–5mm in length. Day flowering, in summer, the flowers are white with a pale pinkish midstripe, about 2.5cm in diameter. Requires bright light; normal cactus compost; minimum temperature 7°C (45°F). *Bolivia (Tarija).*

RAUHOCEREUS **RIOSANIENSIS** Backeb.
Syn: *Browningia riosaniensis* (Backeb.) Rowley

A bushy columnar plant, to 4m high. The bluish-green branches are about 8cm wide and the five to six ribs are divided by furrows into tubercles, each tubercle carrying a woolly areole. There are six to eight reddish spines, some to only 5mm long. Nocturnal flowers, early summer, white, 8–10cm long and about 5cm wide, externally scaly and woolly. Needs bright light; normal cactus compost; minimum temperature 13°C (55°F). *Northern Peru.*

   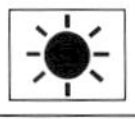 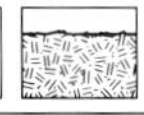 

REBUTIA **AUREIFLORA** Backeb.
Syn: *Mediolobivia aureiflora* (Backeb.) Backeb.

Globular plants, clustering freely. The greenish-violet stems are covered with spirally arranged prominent tubercles set with white areoles. Greyish-white spines consist of 10–16 radials up to 6mm long and one to four centrals 4mm to 2cm or more. The flowers, diurnal, in summer, are yellow-orange and about 4cm wide. Needs filtered light; normal cactus compost; minimum temperature 7°C (45°F). *Argentina (Salta, Jujuy).*

REBUTIA **DEMINUTA** (Weber) Br. & R.
Syn: *Aylostera deminuta* (Weber) Backeb.

A clustering species; the individual stems are dark green, globular, and about 6cm in diameter. It has up to 13 ribs with close-set tubercles and whitish-grey areoles bearing 10–12 brownish radial spines 5–6mm long. Very free-flowering in mid-summer, the flowers are diurnal, a deep orange-red, and about 3cm long. Requires very slight shade; normal cactus compost; minimum temperature 7°C (45°F). *Argentina (Tucuman).*

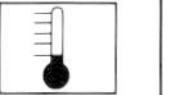

REBUTIA **DONALDIANA** Lau & Rowley

A deep-green globular to cylindrical plant which quickly forms groups. The individual stems are about 8cm in diameter and up to 10cm high. There are 16–18 spiralling ribs with conical tubercles and brown-felted areoles bearing 10–12 white or brown radial spines up to 1.5cm long and four to six rich brown central spines, 2–2.5cm in length. Flowers are a dull orange with bright inner petals up to 1.5cm long: they are summer flowering, and diurnal. Requires partial shade; normal cactus compost; minimum temperature 7°C (45°F). *Bolivia (Santa Cruz).*

REBUTIA **EINSTEINII** Frič
Syn: *Mediolobivia schmiedcheniana* (Köhl.) Krainz var. *einsteinii* (Frič) Backeb.

A most variable clustering plant with pale-green to dark brownish-green stems, 2–3cm thick. It has minute pale to dark-brown spines 3–7mm long, often densely pectinate. The plant shown here is a variety discovered at Quebrada del Toro, Jujuy and not yet botanically described. Flowers are bright yellow, around 2.5cm wide, and are diurnal, appearing in mid-summer. Needs bright light; normal cactus compost; minimum temperature 7°C (45°F). *Argentina (Salta).*

REBUTIA **FABRISII** Rausch

A clump-forming species composed of globular stems about 2cm in diameter and about 14 tuberculate ribs arranged spirally. The areoles are whitish to yellow with numerous similarly coloured spines 2–7mm long. Flowering in summer, and diurnal, the flowers are red, about 3cm long, 2.5cm across. Needs bright light; normal cactus compost; minimum temperature 7°C (45°F). *Argentina.*

REBUTIA **GRANDIFLORA** Backeb.

A dark-green, clump-forming plant about 5cm high, 7.5cm in diameter, globular in shape. It has about 25 spiralling, tuberculate ribs with whitish areoles and about 25 whitish radial spines and usually four centrals which are more brownish. Flowers are bright red and about 6.5cm long; they are diurnal, in summer. Requires a fairly sunny position; normal cactus compost; minimum temperature 7°C (45°F). *Northern Argentina (Salta).*

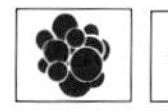

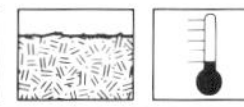

REBUTIA **HELIOSA** Rausch

A small grey-greenish, slightly flattened globular to short cylindrical plant, 1.5–2.5cm in diameter, 2cm high, which offsets freely. It has 35–40 ribs arranged spirally, with low tubercles. The brown-felted areoles have 24–26 comb-like spines up to 1mm long, but no centrals. Day flowering in summer, the flowers are orange or reddish, 4.5–5.5cm long, 4cm in diameter. Requires slight shade; normal cactus compost; minimum temperature 10°C (50°F). *Bolivia (Tarija).*

REBUTIA **HOFFMANNII** Diers & Rausch

Clustering greyish-green plants with more or less globular stems about 3.5–4cm thick, to 5cm high with over 30 tuberculate ribs. The pale-brownish areoles carry numerous pale-yellowish, soft, bristly spines up to 7mm long. Flowers, about 4–4.5cm in diameter, are day flowering in mid-summer; they are orange with a slight tinge of pale lavender. Requires slight shade; normal cactus compost; minimum temperature 10°C (50°F). *Argentina (Salta).*

REBUTIA **MARSONERI** Werd.

A variable species, generally clustering, rarely solitary, with dark-green stems 4cm high, 5cm thick and about 20 tuberculate ribs. The brownish-white areoles bear 30–35 pale-brownish radial spines 3mm to 1.5cm long. Flowers are usually deep yellow, 3–3.5cm wide, and appear by day in summer. Requires slight shade; normal cactus compost; minimum temperature 7°C (45°F). *Argentina (Jujuy).*

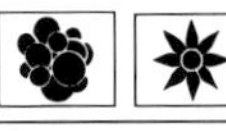

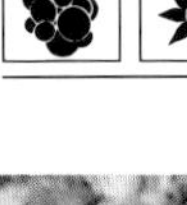

REBUTIA **HELIOSA var. CONDORENSIS** Donald

Greyish-green clustering plants, individually about 3cm high, 4cm in diameter, with 30-40 low-tuberculate ribs. The areoles carry 12–16 white comb-like spines 4mm long. Flowering in summer, and diurnal, the flowers are reddish-purple, 2.5–4cm long. Requires slight shade; normal cactus compost; minimum temperature 10°C (50°F). *Bolivia (Tarija).*

REBUTIA **KUPPERIANA** Böed.
Syn: *Aylostera kupperiana* (Böed) Backeb.

A freely clustering plant with dark leaf-green stems about 3cm in diameter and about 15 tuberculate ribs. The areoles are yellowish, bearing 13–15 whitish-brown radial spines 5–8mm long and one to three darker brown centrals up to 1.2cm in length. Flowers appear by day in summer and are vermilion to bright red, 4cm long, 3.5cm across. Needs a fairly bright position; normal cactus compost; minimum temperature 7°C (45°F). *Bolivia (Tarija).*

REBUTIA **MARSONERI var. BREVISPINA** Donald

In most respects this is similar to the type, but the white areoles have smaller brownish spines, 3–4mm long. A very neat, attractive form. Requirements are the same as for the species. *Northern Argentina.*

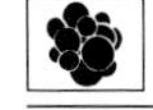

REBUTIA **MINUSCULA** K. Sch.

A free-clustering species. Each stem is globular, with a rather flattened top surface, about 5cm in diameter. It has 16–20 dull-green tuberculate ribs spirally arranged and the small brownish areoles carry about 25–30 whitish radial spines 2–3mm long. It is day flowering in summer with bright red flowers, about 4cm long. Needs a fairly bright light; normal cactus compost; minimum temperature 7°C (45°F). *Argentina (Salta, Tucuman).*

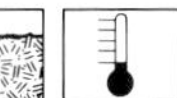

REBUTIA **NARVAECENSIS** (Card.) Donald
Syn: *Aylostera narvaecensis* Card.

A clustering species with greyish-green, somewhat globular stems about 3cm high, 3.5cm in diameter. It has about 18–22 spirally arranged ribs set with low tubercles. The creamy-brown felted areoles bear white or brown spines, 20–30 radials 2–5mm long, and up to six hardly distinguishable centrals. Flowering in summer, the blooms are diurnal, and are a pale rose pink and up to 4.5cm long, 4cm wide. Needs slight shade; normal cactus compost; minimum temperature 10°C (50°F). *Bolivia (Cochabamba).*

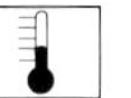

REBUTIA **NIVEA** Ritter

A controversial species closely associated with *R. fiebrigii var. densiseta.* It is a small globose plant up to about 5cm diameter with 20 or more ribs and areoles bearing many fine whitish spines up to 2cm long. The flowers, which are bright yellowish red, are about 2.5cm in diameter and it is day flowering in mid-summer. Needs slight shade; normal cactus compost; minimum temperature 7°C (45°F). *Bolivia.*

REBUTIA **PADCAYENSIS** Rausch

A fresh to greyish-green, semi-globose plant which generally offsets and is up to 2.5cm high, 4cm in diameter. It has 14–16 ribs divided into tubercles 6mm long and wide, with white to brown-felted areoles bearing 12–14 pale yellow, brown-tipped radial spines 5–12mm long. Flowering by day, in summer, the blooms are red with a white throat and a greenish midstripe to the outer segments, about 3.5cm long and across. Requires slight shade; normal cactus compost; minimum temperature 10°C (50°F). *Argentina, Bolivia.*

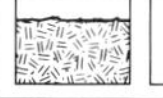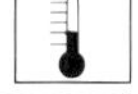

REBUTIA **PSEUDODEMINUTA** Backeb.
Syn: *Aylostera pseudodeminuta* (Ritter & Buin.) Backeb.

Deep-green, solitary stems about 10cm long, 8cm in diameter. There are about 20 ribs divided into tubercles and the brown areoles bear about 10 glassy-white radial spines 3–7mm long, and two to three yellowish centrals 1.2–1.5cm in length. Day flowering in summer, the flowers are carmine red and 3–4cm in diameter. Requires fairly bright light; normal cactus compost; minimum temperature 10°C (50°F). *Argentina (Salta).*

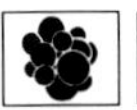     

REBUTIA **PSEUDOMINUSCULA** (Speg.) Br. & R.
Syn: *Aylostera pseudominuscula* Speg.

A group-forming species with somewhat cylindrical, dark-green stems up to about 8cm high, 3–4cm wide. It has about 14 ribs in spiralled rows of tubercles. The spines are brownish: seven to fourteen radials 3–5mm in length, and one to four centrals. Flowers appear by day, in early summer, and are purplish red, about 2.5cm long. Requires slight shade; normal cactus compost; minimum temperature 7°C (45°F). *Argentina (Salta).*

▲

REBUTIA **SENILIS** Backeb.

A deep-green, flattened-globular species which clusters freely. It is up to 8cm high, 7cm across and has about 18 spirally arranged ribs divided into tubercles. Areoles are white and bear about 25 yellowish-white fine spines about 3cm long, often matted together. Appearing by day, in summer, the flowers are carmine red, 3.5cm in diameter. On rare occasions an interesting cristate form develops, and invariably the spiralling arrangement is much in evidence, coupled with the profusion of flowers. Requires a fairly bright position; normal cactus compost; minimum temperature 10°C (50°F). *Argentina.*

   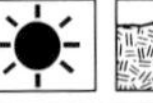 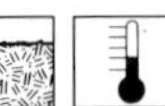

▼

REBUTIA **SPEGAZZINIANA** Backeb.
Syn: *Aylostera spegazzinii* (Backeb.) Backeb.

A more or less globular plant with bright green stems 3–5cm wide, 6–8cm long, forming dense clusters. It has about 18 ribs with quite prominent tubercles, and the whitish-felted areoles bear 14 whitish radial spines up to 4mm long, closely adpressed to the stem, and three to six centrals only to 2mm long. Day flowering in early summer, the flowers are a pale vermilion, 2.5–3cm wide. Needs only slight shade; normal cactus compost; minimum temperature 7°C (45°F). *Argentina (Salta).*

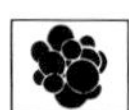     

REBUTIA **SPINOSISSIMA** Backeb.
Syn: *Aylostera spinosissima* (Backeb.) Backeb.

More or less globular plants 5–6cm thick, bright green and clustering freely around the base. There are about 15 or more spirally arranged ribs set with tubercles and the white hairy areoles bear numerous whitish bristle-like radial spines, up to 1cm long, and five to six thicker yellowish-white centrals. Flowers are medium red, 4cm long and 3cm in diameter; they are diurnal, appearing in summer. Requires slight shade; normal cactus compost; minimum temperature 7°C (45°F). *Argentina (Salta), Bolivia (Tarija).*

    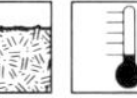 

REBUTIA **WEINGARTIANA** Ritter nom nuda

A doubtful species which might well be included within *Sulcorebutia*. The somewhat globular dark-green stem has about 30 ribs with greyish-white areoles and yellowish-brown spines, both radials and centrals. Flowers are bright yellow, about 2.5cm long, and appear by day in early summer. Requires bright light; normal cactus compost; minimum temperature 7°C (45°F). *Bolivia.*

      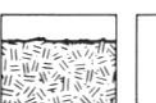 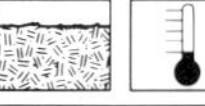

RHIPSALIDOPSIS **GAERTNERI** (Regel) Moran
Syn: *Schlumbergera gaertneri* (Regel) Br. & R.
Epiphyllopsis gaertneri (Regel) Lindinger

A bushy epiphytic species composed of many flat oval joints or segments 4–7cm long, 2–2.5cm broad in a link-like formation. Each joint has three to five tubercles with areoles on each side which carry one or two yellowish bristles. The flowers are scarlet, appearing by day in late spring or early summer. Requires filtered light, not full sun; a porous acid cactus compost; minimum temperature 10°C (50°F). *Brazil (Minas Gerais, Parana).*

   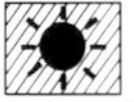 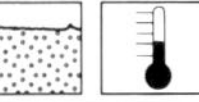 

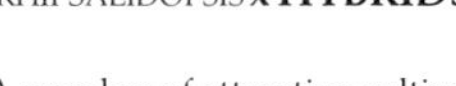

RHIPSALIDOPSIS **x HYBRIDS**

A number of attractive cultivars have been developed in Holland; their exact parentage is not known except that one parent is *Rhipsalidopsis rosea*. They flower in early spring. Requires slight shade; normal cactus compost; minimum temperature 13°C (55°F).

 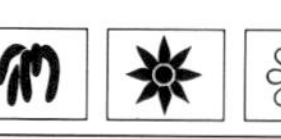    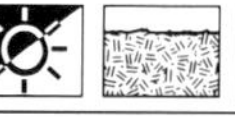  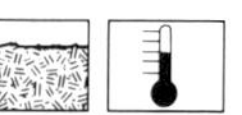

RHIPSALIDOPSIS **ROSEA** (Lageheim) Br. & R.
Syn: *Rhipsalis rosea* Lageheim

A small shrubby plant with erect or pendant stems composed of flat, sometimes angular segments 2–4cm long, to 1cm wide. These usually have fine reddish margins with minute areoles and a few bristly hairs. Rose-pink flowers are borne on the longer areole on the terminal joints; these appear by day in spring and early summer, and are 3–4cm across. Requires a semi-shaded position; an open, enriched compost; minimum temperature 10°C (50°F). *Brazil (forests of Parana).*

RHIPSALIDOPSIS **ROSEA var. ELEKTRA** hort.

These plants are similar to the species, but with deeper green segments and more pronounced marginal areoles. The flowers are purplish pink. Requirements are the same as for the species.

 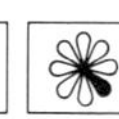  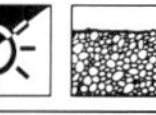 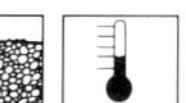

RHIPSALIS **CAPILLIFORMIS** Weber

An elongating, slender-stemmed epiphyte with many very thin pale-green branches 20-40cm long, about 2mm thick, often arranged in whorls. The areoles are minute, but have no bristles or spines. Flowers appear in late spring at the terminal ends of the branches and joints. They are a glossy greenish white, about 7mm long, and day flowering, and are followed by white fruits. Requires semi-shade; normal cactus compost; minimum temperature 10°C (50°F). *Eastern Brazil.*

RHIPSALIS **CASSUTHA (cassytha)** Gaertn.

A pendent bushy epiphyte over 1m in length. The pale-green branches carry cylindrical joints 10–50cm long, 2–4mm thick. Flowers appear by day in early summer and are yellowish white, about 5mm long, 7–8mm wide. They are followed by pale pinkish or white fruits. Needs shade; normal cactus compost; minimum temperature 10°C (50°F). *USA (Florida) to Southern Brazil, Tropical Africa, Sri Lanka.*

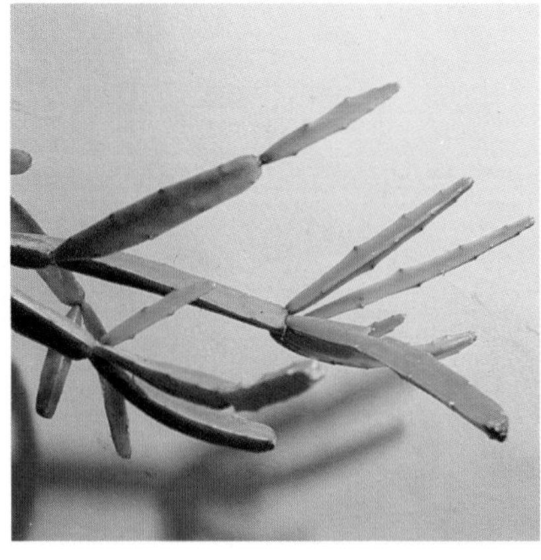

RHIPSALIS **CEREOIDES** Backeb. & Voll

An epiphyte of pendent or semi-erect habit. The branches or joints are usually three-angled, more rarely four-sided, and a dull bluish green, up to between 8 and 15cm in length, and about 1.7cm thick. Small prominent areoles sometimes develop two to four whitish bristles which soon fall. Flowering in late spring, the white flowers are diurnal, growing two to four together, and are about 2cm across. Fruits are pink. Requires slight shade; normal cactus compost; minimum temperature 13°C (55°F). *Brazil (Rio de Janeiro).*

RHIPSALIS **CEREUSCULA** Haw.

A well-known pendent epiphyte which forms a many-branched plant up to 60cm long. The longer stems are 10–30cm in length, while the shorter are arranged in whorls, the joints about 1.5cm long. All branches and joints are cylindrical in shape, and 3–4mm thick. The small areoles have wool and two to four bristles, and the flowers are produced from the tips of short joints. They are 1.5cm long, with whitish petals and pinkish-green sepals and are day flowering, in spring. Requires filtered light; normal cactus compost; minimum temperature 10°C (50°F). *Brazil (Sao Paulo), Argentina, Paraguay.*

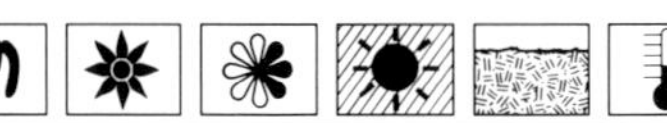

RHIPSALIS **CRISPATA** (Haw.) Pfeiff.

An epiphyte with pale-green, leaf-like joints, 6–12cm long, 2.5–6cm broad. These are slightly wavy-edged with shallow crenations and minute areoles which are spineless. Early summer flowering, the flowers are diurnal, creamy yellow, and about 1.4cm long, followed by white fruits. Needs slight shade, which is essential; normal cactus compost; minimum temperature 13°C (55°F). *Brazil (Sao Paulo, Rio de Janeiro).*

RHIPSALIS **CRISPIMARGINATA** Löefgr.

A semi-erect or pendent species which is epiphytic on forest trees. The thin, pale-green joints are somewhat rounded with a prominent midrib and lateral veins, the margins wavy-edged and lobed. Overall they are 5–8cm long, 4–6cm broad, and have minute areoles. Two or three flowers, which are diurnal, in early summer, are produced from an areole, mainly from the lateral areoles, and are yellowish white, up to 1cm long; these are followed by rose-pink fruits. Needs semi-shade; normal cactus compost; minimum temperature 10°C (50°F). *Brazil (Rio de Janeiro).*

RHIPSALIS **FASCICULATA** (Willd.) Haw.

A much-branching epiphyte with erect or semi-pendent stems. These have more or less cylindrical, pale bluish-green joints 8–10cm long, 4–6mm thick. The areoles are small, slightly woolly and with few bristles. Flowering by day in early summer, the numerous flowers are borne laterally, and are white or pale greenish white and up to 8mm long, 5–7cm wide. Fruits are white. Needs partial shade; normal cactus compost; minimum temperature 13°C (55°F). *Brazil (Bahia).*

RHIPSALIS **GRANDIFLORA** Haw.
Syn: *Lepismium grandiflorum* (Haw.) Backeb.

A cylindrical-stemmed epiphyte up to 1m long, 2cm thick, freely branching dichotomously or in whorls. The greyish-green branches are 5–15cm long, with the areoles slightly depressed. Late spring or early summer flowering, the flowers are diurnal; they are white with pale greenish-white outer segments and up to 2cm wide. Fruits are reddish. Needs protection from full sun; normal cactus compost; minimum temperature 10°C (50°F). *Brazil (Rio de Janeiro).*

   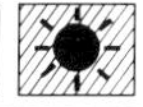 

RHIPSALIS **INCACHACANA** Card.

A deep-green epiphytic species of pendent habit and up to over 1.5m long. It branches freely, with branches 20–30cm long, 4–6cm wide. The yellowish-white areoles are set at intervals along the crenate margins, and bear brownish or yellowish-white bristly hairs about 1.8cm long. Flowers are purple violet, about 1cm long, and are diurnal, flowering in late spring to early summer. This is a useful plant for hanging baskets. Requires slight shade; normal cactus compost; minimum temperature 13°C (55°F). *Bolivia (Incachaca).*

     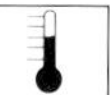

RHIPSALIS **GIBBERULA** Weber
Syn: *Lepismium gibberulum* (Weber) Backeb.

An epiphyte on trees and rocks, this species has greenish to dark greyish-green slightly angular cylindrical joints 10–20cm long, 3–5mm thick. The areoles are slightly woolly, rarely with a few fine bristles, and the flowers are borne laterally, up to 1cm long, 1.4cm wide when fully open. Day flowering in early summer, they are pale yellowish white with greenish or reddish sepals, and are followed by green or red fruits. Requires filtered light; normal cactus compost; minimum temperature 10°C (50°F). *Brazil (Sao Paulo).*

    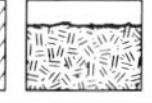 

RHIPSALIS **LINDBERGIANA** K. Sch.
Syn: Probably *Rhipsalis erythrocarpa* K. Sch., a plant collected in East Africa.

A pendent epiphyte with long slender stems and branches up to 30cm or more, the main stems frequently over 1m in length. The branches are cylindrical, 4–5mm thick, and the areoles are close set, rarely with a blackish bristle 2mm long which quickly falls. Pinkish and whitish flowers appear by day in early summer and are about 5mm long. The fruits are pale reddish. Requires fairly bright light; normal cactus compost; minimum temperature 10°C (50°F). *Brazil (Rio de Janeiro).*

   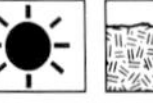  

RHIPSALIS **MICRANTHA** (HBK) DC.

A pendent robust epiphyte with four- to five-angled stems. The joints are usually three-angled or flat, 8mm to a little over 1cm thick and broad, with slight, remote crenations. The areoles are very small and slightly woolly and the flowers, which appear by day in early summer, are white and about 7mm long. Fruits are whitish or pinkish. Requires slight shade; normal cactus compost; minimum temperature 13°C (55°F). *Ecuador, Northern Peru.*

       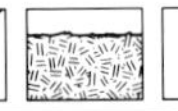   

RHIPSALIS **PENTAPTERA** Pfeiff.

A pale to deep-green bushy epiphyte, more or less erect with many stems up to 40cm high. The joints are five- to six-angled, 7–12cm long, with regularly notched margins and the areoles often have small bristles. Late spring flowering and diurnal, the flowers are white and about 8mm long. Fruits may be white or pink. Requires filtered light; normal cactus compost; minimum temperature 10°C (50°F). *Brazil, Paraguay.*

  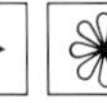   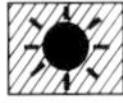  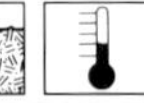

RHIPSALIS **LINEARIS** K. Sch.

A bushy, pendent epiphyte, freely branching, with pale-green stems 60cm or more long. The joints are leaf-like with a prominent midrib, 5–20cm long, 5–7cm wide. The margins are notched, and a small, slightly woolly but spineless areole is set immediately above each notch. Flowering by day in late spring, the flowers, about 1.8cm long, are white and so are the fruits. Requires slight shade; normal cactus compost; minimum temperature 13°C (55°F). *Argentina, Brazil, Paraguay.*

 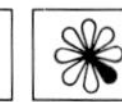   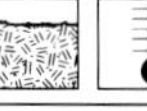 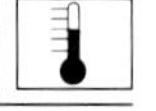

RHIPSALIS **PACHYPTERA** Pfeiff.

A semi-erect, becoming slightly pendent, epiphyte with dark-green, becoming reddish, leaf-like joints 8–20cm long, 5–12cm broad. These have notched margins, a prominent midrib and lateral veins. One to three flowers are borne from each areole; they are yellowish or white and are about 1.5cm long, day flowering, in summer. Fruits are red. Requires partial shade; normal cactus compost; minimum temperature 10°C (50°F). *Brazil (Rio de Janeiro).*

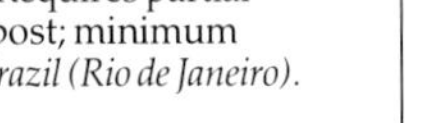

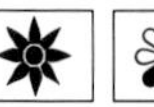  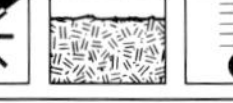  

RHIPSALIS **PLATYCARPA** Pfeiff.

A branching, bushy plant up to about 1m high. The dark-green joints are leaf-like, linear-oblong and narrowing at the base. They are 8–30cm long, 4–5cm wide, with crenate margins and a very prominent midrib. The whole joint is often edged with red. The areoles are slightly woolly and white or pale-yellowish flowers arise mainly from the side areoles. They are about 1.8cm long, and bloom by day in early summer. The fruit is greenish white. Requires partial shade; normal cactus compost; minimum temperature 10°C (50°F). *Brazil.*

  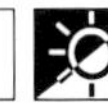 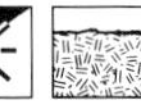 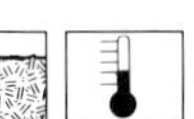

RHIPSALIS **PUNICEO-DISCUS** Lindb.
Syn: *Lepismium puniceo-discus* (Lindb.) Backeb.

A pendent epiphyte with pale green or yellowish-green long soft, fleshy stems, 5–7mm thick. The joints are cylindrical, up to 10cm long, 4mm thick, and are generally a darker green with areoles spirally arranged and ringed in red. Spring-flowering by day, the flowers are a glassy white with reddish-pinkish stamens and are about 1.5cm long. Fruits are at first black, then become yellow. Requires filtered light; normal cactus compost; minimum temperature 10°C (50°F). *Brazil (Minas Gerais).*

   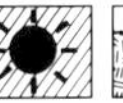 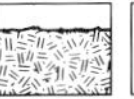 

RHIPSALIS **RHOMBEA** (Salm-Dyck) Pfeiff.

A bushy epiphyte with more or less cylindrical stems, up to 80cm high. The joints are flat or three-angled and 3–12cm long, up to 5cm broad, with a prominent midrib and lateral veins. They are dark green or slightly reddish, especially along the crenate margins. Late spring flowering, the flowers are diurnal, yellowish white, and about 1cm long, with red fruits following. Requires filtered light; normal cactus compost; minimum temperature 10°C (50°F). *Brazil (Sao Paulo).*

   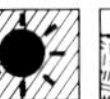  

RHIPSALIS **RAUHIORUM** Barthlott

An attractive epiphyte of forest trees with long pendent bright-green stems. These are two-sided, 30–60cm in length and 1.5–2cm wide. The individual joints have crenate margins and a prominent midrib. Areoles are small and brown, and bear whitish flowers about 1cm long by day in early summer. Fruits are white. It is an ideal plant for hanging baskets. Requires partial shade; normal cactus compost; minimum temperature 13°C (55°F). *Ecuador.*

    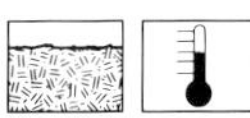 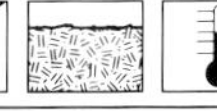

RHIPSALIS **ROBUSTA** Lem.

This is very similar to *R. pachyptera* but it has larger dark-green joints, and these are often three-winged, up to 20cm long, 10cm broad, and quite thick. Areoles are frequently multi-flowered, as many as three to five to each areole. Flowers appear by day in early summer and are pale yellowish white, up to 1.5cm long, 1.8cm across. Fruits are white. Requires slight shade; normal cactus compost; minimum temperature 10°C (50°F). *Brazil (Rio de Janeiro).*

RHIPSALIS **RUSSELLI** Br. & R.

A densely clustering epiphytic species from forested regions growing on trees. The dark-green joints are 15cm long, 5–6cm broad; they are flat with crenate margins edged reddish purple and have particularly prominent veining. Each of the whitish areoles produces either single or many whitish flowers about 3mm long in early summer; these are diurnal. Fruits are purple. Requires slight shade; normal cactus compost; minimum temperature 10°C (50°F). *Brazil (Bahia).*

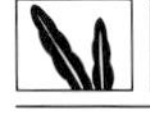    

RHIPSALIS **SULCATA** Weber

An epiphyte whose habitat is uncertain. It is a pale-green, more or less erect plant with spreading branches. The joints are five-angled up to 30cm long, 3–5mm thick, with small reddish areoles set far apart. Spring flowering in the daytime, the flowers are white to pale pinkish, and 1.2cm long. Fruits are white. Requires slight shade; normal cactus compost; minimum temperature 13°C (55°F). *Ecuador?*

 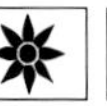  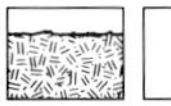

RHIPSALIS **TONDUZII** Weber

A dark-green bushy, pendent epiphyte, with four- to five-angled joints 6–10cm long and 1cm thick. The angles or ribs have prominent notches about 2cm apart, in which the areoles are set. Flowers are whitish, less than 1cm across; they are diurnal, and spring flowering. Fruits are white. Requires shade; normal cactus compost; minimum temperature 13°C (55°F). *Costa Rica.*

RHIPSALIS **SHAFERI** Br. & R.

A rather robust epiphyte with thick cylindrical stems and branches. The dull greyish-green branches, 4–5mm thick, are usually in whorls and have brownish areoles. Flowering by day in late spring, the flowers are greenish white, and about 1cm in diameter. Fruits are white, becoming pink. Needs slight shade; normal cactus compost; minimum temperature 10°C (50°F). *Paraguay.*

    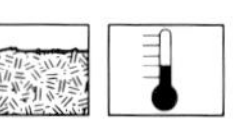

RHIPSALIS **TERES** Steud.

A fresh-green, erect, cylindrical-stemmed epiphyte with many branches. Joints occur in whorls of three to six or more, and are 6–9cm long, 3mm thick. The areoles are very small and reddish. Flowering by day in late spring, the flowers are yellowish white, 1cm long and 1.3cm in diameter. Fruits are white. Needs slight shade; normal cactus compost; minimum temperature 10°C (50°F). *Brazil (Rio de Janeiro, Sao Paulo to Minas Gerais).*

   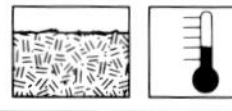

RHIPSALIS **TUCUMANENSIS** Weber
Syn: *Lepismium tucumanensis* (Weber) Backeb.

A pendent epiphyte with cylindrical stems and joints, up to 1cm thick and of varying lengths. The areoles are slightly woolly on the flowering joints, and the flowers appear from the side areoles. Diurnal, and flowering in late spring, the blooms are white, tipped pink, and 1–1.5cm long. Fruits are white, flushed pink. Needs slight shade; normal cactus compost; minimum temperature 10°C (50°F). *Argentina (Tucuman).*

    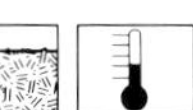

RHIPSAPHYLLOPSIS

RHIPSAPHYLLOPSIS **x ANDREA** (Knebel) Innes
Syn: *Rhipsalidopsis* x *andrea* hort.

A hybrid of *Rhipsalidopsis rosea* and *Rhipsalidopsis gaertneri*, the stems of the former being more apparent. Of pendent habit, these plants are well suited for hanging baskets, flowering in late spring. Requires good light, but not direct sun; normal cactus compost; minimum temperature 13°C (55°F).

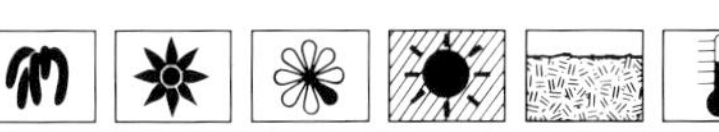

RHIPSAPHYLLOPSIS **x GRAESERI** Werd.
Syn: *Rhipsalidopsis* x *graeseri* (Werd.) Moran

A hybrid of *Rhipsalidopsis gaertneri* and *Rhipsalidopsis rosea* with a similar stem formation. The generic title is derived from the now obsolete *Epiphyllopsis* and *Rhipsalidopsis*. Requirements are the same as for *Rhipsalidopsis rosea*.

SAMAIPATICEREUS

SAMAIPATICEREUS **CORROANUS** Card.

An erect, tree-like columnar species up to 3.5m high with dark green branches, about 15cm in diameter. The branches are more slender, about 4cm wide. It has four to six deeply furrowed ribs with very prominent areoles composed of brownish felt. The spines are brownish, later greyish white, and about five in number, one to 1cm long, the others 2–3mm. Appearing in midsummer the white flowers have a bristly, scaly green tube up to 5cm long, and are nocturnal. Requires full sun; normal cactus compost; minimum temperature 13°C (55°F). *Bolivia (Florida)*.

SCHLUMBERGERA

SCHLUMBERGERA **Sp. nova "Adda Abendroth"**

A new introduction of recent years, this species was discovered by the late Mrs Adda Abendroth in deep forested areas growing as an epiphyte in trees. The zygomorphic flower, 5–7cm long, appears by day in late winter or early spring. The rich deep rose-magenta petals with a white throat makes a unique and beautiful plant. Requires semi-shade; a slightly acid, porous compost; minimum temperature 13°C (55°F). *Brazil (Organ Mountains)*.

   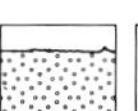 

SCHLUMBERGERA **cv. 'Bristol Amber'** McMillan

One of the results achieved by A. J. S. McMillan of Bristol. The amber-coloured petals are enhanced by the paler throat. It flowers in early winter. Minimum temperature at flowering time 15°C (59°F).

   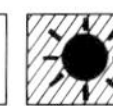 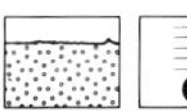 

SCHLUMBERGERA **cv. 'Bristol Queen'** McMillan

A fine multi-coloured cultivar of rich magenta and white, it is very free flowering during late autumn and early winter. Careful watering is essential during the flowering period. Minimum temperature at flowering time 15°C (59°F).

  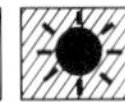 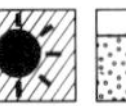 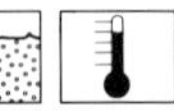

SCHLUMBERGERA **x BUCKLEYI** Hunt
Syn: *Epiphyllum bridgesii* Lem.; *Schlumbergera* x *bridgesii* (Lem.) Löefgr.

This is the popular Christmas Cactus which is of hybrid origin. The stems are composed of flat, oval joints or segments arranged like links, each 2–5cm long, 1.5–2cm wide and notched along both margins. The flowers are zygomorphic, bright red and up to 7.5cm long, appearing by day in late autumn and winter from the areoles at the tips of the uppermost segments. Requires filtered light; a slightly acid, but porous cactus compost; minimum temperature 13°C (55°F).

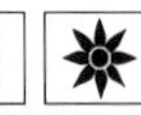   

SCHLUMBERGERA **cv. 'Exotica'** Barthlott & Rauh

A hybrid between *Schlumbergera truncata* and *Schlumbergera opuntioides*, produced in California. Whilst the stem growth becomes elongated, the flowers closely resemble those of *S. truncata*. Ideal for hanging baskets. Requires filtered light; a slightly acid, but porous cactus compost; minimum temperature 13°C (55°F).

SCHLUMBERGERA **cv. 'Bristol Rose'** McMillan

A choice product of the skills of A. J. S. McMillan. The emphasis is on the pinkish-rose tints edging the white and pinkish centres of the petals. It flowers in early winter when careful watering is necessary; minimum temperature at this time 15°C (59°F).

   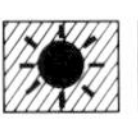 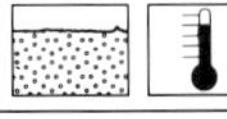

SCHLUMBERGERA **cv. 'Christmas Cheer'**

This cultivar is of Dutch origin. The orange-red petals, the red style and creamy-white stamens with scarlet stigma provide an interesting colour-change. Requires filtered light; a slightly acid, but porous cactus compost; minimum temperature 13°C (55°F).

 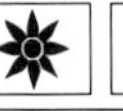  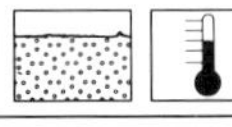

SCHLUMBERGERA **cv. 'Gold Charm'**

A cultivar produced in California, USA and possibly the best yellow-flowered form available. A temperature in excess of 13°C (55°F) is necessary to maintain the deep colouring. Requires filtered light; a slightly acid, but porous cactus compost; minimum temperature 13°C (55°F).

   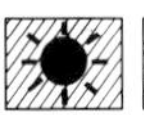 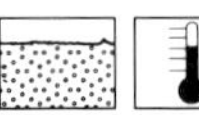

SCHLUMBERGERA **cv. 'Lilac Beauty'** Innes

Produced in the UK. Its parentage is *Schlumbergera truncata* x *Schlumbergera truncata* var. *delicatus*. The colouring of both parents is very obvious. It flowers in late winter. Requires filtered light; a slightly acid, but porous cactus compost; minimum temperature 13°C (55°F).

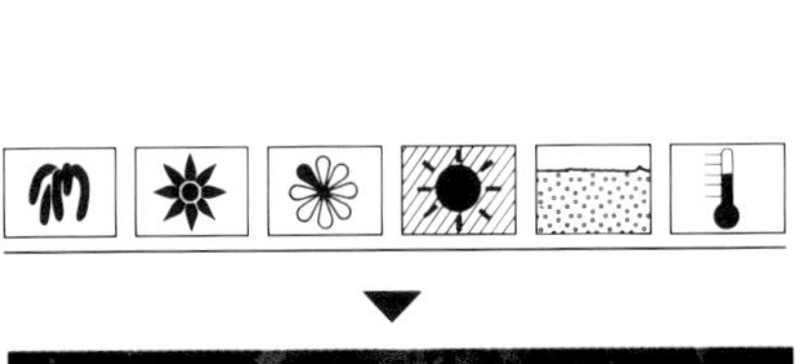

SCHLUMBERGERA **cv. 'Rudolf Zenneck'**

A cultivar of German origin – parentage unknown. Requires filtered light; a slightly acid, but porous cactus compost; minimum temperature 13°C (55°F).

SCHLUMBERGERA **cv. 'Westland'**

A cultivar of Dutch production. Flowers are generally smaller; the varying shades of red in the petals with the white throat provides a colourful display in late winter to very early spring. Requires filtered light; a slightly acid, but porous cactus compost; minimum temperature 13°C (55°F).

SCHLUMBERGERA **cv. 'White Christmas'**

A beautiful cultivar developed in California. It is a prolific-flowering plant bearing a close resemblance to *Schlumbergera truncata* var. *delicatus;* but generally smaller and carrying white blooms. Requires filtered light; a slightly acid, but porous cactus compost; minimum temperature 13°C (55°F).

SCHLUMBERGERA **OBTUSANGULA**
(K. Sch.) D. R. Hunt
Syn: *Epiphyllanthus obtusangulus* (K. Sch.) Berger

An epiphytic species with small oval-shaped joints 2.5–4cm long, 1–2cm broad. These are thick and flat and covered with many greyish areoles on both surfaces. The areoles often have one or two whitish bristles which usually soon fall. Flowering by day in late spring, the flowers are zygomorphic, a purplish violet colour and 4–4.5cm long. Requires slight shade; normal cactus compost; minimum temperature 13°C (55°F). *Brazil (Itatiay-Gebirge).*

SCHLUMBERGERA **OPUNTIOIDES** (Löefgr. & Dusén) D. R. Hunt
Syn: *Epiphyllum opuntioides* Löefgr. & Dusén; *Epiphyllanthus obovatus* (Engelm.) Br. & R.

Stems consist of segments 2.5–6cm long, 1–2cm wide, thick, fleshy, and deep green in colour. They are covered with white areoles with minute spines. Day flowering in late spring; these are zygomorphic, pinkish purple in colour and about 4.5cm long. A brief dry period after flowering is advisable. Requires partial shade; normal cactus compost; minimum temperature 13°C (55°F). *Brazil (Minas Gerais).*

SCHLUMBERGERA **ORSSICHIANA** Barthlott & McMillan

A fascinating epiphyte with pendant stems of flattened segments or joints, each up to 6cm long, 4cm wide. The margins have two to three prominent teeth with areoles set in the angles. Daytime flowers are produced from the tips of terminal joints in late winter and also in late summer; these are zygomorphic, up to 9cm long, 8–9cm across, and are white with reddish margins to the petals. Requires filtered light; a porous acid compost; minimum temperature 13°C (55°F). *Brazil (Serra do Mar).*

   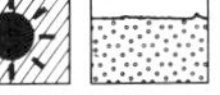 

SCHLUMBERGERA **TRUNCATA** (Haw.) Moran
Syn: *Zygocactus truncatus* (Haw.) K. Sch.

The parent of many attractive cultivars. It is a bright-green pendant epiphytic species from forest regions with linked joints, each 4–5cm long, 1.5–2.5cm broad and flat. The margins have two to four teeth on either side and the areoles have a few fine bristles. Flowers are deep pink or red, zygomorphic, and up to 8cm long, blooming by day in winter. Warmth plus humidity needed. Requires partial shade; an enriched, fairly acid, permeable compost; minimum temperature 13°C (55°F). *Brazil (Rio de Janeiro).*

    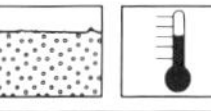

SCHLUMBERGERA **TRUNCATA var. CRENATUS** Borg
Syn: *Zygocactus truncatus* var. *crenatus* Borg

Similar to the species, but with greyish-green joints up to 6cm long, 1.5–3cm broad, with two to four crenate teeth on either side. The areoles have one or two minute white bristles. Flowers appear in winter, and are diurnal, pinkish violet in colour. Requirements are the same as for the species. *Brazil (Rio de Janeiro).*

SCHLUMBERGERA **TRUNCATA var. DELICATUS** (N. E. Br.) Moran
Syn: *Zygocactus truncatus* var. *delicatus* N. E. Br.; *Epiphyllum delicatum* N. E. Br.

Plants are more erect than the species. The joints are more slender and up to 7cm long, dull-green in colour and with three to four very prominent teeth on each side. Flowers appear in daytime in late autumn, and are zygomorphic; they open to pure white with a rose-pink style, white stamens and a crimson stigma. Requirements are the same as for the species. *Brazil (Rio de Janeiro).*

    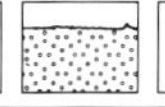 

SCLEROCACTUS **BLAINEI** Welsh & Thorne
Syn: *Sclerocactus spinosior* var. *blainei* (Welsh & Thorne) R. May

Usually solitary, a dark-green, globose species 4–6cm in diameter. The stem is tuberculate and the areoles more or less elliptical in shape, bearing eight to twelve white radial spines 1–1.5cm long and six red or red-tipped white centrals, three of which are hooked, 4–6cm long. Flowering in summer, and diurnal, the flowers are magenta, 4cm long and 2cm in diameter. Needs good light; normal cactus compost; minimum temperature 10°C (50°F). *USA (Nevada).*

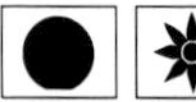   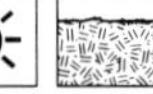 

SCLEROCACTUS **GLAUCUS** (K. Sch.) L. Benson
Syn: *Echinocactus glaucus* K. Sch.; *Pediocactus glaucus* (K. Sch.) Arp

Greyish-green, almost globular plant, 6cm high, 5cm wide with 12 tuberculate ribs, the tubercles protruding beyond. Areoles 9mm apart with dense spination: six to eight whitish radials to 1.9cm long, one to three centrals 2.5cm in length. Flowers diurnal, in summer, and pinkish purple, 3.5cm long to 5cm across. Requires sunshine; normal cactus compost plus a little lime; minimum temperature 10°C (50°F). *USA (Navajoan Desert).*

SCLEROCACTUS **MESAE-VERDAE** (Boissevain ex Hill & Salisb.) L. Benson
Syn: *Coloradoa mesae-verdae* Boissevain ex Hill & Salisb.

Small, usually solitary, greyish-green plants 5–6cm high, 8–9cm wide. There are 13–17 ribs with brownish-grey areoles bearing eight to ten radial spines up to 1cm long, and rarely one central. Flowers are diurnal, in summer, and 4cm across with creamy-yellow petals and purplish-brown sepals. Requires very careful watering; good light; enriched porous compost; minimum temperature 7°C (45°F). *USA (Colorado).*

    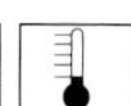

▲

SCLEROCACTUS **PAPYRACANTHUS** (Engelm.) N. P. Taylor
Syn: *Echinocactus papyracanthus* Engelm.; *Toumeya papyracantha* (Engelm.) Br. & R.

A short cylindrical globose plant up to 8cm tall, 3.5cm wide, either solitary or grouping. It has eight to thirteen ribs with prominent tubercles and areoles bearing five to nine whitish radial spines 3–4mm long, and three to four flat, curving centrals 1–2cm in length. The flowers, diurnal in summer, are whitish, about 2cm long, and appear from the crown. It is best grafted. Requires very careful watering; a sunny position; normal cactus compost with a little lime added; minimum temperature 10°C (50°F). *USA (New Mexico, Arizona).*

    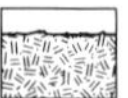 

SCLEROCACTUS **PARVIFLORUS** Clov. & Jott.

A cylindrical plant up to 45cm tall, 9cm wide, but usually remaining globular during the earlier years. The stem is bluish-green and it has 13 ribs with whitish areoles set on prominent tubercles. There are nine to fifteen greyish radial spines up to 3cm long and one to three centrals to 6cm in length. The pinkish purple flowers, which are diurnal, in mid-summer, are 2.5cm long and 2cm across. Requires a sunny bright position, which is essential; normal cactus compost with lime added; minimum temperature 10°C (50°F). *USA (Arizona).*

SCLEROCACTUS **PARVIFLORUS var. INTERMEDIUS** (Peebles) Woodruff & L. Benson
Syn: *Sclerocactus intermedius* Peebles

Very similar to the species in most respects, but differing principally in having longer flowers, up to 5cm, which only open in bright sunlight. Requirements are the same as for the species. *USA (Arizona).*

   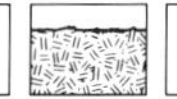 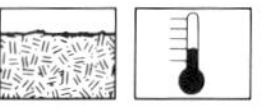

SCLEROCACTUS **POLYANCISTRUS** (Engelm. & Bigelow) Br. & R.
Syn: *Pediocactus polyancistrus* (Engelm. & Bigelow) Arp

A solitary plant, oval or cylindrical, 8–20cm tall, 6–10cm in diameter with a spiny, woolly crown. There are 13–17 slightly tuberculate ribs and the areoles bear white-tipped brown spines, about 20 stiff, curved radials up to 4.5cm long and 10 curved or straight centrals to 12cm long. Flowers appear in summer and are diurnal, rose pink or rarely white, and up to 5.5cm long. Needs sun; normal cactus compost; minimum temperature 10°C (50°F). *USA (Nevada, California).*

SCLEROCACTUS **PUBISPINUS** (Engelm.) L. Benson

The stems of this species are more or less globose, greyish-green, and usually 4–6cm in diameter with prominent tuberculate ribs. Areoles bear about eight white, brown-tipped radial spines up to 2cm long and four centrals about 2.5cm long, the lower hooked and reddish, the upper whitish, and laterals brownish-red. Day flowering, in summer, the flowers are yellow, up to 2.5cm long. Needs sun; normal cactus compost; minimum temperature best at 10°C (50°F). *USA (Utah, Nevada).*

   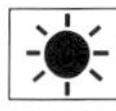 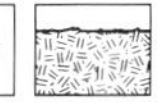 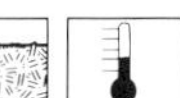

SCLEROCACTUS **PUBISPINUS var. SPINOSIOR** (Engelm.) Welsh
Syn: *Sclerocactus spinosior* (Engelm.) Woodruff & L. Benson

Dark greyish-green stems, globose to cylindrical, with ribs almost hidden by the high tubercles. The areoles have long spines, nine to eleven whitish radials and one to five brownish centrals of varying lengths from 2–5cm. Flowering in summer, the reddish-violet flowers are diurnal and about 4cm long. Requirements are the same as for the species. *USA (Utah, Arizona).*

SCLEROCACTUS **TERRAE-CANYONAE** Heil

Dark greyish-green, stems from 7–11.5cm long, 8–11cm wide with 11–13 ribs, sometimes spiralled. The areoles are woolly, and bear five to thirteen radial spines, one central hooked spine up to 8.2cm long, one upper one up to 5cm and two to four peripheral centrals varying from 2–6.2cm in length. Flowers are pale yellow and about 5cm long and across. They appear by day, in summer. Needs sun; normal cactus compost; minimum temperature 10°C (50°F). *USA (Utah, Colorado, New Mexico).*

SCLEROCACTUS **WHIPPLEI var. HEILII** Castetter, Pierce & Schwerin

A globose to cylindrical species, 15–17.5cm high, 10–15cm in diameter. It has about 13 ribs, with tubercles set about 2cm apart. The downward-pointing areoles bear two to six brown-tipped white spines up to 2cm long and eight to nine brownish centrals. Day flowering in early summer, the rose-pink flowers are 3cm long, 5cm across. Needs sun; normal cactus compost; minimum temperature 10°C (50°F). *USA (New Mexico).*

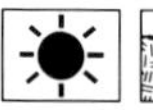

SCLEROCACTUS **SCHLESERI** Heil & Welsh
Syn: *Sclerocactus spinosior* var. *schleseri* (Heil & Welsh) R. May

A green globular plant, rarely offsetting, with stems 3–5cm long and wide and tubercles 5–9mm long. The areoles bear seven to nine brown-tipped white radial spines up to 3cm long, one white upper central 6cm in length, and three curled or hooked dark-red centrals 2–5cm long. Summer flowering, the magenta flowers are diurnal, and up to 2.5cm long. Requires bright light; normal cactus compost; minimum temperature 10°C (50°F). *USA (Nevada).*

SCLEROCACTUS **WHIPPLEI** (Engelm. & Bigelow) Br. & R.
Syn: *Echinocactus whipplei* Engelm. & Bigelow

A globular species up to 7cm high, about 8cm wide. It has 13 ribs and the areoles bear eight to ten greyish-white radial spines and four centrals, the upper one up to 5cm long, the lower hooked, to 3.5cm, and peripherals up to 5cm. Day flowering in summer, the flowers are yellow, about 2.5cm long and across. Requires good light; enriched compost; minimum temperature 10°C (50°F). *USA (Arizona, Utah, Colorado).*

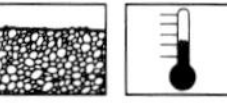

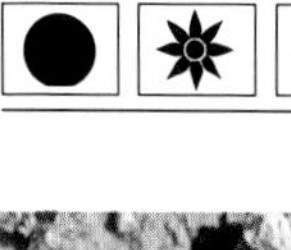

SCLEROCACTUS **WRIGHTIAE** L. Benson
Syn: *Pediocactus wrightiae* (L. Benson) G. K. Arp

A globose plant 5–8.7cm long, 5–7.5cm wide with about 13 tuberculate ribs, the tubercles about 1.2cm long. Areoles bear eight to ten white radial spines up to 1.2cm long and four brownish centrals, 1.2–1.9cm in length, the lower one curved and hooked. Flowers are about 2cm long and across, pale to deep lavender, and appear by day, in summer. Needs good light; normal cactus compost; minimum temperature 10°C (50°F). *USA (Utah).*

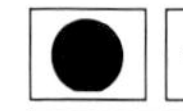

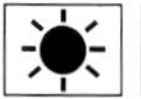
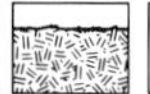
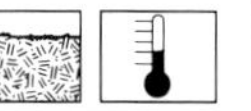

SELELIOCEREUS x **MAYNARDAE** (Paxton) Guill.

An inter-generic hybrid of *Selenicereus grandiflorus* and *Heliocereus speciosa*, originally described in 1847. It has clambering three- to five-angled stems up to 4m in length, 1.5cm thick, with brownish and almost spineless areoles. Flowers are diurnal in summer, about 10cm long to 18cm across when expanded, in shades of rose pink and a deeper red, often more of a pale violet red. Requires a position in filtered light; normal cactus compost; minimum temperature 15°C (59°F).

    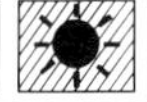  

SELENICEREUS **GRANDIFLORUS** (Mill.) Br. & R.
Syn: *Cereus grandiflorus* Miller

A variable species with trailing or climbing stems up to 5m long, 2–3cm thick. It has five to eight ribs and pale-yellowish woolly areoles bearing seven to eleven yellow spines which become grey. Flowering at night in summer, the blooms are fragrant, about 30cm long and 15cm across, with broad, white petals and narrow, pale yellowish-brown and spreading sepals. Requires semi-shade; a rich porous compost; minimum temperature 15°C (59°F). *West Indies, Mexico.*

 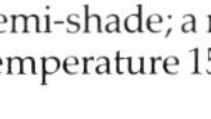      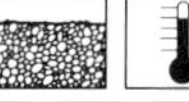   

▼

SELENICEREUS **HALLENSIS** (Weingt.) Weingt.
Syn: *Cereus hallensis* Weingt.

A pale-green climbing species with stems up to 3m long, 1.5cm thick. Five to six ribs and brown areoles on short prominences, often spineless, or have two to six thin, pale-brown spines up to 1cm long. Fragrant flowers in summer, nocturnal, up to 30cm long, 28cm across, with white or yellowish-white petals and reddish or externally yellowish-red sepals. Requires shade; an open acid compost; minimum temperature 15°C (59°F). *Colombia.*

     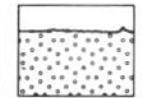   

SELENICEREUS **HAMATUS** (Scheidw.) Br. & R.
Syn: *Cereus hamatus* Scheidw.; *Selenicereus rostratus* (Lem.) Marsh.

A dark-green plant with three- to five-angled stems up to 4m long, 2cm thick. Short spines grow from hooked tubercles are 1cm long. Fragrant flowers at night in summer, with white and yellowish petals in three series and greenish-yellow sepals in two series. Give semi-shade; porous acid compost; minimum temperature 15°C (59°F). *Mexico (Vera Cruz, Jalapa), West Indies.*

   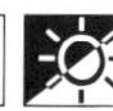 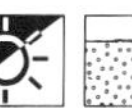 

SELENICEREUS **HONDURENSIS** (K. Sch.) Br. & R.
Syn: *Cereus hondurensis* K. Sch.

An elongating, clambering species with trailing or climbing stems 2cm thick. It has seven to ten low ribs and areoles of dark wool with brown hairs and white bristles. The spines are whitish, 5mm long. Flowers appear in summer, and are nocturnal, about 23cm long, to 18cm across, with creamy-white petals 1.5cm wide and linear, yellowish-green, spreading sepals. Requires a position in filtered light; normal cactus compost; minimum temperature 18°C (64°F). *Honduras.*

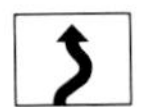   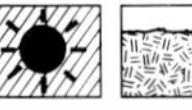  

SELENICEREUS **INNESII** Kimnach

A trailing species, stems up to 2m long, 1.2cm thick. It has six ribs and woolly areoles with one or two thick and three to seven slender pale-brown spines. It is unique within the *Cactaceae* as some plants bear only male flowers (left), others only female (below left), whilst on some plants there are normal flowers (above). Flowering by day in summer, the blooms are normally pinkish white and 4–5cm long, with extended petals up to 6cm across. It makes an ideal plant for hanging baskets. Requires a position in filtered light; normal cactus compost; minimum temperature 15°C (59°F). *St Vincent (West Indies).*

   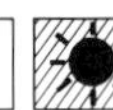 

SELENICEREUS **MACDONALDIAE** (Hook.) Br. & R.
Syn: *Cereus macdonaldiae* Hook.

A long-stemmed, trailing and climbing species. The stems are up to 8m long, 1.5cm thick, and are glossy green, often suffused purple. There are five to seven ribs with brown areoles set on prominent tubercles with a few short spines. Flowers, up to 35cm long, 25cm across, appear at night in summer. The inner petals are white or pale cream and the outer segments yellowish or reddish. Requires shade; an acid compost; minimum temperature 15°C (59°F). *Uruguay, Argentina.*

SELENICEREUS **TESTUDO** (Karw.) F. Buxb.
Syn: *Deamia testudo* Karw.

Remains better known as *Deamia.* It is an epiphytic clamberer, the stems composed of joints up to 25cm long, varying in shape and three- to eight-angled, with aerial roots holding fast to the host tree. The areoles have bristly spines. Flowers appear in summer, and are diurnal, about 25cm long, 15cm across, with white petals and yellowish-green, widely spreading sepals. Requires humidity and semi-shade, which are essential; an open acid compost; minimum temperature 18°C (64°F). *Southern Mexico to Colombia.*

     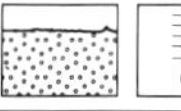

SELENICEREUS **WERCKLEI** (Weber) Br. & R.
Syn: *Cereus wercklei* Weber

An uncommon epiphytic species growing on trees and rocks. The more or less cylindrical stem has about 12 very shallow ribs, 1–2m in length and about 1cm thick and much branching; they are spineless. The white flowers, nocturnal, in summer, are about 12cm long and across when fully expanded and have oblong petals and narrow, greenish-white sepals. Requires relative semi-shade and humidity; an acid compost; minimum temperature 18°C (64°F). *Costa Rica.*

    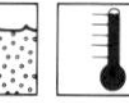 

SELENICEREUS **PTERANTHUS** (Link & Otto) Br. & R.
Syn: *Cereus nycticalus* Link

A remarkable plant with long purplish-green, four- to six-angled stems 2–4cm thick, bearing areoles with whitish wool and short, thick spines about 4mm long. Flowers are nocturnal, appearing in early summer; they are about 30cm long and little more across when fully expanded. The white or pale-cream petals are set like a funnel and the sepals are very slender and long, pale purple externally and recurving. Requires shade; an acid compost; minimum temperature 18°C (64°F). *Mexico, Central America.*

    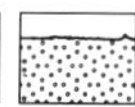 

SETIECHINOPSIS **MIRABILIS** (Speg.) Dehaas.
Syn: *Arthrocereus mirabilis* (Speg.) W. T. Marsh.; *Echinopsis mirabilis* Speg.

A small columnar plant with dark bluish-green stems 10–15cm high, 2–2.5cm thick, rarely branching. It has about 12 ribs and white woolly areoles with nine to fourteen whitish radial spines and one brownish central up to 1.5cm in length. Flowering in summer, the flowers are nocturnal and produced from the top of the stem. They are white and fragrant, shaped like a funnel and up to 12cm long, 3–4cm across. Needs a bright location; normal cactus compost; minimum temperature 10°C (50°F). *Argentina.*

   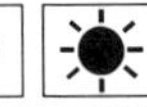 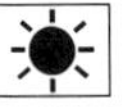  

SICCOBACCATUS
DOLICHOSPERMATICUS (Buin. & Bred.) Braun & Esteves
Syn: *Austrocephalocereus dolichospermaticus* Buin. & Bred.

A cylindrical, erect species. The stems are up to 2m tall, 8cm in diameter, with a brown bristly lateral cephalium. There are 30 ribs with oval woolly areoles bearing yellowish spines 8mm to 2.5cm in length. Nocturnal flowers appear in summer; these are whitish, pinkish externally and 4cm long, 2.5cm across, the tube devoid of scales. Needs sun; normal cactus compost; minimum temperature 15°C (59°F). *Brazil (Bahia).*

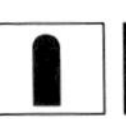    

SICCOBACCATUS **ESTEVESII** Buin. & Bred.
Syn: *Austrocephalocereus estevesii* Buin. & Bred.

A tall, columnar plant, rarely branching, up to 6m high, with green stems 15cm thick. The lateral cephalium consists of creamy-white woolly hairs and red bristles. There are 37–42 ribs, and the brown or greyish areoles carry about 11 radial spines and four centrals, all dark grey, and varying from 5mm to 2cm long. Flowers are nocturnal in summer, 3.5cm long and wide, and are white.
The subspecies *grandiflorus* (Diers & Esteves) Braun & Esteves, from North-eastern Goias is similar to type but with longer flowers.
The subspecies *insigniflorus* (Diers & Esteves) Braun & Esteves, from Minas Gerais, has a more bluish stem and a smaller, more bristly cephalium with a different flower structure.
Requires bright light; normal cactus compost; minimum temperature 15°C (59°F). *Brazil (Goias).*

    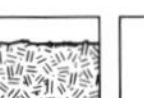 

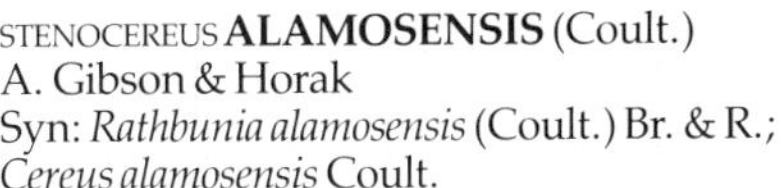

STENOCEREUS **ALAMOSENSIS** (Coult.) A. Gibson & Horak
Syn: *Rathbunia alamosensis* (Coult.) Br. & R.; *Cereus alamosensis* Coult.

A bush-like columnar plant with semi-erect or straggling stems 2–4m in length. In its habitat it is associated with tall scrub country. It has five to eight ribs encircling a stem up to 8cm thick. The areoles appear at 2–3cm intervals, bearing about 12 whitish radial spines, 1–1.5cm long, and one to four centrals up to 5cm in length. Day flowering in summer, the flower is tubular becoming funnel-shaped, with brick-red, recurving petals and 4–10cm long. Requires slight shade; an open, fairly rich compost; minimum temperature 10°C (50°F). *Mexico (Alamos, Sonora).*

    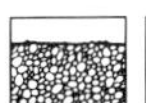 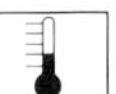

STENOCEREUS **BENECKEI** (Ehrenb.) Backeb.
Syn: *Lemaireocereus beneckei* (Ehrenb.) Br. & R.; *Hertrichocereus beneckei* (Ehrenb.) Backeb.

A columnar plant attaining 2–3m tall. Stems are greyish-green, coated with a white, powdery bloom especially towards the tips. Five to nine ribs, notched at regular intervals, in which are the areoles carrying five grey radial spines, one central to 4cm long. Nocturnal flowers grow from the upper areoles in winter; ivory white, brownish externally and 4–6cm long. Needs sun; a porous enriched compost; minimum temperature 15°C (59°F). *Mexico (Guerrero).*

    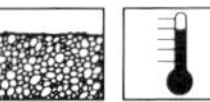

STENOCEREUS **DUMORTIERI** (Scheidw.) Buxb.
Syn: *Lemaireocereus dumortieri* (Scheidw.) Br. & R.; *Isolatocereus dumortieri* (Scheidw.) Backeb.

Columnar plants up to 15m tall, branching freely. The bluish-green branches are 5–7.5cm thick and have five to nine ribs. Areoles bear nine to twenty radial spines about 1cm long, one to four centrals to 3cm, all yellowish white. Flowers 5cm long, white, brownish externally, appear at night in spring. Needs full sun with warmth; normal cactus compost; minimum temperature 13°C (55°F). *Mexico (Hidalgo to Oaxaca).*

   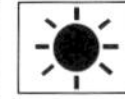 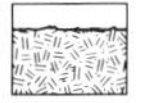 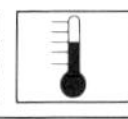

STENOCEREUS **ERUCA** (Brandegee) A. Gibson & Horak
Syn: *Machaerocereus eruca* (Brandegee) Br. & R.

Popularly known as the Creeping Devil, this is a creeping, prostrate plant rooting along its length with only the tips of the stems rising. The stems are 1–3m long, 4–8cm thick with about 12 ribs. The areoles are set about 2cm apart with around 20 greyish radial spines and one dagger-like white central to 3.5cm long. Night flowering in spring, the flowers are pale yellow, 10–12cm long and 4–6cm broad. Requires the sunniest position possible; very porous enriched cactus compost; minimum temperature 10°C (50°F). *Mexico (Baja).*

    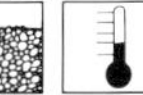

STENOCEREUS **GUMMOSUS** (Brandegee) A. Gibson & Horak
Syn: *Machaerocereus gummosus* (Engelm.) Br. & R.

Bushy, columnar plant to 1m tall, branching from base. Stems greyish-green, 4–6cm thick. Eight to nine ribs with areoles at 2cm intervals, bearing eight to twelve radial spines to 1cm long and four to six centrals, 4cm in length. Nocturnal flowers in early summer, are 10–14cm long on a slender tube, and purplish red. Needs a bright sunny position; calcareous, enriched porous compost; minimum temperature 13°C (55°F). *Mexico (Baja).*

    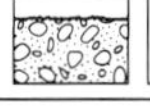 

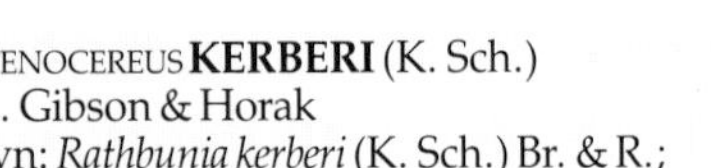

STENOCEREUS **KERBERI** (K. Sch.) A. Gibson & Horak
Syn: *Rathbunia kerberi* (K. Sch.) Br. & R.; *Cereus kerberi* K. Sch.

Bright-green bushy, columnar species, 2m tall, branches 4–7cm thick. Four crenated ribs with brownish areoles carrying 10–16 greyish radial spines 2cm long, and one to four central spines 3–5cm long. Daytime flowers in summer, deep pink and 10–12cm long with a red scaly ovary and reddish scaly tube. Requires bright light; normal cactus compost; minimum temperature 13°C (55°F). *Mexico (Colima).*

STENOCEREUS **MARGINATUS** (DC.) Buxb.
Syn: *Marginatocereus marginata* (DC.) Backeb.; *Pachycereus marginatus* (DC.) Br. & R.

Tall, tree-like, greyish-green plants eventually reaching 3–7m high, to 30cm thick. There are five to seven ribs with areoles set close. The brownish spines are thick, to 1.5cm long, but soon falling; there are seven to nine radials and one central. Flowers are diurnal, growing in summer at the tips of the stems, and are white, reddish externally, and 4–5cm long. Requires full sunshine; normal cactus compost; minimum temperature 10°C (50°F). *Mexico*.

   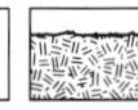 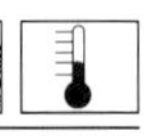

STENOCEREUS **MARTINEZII** (G. Ort.) Bravo
Syn: *Lemaireocereus martinezii* G. Ort.

A dark-green columnar plant up to 5m tall with nine to twelve or more ribs bearing prominent dark reddish-brown areoles. The spines are dark brown, almost black, and consist of seven to eleven radials 2–10mm long, and three centrals, the lower, the longest, up to 2.5cm. Flowers are whitish pink . Possibly night flowering in summer, requiring an open sunny position; normal cactus compost; minimum temperature 10°C (50°F). *Mexico (Sinaloa, Mazatlan).*

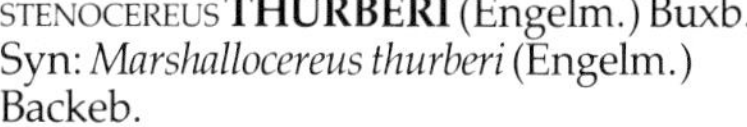

STENOCEREUS **THURBERI** (Engelm.) Buxb.
Syn: *Marshallocereus thurberi* (Engelm.) Backeb.

Greyish-green columnar plant 2–3m high, branching from base. Branches 15cm across , with 12–17 prominent ribs and brown areoles 1–2cm apart. Spines black, turning grey; seven to nine radials 1cm long, and one to three centrals 2–5cm in length. Flowers diurnal, in summer, about 7cm long, with pink petals and red sepals. Needs bright sunlight; normal cactus compost; minimum temperature 10°C (50°F). *USA (Texas), Mexico (Baja California).*

   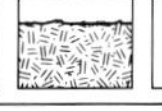 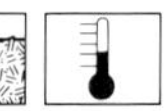

STENOCEREUS **THURBERI fma CRISTATA**

Very occasionally a fasciated fan-like formation develops at the tips of the stems creating an interesting feature about 60cm in diameter. This picture was taken in the Baja California (Mexico).

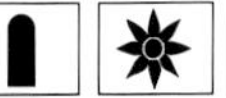    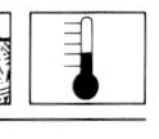

STENOCEREUS **TRELEASII** (Br. & R.) Backeb.
Syn: *Lemaireocereus treleasii* Br. & R.

A columnar, rather weak-stemmed species, more or less erect and branching from the base. The stems are only 4–8cm thick and have 14–20 ribs, regularly notched, with whitish areoles bearing eight to ten small radial spines and one or two longer yellowish-grey centrals. Flowers, which are diurnal, appearing in summer, are 4–5cm long and pinkish purple in colour. Needs good light; normal cactus compost; minimum temperature 13°C (55°F). *Mexico (Oaxaca).*

    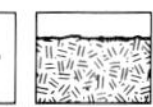 

× STENOMYRTILLUS

x STENOMYRTILLUS

A bi-generic title provided by Rowley in 1980 for natural hybrids between *Stenocereus* and *Myrtillocactus*. Shown here is one of the few discovered, and the peculiar features of both genera are clearly obvious. So far the plant remains un-named. *Mexico.*

STEPHANOCEREUS

STEPHANOCEREUS **LEUCOSTELE** (Gürke) Berger

A rare, columnar plant, up to 3m tall and 10cm thick in its habitat. The bluish-green stems have 12–18 ribs, branching from well above the base, and the areoles are about 1.5cm long with white hairs and about 20 white, later brownish, radial spines, 5mm to 1.5cm in length, and one or two yellowish centrals 3–4cm long. Flowers are borne in a densely woolly and hairy cephalium which is subsequently grown through, but the encircling cephalium still persists and is likely to flower in following seasons. Several white flowers are produced up to 7cm long with a yellowish, scaly tube; these are nocturnal, appearing in summer. The green fruits of *Stephanocereus* develop soon after flowering. These are oval, and about 5cm long, and remain on the plant for many weeks before ripening. Requires a bright sunny position; normal cactus compost; minimum temperature 13°C (55°F). *Brazil (Bahia).*

   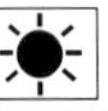 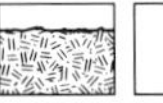

STETSONIA

STETSONIA **CORYNE** (Salm-Dyck) Br. & R.

A tree-like, columnar species 5–8m tall, the trunk up to 40cm thick at the base. Stems are bluish green, 9–10cm in diameter, and have eight to nine ribs. The areoles carry brownish-yellow spines which later turn glossy black, seven to nine radials up to 3cm long, and one central to 8cm in length. Flowers, up to 15cm long, are nocturnal in summer and consist of a long scaly tube tipped with white inner petals, glossy green externally. Requires good light and warmth; normal cactus compost; minimum temperature 13°C (55°F). *Bolivia, Argentina.*

   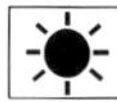 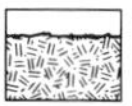 

STROMBOCACTUS **DISCIFORMIS** (K. Sch.) Br. & R.
Syn: *Echinocactus disciformis* K. Sch.

A greyish-green, globular plant, 5–12cm in diameter, only very rarely offsetting. It is slightly flattened on the top with a few persistent white spines at the centre. The 12–18 ribs are formed into flat, closely set rhomboid tubercles which are raised in the centre, each with a whitish areole bearing one to five whitish spines 1.5cm long. A summer, diurnal species, the flowers are white or yellowish and about 4cm across. The cristate form of *Strombocactus disciformis* is rarely encountered, and this invariably provides two crowns. Careful watering is required, and the plant should be kept dry in winter. Needs full sun; a mineral compost; minimum temperature 10°C (50°F). *Mexico (Hidalgo).*

    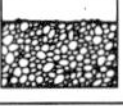 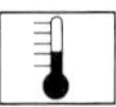

STROPHOCACTUS **WITTII** (K. Sch.) Br. & R.

An extreme rarity, this is a climbing epiphyte with flattened stems 4–5m in length, 3–8cm wide. These have a prominent centre vein from which aerial roots appear along its length to ensure persistent climbing. The areoles are closely set along the finely toothed margins, sometimes with fine bristle-like spines up to 1cm long. The summer flowers are nocturnal, white with pinkish outer petals and up to 25cm long. Requires semi-shade; normal cactus compost; minimum temperature 21°C (70°F). *Brazil (Manaos).*

SUBPILOCEREUS **REPANDUS** (L.) Backeb.

A tall columnar plant, often tree-like in its habitat, reaching to 10m or more high. It has many greyish to bluish-green branches, each up to about 10cm in diameter. There are eight to twelve ribs about 1cm high, and the greyish-white areoles have numerous fine, whitish bristle-like spines and one or more centralized spines, to 5cm in length. Funnel-shaped flowers, 10cm long and 4cm across, with white inner petals and greenish-white or pale-pinkish outer segments, and are nocturnal, in summer. Needs sun; normal cactus compost; minimum temperature 18°C (64°F). *Curacao.*

SULCOREBUTIA **BREVIFLORA** Backeb.
Syn: *Sulcorebutia haseltonii* (Card.) Donald

The brownish-green stems are more or less globular, up to 6cm wide and 4cm high. The plant has about 20 ribs, and the areoles are 3–5mm long with whitish wool, each with about 12 bristle-like, yellowish pectinate spines 1cm long. Mid-summer flowering, and diurnal, the flowers are usually yellow, about 2.5cm long and across. Needs a bright position; normal cactus compost; minimum temperature 10°C (50°F). *Bolivia (Cochabamba).*

SULCOREBUTIA **CRISPATA** Rausch

Generally a clustering species with greyish-green stems about 2.5cm high, 3.5cm thick and about 13 spirally arranged ribs. The areoles are about 4mm long with brown or whitish wool and bear 20–30 white to pale-brown radial spines from 5mm to nearly 2cm in length. Flowering by day in mid-summer, the flowers are magenta, about 3cm long and wide. Requires bright light; normal cactus compost; minimum temperature 10°C (50°F). *Bolivia (Chuquisaca).*

SULCOREBUTIA **GLOMERISETA** (Card.) Ritter
Syn: *Rebutia glomeriseta* Card.

A clustering plant formed of many individual dull-green stems, each up to 6cm high and wide, with about 20 spiralling ribs. The brown or white-felted areoles are about 3mm long, and there are numerous yellowish or brownish-yellow spines, radiating in series, 2–3cm long. It is summer flowering, and diurnal, with pale to deep, almost orange-yellow flowers, about 2.5cm long, 1.5cm wide. Requires bright light, which is essential; normal cactus compost; minimum temperature 10°C (50°F). *Bolivia.*

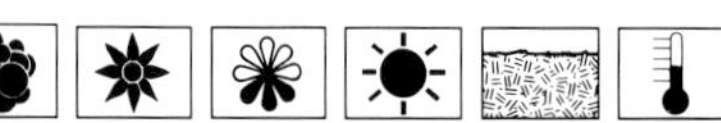

SULCOREBUTIA **GLOMERISPINA** (Card.) Buin. & Donald
Syn: *Rebutia glomerispina* Card.

Slightly globular plants with a tendency to group. The dark grey-green stems are 2cm high, 3cm wide, with about 20 spiralling ribs. Areoles are about 3mm long with whitish wool, and there are 10–14 brownish radial spines from 5–10cm or more, with occasionally one or more central which is similar. The flowers are a deep reddish purple, about 3cm long, 2cm wide, and appear by day in summer. Requires bright light; normal cactus compost; minimum temperature 10°C (50°F). *Bolivia (Cochabamba).*

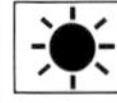

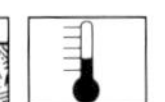

SULCOREBUTIA **KRAHNII** Rausch

A slow-growing, dull-green clustering species with flattened, globular stems up to 5cm high, 6–8cm wide. It has 30 or more spiralling ribs and white woolly areoles about 4mm long, with 20–24 white to brownish radial spines 1cm long and three to seven dark-brown centrals about 1.2cm. The flowers are yellow, about 2.5cm long and across, appearing by day, in summer. Requires bright sun; normal cactus compost; minimum temperature 10°C (50°F). *Bolivia (Santa Cruz).*

    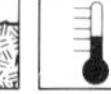

▲

SULCOREBUTIA **MENESESII** (Card.) Buin. & Donald

A dark greyish-green clump-forming species. Each globular stem is about 4cm high, 5–6cm thick, with about 14–18 spiralling ribs. The white woolly areoles are about 6mm long and bear 10–15 brown-tipped whitish radial spines from 5mm to 3cm or more long. Flowers are diurnal, appearing in summer; they are pale to bright yellow, 4cm long and 3.5cm in diameter. Requires bright light; normal cactus compost; minimum temperature 10°C (50°F). *Bolivia (Cochabamba).*

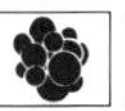    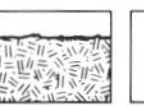

SULCOREBUTIA **LANGERII** Falken. & Neumann

A dark reddish-green, globose, solitary species, only rare clustering, 2–2.5cm in diameter. It has about 14 tuberculate ribs and pale-brownish areoles bear 21–25 bristly, mostly brownish-white pectinate spines up to 3mm long. Day flowering in summer, the flowers are bright yellow. Needs bright light; normal cactus compost; minimum temperature 10°C (50°F). *Bolivia (Santa Cruz).*

    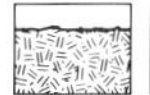 

SULCOREBUTIA **PAMPAGRANDENSIS** Rausch

A greyish-green, more or less solitary species, 4cm high, 7cm wide, with 18–26 spiralling ribs. The white woolly areoles, up to 8mm long, bear 16–25 pale-brownish or yellowish radial spines 6–9mm long and one, sometimes three to four, brown-tipped yellowish centrals to 1.5cm in length. Flowers appear in summer, and are diurnal; purple or magenta, they are 3.5cm long, 4.5cm in diameter. Requires bright light; normal cactus compost; minimum temperature 10°C (50°F). *Bolivia (Cochabamba).*

   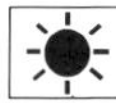  

▲

SULCOREBUTIA **RAUSCHII** Frank

A clustering plant composed of small blackish-green or purplish-green stems about 2cm high, 3cm in diameter with up to 16 spiralling ribs. The areoles are almost bare, about 2mm long with 11–12 minute dark or yellowish radial spines about 1mm in length, rarely one or two centrals. Day flowering in early to mid-summer, the flowers are magenta pink or purple, 3cm long and across. Needs a bright sunny position; normal cactus compost; minimum temperature 10°C (50°F). *Bolivia (Chuquisaca).*

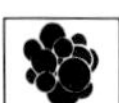    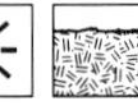 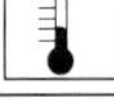

SULCOREBUTIA **TIRAQUENSIS** (Card.) Ritter **var. BICOLORISPINA** Knize

One of many forms of this popular species. It is a grouping plant with bluish-green stems 8cm high, 7cm wide with 16 to possibly 28 ribs arranged spirally. The white woolly areoles are about 4mm long, 3mm wide and bear 30–40 or more fine white radial spines 5mm to 1cm in length, and eight to twelve dark glossy brown centrals up to about 2cm long. Flowering by day in mid-summer, the flowers are a glossy purplish pink, about 3cm long, 2–3cm in diameter. Needs bright light; normal cactus compost; minimum temperature 10°C (50°F). *Bolivia (Cochabamba).*

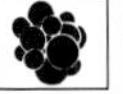    

SULCOREBUTIA **TIRAQUENSIS var. SPINOSIOR** Ritter

A solitary, then clustering plant with dark-green stems about 6cm high and thick and about 21 spiralling ribs. The areoles have whitish wool and are about 5mm long. They bear about 25–30 or more yellowish-white or brownish radial spines about 6mm long, and about 10–12 dark-brownish centrals to 1cm in length. Day flowering in mid-summer, the red flowers are prolific; they are about 2.5cm long and wide. Needs sun; normal cactus compost; minimum temperature 10°C (50°F). *Bolivia (Cochabamba).*

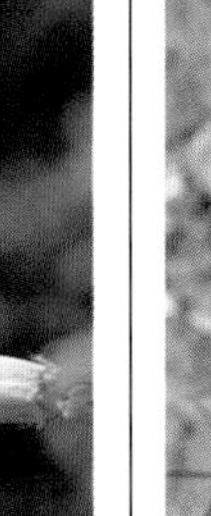

TACINGA **FUNALIS** Br. & R.

A tall species, up to about 12m high in its habitat. The bright-green stems are cylindrical, 1–1.5cm thick, and frequently branching. When young they have small, quickly deciduous leaves. The areoles are brownish with white glochids, but no spines. Flowers are nocturnal, in summer, borne on the upper part of the stems. They are pale green, the few petals reflexed and rolled back against the long floral tube, in all 7–8cm long. Requires slight shade; normal cactus compost; minimum temperature 13°C (55°F). *Brazil (Bahia).*

    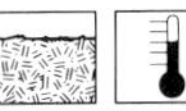

TACINGA **BRAUNII** Esteves

A very recent discovery and only described in 1989. Whilst in certain features it is similar to *T. funalis,* the greyish to reddish-green stems are flattened and have regularly arranged pale-brownish areoles and minute white glochids but no spines. Flowers are nocturnal in summer, invariably produced from near the tips of the stems, and are pale greenish white, 8cm or more long. Needs a fairly bright position; normal cactus compost; minimum temperature 13°C (55°F). *Brazil.*

   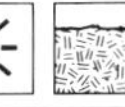 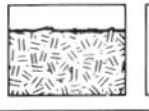 

TEPHROCACTUS **ALEXANDERI** (Br. & R.) Backeb.
Syn: *Opuntia alexanderi* Br. & R.

A clump-forming species with greyish-green, globose joints 2–3cm thick. The areoles are very small and closely arranged on prominently raised warts. Spines are a dark greyish brown, up to about 4cm in length, and flexible. It is day flowering in summer with pale, pinkish-white flowers about 4cm across. Requires a sunny position; slightly calcareous compost; minimum temperature 10°C (50°F). *Argentina (La Rioja).*

   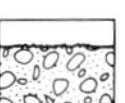 

TEPHROCACTUS **ARTICULATUS** (Pfeiff.) Backeb.

A greyish-green, grouping plant, the joints more or less cylindrical in shape, and about 5cm long. Small areoles have very short brown glochids and no spines except deep reddish-brown, awl-shaped ones which appear at the tips of the joints but soon fall. The flowers, which appear by day in summer, are white or pale pinkish, 3–4cm across. Needs a sunny position; normal cactus compost; minimum temperature 10°C (50°F). *Argentina (Mendoza).*

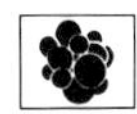   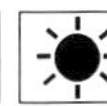 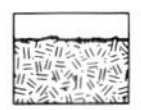 

TEPHROCACTUS **ARTICULATUS** (Pfeiff.) **var. INERMIS** (Speg.) Backeb.
Syn: *Opuntia inermis* Speg.; *Tephrocactus strobiliformis* (Berg.) Backeb.

This variety has thick, cylindrical, green or brownish-green stems, 10cm long, 2.5cm thick with tubercle-like prominences tipped with a white areole, but spineless. The glochids are minute, and pale brownish. Flowering in summer, it is diurnal, with pale pinkish-white flowers about 5cm across. Requires sun; slightly calcareous cactus compost; minimum temperature 10°C (50°F). *Argentina (Mendoza).*

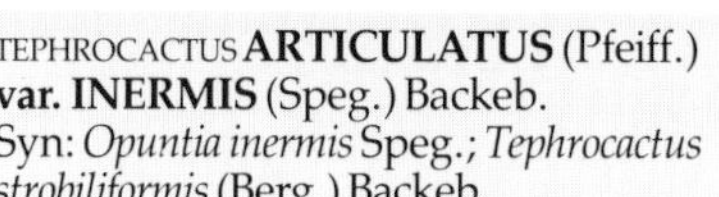

TEPHROCACTUS **ARTICULATUS** (Pfeiff.) **var. OLIGACANTHA** (Speg.) Backeb.

A low-growing, clumping species with dull bluish- or greyish-green joints, globose in shape, and up to 5cm long, 3.5cm wide. Small brownish areoles bear one or two flat greyish-whitish spines, 6–8cm in length, which are twisted and flexible. The pale pinkish-white flowers, about 3cm long, appear by day in mid-summer. Requires a sunny position; normal cactus compost; minimum temperature 10°C (50°F). *Argentina (San Juan).*

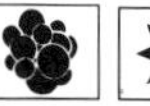    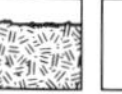 

TEPHROCACTUS **ARTICULATUS var. SYRINGACANTHUS** (Pfeiff.) Backeb.

A low-growing variety with short, jointed stems up to 5cm thick, and almost round, the joints set one on another. The areoles are large with brown glochids and one or two fairly stiff, greyish-white or pale-brownish flattened spines 5–10cm long, 3mm broad. Summer flowering, and diurnal, the flowers are white to pink, and about 10cm diameter. Requires full sun; slightly calcareous cactus compost; minimum temperature 10°C (50°F). *Western Argentina.*

TEPHROCACTUS **DACTYLIFERUS** (Vaup.) Backeb.

Greyish-green stems about 7cm long and up to 4cm thick, forming small clusters. The yellowish-white areoles are minute, with numerous glochids and one or two yellowish-brown spines, 0.5mm long at the most. Flowers are yellowish-orange, about 5cm long, and are diurnal, flowering in summer. Requires very slight shade; normal cactus compost; minimum temperature 7°C (45°F). *Southern Peru.*

TEPHROCACTUS **DIMORPHUS** (Förster) Backeb.

The plant is usually up to about 20cm high, with stems composed of small oval, bright-green joints up to 2.5cm long and thick. Areoles are white-felted with bright yellow glochids and at the most six to eight, more usually three to four, pale-brownish spines, varying in size from up to 2cm or more. It is summer flowering, and diurnal, with bright yellow flowers up to 5cm across when fully open. Requires bright light; normal cactus compost; minimum temperature 7°C (45°F). *Southern Peru (Pampa).*

TEPHROCACTUS **GEOMETRICUS** (Cast.) Backeb.

A greyish-green plant to about 15cm tall. The joints are almost rounded, to 3.5cm long and thick, and the brownish areoles have minute bristly glochids and three to five whitish or brown spines from 5mm to 1cm in length, these soon falling. Flowers are white, about 3cm long, and appear by day in mid-summer. Needs sun; normal cactus compost; minimum temperature 10°C (50°F). *Argentina (Catamarca).*

TEPHROCACTUS **GLOMERATUS** (Haw.) Backeb.

A most variable species; the one featured would appear to have escaped adequate description. A clumping plant, with dull-greenish joints about 3cm long, 1–1.5cm thick. The areoles are small and yellowish-felted with yellowish glochids. There are usually three greyish-white spines to each areole, about 1.5cm long. Flowers are unknown, but are obviously summer flowering, and diurnal. Requires a sunny position; normal cactus compost; minimum temperature 10°C (50°F). *Argentina (San Juan).*

TEPHROCACTUS **MOLINENSIS** Speg.
Syn: *Opuntia molinensis* Speg.

Closely allied to *T. diademata*, it is a cushion-forming species with the greyish-green joints densely crowded together. The stems or joints are 3–4cm long, 1.8–2.5cm thick. Spineless, they are tuberculate and have areoles bearing tufts of greyish glochids. The flowers, day flowering, in summer, are red, and about 4cm in diameter. Needs very slight shade; normal cactus compost; minimum temperature 10°C (50°F). *Argentina (Molinos, Salta).*

TEPHROCACTUS **RAUHII** Backeb.
Syn: *Opuntia floccosa* var. *rauhii* Backeb.

The stems of this species are relatively green but covered in dense wool. They are up to 25cm long, 8cm thick, often generally smaller in cultivation, with minute areoles and one yellow-tipped white spine to 1.5cm long and numerous curly white woolly hairs. The flowers are yellowish, about 3.5cm across, and appear by day, in summer. Requires sun; slightly calcareous cactus compost; minimum temperature 10°C (50°F). *Southern Peru.*

    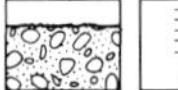 

TEPHROCACTUS **RUSSELLII** (Br. & R.) Backeb.

A clump-forming species with dull-greenish stems 2–4cm long. The areoles are pale yellow with fairly long glochids to 2mm in length and there are two to six white or yellowish spines 2–3cm long. Flower details are unknown. Requires bright sunlight; normal cactus compost; minimum temperature 10°C (50°F). *Argentina (Mendoza).*

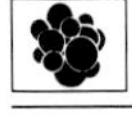   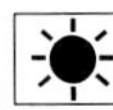 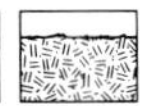

TEPHROCACTUS **WEBERI** (Speg.) Backeb.

A clump-forming species with clusters up to 15cm or more high, 30cm broad. The dark-green joints are up to 6cm long, 2cm thick with closely set areoles each bearing five to seven brown to reddish-brown spines about 5cm in length and more or less upward pointing. Summer flowering, and diurnal, the flowers are yellow, about 2cm long. Needs bright light, which is essential; normal cactus compost; minimum temperature 10°C (50°F). *Argentina (San Carlos).*

    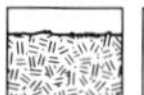

THELOCACTUS **BICOLOR** (Galeotti ex Pfeiff.) Br. & R.
Syn: *Ferocactus bicolor* (Galeotti ex Pfeiff.) N. P. Taylor; *Echinocactus bicolor* Galeotti

A bluish-green species, globular to cylindrical in shape and up to 10cm in diameter. It has eight to thirteen straight or slightly spiralled ribs with areoles bearing eight to thirteen reddish, radial spines up to 3cm long, and four slightly flat red centrals, 3.5cm. Flowers are diurnal, in summer, up to 6cm long and across, and a dark violet red. Requires a bright sunny position; normal cactus compost; minimum temperature 10°C (50°F). *USA (Texas), Mexico (Central).*

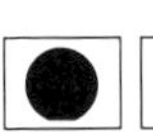 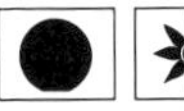      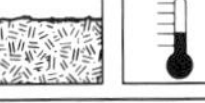

THELOCACTUS **BICOLOR var. TRICOLOR** K. Sch.

Possibly only a colour form of the species. The stems are densely spiny, with red, deep-orange or red and white spines. Flowers also differ in colour; these are deep reddish or more rarely white, and about 6cm in diameter. Requirements are the same as for the species. *Northern Mexico.*

      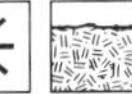   

THELOCACTUS **CONOTHELE** (Regel & Klein) F. Knuth
Syn: *Echinocactus conothelos* Regel & Klein

The greyish-green stems are more or less globular to short cylindrical, 10cm high, to 7.5cm in diameter. There are 10–12 slightly spirally arranged tuberculate ribs, and 14–16 white radial spines to 1.8cm long with two to four pale-brownish centrals 1.5–3.5cm in length. Day flowering in summer, the flowers are a rich purple, 3.5cm across. Requires full sun; normal cactus compost; minimum temperature 10°C (50°F). *Mexico (Tamaulipas).*

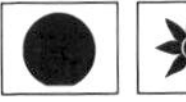        

THELOCACTUS **CONOTHELE var. ARGENTEUS** Glass & Foster

A pale-green, sub-globose plant up to 8cm high, 13cm thick, with prominent tubercles obscured by silvery white spines: there are about 20 radials 2–3cm long, and four creamy-white centrals to 5cm in length. The flowers are a pinkish purple, 3.5–4cm across, and appear by day in summer. Requirements are the same as for the species. *Mexico (Nuevo Leon).*

    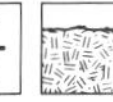 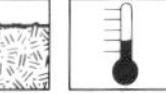

THELOCACTUS **CONOTHELE var. AURANTIACUS** Glass & Foster

Similar in most respects to the species, this variety is 10cm high, 11cm wide and pale green with ribs divided into prominent tubercles. There are 17–23 yellowish-white radial spines 1–2cm long, and four greyish-brown centrals 2–5.5cm in length. Flowers, diurnal, and summer blooming, are bright yellow, about 3.8cm long. Requirements are the same as for the species. *Mexico (Nuevo Leon).*

   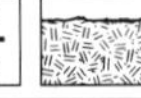 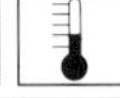

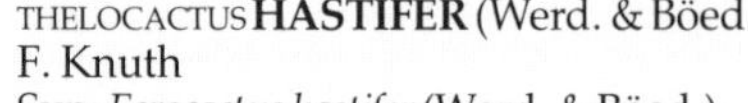

THELOCACTUS **HASTIFER** (Werd. & Böed.) F. Knuth
Syn: *Ferocactus hastifer* (Werd. & Böed.) N. P. Taylor

A pale greyish-green globular, solitary species, only rarely offsetting, 10–15cm high, 6–9cm thick. It has 18–20 tuberculate ribs and white woolly areoles when young. The spines are white: 20–25 radials to 1.5cm long and four centrals to 3cm in length. Summer flowering, and diurnal, the flowers are pinkish with a violet-pinkish centre to the petals. Requires full sun; normal cactus compost with a little lime added; minimum temperature 10°C (50°F). *Mexico (Coahuila, Nuevo Leon).*

THELOCACTUS **CONOTHELE var. MACDOWELLII** (Rebut ex Quehl) Glass & Foster
Syn: *Echinomastus macdowellii* (Rebut) Br. & R.; *Neolloydia macdowellii* (Rebut) H. E. Moore

Dull-green globular plants 10–12.5cm in diameter, with about 30 ribs. Radial spines number 15–27, and are white, to 3cm in length; there are three to four yellowish, flattened centrals, 2.5–5.5cm long. The deep-pink flowers are day flowering in summer, and are 4–5cm long. Requirements are the same as for the species. *Mexico (Nuevo Leon, Coahuila).*

    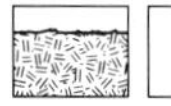 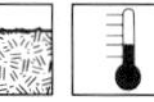

THELOCACTUS **FLAVIDISPINUS** Backeb.
Syn: *Ferocactus bicolor var. flavidispinus* (Backeb.) N. P. Taylor

Rather similar to *T. bicolor*, this plant is a dark brownish green with about 8–13 ribs. There are 12–20 pale to darker brown spines, including one central, up to 4cm long. Summer flowering, and diurnal, the flowers are purplish red, and about 5cm in diameter. Needs sun; normal cactus compost; minimum temperature 10°C (50°F). *USA (Texas).*

   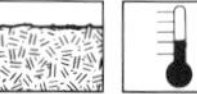

THELOCACTUS **HASTIFER**

THELOCACTUS **HETEROCHROMUS** (Weber) van Oosten
Syn: *Ferocactus heterochromus* (Weber) N. P. Taylor; *Echinocactus heterochromus* Weber

A semi-globular, solitary glaucous-green species up to about 15cm in diameter with eight to nine tuberculate ribs. The spines are brownish with reddish and yellowish markings; there are seven to ten radials 2–3cm long and one to three centrals to 4cm in length. Flowers, pale violet with a deeper throat and up to 6cm long, appear by day. Requires sunshine; normal cactus compost; minimum temperature 10°C (50°F). *Mexico (Coahuila).*

THELOCACTUS **HEXAEDROPHORUS** (Lem.) Br. & R.

A bluish- to greyish-green more or less globular plant, rarely offsetting, about 15cm thick. The 12–13 ribs are divided into six-sided tubercles and there are six to nine yellowish radial spines up to 2cm long and one central, which is often absent, to 3cm. Flowers are pinkish with a prominent creamy-white centre, and 6cm long; these appear by day, in summer. Requires sun; normal cactus compost; minimum temperature 10°C (50°F). *Mexico (San Luis Potosi).*

THELOCACTUS **HEXAEDROPHORUS var. FOSSULATUS** (Scheidw.) Backeb.
Syn: *Thelocactus fossulatus* Br. & R.; *Thelocactus hexaedrophorus* var. *decipiens* Berger

The dark greyish-green or bluish-green stems are about 15cm thick, with brown or yellowish radial spines 2.5 to 3.5cm long and one central 4.5cm in length. Flowering in summer, by day, the flowers are almost white with faint, pale-pink suffusions, and are about 4.5cm across. Requirements are the same as for the species. *Mexico (San Luis Potosi).*

THELOCACTUS **LEUCACANTHUS** (Zucc.) Br. & R.
Syn: *Ferocactus leucacanthus* (Zucc.) N. P. Taylor

A short cylindrical plant up to 15cm high, 8cm in diameter, later off-setting. The pale-green stems are divided into eight to thirteen ribs consisting of conical tubercles about 1cm high. There are seven to twenty yellowish to greyish radial spines up to 3cm long and one central. Day flowering in summer, flowers are a pale to deep yellow, 4–5cm long. Requires a sunny location; slightly calcareous cactus compost; minimum temperature 10°C (50°F). *Mexico (Hidalgo).*

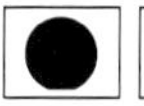    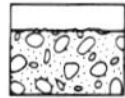 

THELOCACTUS **LEUCACANTHUS var. SCHMOLLII** Werd.
Syn: *Thelocactus schmollii* Werd.

A smaller, greyish-green globular plant which is group forming. It has about 12 tubercled ribs and many greyish-white spines: six or more radials, often one central, all to about 1.5cm long. Flowers are a deep violet red, about 4cm long. Requirements are the same as for the species. *Mexico (Queretaro).*

THELOCACTUS **RINCONENSIS** (Pos.) Br. & R.

A solitary plant, grey-green or bluish-green and about 12cm in diameter, 6–8cm high. It has white wool in the crown and usually 13 ribs divided into conical compressed tubercles with three to four greyish-brown or brownish-black spines up to 1.5cm long. An early summer, day flowering species, the flowers white with tinges of rose pink and about 4cm long. Requires sun; a calcareous cactus compost; minimum temperature 13°C (55°F). *Mexico (Nuevo Leon).*

THELOCACTUS **RINCONENSIS var. NIDULANS** (Quehl) Glass & Foster
Syn: *Thelocactus nidulans* (Quehl) Br. & R.

The stems, to 20cm in diameter, are generally solitary with up to 20 ribs and large tubercles to 2cm high. There are five to eleven radial spines, usually about 5mm long, occasionally up to 3cm in length, and generally four central spines to 6cm long; these are brownish becoming grey. Day flowering in summer, the flowers are whitish with a pinkish mid-stripe, and 4cm long, 4.5cm across. Needs very bright light; calcareous cactus compost; minimum temperature 10°C (50°F). *Mexico (Southern Coahuila).*

THELOCACTUS **RINCONENSIS var. PHYMATOTHELE** (Pos.) Glass & Foster
Syn: *Thelocactus phymatothelos* Pos.

Mostly a solitary plant, it is 9–15cm in diameter with a compressed top, greyish-green in colour. It has 13 ribs divided into very prominent angled tubercles, each up to about 1cm high. There are one to three very short spines, which may be absent; where present they are usually 2mm, rarely up to 2–3cm in length. Flowers are white with a pinkish mid-stripe, about 4cm in diameter, and appear by day in summer. Requirements are the same as for the species. *Mexico (Coahuila).*

   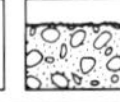 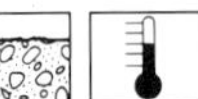

▲

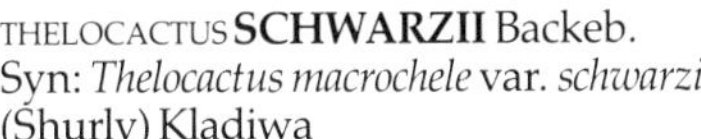

THELOCACTUS **SCHWARZII** Backeb.
Syn: *Thelocactus macrochele* var. *schwarzii* (Shurly) Kladiwa

Bluish-green globular plants up to about 6cm high, 5.5cm in diameter with about 13 ribs. The areoles are whitish, bearing 13–14 reddish, yellowish-tipped radial spines to 2cm long, but no centrals. Day flowering in summer, the flowers are pale reddish purple, and up to 8.5cm in diameter. Requires sun; normal cactus compost; minimum temperature 10°C (50°F). *Mexico (Tamaulipas).*

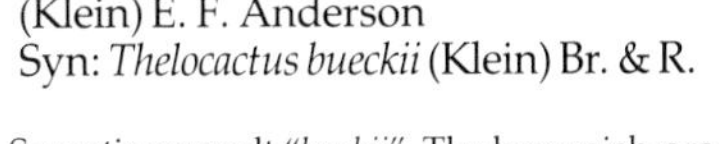

THELOCACTUS **TULENSIS var. BUECKII** (Klein) E. F. Anderson
Syn: *Thelocactus bueckii* (Klein) Br. & R.

Sometimes spelt *"buekii"*. The brownish-green stems are mostly solitary, depressed globose in shape and 15–18cm in diameter. Ribs are divided into distinct, pointed, angular tubercles up to 2.5cm wide at the base. Spines, orangey brown becoming greyish, consist of seven to ten radials 1.5–2.5cm or more long and one or two centrals to 5.5cm in length. The dark purplish-red flowers, up to 5cm long and wide, are diurnal, in summer. Requirements are the same as for the species. *Mexico (Tamaulipas).*

     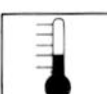

THELOCACTUS **TULENSIS** (Pos.) Br. & R.
Syn: *Thelocactus tulensis* var. *"longispinus"* nom nud.

The stems are dark greyish green, globular and 12–25cm high. It has eight to thirteen ribs divided into close-set, conical tubercles up to 2cm high. There are six to eight whitish radial spines, 1–1.5cm long; centrals, where present, are up to 3cm in length. Flowering in daytime, in summer, the flowers are about 2.5cm long, and are pinkish with a reddish mid-stripe, more rarely yellowish (as shown). Requires sun; normal cactus compost; minimum temperature 10°C (50°F). *Mexico (Tamaulipas, San Luis Potosi).*

     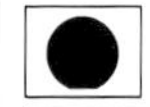

THELOCACTUS **TULENSIS var. MATUDAE** (Sanchez-Mejorada & Lau) E. F. Anderson
Syn: *Thelocactus mutadae* Sanchez-Mejorada & Lau

The plant has glaucous-green stems 12–16cm in diameter with long, prominent tubercles 2.2–2.5cm long. Spines are whitish or brownish: about seven radials to 1.7cm long and four centrals to 2cm in length. Flowers are a deep vivid purple-pink, up to 8cm wide, and are diurnal, in summer. Requirements are similar to those for var. *bueckii*. *Mexico (Tamaulipas).*

   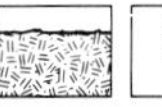 

THRIXANTHOCEREUS **BLOSSFELDIORUM** (Werd.) Backeb.
Syn: *Espostoa blossfeldiorum* (Werd.) Buxb.

A tall, erect columnar plant up to 4m high, rarely branching. The stems are about 10cm thick and there are 18–25 ribs with closely set, woolly areoles. These bear 20–25 radial spines about 8mm long, and six to seven dark-brown centrals to 3cm long. A pseudocephalium develops once the plant is about 60–80cm high; this consists of dense tufts of yellowish-white hairs and numerous white or dark-brown bristles. Creamy-white nocturnal flowers appear in mid-summer, up to 6cm long. Requires sun and warmth; normal cactus compost; minimum temperature 13°C (55°F). *Northern Peru.*

   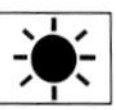 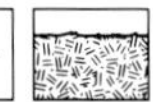 

THRIXANTHOCEREUS **CULLMANNIANUS** Ritter

A greyish-green columnar plant to 2m high, with stems 3–6cm thick and 18–24 ribs. White woolly areoles bear numerous very fine, thread-like white, sometimes brown-tipped, spines from 5mm to 3cm in length. The lateral cephalium forms once the plant is about 50cm high and is composed of dense whitish or brownish spines, which are 1–3cm long. Summer flowering, the flowers are nocturnal, white, and 4–6cm long. Needs bright light; slightly calcareous cactus compost; minimum temperature 13°C (55°F). *Northern Peru (Cajamarca).*

    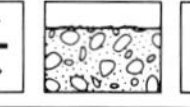

TRICHOCEREUS **ANGELENSIS** (Weber) Kreuringer
Syn: *Lobivia andalgalensis* (Weber) Br. & R.; *Helianthocereus andalgalensis* (Weber) Backeb.

The grass-green stems are about 30cm long, 5–9cm thick, with 13–17 ribs. Areoles are brownish white and fairly close-set with eight to eleven golden-yellow radial spines and one or two longer centrals to 2.5cm. Summer flowering, and diurnal, the flowers are bright red, about 6cm or a little more long. Requires a sunny position; normal cactus compost; minimum temperature 10°C (50°F). *Argentina (Catamarca).*

    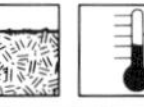

TRICHOCEREUS **ANGELESII** Kiesl.

A somewhat sprawling, cylindrical-shaped, dull-greenish species with stems about 60cm or more in length, branching from the base. It has 20 or more ribs and the areoles bear brown spines which become more yellowish. Little is known of this plant and it is not generally in cultivation. Flowers are unknown. Where they are available, the plants need full sun; normal cactus compost; minimum temperature 10°C (50°F). *Argentina (Salta).*

   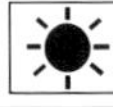  

TRICHOCEREUS **FORMOSUS** (Pfeiff.) Ritter
var. MAXIMA (Backeb.)
Syn: *Soehrensia formosa* (Pfeiff.) Backeb.
var. *maxima* Backeb.

A greyish-green, more or less cylindrical plant reaching over 2m high in its habitat, and 40cm in diameter, with 15–35 or more ribs. The spines are yellowish brown: eight to sixteen very fine, flexible radials and five to eight centrals about 7cm in length. Day flowering, in mid-summer, the flowers are bright yellow and about 8cm long. Needs bright sun; normal cactus compost; minimum temperature 10°C (50°F). *Northern Argentina.*

    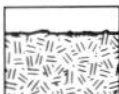 

TRICHOCEREUS **BRUCHII** (Br. & R.) Ritter
Syn: *Soehrensia bruchii* (Br. & R.) Backeb.

A dark-green globular to somewhat elongating plant up to about 20cm in diameter. It has about 50 ribs with large, brownish-white areoles and pale-brownish spines: nine to fourteen radials and about four centrals up to 2cm long. The flowers are deep red, about 5cm in diameter, and come out by day, in summer. Needs sun; normal cactus compost; minimum temperature 10°C (50°F). *Argentina (Jujuy, Catamarca).*

TRICHOCEREUS **CHILOENSIS** (Colla) Br. & R.

A dull-green, variable species of columnar growth to about 3m tall and 12cm thick. It has 10–15 ribs with large, whitish areoles set below prominent notches, about 2cm apart. The spines are yellowish, later greyish, consisting of eight to twelve radials to 4cm long, and one to four centrals 5cm or more in length. Flowers are borne laterally in summer, and are nocturnal; they are white with greenish, brown-edged outer segments and about 15cm long. Needs good light; normal cactus compost; minimum temperature 10°C (50°F). *Chile.*

  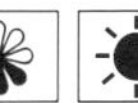 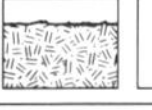

TRICHOCEREUS **FULVILANUS** Ritter

A dark greyish-green columnar species 1–1.5m tall with stems 4–7cm thick and eight to thirteen deeply notched ribs. The areoles are large, and white-felted, bearing brownish spines which gradually turn to grey; nine to twelve are radials, 1.5–3cm long, and there are two to four centrals 3–15cm in length. Nocturnal, and summer flowering, the flowers are white and fragrant, and 9–12cm long. Requires a sunny position; normal cactus compost; minimum temperature 10°C (50°F). *Chile (Taltal).*

TRICHOCEREUS **GRANDIFLORUS** (Br. & R.)
Syn: *Lobivia grandiflora* Br. & R.; *Helianthocereus grandiflorus* Backeb.; *Trichocereus rowleyi* Kiesling

A bright-green, mostly solitary plant up to 35cm tall, 6cm thick, with about 14 ribs. Areoles are set about 1cm apart with yellowish spines, eight to twelve or more radials and one central, up to 1cm long. Day flowering in mid-summer, the flowers are a deep bright red, and 8–10cm long. Needs a sunny position; normal cactus compost; minimum temperature 10°C (50°F). *Argentina (Catamarca).*

  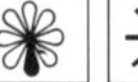  

TRICHOCEREUS **HUASCHA** (Weber) Br. & R.
Syn: *Helianthocereus huascha* (Weber) Backeb.; *Echinopsis huascha* (Weber) H. Friedr. & Rowley

A dark-green, much-branching species with stems 50–90cm tall, 5–8cm thick, and 12–18 ribs. The whitish-brown areoles are very close-set and bear nine to eleven brownish radial spines to 4cm long, and one or two centrals to 6cm in length. Mid-summer flowering, and diurnal, the flowers are golden yellow (below) or red (above), 7–10cm long. Needs sun; normal cactus compost; minimum temperature 10°C (50°F). *Argentina (Catamarca).*

  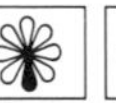  

TRICHOCEREUS **PASACANA** (Weber) Br. & R.
Syn: *Cereus pasacana* Weber

A tall, almost giant, species, reaching up to 5m in its habitat. The stems are 30–50cm thick, branching from near the base to form a tree-like specimen. It has 15–35 ribs with brownish areoles bearing brownish or reddish-brown spines varying from 4mm to 1.5cm long. Flowering in summer, and diurnal, the blooms are white and up to 12cm long. The fruit is said to be edible. Needs full sun; normal cactus compost; minimum temperature 10°C (50°F). *Argentina, Bolivia.*

    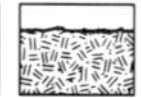 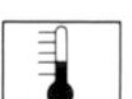

TRICHOCEREUS **SANTIAGUENSIS** (Speg.) Backeb.

A bluish-green columnar plant up to about 7m high, with stems about 10cm thick. It has about 10 ribs with whitish areoles set about 1.5cm apart and bearing short radial spines 5mm to 1cm long, with one central 1–2cm in length. The flowers, appearing by day in summer, are 20cm long, funnel-shaped, and creamy white. Needs bright light; normal cactus compost; minimum temperature 13°C (55°F). *Argentina.*

TRICHOCEREUS **SHAFERI** Br. & R.

A fairly tall, bright-green plant up to about 50cm high, 12.5cm thick. It usually has 14 prominent ribs 1cm or more high, and the whitish areoles are set 5–7mm apart, bearing about 10 yellowish spines up to 1.2cm in length. White flowers appear in summer and are up to about 15cm long. They bloom by day or night. Requires good light; normal cactus compost; minimum temperature 10°C (50°F). *Argentina (Salta).*

TRICHOCEREUS **SMRZIANUS** (Backeb.) Backeb.
Syn: *Echinopsis smrziana* Backeb.

A dark-green columnar plant 40–50cm tall, and up to 16cm in diameter, with about 15 broad ribs. The yellowish-brown areoles bear up to 14 whitish or yellowish spines up to 1cm long. It flowers in early summer in the late afternoon; the flowers are white, 12cm long and in diameter. Requires a sunny position; normal cactus compost; minimum temperature 13°C (55°F). *Northern Argentina.*

TRICHOCEREUS **SPACHIANUS** (Lem.) Ricco.
Syn: *Echinopsis spachianus* (Lem.) H. Friedr. & Rowley

Tall, dark-green columnar plants up to 2m high and to 6cm thick, freely branching from the base, with 10–15 ribs. The areoles are yellowish becoming grey, and bear yellowish-brown spines, 8–10 radials and one, often two or three, centrals all about 1cm long. Night flowering in mid-summer, the flowers are about 20cm long, to 15cm across, with white inner petals and greenish outer segments. Needs a bright position; normal cactus compost; minimum temperature 10°C (50°F). *Western Argentina.*

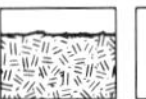

TRICHOCEREUS **TARIJENSIS** (Vaup.) Werd.
Syn: *Cereus tarijensis* Vaup.; *Helianthocereus tarijensis* Backeb.

A dark-green columnar plant up to about 1.5m tall, with stems about 25cm thick. It has about 15 ribs with yellowish-brown areoles, which later become greyish. There are 10–17 reddish-brown spines, including three to four centrals, up to 4cm or more long. Flowers are bright red and 10cm long; these are diurnal, appearing in summer. Needs full sun; normal cactus compost; minimum temperature 10°C (50°F). *Argentina (Tucuman).*

TRICHOCEREUS **TARIJENSIS** (Vaup.) **var. POCO** (Backeb.) Ritter
Syn: *Trichocereus poco* Backeb.; *Helianthocereus poco* (Backeb.) Backeb.

A dark greyish-green columnar plant to over 1.5m tall, 20–35cm thick. It has about 25 ribs, and the greyish areoles bear 12–18 brownish radial spines up to 4cm in length, and six to nine shiny brownish-yellow centrals to 7cm long. Summer flowering, and diurnal, the flowers are reddish purple, up to 12cm long. Needs bright sunlight; normal cactus compost; minimum temperature 10°C (50°F). *Northern Argentina, Bolivia.*

TRICHOCEREUS **TERSCHECKII** (Parm.) Backeb.

A columnar species up to 12m tall, branching from the base or above, the branches about 15cm thick. It has 8–14 narrowly furrowed ribs and large pale-brownish areoles about 1.5cm in diameter, set at 3cm intervals, with eight to fifteen yellowish spines 8–10cm in length. Night flowering in summer, the flowers are white, brown externally, and up to 20cm long, 12cm across. Requires good light; normal cactus compost; minimum temperature 13°C (55°F). *Northern Argentina.*

TRICHOCEREUS **THELOGONUS** (Weber) Br. & R.

A rather weak-stemmed species, semi-erect or sprawling. The stems are dark green and up to 1.5m long, 5–8cm thick, branching freely, with about 12 broad ribs. The brownish areoles are about 1cm apart, bearing yellow spines which become greyish, about six straight radials 1–2cm long, and one central to 4cm in length. Flowers are nocturnal, in summer; they are about 20cm long and in diameter when fully expanded. Needs sun; normal cactus compost; minimum temperature 10°C (50°F). *Northern Argentina.*

TURBINICARPUS **LAUI** Glass & Foster
Syn: *Strombocactus laui* (Glass & Foster) Mays; *Neolloydia laui* (Glass & Foster) E. F. Anderson

A solitary, dull-green sub-globose species up to 1.5cm high, 3.5cm wide. It has five to six ribs divided into prominent rhomboidal tubercles, three or four to a spiral and up to 5mm high. Minute areoles bear about six glassy-white spines 5–7mm long. Flowers are diurnal in early summer, white or pinkish and up to 3.5cm long. Requires a bright position; a permeable, mineral and enriched compost; minimum temperature 13°C (55°F). *Mexico (San Luis Potosi).*

    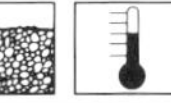

TURBINICARPUS **LAUI cv. 'Old Baldy'**

A small globular dull-green plant 3.5–4cm in diameter with four-angled tubercles arranged spirally and tipped with white areoles. The spines are pale yellowish brown, very twisted and curved and it has whitish flowers. Requirements are the same as for the species.

 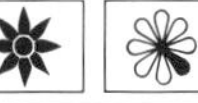  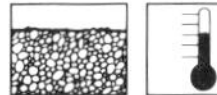 

TURBINICARPUS **LOPHOPHOROIDES** (Werd.) Buxb. & Backeb.
Syn: *Strombocactus lophophoroides* F. Knuth & Buxb.; *Neolloydia lophophoroides* (Werd.) E. F. Anderson

A small globular plant 3–4cm in diameter, greyish or bluish-green. About 12 ribs divided into tubercles tipped with small woolly areoles. Usually three to five brownish to blackish spines. Flowers are diurnal in summer, appearing in the woolly crown; they are pink or white, and about 3.5cm in diameter. Needs a bright location; a porous mineral enriched compost; minimum temperature 13°C (55°F). *Mexico (San Luis Potosi).*

       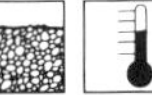 

TURBINICARPUS **PSEUDOMACROCHELE** (Backeb.) Buxb. & Backeb.
Syn: *Strombocactus pseudomacrochele* Backeb.; *Neolloydia pseudomacrochele* E. F. Anderson

Dull-green, miniature plants. Heads 3–4cm in diameter, with ribs divided into small tubercles, white terminal areoles bear six to eight adpressed spines. Diurnal flowers in summer, about 3.5cm in diameter, pale pinkish, with a pale-reddish median stripe. Keep dry in winter; bright sun; enriched mineral compost; minimum winter temperature 10°C (50°F). *Mexico (San Luis Potosi).*

    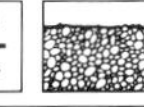 

TURBINICARPUS **PSEUDOPECTINATUS** (Backeb.) Glass & Foster
Syn: *Normanbokea pseudopectinatus* Kladiwa & Buxb.; *Pelecyphora pseudopectinatus* Backeb.

This has also been included within *Neolloydia*. It is a dull-green, small globular species 2.5–5cm in diameter, often slightly elongating. There are 24 or more ribs divided into slightly spirally arranged tubercles which are hatchet-shaped and each tipped with a white areole and numerous white spines in a comb-like formation. The flowers are diurnal, appearing in summer; they are pink, the outer segments having a reddish median line, and are about 3cm across. Requires to be kept dry in winter; a bright position; a permeable enriched mineral compost; minimum temperature 13°C (55°F). *Mexico (Tamaulipas).*

    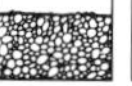

TURBINICARPUS **PSEUDOMACROCHELE var. KRAINZIANUS** (Frank) Glass & Foster
Syn: *Toumeya krainziana* Frank; *Strombocactus pseudomacrochele* var. *krainzianus* Rowley

A dark-green miniature species, 2–3.5cm wide, 3–4cm high, with about 11 spiralled, tubercled ribs. White woolly areoles carry six to eight yellowish-grey twisting spines up to 3cm long. The flowers are terminal, greenish cream in colour and up to 2cm long, appearing by day in summer. Requirements are similar to those of the species. *Mexico (uncertain).*

    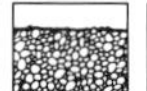 

TURBINICARPUS **SCHMIEDICKEANUS** (Böed.) Buxb. & Backeb.
Syn: *Neolloydia schmiedickeana* (Böed.) E. F. Anderson; *Echinocactus schmiedickeanus* Böed.

A solitary or grouping plant with stems to 4cm wide, 5cm high. There are 10–12 ribs divided into four-angled pyramidal tubercles with white areoles and one to four curved spines to 2.5cm long. Flowers, diurnal in summer, are pale pink with a darker median line, to 2.5cm across. Needs to be kept dry in winter; a sunny position; porous, calcareous enriched compost; minimum temperature 13°C (55°F). *Mexico (Tamaulipas).*

   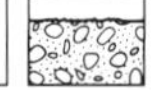 

TURBINICARPUS **SCHMIEDICKEANUS var. DICKISONIAE** Glass & Foster

Stems are up to 3cm wide, dark greyish-green and almost globular in shape. The tubercles are arranged in eight to thirteen spirals, each bearing about 23 fine, white radial spines about 2.5mm long and one to three greyish-brown twisted centrals to about 2cm long. Flowers, about 2cm long, 1.7cm wide when expanded, are white, sometimes with a reddish centre stripe. Requirements are the same as for the species. *Mexico (Nuevo Leon).*

    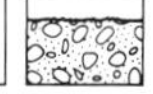 

TURBINICARPUS **SCHMIEDICKEANUS var. GRACILIS** Glass & Foster
Syn: *Neolloydia schmiedickeana* var. *gracilis* (Glass & Foster) E. F. Anderson

The variety has a bright-green solitary stem, 1.5-2cm wide, or including the tubercles 3cm broad. These are almost terete, up to 7mm long and bearing thin, papery spines from the areoles: one to three white radials, 2mm long, and one greyish central, 1.8–2.3cm. Flowers are pure white, 2cm long, and 1.5cm across; they are diurnal, appearing in summer. Requirements are the same as for the species. *Mexico (Nuevo Leon).*

   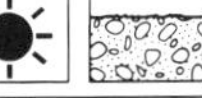 

▲

TURBINICARPUS **SCHMIEDICKEANUS var. MACROCHELE** (Werd.) Glass & Foster
Syn: *Strombocactus macrochele* Werd. & Backeb.

This plant is similar to the species, but invariably solitary and smaller, 3cm high, 4cm wide. The tubercles bear whitish areoles and three to four curved and twisted spines 4cm or more long. Flowers are diurnal, white, and somewhat trumpet-shaped, borne in the crown. Requirements are similar to those for the species. *Mexico (San Luis Potosi).*

TURBINICARPUS **SCHMIEDICKEANUS var. KLINKERIANUS** (Backeb. & Jacobsen) Glass & Foster
Syn: *Toumeya klinkerianus* (Backeb. & Jacobsen) Bravo & W. T. Marsh

Solitary, globular, and a dull brownish-green, 3cm high, 3–4cm wide. Ribs are divided into low, broad tubercles 5mm high, 4mm thick, which are tipped with a small areole bearing three incurving spines, the upper two short and soon falling, the lower about 9mm long. Flowers are white to cream, about 1.4cm long, with wide-spreading petals. Requirements are the same as for the species. *Mexico (Tamaulipas).*

   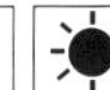  

TURBINICARPUS **SCHMIEDICKEANUS var. SCHWARZII** (Shurly) Glass & Foster
Syn: *Strombocactus schwarzii* Shurly; *Turbinicarpus polaskii* Backeb.

A solitary plant, pale green to bluish- or brownish-green, and 4–5cm in diameter. The tubercles are arranged in five to eight spirals, flattened and four-angled, and the spines are up to 2cm long. Flowers are white or purple, 3cm long and 4cm across when expanded. Requirements are similar to those for the species. *Mexico (San Luis Potosi).*

TURBINICARPUS **VALDEZIANUS** (Möller) Glass & Foster
Syn: *Pelecyphora valdeziana* Möller; *Normanbokea valdeziana* Kladiwa & Buxb.

An attractive sub-globose miniature plant named for Möller's mother-in-law. It has a long subterranean stem, 1–3.5cm in diameter, with only the rounded top exposed. The bluish-green ribs are divided into tubercles arranged spirally, and are four angled, 3mm long and wide. There are numerous white and hair-like spines up to 2mm long and horizontally spreading. Flowers are reddish purple, up to 2cm long and wide: these are diurnal, flowering in summer. A white-flowered variety is also known, referred to as var. *albiflora* (left), the flower colour being the only difference. The cristate form (below left) which only rarely is encountered is a much sought-after and attractive plant. Requires a sunny position; slightly calcareous compost; minimum temperature 13°C (55°F). *Mexico (near Saltillo, Coahuila).*

  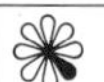  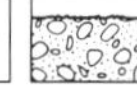

TURBINICARPUS **VALDEZIANUS cv. 'Torito'**

A dark-green globular plant of only dwarf dimensions. The ribs are divided into rhomboid tubercles about 3mm long and broad. Areoles are greyish white and bear seven to eight brownish-grey spines. Flowers are whitish with a faint deep-pinkish mid-stripe. Requirements are the same as for the species.

    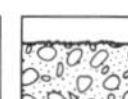 

UEBELMANNIA **GUMMIFERA** (Backeb. & Voll) Buin.
Syn: *Parodia gummifera* Backeb. & Voll.

A greyish-green, globular, slightly elongating plant up to about 10cm high, 6–7cm in diameter. It has about 32 ribs closely encompassing the body with small greyish-white areoles each with three radial spines to 5mm long, one downward pointing, two lateral, and one longer, slightly upward-pointing central. Flowers appear by day in summer in the crown of the plant and are bright yellow, 2cm long, 1.5cm wide. Needs a sunny position, which is essential; porous, slightly calcareous compost enriched with humus; minimum temperature 15°C (59°F). *Brazil (Minas Gerais).*

     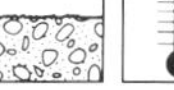

UEBELMANNIA **BUININGII** Donald

A dark-green or brownish-red, somewhat globular plant totally covered with minute waxy scales. The stem is about 8cm in diameter and up to 10cm high, and it has 16–18 ribs with close-set, heavily spined areoles. These spines are reddish-brown, mostly semi-erect; two to four are about 5–6mm long, and there are usually four longer, 1–1.5cm in length. Flowers, diurnal in summer, are funnel-shaped, bright yellow, and up to 2.7cm long, about 2cm across. Needs a humid, slightly shaded position; a porous acid compost; minimum temperature 15°C (59°F). *Brazil (Minas Gerais).*

    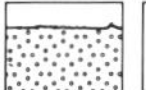 

UEBELMANNIA **MENINENSIS** Buin.

A rather globose-cylindrical-shaped green plant to 50cm high, 10cm in diameter, with up to 40 ribs. The areoles are brownish, each bearing one upward-pointing and one downward-pointing greyish blackish spine about 2cm long, which provides a formidable covering to the stem! Flowers are diurnal, appearing in summer; they are yellow, 2–3.5cm long and across. Requires full sun; a slightly acid cactus compost; minimum temperature 15°C (59°F). *Brazil (Minas Gerais).*

UEBELMANNIA **PECTINIFERA var. HORRIDA** Braun

This is very similar to the type species but is basically green, and the whitish-grey spines tend to be more widely spreading. Flowers are yellow, almost hidden by the terminal spination! Requirements are the same as for the species. *Brazil (Northern Minas Gerais).*

UEBELMANNIA **PECTINIFERA** Buin.

A distinctive and attractive globular plant which becomes slightly columnar, up to 50cm high, 10–15cm in diameter and reddish, almost blackish-brown in colour. It has 15–18 pronounced ribs with closely set areoles bearing a number of straight dark-brownish central spines – no radials. These are up to 1.5cm long, producing an interesting comb-like effect. Flowering by day in summer, the blooms are about 1.5cm long and 1cm across. Requires a sunny position with humidity; permeable enriched, slightly calcareous compost; minimum temperature 15°C (59°F). *Brazil (Minas Gerais).*

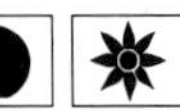   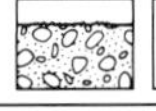 

UEBELMANNIA **PECTINIFERA var. PSEUDOPECTINIFERA** Buin.

This is very similar to the species except that the body colour is green without many spots. Ribs are similar, but the spination tends to spread laterally, not in a comb-like formation. Flowers and cultivation requirements are the same as for the species. *Brazil (Minas Gerais).*

    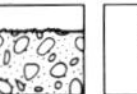 

VATRICANIA

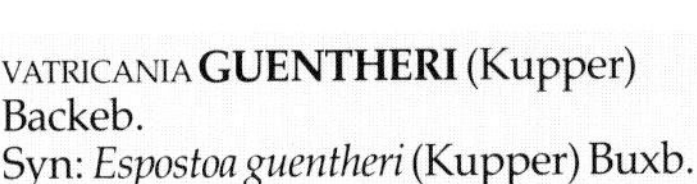

VATRICANIA **GUENTHERI** (Kupper) Backeb.
Syn: *Espostoa guentheri* (Kupper) Buxb.

Similar to species of *Espostoa* where it properly belongs. It is a pale-green columnar plant 2m or more tall, to 10cm thick, branching from the base, with about 27 ribs. The yellowish-white areoles bear around 25 spines from 5mm to 1.5cm long. Composed of reddish-brown bristles up to 6cm long and brownish-yellow hairs and wool. Yellowish white flowers occur in early summer. Requires sun; normal cactus compost; minimum temperature 13°C (55°F). *Bolivia.*

   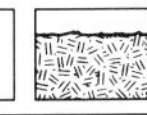 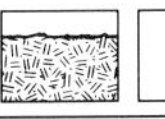 

WEBERBAUEROCEREUS

WEBERBAUEROCEREUS **JOHNSONII** Ritter

A bushy columnar plant, often tree-forming in its habitat and up to 6m tall! In cultivation it is usually columnar to 1.5m tall, with stems 7–9cm in diameter. It has 30–35 ribs with brown areoles 3mm wide bearing golden-yellow spines. The more or less terminal flowering zone has larger areoles and more numerous spines up to 50 in number, and to 6cm long. Flowers are nocturnal; they are white or pale pinkish white, about 11cm long, and appear in early summer. Requires bright light; normal cactus compost; minimum temperature 13°C (55°F). *Peru (Cajamarca).*

  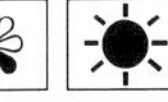 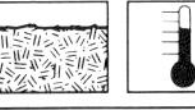

WEBEROCEREUS

WEBEROCEREUS **BIOLLEYI** (Weber) Br. & R.
Syn: *Cereus biolleyii* Weber

An epiphytic trailing or climbing species. It has cylindrical or irregularly angled stems up to 80cm long, rarely exceeding 5mm thick, and often branching. The areoles are small and far apart, with rarely one to three very fine spines. Flowers, nocturnal in summer, are 3–5cm long and in diameter, and have fleshy, dark-pink outer petals and longer, pale-pink inner segments. Needs a semi-shaded position, which is essential, plus humidity; a porous acid compost; minimum temperature 15°C (59°F). *Costa Rica.*

    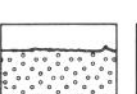 

WEBEROCEREUS **BRADEI** (Br. & R.) D. R. Hunt
Syn: *Phyllocactus bradei* Vaup.; *Eccremocactus bradei* (Vaup.) Br. & R.

An epiphytic species with thick, flat, leaf-like stems. The joints or branches are 30–40cm long, 5–10cm wide, and about 5mm thick, with wavy edges and very small areoles bearing a single short spine. Flowers, nocturnal in summer, appear from the upper areoles. They are white, pale pinkish externally and 6–7cm long, the fleshy petals only slightly expanding. Requires filtered light; an enriched porous compost; minimum temperature 18°C (64°F). *Costa Rica.*

    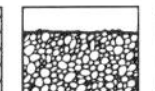 

WEBEROCEREUS **GLABER** (Eichl.) D. R. Hunt
Syn: *Cereus glaber* Eichl.; *Werckleocereus glaber* (Eichl.) Br. & R.

An epiphytic species climbing by means of aerial roots. It has glaucous-green stems 2–3m long, about 2cm thick, which are three-angled and more or less toothed. The areoles are small with brownish wool and one or two very short spines. Nocturnal flowers appear in mid-summer; these are cup-shaped and 10–12cm long. The inner petals are white, slightly serrated and the outer petals are pale greenish brown. Requires partial shade; normal cactus compost; minimum temperature 15°C (59°F). *Guatemala.*

WEBEROCEREUS **TONDUZII** (Weber) D. R. Hunt
Syn: *Cereus tonduzii* Weber; *Werckleocereus tonduzii* (Weber) Br. & R.

Epiphytic trailing or climbing species with pale greyish-green, two- to three-angled stems, the angles mostly rounded, more rarely toothed. The stems are 3–4m or more long, 2–3cm thick, small areoles with a few weak spines. Flowers are nocturnal in summer, inner petals yellowish and the outer ones brownish pink. Requires semi-shade; porous acid compost; minimum temperature 15°C (59°F). *Costa Rica.*

    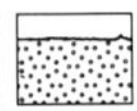 

▲

WEINGARTIA **LANATA** Ritter

A globular species, with the stem about 17cm thick and about 14 ribs. The areoles are elongated, bearing 12–16 yellowish-white, dark-tipped radial spines 1–4cm long, and 10–15 similarly coloured centrals from 1.5–5cm in length. Summer flowering, and diurnal, the flowers are bright yellow, 2.7–3.3cm long, and 2–3cm in diameter. Requires bright light; normal cactus compost; minimum temperature 10°C (50°F). *Bolivia (Chuquisaca).*

   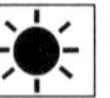 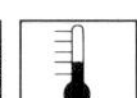

WEINGARTIA **MULTISPINA** Ritter

A pale-green, semi-globular plant about 14cm in diameter, covered with large prominent conical tubercles about 7mm long. The areoles are 6–8mm long, 3–4mm wide with whitish-brown wool. The spines are yellowish or slightly brownish consisting of 25–30 radials to 1cm long and 25–30 centrals up to 2cm in length. Flowering in summer, and diurnal, the flowers are bright yellow, about 2cm long, 1.5cm wide. Requires bright light; normal cactus compost; minimum temperature 10°C (50°F). *Bolivia (Cochabamba).*

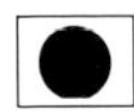    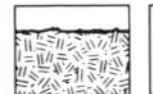 

WEINGARTIA **NEOCUMMINGII** Backeb.

A most variable species; the bright to dark-green stems are semi-globular, and up to 20cm high, 10cm thick, with about 16–18 tuberclate ribs. Areoles bear 16–20 yellowish, brown-tipped radial spines up to 1.5cm long and about six more centrally placed spines which are thicker. Day flowering in summer, the flowers are orange, shading to a yellow throat, and 2.5cm long. Requires a bright location; normal cactus compost; minimum temperature 10°C (50°F). *Bolivia (Florida).*

WEINGARTIA **NEOCUMMINGII var. MAIRANENSIS** Donald
Syn: *Weingartia "hajekiana"* Knize

Apparently this is somewhat similar to the species but is of more cylindrical growth. The spines are orange or brownish, and fewer in number, and the flowers are bright yellow. Requirements are the same as for the species. *Bolivia (Santa Cruz).*

    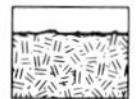 

WEINGARTIA **NEUMANNIANA** (Backeb.) Werd.
Syn: *Spegazzinia neumanniana* Backeb.; *Rebutia neumanniana* (Backeb.) D. R. Hunt

Small greyish-green, more or less globular plants up to 7cm long, 5cm in diameter with 13–15 notched ribs. The areoles are set about 1cm apart, and bear reddish-brown spines, about six radials and one central up to 2cm or a little longer. Day flowering in summer, the flowers are orange-red with pointed petals, and are about 2.5cm long and across. Requires bright light; normal cactus compost; minimum temperature 10°C (50°F). *Northern Argentina.*

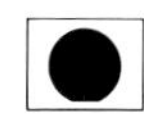     

WILCOXIA **ALBIFLORA** Backeb.

All *Wilcoxia* species are possibly synonymous with *Echinocereus*. This is a freely branching, clambering species with dark-green slender stems up to 20cm or more long, 6mm in diameter, and somewhat cylindrical in shape. It has nine to twelve ribs set with small brown areoles bearing 10–12 yellowish spines about 1mm long. The flowers, diurnal in mid-summer, are produced from near the tips of the stems; they are white with a greenish-brown throat, and are about 2cm long. Requires a little protection from full sun; normal cactus compost; minimum temperature 10°C (50°F). *Mexico.*

    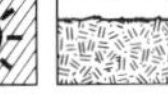 

WILCOXIA **POSELGERI** (Lem.) Br. & R.
Syn: *Echinocereus poselgeri* Lem.

Fairly rigid, erect bushy plants with dark-green, branching stems up to 60cm long, and 1.5cm or more thick. It has eight to ten shallow ribs with close-set areoles carrying greyish-white spines, eight to nine radials to 2mm long, and one or two centrals 8mm or so long. Flowering in summer, the blooms open after midday but close at night; they are pale purplish pink with a reddish throat, and 4–5cm long. Requires a somewhat filtered light; normal cactus compost; minimum temperature 10°C (50°F). *USA (Texas), Mexico (Coahuila).*

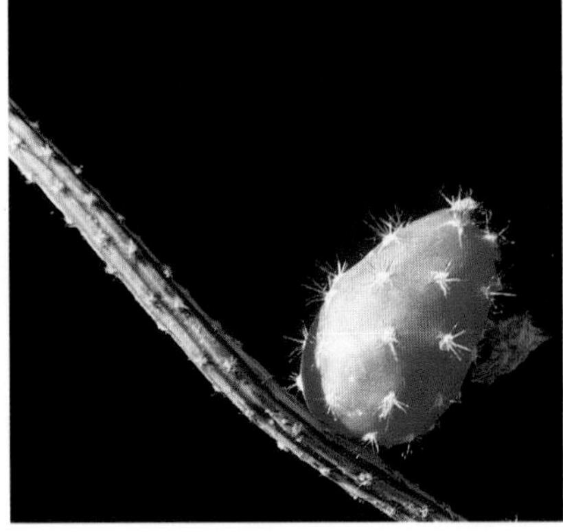

WILCOXIA **STRIATA** (Brandegee) Br. & R.

A long, bluish to greyish-green slender-stemmed species up to 1m in length and 5–8mm thick. It has eight to nine very narrow, low ribs and the areoles, up to 1cm apart, bear nine to ten almost minute blackish-brown radial spines. Flowers are diurnal, blooming in summer. They are produced laterally, and are reddish purple, about 10cm long, and are followed by large red fruits 3–4cm long. The plant has tuberous roots, which are often up to 40cm long. Needs slight shade; very porous cactus compost; minimum temperature 13°C (55°F). *Mexico (Baja and islands).*

WILCOXIA **VIPERINA** (Weber) Br. & R.
Syn: *Cereus viperina* Weber; *Cullmannia viperina* (Weber) Distef.

A bushy species with many greyish-green, long trailing stems to nearly 3m in length, about 2cm thick, and quite velvety. It has eight to ten ribs with small blackish areoles bearing blackish spines: eight to nine radials about 4mm long, and three to four centrals which soon fall. The flowers appear laterally along the stems, and are glossy red, about 8cm long, 4cm across; they are diurnal, in summer. Requires very good light; normal cactus compost; minimum temperature 13°C (55°F). *Mexico (Puebla).*

WILMATTEA **MINUTIFLORA** (Br. & R.) Br. & R.
Syn: *Wilmattea viridiflora* (Vaup.) Br. & R.

An epiphytic climbing or clambering plant from forested regions. It has elongated three-angled, dark-green stems and joints 1.5–2.5cm wide, with evenly crenate margins. The areoles are about 3cm apart and have usually one to three minute, almost hair-like yellowish to black spines, about 1mm long. Flowers appear in early summer, and are nocturnal and fragrant. They are 3–3.5cm long, 8–9cm wide when fully open. The elegant unopened flower has a short tube and a small ovary, which are covered with green triangular scales, edged at the tips with brownish-red. Requires slight shade; normal cactus compost; minimum temperature 13°C (55°F). *Guatemala, Honduras.*

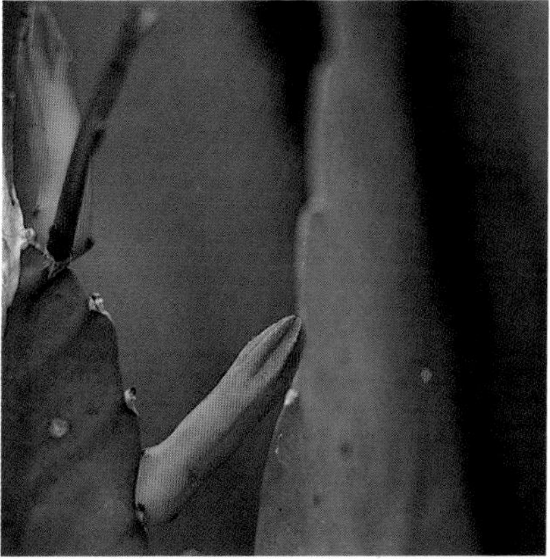

WITTIOCACTUS **AMAZONICUS** (K. Sch.) Rauschert
Syn: *Wittia amazonica* K. Sch.; *Disocactus amazonicus* (K. Sch.) D. R. Hunt

Indeed a rarity. Stems are leaf-like, notched at intervals. They are 15–40cm long, 4.5–9cm wide, with many branches, mostly pendent, spineless and epiphytic. Day flowering in early summer, the flowers are pink and almost cylindrical, the bluish tips scarcely open. Requires filtered light; normal cactus compost; minimum temperature 18°C (64°F). *Peru (Leticia, Tarapoto).*

AUTHORS OF CACTUS TITLES

The following is an alphabetical list of botanists, researchers and so on who have given their names to cacti finds, along with their recognized abbreviations.

Akers (J Akers, US botanist)
Alex. (E J Alexander, US botanist)
And. (E F Anderson, US botanist)
Arech. (J Arechavaleta, Uruguayan botanist)
Arp
Audot
Backeb. (C Backeberg, Germany)
Baird (R O Baird)
Barber (J T Barber, British horticulturalist)
Barthlott (W Barthlott, German botanist)
Baum (B R Baum)
Beahm (US horticulturalist)
Benson B W
Benson L (Lyman Benson, US botanist)
Berger (Alwin Berger, German researcher)
Bigel. (J Bigelow, US botanist)
Böed. (F Böedecker, German researcher)
Boiss. (C H Boissevain)
Boom (B K Boom, Dutch researcher)
Borg (J Borg)
Brand. (K Brandegee, US botanist)
Brandegee (T S Brandegee, US botanist)
Brandt (F H Brandt)
Braun (P J Braun)
Bravo (Helia Bravo-Hollis)
Bred. (J A Brederoo)
Bregman
Britt. (see Br. & R.)
Br. & R. (N L Britton & J N Rose, US botanists)
Buchenau (F G Buchenau)
Buin. (A F H Buining, Dutch botanist)
Buxb. (Franz Buxbaum, German botanist)
Byl. (R S Byles, British botanist)
Cactus Pete (US horticulturalist)
Campos-Porto (Brazilian botanist)
Card. (M Cardenas, Bolivian botanist)
Castañ. (M Castañeda)
Cav. (A J Cavanilles, Spanish botanist)
Cels (J M Cels, French horticulturalist)
Clokey (I W Clokey)
Clov. (E U Clover)
Colla (A Colla, Italian botanist)
Cons. (M Console, Italian botanist)
Coolidge (US horticulturalist)
Coult. (T Coulter)
Coult. J M (John M Coulter, US botanist)
Craig (R T Craig, US botanist)
Croiz. (L C M Croizat, US botanist)
Cutak (L Cutak, US cactus authority)
Dams (E. Dams, German librarian)
Dän. (A U Däniker, Swiss botanist)
Dawson (E Y Dawson, US botanist)
DC. (Augustin Pyramus de Candolle, Swiss botanist)
Diers
Dietr. (A G Dietrich, German botanist)
Distef. (C Distefano, Sicilian botanist)
Don G
Donald (J D Donald, British researcher)
Dusén (P Dusén)
Earle (W Hubert Earle, US researcher)
Ehrenb. (Carl Ehrenberg, German authority)
Eichl. (F Eichlam)
Ekm. (H or E Ekman)
Engelm. (George Engelmann, US authority)
Esteves (E Esteves Pereira)
Farwig
Fechs. (H Fechser, Argentinian researcher)
Fittkau (H W Fittkau, Mexican priest)
Fobe (F Fobe, German researcher)
Fischer
Först. (C F Förster, German botanist)
Fort & O'Barr (US horticulturalists)
Foster (Robert A Foster)
Frank (G Frank from Austria)
Frič (Alberto V Frič, Czech cactus authority)
Friedr. (H C Friedrich, German botanist)
Gaertn. (J Gaertner, German botanist)
Gal. (H G Galeotti, Belgian authority)
Gat. (H E Gates)
Gentry (A Gentry, US authority)
Gibson A (A Gibson, US botanist)
Gill. (J Gillies, Scottish authority)
Glass (C Glass, also linked with R Foster)
Goss. (R Roland Gosselin, French researcher)
Graham
Greene (E L Greene, US botanist)
Griffiths (Dr D Griffiths)
Griseb. (A H R Grisebach)
Guill. (A Guillaumin)
Gürke (M Gürke, German botanist)
Haage Jr. (F Haage, German horticulturalist)
Haage W. (Walther Haage, German horticulturalist)
Haw. (Adrian H Haworth, British botanist)
H.B.K. (F A von Humboldt, A A Bonpland, C S Knuth, German/French botanists)
Heath (P V Heath, British authority)
Heese (E Heese, German cactus enthusiast)
Hensl. (J S Henslow, British botanist)
Herrera (F L Herrera y Garmendia, Peruvian botanist)
Hester (J Pinckney Hester)
Hildm. (H Hildmann, German authority)
Hook. (Sir W J Hooker, British botanist)
Hopff. (C Hopffer, German authority)
Horak (B Horak)
hort. (attributed to horticulture)
Hoss. (C C Hosseus, German/Argentinian botanist)
Houghton (A D Houghton)
How (Foon-Chew How)
Hunt (D R Hunt, British botanist)
Hutch. (P C Hutchison, US botanist)
Innes (Clive Innes, British horticulturalist)
Ito (Y Ito, Japanese botanist)
Jacobi (G A von Jacobi, German botanist)
Jacobsen (Hermann Jacobsen, German authority)
Johnson (H Johnson, US horticulturalist)
Jott. (M L Jotter)
Karsten (G K W H Karsten, German botanist)
Karw. (W Karwinsky von Karwin, German botanist)
Kayser (K Kayser)
Ker (J Bellenden Ker-Gawler, botanist)
Kiesling (R Kiesling, Argentinian botanist)
Kimn. (Myron Kimnach, US botanist)
Kladiwa (L Kladiwa, Austrian authority)
Klein (W Klein, US authority)
Knebel (Curt Knebel, German horticulturalist)
Knuth F (F M Knuth, Danish botanist)
Krainz (Hans Krainz, Swiss researcher)
Krzgr. (K G Kreuzinger, Czech authority)
Kupper (W Kupper, German botanist)
L. (Carl von Linné, Swedish botanist)
Lab. (J Labouret, cactus authority)
Lag. (M Lagasca y Seguro, Spanish botanist)
Lagerh. (N G von Lagerheim, Swedish botanist)
Lam. (J B P A de Monet de Lamarck, French botanist)
Lau (A Lau, German/Mexican botanist)
Lauterb. (Karl A G Lauterbach)
Lawr. (G Lawrence, British researcher)
Lehm. (J G C Lehmann, German botanist)
Lem. (Charles A Lemaire, French botanist)
Leon (A P Leon, Cuban researcher)
Liebn. (F Liebmann)
Lindb. (G A Lindberg)
Lindinger (K H L Lindinger)
Lindl. (J Lindley, British botanist)
Linds. (G Lindsay, US botanist)
Link & Otto (Heinrich F Link & Christoph F Otto, German botanists)
Linke (A Linke, German cactus authority)
Liogier
Lodd. (C Loddiges, British botanist)
Loefgr. (A Loefgren, Swedish botanist)
Macbr. (J Macbride)
MacDoug. (T B MacDougall, Scottish/ Mexican botanist)
Marn.-Lap. (J Marnier-Lapostelle, French researcher)
Marsh. (W T Marshall, US researcher)
Mart. (Karl F P von Martius, German botanist)
Mathsson (A Mathsson)
Mey. R (Rudi Meyer)
Meyen (F J F Meyen)
Meyran (J Meyran, Mexican researcher)
Mill. (P Miller, British botanist)
Miquel (F A W Miquel, Dutch botanist)
Mir. (G F Miranda)
Möll. (L Möller, German researcher)
Monmonier T M (US horticulturalist)
Monv. (M de Monville, French cactus collector)
Moore H E (US botanist)
Moran (R V Moran, US botanist)
Morr. E (C J E Morren, Belgian botanist)
Mühlpf. (F Mühlenpfordt, German researcher)
Munz (P A Munz)
Nic. (E A Nicolai, German botanist)
Nutt. (T Nuttal, British/US botanist)
Ok. (O Kafor)
Orc. (C R Orcutt, US botanist)
Ort. G (G Ortega)
Parish (S B Parish)
Parm. (A A Chevalier de Parmentier, French researcher)
Parry (W or C Parry)
Parsons (S H Parsons)
Passmore J (British horticulturalist)
Paxton (J Paxton)
Pfeiff. (Ludwig G K Pfeiffer, cactus researcher and writer)
Phil. (R A Philippi, German/Chilean botanist)
Porter D M (US botanist)
Poselg. (H Poselger, German researcher)
Purp. (J A Purpus, German researcher)
Quehl (L Quehl, German researcher)
Raf. (C S Rafinesque-Schmaltz, Italian /US botanist)
Rauh (Prof W Rauh, German botanist)
Rausch (Walter Rausch, German researcher)
Rauschert (S Rauschert)
Rebut (P Rebut, French researcher)
Regel (E A von Regel, German botanist)
Reichenb. (F Reichenbach, German researcher)
Reppenhagen
Ricco. (V Riccobono, Italian botanist)
Riha
Ritter (F Ritter, German researcher/writer)
Rodr. (J D Rodriguez, Spanish botanist)
Rogozinski
Rojas (N Rojas Acosta)

Rose (see Br. & R.)
Rost (G Rost)
Rowley (Gordon Rowley, British botanist)
Rümpl. (T Rümpler, German researcher)
Runge (C Runge, early-day cactus collector, US)
Sadovsky C
Salisb. (R A Salisbury)
Salm.-Dyck. (Joseph Fürst Salm-Reifferscheid-Dyck, notable author)
Sanchez-Mejorada H
Sand. (H F C Sander, British/German researcher)
Scheer (F Scheer, British researcher)
Scheidw. (J Scheidweiler, Belgian/German plantsman)
Schelle (E Schelle, German plantsman)
Sch. K (Karl M Schumann, German botanist)
Schmoll (F Schmoll, cactus researcher)
Schütz (B Schütz, Czech researcher)
Shurley (E W Shurley, British researcher)
Slaba
Speg. (Carlos Spegazzini, Italian/Argentinian botanist)
Spreng. (K P J Sprengel, German botanist)
Stein (B Stein, German researcher)
Steeg (van der Steeg)
Steele C (US horticulturalist)
Stephans Ed. (US horticulturalist)
Steud. (E G von Steudel)
Steyerm. (Julian A Steyermark)
Stoddart (US horticulturalist)
Taylor N P (British researcher)
Theunissen
Tiegel (E Tiegel, German researcher)
Torrey (J Torrey, US botanist)
Tsuda
Unger (Franz J A N Unger)
Unger G (Gottfried Unger)
van Oosten
Vaup. (F Vaupel, German botanist)
Vellozo (J M da Conceicão Vellozo, Brazilian botanist)
Voll (O Voll, German/Brazilian researcher)
Wagner (J or H Wagner)
Walp. (W G Walpers, German botanist)
Walton F A (US horticulturalist)
Wats. S (S Watson, US botanist)
Weber (Frederic A C Weber, French researcher)
Weingt. (W Weingart, German researcher)
Wendl. (J C Wendland, German cactus authority)
Weniger H L (US botanist)
Werd. (E Werdermann, German botanist)
Wessn. (W Wessner, authority on South American cacti)
Willd. (K L Willdenow, German botanist)
Wright Y
Wressey Cocke
Zecher
Zimm. (F or W Zimmermann)
Zucc. (Joseph G Zuccarini, German botanist)

GLOSSARY

Acuminate Tapering to a point.
Acute Pointed.
Aerial root Roots produced on stems above ground, usually in *epiphytes*.
Areole The cushion-like growing point of a cactus.
Axil The angle between stem and branch.
Bract A modified or reduced leaf.
Bristle A stiffened hair.
Calcareous Of or containing lime or chalk.
Callus New tissue which forms over a cut.
Calyx The ring of *sepals* that surrounds the petals of a flower before it opens.
Capsule The dry seed-case.
Caudex The woody or fleshy 'stem' developing at or below ground level, with growing points.
Caudiciform Having a *caudex*.
Central spines Those arising from the centre of the *areole*.
Cephalium A densely woolly, bristly 'head' formed on certain cacti.
Cordate Heart-shaped.
Corolla The collective name for the petals.
Corona The centre of the flower surrounding the *stamens* and style – the crown.
Cristate The *monstrosus* growth development in plants.
Cultivar A hybrid produced by cultivation.
Dentate Toothed.
Diurnal Day flowering.
Endemic Regularly or only found in (a certain region or country).
Entire Smooth margins or edges.
Epiphyte Plant growing on another, but not parasitic.
Exotic Usually referring to tropical or sub-tropical plants.
Exserted Protruding from.
Family Taxonomic grouping of similar genera.
Farinose Having a mealy appearance.
Floccose Woolly-hairy.
Form (fma.) A more or less minor variation of a species or variety.
Genus Taxonomic grouping of plants with similar characteristics. Represented by the first element in a botanical name.
Glabrous Smooth – without hairs or wool.
Glaucous Covered with a wax-like bloom.
Globose Globular, spherical.
Glochid Tuft of bristly hairs on the areole.
Habitat The natural home of a plant.
Head A close-set group of flowers.
Humus Decomposed organic matter.
Hybrid A plant created by crossing two different *species* or varieties.
Inflorescence Arrangement of flowers of plant; collective flower of plant.
Internode Section of stem between two nodes.
Joint A section of stem.
Lateral A shoot or branch coming out of the main stem.
Latex A milky sap exuding from stems.
Margin Edge of petal.
Monotypic The only species within a *genus*.
Monstrose An abnormal, irregular stem growth.
Naturalized Referring to plants flourishing away from their natural habitat.
Nomen Nudum Abbreviated n.n. A title lacking valid description.
Obtuse Blunt or partially rounded.
Offset Section of plant capable of rooting.
Ovate Broadly elliptic – egg-shaped.
Ovary Lower part of a flower, containing the ovules.
Panicle Many-flowered *inflorescence*.
Pectinate Arranged in a comb-like manner.
Pendant Inclined downwards; hanging.
Perianth Outer part of flower.
Plumose Feathery – covered with fine hairs.
Procumbent Growing along the ground.
Prostrate Low growing.
Pseudocephalium Usually a lateral *cephalium*.
Pubescent Covered with fine, minute hairs.
Radial spines The *spines* arranged around the edge of the areole.
Recurved Curved backwards.
Reflexed Curved downward.
Resting period The period of dormancy in a plant.
Ribs Sections of the stem forming raised ridges, usually more or less vertical.
Saxicolous Refers to plants growing on rocks.
Scales Thin, leaf-like structures.
Sepals Leaf-like structures surrounding and protecting the petals of a flower. Collectively known as the *calyx*.
Serrate Saw-edged.
Simple Solitary.
Sp.n. *Species nova:* newly discovered.
Species An individual or closely related group of plants within a genus.
Spines Thorn-like modified leaves.
ssp. Sub-species: plants with similarities but differing in certain features.
Stamen The male fertilizing organ of flowering plants, including the anther, which contains the pollen.
Stigma The tip of the style, on which the pollen is deposited.
Sub-genus A division of a genus.
Succulent Any plant which stores water in fleshy stems and/or leaves.
Synonym Title already known under a different name.
Taxon Taxonomic group, e.g. genus.
Taxonomy Principles of classification, in the natural sciences.
Terete Smooth and rounded.
Tube The tubular section of the flower above the ovary, bearing the petals etc.
Tuber Fleshy, swollen section of a root or underground stem, storing food for the plant.
Tubercle Small wart-like swelling or growth.
Type The principal example of a genus or species.
Undulate Having wavy edges.
Variety Any distinct form of species or *hybrid*.
Viable Able to survive and develop.
Wart An irregular growth (see *tubercle*).
Whorl Ring of leaves or branches surrounding the stem of a plant.
Wool Dense covering of fine, soft hairs.
Zygomorphic Having one single plane of symmetry.

USEFUL ADDRESSES

The following is a list of societies and current publications specializing in (or frequently featuring) cacti & other succulent plants

AfM
Mitteilungsblatt des Arbeitskreises fuer Mammillarienfreunde e. V.
Erikastrasse 9, D6650 Homburg/Saar, West Germany

AGAVE
quarterly Magazine of Desert Botanical Garden, 1201N. Galvin Parkway, Phoenix, AZ 85008, USA. (See also *Saguaroland Bulletin*)

ALOE
published by the South African Aloe & Succulent Society, Box 1193, Pretoria 0001, Republic of South Africa

ANACAMPSEROS
Australian National Cactus & Succulent Journal
Succulent Publications of South Australia, P.O. Box 572, Gawler, South Australia 5118

ASKLEPIOS
published by the International Asclepiad Society, 6 Woodland Rise, Wakefield, West Yorkshire WF2 9DL, UK
American rep: Dana Craig, 67 Hill St., Norwood, MA 02062, USA

BALTIMORE AREOLE
published by the Cactus & Succulent Society of Maryland, 20 Perhall Court, Baltimore, MD 21236, USA

BOTHALIA
Botanical Research Institute, Div. of Ag. Info.,
Dept. of Ag. Tech. Serv., Private Bag X144, Pretoria, Republic of South Africa

BRADLEYA
Yearbook of British Cactus & Succulent Journal
Herbarium, Royal Botanical Gardens, Kew, Richmond, Surrey TW9 3EA, UK

BRITISH CACTUS & SUCCULENT JOURNAL
published by the British Cactus and Succulent Society, 8 Stonehouse Close, Cubbington, Leamington Spa CV32 7LP, UK. (See also *Prickly Paragraphs*)

BULLETIN
published by the Mesembryanthemum Study Group
American rep: Steven Brack, Mesa Garden, P.O. Box 72, Belen, NM 87002, USA

BULLETIN OF THE EPIPHYLLUM SOCIETY OF AMERICA
4400 Portola Ave., Los Angeles, CA 90032, USA

CACTACEAS Y SUCULENTAS MEXICANAS
2a de Juarez 42, Col. San Alvaro 02090, Tacuba, Mexico 17 DF, Mexico

CACTOCHAT
newsletter of the Cactus and Succulent Society, 3 Kinsey Terrace, Christchurch 2, New Zealand

CACTUS & SUCCULENT JOURNAL OF NEW SOUTH WALES
published quarterly. 542 Grand Junction Rd., Northfield, S.A. 5085, Australia

CACTUS & SUCCULENT SOCIETY OF AMERICA NEWSLETTER
3602 W. 157th St., Lawndale, CA 90260, USA

CACTUS CHATTER
published by the Oregon Cactus & Succulent Society, 27821 SE Sun Ray Drive, Boring OR 97009, USA

CACTUS CHRONICLE
bulletin of the Los Angeles Cactus & Succulent Society, 5149 Jeffdale Ave., Woodland Hills, CA 91364, USA

CACTUS COMMENTS
New York Cactus & Succulent Society, 312 W. 49th St., New York, NY 10019, USA

CACTUS CORNER NEWS
Fresno Cactus & Succulent Society, 3015 Timmy, Clovis, CA 93612, USA

CACTUS COURIER
San Jose Cactus & Succulent Society, 2568 Crystal Dr., Santa Clara, CA 95051, USA

CACTUS DIGEST
Henry Shaw Cactus & Succulent Society, Missouri, 2004 Ridgedale Dr., High Ridge, MO 63049, USA

CACTUS FACTUS
Toronto Cactus & Succulent Society, 24 Criscoe St., Toronto, Ont., M6N 3Y9 Canada

CACTUS STICKER
Las Vegas Cactus & Succulent Society, 3656 Lakeshore Lane, Las Vegas, NV 89115, USA

CENTRAL SPINE
Central Arizona Cactus & Succulent Society, 3102 W. Anderson Dr., Phoenix, AZ 85023 USA

THE CHILEANS
32 Forest Lane, Kirklevington, Yarm TS15 9LY, UK

COS (Cacti & Other Succulents)
8591 Lochside Drive, Sidney, B.C. V8L 1M5, Canada

ECHINOCEREANAE
the Official Bulletin of the Echinocereanae Society, 22 Collina St., Mitcham 3132, Victoria, Australia

EPIPHYTES
Journal of the Epiphytic Plant Study Group
editor: John Horobin; American rep: Seymour Linden; subscriptions to Chris Dawson, 1 Belvidere Park, Great Crosby L23 0SP, UK

EUPHORBIA
yearbook published by Strawberry Press, 227 Strawberry Drive, Mill Valley, CA 94941, USA

EUPHORBIA STUDY GROUP
101 Beach Road, Hartford, Northwich CW8 3AB, UK
American rep: Herman Schwartz, 227 Strawberry Drive, Mill Valley, CA 94941, USA

ESSEX SUCCULENT REVIEW
Quarterly journal
49 Chestnut Glen, Hornchurch, Essex, UK

FLOWERING PLANTS OF SOUTH AFRICA
published by Botanical Research Institute, Div. of Ag. Info., Dept. of Ag. Tech. Serv., Private Bag X144, Pretoria, Republic of South Africa

FOUR C'S
Confederation of Country Cactus Clubs, Australia, 542 Grand Junction Rd., Northfield, S.A. 5085, Australia

GAZETTE
journal of Peperomia and Exotic Plant Society, P.O. Box 1033, Fort Richey, FL 34673, USA

HAWORTHIAD
journal of the Haworthia Society,
Wades Barn Cottage, Buckden, near Skipton, N. Yorkshire, BD23 5JA, UK
American rep: Dennis Plath, 689 Estonia Court, San Jose, CA 95123, USA

HOBBY GREENHOUSE
journal of the Hobby Greenhouse Association, 8 Glen Terrace, Bedford, MA 01730, USA

HOYA SOCIETY/WEST COAST
PO Box 5130, Central Point, OR 97501, USA

USEFUL ADDRESSES

INDOOR GARDEN
newsletter of the Indoor Gardening Society
944 S. Munroe Road, Tallmadge, OH 44278, USA

INTERNATIONAL CACTUS & SUCCULENT SOCIETY
P.O. Box 691, Breckenridge, TX 76024, USA

THE JOURNAL OF THE ECHEVERIA SOCIETY
Camino Real a Calipan Km 3, Barranca de las Minas, 75980 Coxcatlan, Pue., Mexico

KAKTEEN/Sukkulenten
Pillnitzer Strasse 26, Dresden 8019, East Germany

KAKTEEN UND ANDERE SUKKULENTEN
Ahornweg 9, D-7820 Titisee-Neustadt, West Germany

KAKTOS KOMMENTS
publication of the Houston Cactus & Succulent Society,
11015 Sage Orchard Lane, Houston, TX 77089, USA

KAKTUS
publication of the Nordisk Kaktusselskab, Otto Forum Sorensen, Viemosebro 14, 2610 Rodovre, Sweden

KAKTUSI IN DRUGE SOCNICE
published by the Cactus Friends Society of Slovenia, Topol 17, 61215 Medvode, Yugoslavia

KAKTUSY
Riegrova 112, 25263 Roztoky u. Prahy, Czechoslovakia

KAKTUSZKEDVELOK
Kerteszmernok, Debrecen, 10, Botanikus kert, Hungary

LITERATURSCHAU KAKTEEN
1136 Berlin, Bataton Strasse 48, East Germany

MID-IOWA CACTUS & SUCCULENT SOCIETY NEWSLETTER
3417 Bel Aire Road, Des Moines, IA 50310, USA

MITTEILUNGEN DER BOTANISCHEN STAATS-SAMMLUNG-MUENCHEN
Menzinyer Strasse 67, D-8000 München 19, West Germany

THE NEW ZEALAND CACTUS & SUCCULENT JOURNAL
164 Massey Street, Frankton Ph. Ham. 76-240, New Zealand

OMAHA CACTUS & SUCCULENT SOCIETY NEWSLETTER
Drawer U, Griswold, IA 51535-0620, USA

PALOMAR CACTUS & SUCCULENT SOCIETY BULLETIN
P.O. Box 840, Escondido, CA 92025, USA

PAPYRACANTHA FOR THE CACTOPHILE
published bi-monthly
Box 103, Kent, Ohio 44240, USA

A PERIODIC JOURNAL OF PATAPHYSICAL SUCCULENTOSOPHY TAJOPS
1341 Williamson, Madison, W1 53703, USA

THE POINT
Washington: Cascade Cactus & Succulent Society publication: Box 551, Both ell, WA 98041-0551, USA

PRICKLY PARAGRAPHS
published by the British Cactus & Succulent Society, 8 Stonehouse Close, Cubbington, Leamington, CV32 7LP, UK. (See also *British Cactus & Succulent Journal)*

REPERTORIUM PLANTARUM SUCCULENTARUM
Mythenquai 99, CH 8002 Zürich, Switzerland

SAGUAROLAND BULLETIN
publication of the Desert Botanical Garden, 1201 N. Galvin Parkway, Phoenix, AZ 85008, USA. (See also *Agave)*

SEDUM SOCIETY NEWSLETTER
published by Keith Powell, 8 Gibsons Green, Heelands, Milton Keynes, Buckinghamshire, MK13 7NH, UK
American Rep: Micki Crozier, Rt. 2, Box 130, Sedgwick, KS 67135, USA

SEMPERVIVUM FANCIERS ASSOCIATION
37 Ox Bow Lane, Randolph, MA 02368, USA

THE SEMPERVIVUM SOCIETY JOURNAL
published by the Sempervivum Society, 11 Wingle Tye Rd., Burgess Hill, Sussex, UK

SLIGHTLY SKINNY SHEET
bulletin of the Sunset Succulent Society, 7326 Ogelsby Avenue, Los Angeles, CA 90045, USA

SPINAL COLUMN
Michigan Cactus & Succulent Society publication, 3921 Auburn Drive, Royal Oak, MI 48072, USA

THE SPINE
bulletin of the Cactus & Succulent Society of Australia, 3 Bruce Street, North Frankston, 3200, Australia

STACHELPOST
Wallufer Strasse 30 2/10, 6502 Mainz-Kostheim, West Germany

SUCCULENTA
published by the Nederlands-Belgische vereniging van cactussen en andere vetplanten, P.O. Box 3240, NL-4700 GE Roosendaal, Netherlands

SUCCULENTES
Jardin Exotique, B.P. 105, Monte Carlo, MC 98002, Monaco

VELD & FLORA
Botanical Society of South Africa, Kirstenbosch, Claremont, 7735 Cape, Republic of South Africa

THE XEROPHYTE
67 Hill St., Norwood, MA 02062, USA

ZONEMAG
72 Church Lane Ave., Hooley, Coulsdon, Surrey, CR3 3RT, UK

INDEX

Species names which appear in italic, represent plant names which have been superseded.

Credits

The authors and publishers have made every effort to identify the copyright owners of the pictures used in this book; they apologize for any omissions and would like to thank the following:

Dr. W. Barthlott
Mary Bellerue Bleck
Pierre Braun
Dennis Cowper
Edi Day
John Donald
Stan Farwig
Robert Foster
Charles Glass
Ed Greenwood
Kenneth Heil
Robert Holt
Clive Innes
Myron Kimnach
Felix Kraehenbuehl
Alfred B. Lau
B.E. Leuenberger
A.J.S. McMillan
Dr. W. Rauh
Tegelberg Nurseries
John N. Trager
V. Turecek
Dale A. Zimmermann